This is a *tour de force* that examines in often distressing detail the character of settler colonialism in Israel/Palestine. Its special contribution is to argue that for decades, surveillance in multiple forms has been a central from of governance enabling the Israeli regime. Its meticulous, measured and mature scholarship makes it indispensable to our understanding of the past, present and possible futures of Israel and the Palestinians.

David Lyon, *Director of the Surveillance Studies Centre, Queen's University*

In this book, Zureik articulates the centrality of bio-political racism in the Israeli settler colonial surveillance regime. By Historicizing Israel's colonialism, he turns our attention to the devastating power of surveillance in the present time, or what he calls the "brutal pursuit" to monitor people and masses of information. Through his work, the author continues his already outstanding and original contributions to surveillance and settler colonial studies, as well as to our expanding knowledge and understanding of the continued dispossession of Palestine.

Nadera Shalhoub-Kevorkian, *Lawrence D. Biele Chair in Law, Hebrew University of Jerusalem*

Decades of careful reading, writing, and research have gone into this impressive volume; a must-read for serious scholars of Palestine, Israel and the Middle East.

James Ron, *Harold E. Stassen Chair of International Affairs, University of Minnesota*

ISRAEL'S COLONIAL PROJECT IN PALESTINE

Colonialism has three foundational concerns – violence, territory, and population control – all of which rest on racialist discourse and practice. Placing the Zionist project in Israel/Palestine within the context of settler colonialism reveals strategies and goals behind the region's rules of governance that have included violence, repressive state laws, and racialised forms of surveillance.

In *Israel's Colonial Project in Palestine: Brutal pursuit*, Elia Zureik revisits and reworks fundamental ideas that informed his first work on colonialism and Palestine three decades ago. Focusing on the means of control that are at the centre of Israel's actions toward Palestine, this book applies Michel Foucault's work on biopolitics to colonialism and to the situation in Israel/Palestine in particular. It reveals how racism plays a central role in colonialism and biopolitics, and how surveillance, in all its forms, becomes the indispensable tool of governance. It goes on to analyse territoriality in light of biopolitics, with the dispossession of indigenous people and population transfer advancing the state's agenda and justified as in the interests of national security. The book incorporates sociological, historical, and postcolonial studies into an informed and original examination of the Zionist project in Palestine, from the establishment of Israel through to the actions and decisions of the present-day Israeli government.

Providing new perspectives on settler colonialism informed by Foucault's theory, and with particular focus on the role played by state surveillance in controlling the Palestinian population, this book is a valuable resource for students and scholars interested in the Arab-Israeli conflict and colonialism.

Elia Zureik is Head of the department of sociology and anthropology at the Doha Institute for Graduate Studies in Qatar, and is Professor Emeritus of Sociology at Queen's University in Ontario, where he is the holder of the Research Excellence Award.

Routledge Studies on the Arab-Israeli Conflict
Series editor: Mick Dumper
University of Exeter

The Arab-Israeli conflict continues to be the centre of academic and popular attention. This series brings together the best of the cutting edge work now being undertaken by predominantly new and young scholars. Although largely falling within the field of political science, the series also includes interdisciplinary and multidisciplinary contributions.

1 **International Assistance to the Palestinians after Oslo**
Political guilt, wasted money
Anne Le More

2 **Palestinian Political Prisoners**
Identity and community
Esmail Nashif

3 **Understanding the Middle East Peace Process**
Israeli academia and the struggle for identity
Asima A. Ghazi-Bouillon

4 **Palestinian Civil Society**
Foreign donors and the power to promote and exclude
Benoît Challand

5 **The Jewish-Arab City**
Spatio-politics in a mixed community
Haim Yacobi

6 **Zionist Israel and Apartheid South Africa**
Civil society and peace building in ethnic-national states
Amneh Daoud Badran

7 **The Political Right in Israel**
Different faces of Jewish populism
Dani Filc

8 **Reparations to Palestinian Refugees**
A comparative perspective
Shahira Samy

9   Palestinian Refugees
    Identity, space and place in the Levant
    Edited by Are Knudsen and Sari Hanafi

10 The Rise and Fall of Arab Jerusalem
    Palestinian politics and the city since 1967
    Hillel Cohen

11 Trans-Colonial Urban Space in Palestine
    Politics and development
    Maha Samman

12 Zionism and Land Tenure in Mandate Palestine
    Aida Asim Essaid

13 Women, Reconciliation and the Israeli-Palestinian Conflict
    The road not yet taken
    Giulia Daniele

14 UNRWA and Palestinian Refugees
    From relief and works to human development
    Edited by Sari Hanafi, Leila Hilal and Lex Takkenberg

15 The Naqab Bedouin and Colonialism
    New perspectives
    Edited by Mansour Nsasra, Richard Ratcliffe, Sarab Abu Rabia-Queder and Sophie Richter-Devroe

16 Israel-Palestine in the Print News Media
    Contending discourses
    Luke Peterson

17 The Re-Emergence of the Single State Solution in Palestine-Israel
    Countering an illusion
    Cherine Hussein

18 Students and Resistance in Palestine
    Books, guns and politics
    Ido Zelkovitz

19 Political Conflict and Exclusion in Jerusalem
    The provision of education and social services
    Rawan Asali Nuseibeh

20 Israel's Colonial Project in Palestine
    Brutal pursuit
    Elia Zureik

21 Palestinians in Jerusalem and Jaffa, 1948
    A tale of two cities
    Itamar Radai

ISRAEL'S COLONIAL PROJECT IN PALESTINE

Brutal pursuit

Elia Zureik

LONDON AND NEW YORK

First published 2016
by Routledge
2 Park Square, Milton Park, Abingdon, Oxon OX14 4RN

and by Routledge
711 Third Avenue, New York, NY 10017

Routledge is an imprint of the Taylor & Francis Group, an informa business

© 2016 Elia Zureik

The right of Elia Zureik to be identified as author of this work has been asserted by him in accordance with sections 77 and 78 of the Copyright, Designs and Patents Act 1988.

All rights reserved. No part of this book may be reprinted or reproduced or utilised in any form or by any electronic, mechanical, or other means, now known or hereafter invented, including photocopying and recording, or in any information storage or retrieval system, without permission in writing from the publishers.

Trademark notice: Product or corporate names may be trademarks or registered trademarks, and are used only for identification and explanation without intent to infringe.

British Library Cataloguing-in-Publication Data
A catalogue record for this book is available from the British Library

Library of Congress Cataloging-in-Publication Data
Names: Zureik, Elia, author.
Title: Israel's colonial project in Palestine : brutal pursuit / Elia Zureik.
Description: New York, NY : Routledge, 2016. | Series: Routledge studies on the Arab-Israeli conflict
Identifiers: LCCN 2015021943| ISBN 9780415836074 (hardback) | ISBN 9781315661551 (ebook) | ISBN 9780415836104 (pbk.)
Subjects: LCSH: Israel-Arab War, 1967—Occupied territories. | West Bank. | Gaza Strip. | Military occupation. | Land settlement—Government policy—Israel.
Classification: LCC DS127.6.O3 Z87 2016 | DDC 956.95/305—dc23
LC record available at http://lccn.loc.gov/2015021943

ISBN: 978-0-415-83607-4 (hbk)
ISBN: 978-0-415-83610-4 (pbk)
ISBN: 978-1-315-66155-1 (ebk)

Typeset in Bembo
by Swales & Willis, Ltd, Exeter, Devon, UK

For Mary, whose insightful questions made the book all the better
and
For Jordan and Zachary, who I hope will grow up in a more peaceful world where sovereign Palestine is a reality

CONTENTS

Preface		*xii*
Acknowledgements		*xvii*
	Introduction	1
1	Researching Palestine and the Palestinians: a road map	9
2	Zionism and colonialism	49
3	Colonialism as surveillance	95
4	Biopolitics, eugenics, and population discourse	135
5	From calibrated suffering to necropolitics	161
6	The Internet and acts of everyday resistance	179
	Conclusion	209
References		*215*
Index		*263*

PREFACE

Intellectuals are never free-floating individuals with no ideological moorings. For the present purpose, there is more purchase in Antonio Gramsci's (1991) differentiation of the organic intellectual from the traditional intellectual – the one who represents the aspirations of the masses from the one who is bound to the dominant strata of society – than there is in Karl Mannheim's (1991) notion of the detached intellectual. The purpose here is to underscore the "sociology of knowledge" axiom that ideas are formed in a social context where positioning of the self and liminality are key markers.

The journey from Palestine to North America half a century ago was an act of severance for me. To my mind, coming to the United States at the age of twenty-one was not just a journey in search of higher education and eventual return to Acre, my home town in northern Palestine, but also an act signalling the beginning of a new phase in my life that is now nearing its finale. For me, at one level, it was a voluntary act of an immigrant in search of better life chances in the face of discrimination in the Jewish state on account of my minority status. If anything, the sociological literature tells us that voluntary immigrants are likely to remain and settle in their adopted country or countries, as was the case with me. At another level, my immigration in the early 1960s came at a time when so-called "twentieth-century globalisation" was at its height, but it was also a continuation of this phenomenon from early in the century, when my father had made a nonvoluntary trip to the United States after graduating from the American University in Beirut in order to evade being drafted into the Ottoman Army. In his case, he returned to Acre after spending close to three decades in New York.

I occupied different roles on the way to becoming a university student – first in the United States, then in Canada, and finally in Britain – and later to becoming an academic. There is nothing unique about this journey. A countless number of people travelled this road before me and have done so since then – although I must say that in the aftermath of the attack of 11 September 2001 on the

United States, the size of the foreign student population in US universities has dwindled significantly. The more interesting aspect of this journey is that I experienced different ways of positioning myself vis-à-vis others – inside and outside academia. This positioning of the self is different from the modernist notion of role taking, which is characterised by fixity. Surely, the argument goes, we occupy different roles, even interpret the same roles differently, but we are still tied to a prescribed script, and we follow the script more or less faithfully. This is not the case with what I mean by "positioning." A positioning of the self as well as the Other implies:

> ... incorporating both a conceptual repertoire and a location for persons within the structure of rights for those that use that repertoire. Once having taken up a particular position as one's own, a person inevitably sees the world from the vantage point of that position and in terms of the particular images, metaphors, storylines and concepts which are made relevant within the particular discursive practice in which they are positioned. At least a possibility of notional choice is inevitably involved because there are many and contradictory practices that each person could engage in. (Davies and Harre 1990, 46)

The point I am stressing is that there is no unitary or even essential self that is universal and timeless. The self is reflexive, historical, interactive, and contextualised. As a result, we experience a contradictory positioning of our various selves when we are subjected to constitutive discourses, but at the same time we negotiate and even resist these discourses. After all, this is the productive aspect of disciplinary power, to invoke Michel Foucault (1977, 194). Some of these observations are not new. Sociology has dealt with the self in various venues, including symbolic interaction (Blumer 1986), dramaturgy (Goffman 1959), small group dynamics (Bales 1955), action theory (Parsons and Shils 1962), structuration theory (Giddens 1984), and identity and subjectivity via cultural studies (Hall and Du Gay 1996). But it is also the case that, for Palestinians, both land dispossession and the 1948 Nakba (Catastrophe), which was accompanied by ethnic cleansing, have been central to understanding identity formation across generations.

Let me state a caveat at the outset. I am not espousing a form of relativism or solipsism, or the idea that "you have to be one to know one," to quote the philosopher Brian Fay (1996, 9). Similar to Fay, I subscribe to what I call "multicultural epistemology," by which I mean the need to bring to bear points of view from the margin, views that are excluded in a system of domination and hegemony (Gramsci 1991), which Fraser (2013, 142) calls "the discursive face of power." My position here is not all that different from Sandra Harding's (2004) notion of "standpoint epistemology." It also resonates with Edward Said's (1993) "resistance culture" on the part of the marginalised. In questioning and critiquing Western views, there is the temptation to present an alternative, relativist, even essentialist, view based on the experience of the marginalised Other. In a statement that has an air of multicultural epistemology to it, Said (1996, 217) warns against ascribing superiority to any one experience or system of thought over another:

A confused and limiting notion of priority allows that only the original proponents of an idea can understand and use it. But the history of culture is the history of cultural borrowings. Cultures are not impermeable, just as Western science borrowed from Arabs, they had borrowed from India and Greece. Culture is never just a matter of ownership, but rather of appropriations, common experiences, and interdependencies of all kinds among different cultures. This is a universal norm.

The fusion of cultures, it must be stated, is carried out against a backdrop of the borderline intellectual's liminal status as an émigré, expatriate, exile, or refugee. This liminality positions intellectuals in an in-between border zone that separates them from the dominant society and at the same time marks them as outsiders in the society of origin (Ghanim 2006). It expresses a feeling of ambivalence about both inclusion in and exclusion from the spheres of citizenship, nationality, and culture. Liminality is crucial to the borderline intellectual because, as Homi Bhabha (1994) points out, it fosters reflexive thought, which enables intellectuals to transfer their individual subjectivity to collective objectivity, although this occurs in varying degrees, depending on political circumstances and the intellectuals in question. Liminality allows individuals to move between spaces and time periods, testing the threshold of survival. In *Representations of the Intellectual*, Said (1996, 49) captures the liminality of the émigré intellectual:

> The exile therefore exists in a median state, neither completely at one with the new setting nor fully disencumbered of the old, beset with half-involvements and half-detachments, nostalgic and sentimental at one level, an adept mimic or a secret outcast on another. Being skilled at survival becomes the main imperative, with the danger of getting too comfortable and secure constituting a threat that is constantly to be guarded against.

A full appreciation of the debate surrounding the self demands a brief mention of the relationship between the self and memory. The self is not the product of solitary experience as in René Descartes' dictum "I think, therefore I am." One's self and identity extend back in time to whatever one remembers of their past. After all, what is the self without memory? However, a recent surge in memory studies shows that memory can play tricks on us – in fact, many tricks – or as some psychologists have claimed, memory has "seven sins." A saving grace of memory distortions and biases – due, for example, to our need to reduce cognitive dissonance – is that we are more likely to remember encoded information about the self than about others through the so-called "self-reference effect" (Schacter 2002, 233–34).

As a Palestinian who spent the first two decades of his life – until the completion of high school – in Palestine and in what became Israel, I experienced significant regime change, from living under British imperialism to later experiencing Zionist colonialism. Each regime ushered in its own system of occupation and domination, but the one that had an enduring effect on my formative years and structured my worldview, self-positioning, and subsequent intellectual endeavours was Israel's form of settler colonialism. Intellectually, this experience culminated in my first book more than three decades ago, *The Palestinians in Israel: A Study in Internal Colonialism* (Zureik 1979). I consider this book to be a continuation of my ongoing attempts to understand and situate the Palestinian experience in the nexus of the "colonial moment," which, as Joseph Massad (2001, 9) notes:

> ... is the moment when colonialism establishes a state-framework on a colonized territory/country, either replacing an existing state structure or inaugurating one where it had not existed before. This inaugural moment establishes the political, juridical, administrative, and military structures of the colonized territory/country, effectively rendering it a nation-state (laws of nationality, governance, and citizenship are codified, borders and maps are drawn up, bureaucratic divisions and taxonomies of the territory and the population are imposed, conscription and/or induction of colonized men into colonial military structures is established). This moment constitutes a radical discontinuity with what existed before the colonial encounter.

It was revealing of the ideological mood in Israel that when the reviews of my above-mentioned book began to appear in the 1980s, Israeli academics labelled it a biased publication for adopting the colonialism perspective. The late Baruch Kimmerling (1980, 77), who eventually became one of the most vociferous academic critics of Israeli policies toward the Palestinians, described my book at the time as "war by other means." Within a decade, however, the tone of reviews had changed significantly. Rather than dismissing my book as merely a "Palestinian perspective," with all the reservation that this view implies for the Western reader, reviewers began to embrace my book as "pioneering" for its application of the colonialism model (Yiftachel 2008, 88), which eventually culminated in the text's being acknowledged by critics and appreciative authors alike as essential reading on the early sociology of the Palestinians in Israel. How to account for this shift? Three main factors contributed to this change of tone. First, a stream of critical writings by Palestinians about the treatment of their society in Western and Israeli scholarship eventually penetrated academic discourse about Palestine. Second, there were changes taking place in Israeli social science, and so-called "post-Zionist" writings emerged that began to question the orthodoxy and the straitjacket interpretations of the Palestinians' circumstances by Israeli society. A third factor relates to developments on the ground, particularly Israel's occupation of the West Bank and Gaza in 1967, which was blatantly colonial by various accounts, including those of Israeli writers.

Thus two points of departure define my intellectual self-positioning in this project. First is the fact that for a century the Palestinians have been struggling for self-determination, often at a very high human and existential cost. Israel's brutal pursuit of Palestinian colonisation remains a defining feature of its reactions to Palestinian resistance. The tragedy is that the Jewish state is following a path similar to that adopted by European states toward their Jewish minorities. Sygmunt Bauman, an internationally acclaimed Polish sociologist with strong family connections to Israel, has remarked that Israel is "taking advantage of the Holocaust to legitimize unconscionable acts," such as the West Bank wall, which he compares to the wall built around the Jewish ghetto of Warsaw (in Frister 2011). Among the approximately 80 million refugees currently displaced around the globe, close to 6 million are Palestinian refugees, who comprise more than half of the global population of the Palestinian people and have constituted one of the largest national groups with this unenviable status for about sixty years. Second, the fact that Palestine experienced several colonial regimes in its modern history – starting with the Ottoman Empire and followed by imperial Britain, Zionist colonisers, the Israeli state, and Egyptian and Jordanian occupiers – makes colonialism the second defining feature in my intellectual self-positioning.

The research for this book has been a continuous effort that followed the publication of my first book on Palestine (Zureik 1979). Published material that is used in some of these chapters has been updated and cast in an expanded theoretical-conceptual framework to reflect ongoing innovations in researching the Palestinians. Whereas the first book dealt mainly with the Palestinians in Israel, the current one expands the focus and addresses the conditions of the Palestinians in all of historical Palestine, west of the Jordan River, and in exile. Yet, as the title of this book conveys, Israel's dominant role as dispossessor of the Palestinians remains paramount in this intellectual undertaking.

ACKNOWLEDGEMENTS

This book is the culmination of research conducted over several decades. During this time, I benefited immensely from associations and exchanges with colleagues in many countries and from different disciplines and political orientations. Individual acknowledgements here can only be sketchy. Salim Tamari, director of the Institute of Palestine Studies, provided me with research facilities when I spent two sabbaticals there in the early 1990s and during my frequent visits thereafter, and he exposed me to fascinating sojourners who always had interesting things to say about Palestine. Salim's wit and ability to narrate Palestinian history from a sociological angle brought historical biographies to life and enriched my understanding of Palestine. Andre Mazzawi, who now teaches at the University of British Columbia, and with whom I cemented a lasting intellectual exchange and friendship after we met during one of my trips to Palestine, is the consummate observer and interpreter of Palestinian life. Andre, with his sociological imagination and philosophical-humanistic bent, has proved to be invaluable in reading and commenting on my writings over the years. His feedback has invariably improved my arguments and made my texts less obtuse. Fouad Moughrabi, a political scientist at the University of Tennessee and a colleague of more than forty years, travelled with me on several occasions to Palestine and other Middle Eastern countries on research missions. Our efforts have yielded collaborative work over the years. I continue to treasure our friendship and intellectual exchanges. Anthropologist Efrat Ben-Ze'ev, at Hebrew University's Truman Centre in Jerusalem, shared with me her anthropological research on memory and always provided me with much needed Hebrew sources for my research.

I am indebted to many colleagues for their willingness to share their work, both published and unpublished. The generosity shown in also giving me their time is deeply appreciated. I single out sociologist Rita Giacaman and anthropologist Rema Hammami of Bir Zeit University, who over the years have provided me with work in progress, published articles, and survey data about the human cost of occupation for the Palestinians, particularly its impact on the mental health of youth and women. Nadera Shalhoub-Kevorkian, a criminologist at the Hebrew University, single-handedly launched studies into domestic violence and violence against women. These studies have become lightning rods for situating the experience of Palestinian women in the context of traditional masculine Arab society and Israeli domination. Political scientist Ahmad S'adi, of Ben-Gurion University, enriched my knowledge of Israeli governmental control and surveillance of Palestinians through his meticulous archival research on Israeli bureaucracy. Neve Gordon, also in political science at Ben-Gurion University, prepared the only publicly available report about the political economy of the surveillance industries in Israel that I know of. His report, for which I am grateful, fed into my ongoing interests in surveillance.

Sari Hanafi, a prolific writer and head of the Sociology Department at the American University in Beirut, who himself epitomises the predicament of Palestinian intellectuals living a liminal existence, continues to boldly experiment with sociological theories in order to gain deeper understanding of the Palestinian predicament, particularly the position of Palestinian refugees in exile. Psychologist Vivian Khams, also at the American University in Beirut, continues to publish extensively on the impact of violence and occupation on Palestinian family life in the West Bank and Gaza. Her meticulous empirical research enriched my understanding of Palestinian society under duress. Honaida Ghanim, who was awarded distinction for her doctoral thesis in sociology at the Hebrew University and whose work on the liminality of Palestinian intellectuals enriched my work, always graciously answered my questions and provided me with much needed sources. Amal Jamal, of the Political Science Department at Tel-Aviv University, made available to me his work in progress that had direct relevance to the intersection between race and surveillance, which proved to be immensely useful for understanding the way surveillance and control unfold in colonial and ethnically bound societies. My fruitful association with Aziz Haider dates back to the mid-1980s, when he was a fresh graduate with a doctorate in sociology from the Hebrew University. Thirty years later, Aziz has emerged as one of the most authentic empirical analysts of and commentators on the Palestinian minority in Israel. His views are sought after by policymakers and others, including me. Although my acquaintance with anthropologist Helga Tawil-Souri at New York University is fairly recent, I am grateful to have met her and for the privilege of reading her work on culture as a form of resistance. Orub El-Abed, currently a doctoral candidate in the School of Oriental and African Studies at London University, has managed to write the only comprehensive, published study of Palestinian refugees in Egypt. She was always ready to share her work in progress.

For nearly four decades, Queen's University provided me with a stable environment that enabled me to carry on with my teaching and research unimpeded. Starting in the mid-1980s, I began developing an interest in surveillance as it applied to the workplace and society at large. Eventually, my interests in Palestine and surveillance merged, as will be apparent in this book. This cross-fertilisation was enhanced through my collaboration with David Lyon, an internationally recognised scholar in surveillance studies who directs the Surveillance Studies Centre at Queen's University. During the final days of this project, I enjoyed a stimulating environment at the Doha Institute for Graduate Studies in Qatar, where I am now head of the program in sociology and anthropology.

The editorial work of Sarah Cheung, Ben Bigio, and Robert Lewis made the manuscript all the more readable.

Elia Zureik
Doha, Qatar
February 2015

INTRODUCTION

Ian Lustick (1980, 64), an astute observer and scholar of the Israeli-Palestinian conflict, has remarked, "What has been most striking about the position of the Palestinian Arab community that has lived in Israel since 1948 has been its political acquiescence." There is some truth to this statement, even today, in spite of the opposition to – and at times violent confrontations with – police and other state agencies, for which the Palestinians have paid dearly with their lives (Dalal 2003). This acquiescence, however, should not be interpreted to mean that the state has succeeded in pacifying the Palestinians into accepting their subordinate position in Israeli society. Political scientist Amal Jamal (2013, 245) claims that Israel has "manufactured the quiet Arab." This has occurred even as the state has pursued persistent surveillance techniques and at times brutal policies to subdue and thwart active Palestinian aspirations both in Israel and in the West Bank and Gaza.

From the outset, however, unlike other (post)colonial states, Israel had no intention of integrating the Palestinian community into its socioeconomic and political fabric. In the words of anthropologist Patrick Wolfe (2012, 136):

> Zionist policy in Palestine constituted an intensification of, rather than a departure from, settler colonialism. In stark contrast to the Australian or United States models, for instance, Zionism rigorously refused, as it continues to refuse, any suggestion of Native assimilation . . . Zionism constitutes a more exclusive exercise of the settler logic of elimination than we encounter in the Australian and US examples.

Since its early days, the main focus of Israel has been to depopulate Palestine of its original inhabitants, denationalise its refugees, and seize Palestinian land and property in order to accommodate Jewish settlers and actualise the Zionist project. The question is how to achieve these objectives under the banner of democracy while keeping the Palestinians in check and preventing them from forming an organised opposition that would amount to what the state labels a fifth column. To his credit, Lustick (1980) advanced his "group control" model early on, instead of focusing on ethnic identification as a mode of explanation, something that remains in vogue to this day among social scientists who write about a deeply divided Israeli society. This form of control, he argues, is exercised through co-optation, dependence, and segmentation of the Palestinian minority at various political, economic, and societal levels. Although he acknowledges that one can infer that Israel's attitudes to the Palestinian minority arose from an overarching Zionist ideology, he contends that what actually transpires amounts to an *unintended* consequence of the unfolding events of 1948: the actual "policies towards the Palestinians emerged as by-products of the new regime's efforts to cope with the difficult problem of sudden statehood" (ibid., 65).

I contend that the Zionist leadership, beginning in the 1950s, implemented preordained and meticulous plans to control and dispossess the Palestinians (Ariel 2013). About the same time that Lustick (1980) presented his model, I published my book *The Palestinians in Israel: A Study in Internal Colonialism* (Zureik 1979). More than three decades later, my study remains a testimony to the fact that the colonialism framework once shunned by academic researchers is now being acknowledged by a wider segment of mainstream academic writers as an important contribution to the sociological study of the Palestinian population. Colonialism is the system of control that I chose to work with at the time and to which I now return in an attempt to investigate the means by which the State of Israel carries out its form of settler colonialism in both Israel and the occupied territories. As will become apparent, I try to explain the predicament of the so-called "quiet" or quiescent Palestinians through understanding the minutiae of the control and surveillance that the state exercises over the physical, socioeconomic, and psychological well-being of the Palestinians under the umbrella of Zionism.

Theoretical focus

> It would be difficult not to recognise Israel's past and ongoing illegal seizure of Palestinian land, the racialisation of every aspect of daily life, and the large-scale and piecemeal demolition of Palestinian homes, destruction of livelihoods, and efforts to destroy the social and family fabric, as decimation by concerted and concentrated colonial design. These are the well-honed practices of regimes that define colonialisms and have flourished across the imperial globe. (Stoler 2010a)

This quotation from the distinguished anthropologist Ann Laura Stoler's statement in support of the Boycott and Divestment Campaign – a reaction to Israel's practices in the West Bank and Gaza – captures the theoretical and empirical concerns of this study in focusing on the relationship between colonialism, biopolitics, and territory.

At a time when the governments of industrialised nations and spokespersons of leading international organisations sing the praises of globalisation, it may seem intellectually quaint – if not out of place entirely – to resuscitate a discussion of colonialism. This is only true if one limits the discussion to mainstream neoliberal social science, which sees in globalisation a defining transition to a so-called "interconnected" and "networked" world where borders and the nation-state are on the wane. As Wendy Brown (2010) clearly demonstrates, the mushrooming of barriers (e.g., walls, fences, and checkpoints) between and within states challenges the globalisation thesis.

As far back as the seventeenth century, if not earlier, European colonialism had already left an enduring mark on modern nation-states, particularly those of the postcolonial variety. In discussing the "colonial present" in Iraq, Afghanistan, and Palestine, cultural geographer Derek Gregory (2007, 7) remarks that "while they may be displaced, distorted, and (most often) denied, the capacities that inhere within the colonial past are routinely reaffirmed and reactivated in the colonial present." John Strawson (2002, 363–64) echoes this sentiment when he remarks that "while colonialism has withered, a postcolonial world has taken shape in which the world replicates elements of the old order through which the West assumes a centrality against the periphery of the ex-colonies." It is not only the territorial, economic, legal, and political dimensions of colonialism that have left their mark, and that are reproduced in the colonial present, but as the late Edward Said (1978, 1993) noted – a point reiterated by Gregory (2007) – so too did Orientalism's colonising culture and its discursive instruments of power (see Dirks 1992).[1] Colonialism has three foundational concerns – violence, territory, and population control – all of which rest on racialist discourse and practice. It is also transformative, albeit under conditions of duress during which colonialism transforms the life of indigenous people beyond their choosing and control. It is concerned with "disabling old forms of life by systematically breaking down their conditions, and with constructing in their place new conditions so as to enable – indeed to *oblige* – new forms of life to come into being" (Scott 1998, 26, emphasis in original).

Settler colonialism, the central concept underlying this book, is intrinsically associated with the dispossession of indigenous populations through violence, repressive state laws and practices, and racialised forms of monitoring (currently referred to as racial profiling), each of which has become an essential tool of governance today; such laws and practices extend from informal to technologically sophisticated formal means of monitoring and control. Two key elements of control concern us. The first is the relationship between colonialism and what Michel Foucault terms "biopolitics," a relationship that is not explored by him in the colonial context and that remains understudied,[2] even though the European states with which Foucault dealt – aptly labelled by Brad Evans (2010, 414) the "colonial heartland" – were invariably colonising states in one form or another (Stoler 1995; Venn 2009). Although I agree with Said's statement that "Foucault ignores the imperial context of his own theories" (in Stoler 1995, 5n8), Foucault's observations on the modern nation-state, racism, and population management are germane to understanding the workings of colonial states. Robert J.C. Young (1995, 5) captures the relevance of Foucault's discourse analysis, where power and knowledge are conjoined, to understanding racism and colonialism, even though Foucault did not deal with colonialism head on:

> Whether early or late, so much of Foucault seems to be applicable to the colonial arena – his emphasis on forms of authority and exclusion, for example, or his analysis of the operations of the technologies of power, of the apparatuses of surveillance. Foucault's own concepts have themselves become productive forms of conceptual power and authority.

According to Foucault (2003, 245), "biopolitics deals with the population, with the population as a political problem, as a problem that is at once scientific and political, as a biological problem and as power's problem." Thus conceived, "biopolitics is a form of politics that entails the administration of the processes of life at the aggregate level of life processes" (Duffield 2007, 5). This is to be distinguished from disciplining, which is applied at the level of the individual. Management of life is made possible with the ascendancy of demographic knowledge through the application of statistical techniques, economic planning, and medical science. As underscored by Foucault (2003, 254) in *Society Must be Defended*, the transition from sovereignty to governmentality in the eighteenth century saw the state exercise biopolitical power that "takes life as both its object and its objective."[3] If by "the right of sovereignty" is meant "the right to 'take' life and 'let' live," the new right ushered into the eighteenth century by liberalism meant "the right to make live and to let die" (ibid., 241); the emphasis of the former is on death, and that of the latter is on life. Thus it was in this context that biopower emerged to replace sovereign power (Legg 2005, 139). In Foucault's words (1978, 138), "the old power of death that symbolized sovereign power was now carefully supplanted by the administration of bodies and the calculated management of life." Patricia Clough and Craig Willse (2010, 49) draw our attention to the important point that biopolitics is not applied in a blanket fashion in managing and enhancing the well-being of the population; rather, "Foucault argues it is a form of racism that allows for death in biopolitics, the death of some populations that are marked as inferior and harmful to the larger body of the nation."

In discussing colonialism and biopolitics, it is necessary to speak of racism, as well as surveillance – a central tool of governance. Although racism has existed in various forms since antiquity, modern European *state* racism, according to Foucault, emerged in the eighteenth century as a tool to serve the state's interests and defend society from within. The nation-state racism that Foucault addresses is anchored in cultural and ethnic differences, not in any essentialist, biological considerations; it is, to use Etienne Balibar's (1991) phrase, a "neo-racism," which refers to "a racism without races . . . whose dominant theme is not biological heredity but the insurmountability of cultural differences" (in Montag 2002, 118). However, in pursuing a racialist agenda through the "calculated management of life" (Foucault 1985, 140), state racism in the twentieth century, enacted in a world saturated with refugees and displaced people (Arendt 1943), had the effect of pushing Foucauldian biopolitics into what Georgio Agamben (1998) and Achille Mbembe (2003) call, respectively, "thanatopolitics" and "necropower" (the politics or the power of death).[4] Patrick Wolfe (2006, 387) draws a similar inference, labelling settler colonialism as "inherently eliminatory" of indigenous populations, although "not invariably genocidal." According to Wolfe (2011), "Race is colonialism speaking." Thus the place of race and racism is central to the discussion of biopolitics as a technology of colonial power and population management, as demonstrated by Matthew Hannah (2011) in his work on biopolitics, as well as in his analysis of the ways that the nineteenth-century American census played a crucial surveillance role in managing and constructing the territory and lives of Native Indians (Hannah 2000). Of interest in this context is how the Israeli colonising state strives to constitute and discipline Palestinians in Israel and the occupied Palestinian territories (OPT) as "dangerous populations" (Kemp 2004), by deploying a gamut of surveillance and control technologies that extend from informal, bureaucratic, and discursive to behavioural and technologically sophisticated (Berda 2013). When it comes to methods of control over the Palestinians, Israel is best described, according to historian Ilan Pappé (2008), as a "*Mukhabarat* state," meaning in Arabic an intelligence or surveillance state – a label that applies to the neighbouring Arab states as well.

If colonialism is the context in which this study unfolds, surveillance, in its material, corporeal, and discursive forms, is its indispensable tool of governance. Surveillance of individuals, groups, and populations is accomplished through soft and hard technologies that involve information gathering by means of bureaucrats, informants and collaborators, direct observation, census taking, territorial mapping, categorical sorting, cross-referencing of identities in databases for the sake of profiling individuals, wiretapping, and more recently, the deployment of sophisticated electronic identification systems, from Internet filtering, closed-circuit television, geopositioning systems, biometric profiling, and iris scanning to radio frequency identification and behavioural profiling (Whitaker 2011), all of which involve what Ben Anderson (2011, 205) labels "affective tools of war." These techniques and their application depend on the objective and location of the surveillance network; they vary historically and according to the spatial configuration of the territory in question, its population size and distribution, and the ability of the coloniser to combine, in the case of automated and electronic surveillance, the use of these various technologies in what Kevin Haggerty and Richard Ericson (2000) call "the surveillant assemblage." In the context of urban warfare and counterinsurgency – as in Palestine, Afghanistan, Iraq, and Chechnya, to name a few salient areas of national and ethnic conflict – biopolitics is considered an integral part of colonial strategy against guerrilla warfare, whereby so-called "anticipatory action," based on prior assessments and on models for forecasting levels of insurgency, is utilised to target and pre-empt oppositionary sectors of the population (Anderson 2011). No matter how thorough the surveillance of the population and its classification into loyal and insurgent groups by means of simulations and modelling techniques – and this is not to support the logic of such surveillance – the civilian population ends up bearing the brunt of so-called "collateral damage." The use of drones by Israel in the OPT and by the United States in Iraq, Afghanistan, and Yemen is an excellent example.

The second feature that concerns this study and complements the first is the place of territory in the exercise of surveillance and control in colonial states. In Patrick Wolfe's words (2006, 388), "territoriality is settler colonialism's specific, irreducible element"; it determines individual (im)mobility, access to land, use of time, economic viability, and indeed life chances. As will be demonstrated in this study, biopolitics and territoriality intersect at various levels to advance the state's racialised agenda, and they are framed by Western-based colonial law to facilitate the seizure of territory, privatisation of communal land, dispossession of indigenous people, and population transfer. In pursuit of their objectives, colonial regimes rely on systems of corporeal identification and enforcement of policing at borders, frontiers, and checkpoints, where bodily inspection, psychological humiliation, and the accompanying violation of privacy are carried out routinely in the name of state security to the detriment of freedom of movement and population mobility. It is important to point out that population identification systems, such as census taking and identification cards, are common to all states (Bennett and Lyon 2008; Torpey 1998) and are essential for state planning and modernisation in general. In the case of colonial regimes, however, identification systems are distinguished by their discriminatory practices and racialised targeting of the population, thus creating a rigid stratification of citizens, subjects, and noncitizen immigrants, displaced people being an example of the latter.

Beyond, and directly related to these two key concerns, this study also deals with the relationship between colonial law, a hallmark of which is the state of exception, and national security, in whose name surveillance, control, and violence are exercised and justified. In *Security, Territory, Population: Lectures at the College de France, 1977–1978*, Foucault (2007, 108) notes that governmentality conceives of "power that has the population as its target, political economy as its major form of knowledge, and apparatuses of security as its essential technical element." To quote Giorgio Agamben (2002, 2), security has "now become the sole criterion of political legitimation." Furthermore, the study clarifies the connections between what appears to be two separate intellectual pursuits: the mushrooming field of surveillance studies on a global scale, on the one hand, and the study of a regional ethno-national conflict that is the product of nineteenth-century colonialism, on the other. In doing so, this book aims to fill a lacuna in Middle East research by situating discussions about surveillance and discipline in Israel/Palestine in the context of the colonial experience as it relates to the control of territory and the management of population.

Chapter outline

Chapter 1 is a road map of academic research on Palestine and the Palestinians during the last half-century. It provides the reader with a tour of what I consider to be worthy research from a variety of disciplines and perspectives in order to demonstrate the evolution of studying a people who have been locked in a national struggle for more than a century and who have been living in dispersal since 1948. The chapter highlights the contribution of this study to complementing existing critical research, including the role of surveillance in governance.

Chapter 2 takes the reader into a discussion of colonialism and its relevance both to the Zionist project, which culminated in the establishment of Israel in 1948, and to the continued colonisation of the occupied Palestinian territories since 1967. Because of the contested nature of the debate surrounding settler colonialism in its Israeli manifestation, the chapter initially delineates the main features of colonialism as a prelude to discussing the claims and counterclaims in the debate over Herzlian Zionism. It pays special attention to what I call "breaching the consensus" regarding the nature of Israel and Zionism, as well as to the official use of obfuscatory language and rhetoric in describing Israeli colonial policies.

Chapter 3 traces the specifics of surveillance and information gathering in Palestine's colonial past and present. The chapter provides an overview of the historical antecedents for present-day surveillance practices in order to highlight the role of colonialism in innovating the development and transfer of surveillance technologies across the colonies and its part in occasioning their eventual deployment in the home country under what Foucault calls the "boomerang effect" (see Legg 2007, 266).[5] I note the place of Palestine in Britain's colonial surveillance systems and how attempts to rule Palestine have relied on the adoption of British methods of surveillance and control developed in India, Egypt, and other colonies. In addition to dealing with advanced surveillance technologies, the chapter pays special attention to bureaucratic and informal face-to-face surveillance that was (and is) used minutely by Israel to control the Palestinian population in Israel proper. The chapter summarises postcolonial state use of micropower in its capillary form through reference to several case studies of surveillance in Israel/Palestine involving identity cards, mobility across borders and checkpoints, the disciplining of memory, and the racialised use of time.

Chapter 4 situates the Israeli discourse on demography and population management, and the contradictions arising therein, as aspects of biopolitics in a colonial context. A brief detour addresses the place of eugenics as a component of biopolitics in Zionist colonial discourse going back to the early part of the twentieth century. Two aspects of the debate surrounding biopolitics are examined: first, at the institutional level, the impact of racialised government legislations and strategies bearing upon the demography debate are scrutinised in order to understand how Israeli "society is defended," to use Foucault's phrase, by reaffirming the geopolitical boundary of the state through racialisation of the Palestinians; second, at the societal level, a review of the public discourse and public opinion data that highlight the place of racism in Israeli society is undertaken. My intention here is to gauge the extent of convergence in the levels of Israeli-Jewish racism among the public, governmental, and private spheres.

Chapter 5 demonstrates the nature of Israeli violence and how the state resorts to pseudoscientific explanations in order to account for its lethal policies toward the Palestinians. Chapter 6 analyses the use of the Internet by Palestinians as a discursive means to mobilise and resist hegemonic control. The study concludes with reflections on Zionism and Israeli colonialism, as one of the last vestiges of modern colonialism in the twenty-first century, and its confrontation with the Palestinians.

Notes

1 Gregory's inspiration for treating culture as *sui generis* is the work of Said (1978; see also Said 1993). Gregory (2007, 16) claims, "The colonial present is not produced through geopolitics and geoeconomics alone" but "is also set in motion through mundane cultural forms and cultural practices that mark other people as irredeemably 'Other' and that license the unleashing of exemplary violence against them." For an application of the Orientalist paradigm in the analysis of Israeli historiography and its treatment of the Palestinians, see Gerber (2003) and Piterberg (2008).
2 Although he generally agrees that Foucault did not pursue the connection between colonialism and racism, Warren Montag (2002, 121) remarks that Foucault's position can best be described as postcolonial:

> It is at this point that my reading of Foucault's treatment of biologistic racism diverges from that of Stoler[,] who tends to present Foucault's argument as internally consistent, even if she finds fault with it in certain crucial respects, notably the text's neglect of the importance of colonialism in the formation of modern racism. I would also say that the racism that Foucault analyzes is perhaps best regarded as "postcolonial" racism, a racism that accompanies not movements of conquest, settlement and administration, but rather the demographic flow of the Other from the former colonies back to the "core."

3 For a critique of Foucault's discussion of the population problem and his failure to anchor it in a concrete empirical-historical moment, see Curtis (2002) and Dupont and Pearce (2001). A competent empirical work on nineteenth-century Egypt that complements Foucault's discussion of population is provided by Fahmy (2010).
4 Although not discussed in any detail, Foucault acknowledged thanatopolitics as a biopolitical option of the state: "Since the population is nothing more than what the state takes care of for its own sake, of course, the state is entitled to slaughter it, if necessary. So, the reverse of biopolitics is thanatopolitics" (in Martin, Gutman, and Hutton 1988, 160). For a useful discussion of Agamben's bare life and sovereignty as they relate to Foucault's biopower, see Genel (2006).
5 In *"Society Must Be Defended": Lectures at the College de France, 1975–1976*, Foucault (2003, 103) states, "It should never be forgotten that while colonization, with its techniques and its political and juridical weapons, obviously transported European models to other continents, it also had a considerable boomerang effect on the mechanisms of power in the West, and on the apparatuses, institutions and techniques of power."

1

RESEARCHING PALESTINE AND THE PALESTINIANS

A road map

It is estimated that at the end of 2012 the number of Palestinians worldwide was 11.6 million – of whom 4.4 million resided in the West Bank (2.7 million) and Gaza (1.7 million), 1.4 million in Israel, 5.1 million in neighbouring Arab countries, and 655,000 in the rest of the world. By 2020, it is projected that the number of Palestinians in historical Palestine alone, west of the Jordan River, will reach 7.2 million – compared to 6.9 million Jews (PCBS 2011b).[1] Of the total number, 5.1 million Palestinians and their descendants are officially classified as refugees, according to the United Nations Relief and Works Agency (PCBS 2012). No doubt, the total number of refugees and their descendants is larger since not every Palestinian who became a refugee in 1947–48 registered with the UN agency.

Figure 1.1 displays the growth of the Palestinian population over more than a century, starting in the 1880s with the first Zionist settler-colonisation of Palestine and ending in 2012. At the time of the Balfour Declaration in 1917, in which the British government promised the Zionists a national home for the Jews, the Palestinians constituted 90 per cent of the population and the Jews a mere 10 per cent (Zureik 2001). On the eve of the United Nations 1947 resolution to partition Palestine, 67 per cent of the population was Arab and 33 per cent Jewish. Following the establishment of Israel in 1948 and the flight and expulsion of the Palestinian population in 1947–48, the remaining Palestinians numbered 160,000, around 20 per cent of the combined Arab and Jewish populations. Now they number 1.3 million people.

For more than a century, which is probably longer than any other national group in recent memory, the Palestinians have struggled for self-determination; they exist largely as a community that is closely administered and monitored by outsiders. Notwithstanding their current attempts at state building, the Palestinians

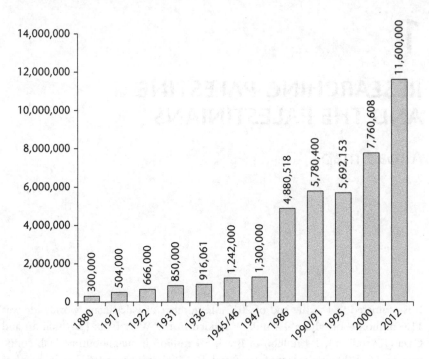

FIGURE 1.1 Growth of the Palestinian people, 1880–2012

for the most part have lived for two-thirds of a century as refugees, exiles, and minorities – both in their homeland and elsewhere. And prior to that, they lived as an occupied people throughout the modern period, ruled first by the Ottomans, then by the British, Jordanians (in the West Bank), and Egyptians (in Gaza), and finally by the Israelis. It must be said, however, that Ottoman and British rule did not entail loss of Palestinian citizenship, as occurred during Israeli colonisation and occupation. Others prefer to label the Palestinian experience under Israeli rule "denationalisation" (Abu-Zahra and Kay 2013, 5). The 1948 Nakba (Catastrophe), as it is known in Arabic, and the dispersal of the Palestinians as a result of the establishment of Israel brought them under close scrutiny by different administrative regimes belonging to several so-called "host countries," including the military-administrative apparatus of Israel and the neighbouring Arab states, a UN organisation in charge of refugees, and what is referred to euphemistically as the "international community." As descendants of minorities and refugees going back five generations, the majority of Palestinians today live under surveillance of one form or another from cradle to grave. Their numbers are contested, their demography is analysed and debated endlessly, their movement across international borders is closely monitored, their activities are routinely scrutinised for political content, and their citizenship status is a perennial topic of discussion. In short, the Palestinians have experienced what sociologists call administrative social sorting of one form or another involving intrusive monitoring, data gathering, and population categorisation. For this reason, surveillance, monitoring, control, and resistance are discussed in this study since they are essential ingredients for understanding Palestinian society – or for that matter, any society (refugee or otherwise) whose existence is controlled and monitored by outsiders. As this study shows, these systems of control are spatial, temporal, local, regional, and global. They include colonial state policies, both past and present, legal impositions to facilitate dispossession and land expropriation, and population containment. Israel, whose establishment contributed directly to the Nakba, occupies a central place throughout this monitoring process and in my analysis of its apparatuses.

This chapter highlights the theoretical, methodological, and conceptual issues related to the study of Palestinian society in its dispersal under various statuses. It provides a road map for the macro- and micro-developments at the individual, communal, and institutional levels while highlighting the contribution of this study in light of existing research on the Palestinians. As mentioned above, social sorting via population count and categorisation, spatial arrangements, (im)mobility, and overall monitoring occupy a special place in this study. As pointed out in the coming chapters, social sorting, recordkeeping, and databases are forms of discursive power that aim to constitute the subject. This chapter does not report on empirical findings as such, except by way of examples, but interrogates the relevant theoretical and methodological literature so as to set the stage for understanding Palestinian society in terms of available data to be analysed in subsequent chapters.

This chapter draws upon a variety of disciplines in the social sciences and humanities in order to familiarise the reader with the scope of published and evolvingresearch on Palestine and the Palestinians. To begin with, it provides a thematic overview of this research, with a separate treatment of research on Palestinian refugees. Following this, it proceeds to address six separate theoretical and methodological perspectives: the near absence of the colonialism model in mainstream academic writings about the Zionist project in Palestine and the use of surveillance techniques for the purpose of ruling; the qualitative-quantitative divide in social science, with special reference to ethnography; critical assessment of Michel Foucault's treatment of power; the utility of constructivist analysis; the problem of order and conflict resolution, and the role of globalisation, networking, electronic communication, and transnationalism in shaping the lives and identities of refugees and migrant communities. Several issues introduced in the next section are taken up again in the subsequent section's discussion of theoretical and methodical perspectives.

Thematic overview

Academic studies of contemporary Palestine and the Palestinians have come a long way since they first made their debut in the early 1960s – when, generally speaking, social science studies of the Middle East were mostly dominated by functionalism and modernisation theory (Bill and Leiden 1976; Lerner 1958; Zartman 1980), on the one hand, and by their traditional nemeses of Marxist studies and dependency theory (Asad and Owen 1983; Rodinson 1973; Turner 1984), on the other. This does not mean that the modernisation school and its functionalist-theoretical underpinnings have been totally eclipsed (Sa'di 1997); nor does it mean that Marxism has succeeded in laying to rest the once-popular modernisation approach. Rather, alongside the functionalist-Marxist divide, most apparent in sociology, political science, and to some extent, anthropology, we see several additional approaches making headway in our understanding of Palestinian society. These competing schools, espousing different theoretical and methodological orientations, come from a variety of disciplines, including sociology, anthropology, social history, historical studies of colonialism, postcolonial and culture studies, human rights and sociolegal studies, criminology, geography, and more recently, contributions from women's studies, visual studies, medical sociology, social studies of science, globalisation, Internet and cyberstudies, and transnational research.

Cultural studies

Cultural studies that are anchored in the humanities display a variety of subapproaches encompassing deconstruction, postcolonialism, literary criticism, poststructuralism, postmodernism, and semiotics – all of which have been deployed in one form or another in the study of Palestinians with varying degrees of frequency and sophistication (Harlow 1996; Lavie 1996; Peteet 1994a; Potoc 1998; Said 1985; Sherwell 1996; Tawil-Souri 2011). Notwithstanding its historical roots in functionalism and service to colonialism (Asad 1973), anthropological and ethnographic research on the everyday life, memory construction, and oral history of Palestinian society has made important contributions to its analysis (Ben-Ze'ev 2000, 2011; Farah 1998; Masalha 2012; Sa'di and Abu-Lughod 2007; Sayigh 1979). Ethnographic studies of marginalised communities such as refugees and people living under occupation demonstrate the importance of such research in uncovering everyday experiences, particularly with regard to strategies of coping and resistance among subaltern groups.

Counting Palestinians

The peculiar situation of the dispersal of Palestinians under various political and administrative regimes has made it difficult for researchers to freely access comprehensive and reliable statistical data, thus encouraging the use of ethnography and the case study approach, with a special focus on everyday life. Nevertheless, quantitative data are available on Palestinians in Israel through the publications of the Israel Central Bureau of Statistics (ICBS), and to a limited extent population data are available on Palestinian refugees who are registered with the United Nations Relief and Works Agency (UNRWA), an agency that is responsible for their humanitarian needs. The Oslo agreement of 1993 between Israel and the

Palestine Liberation Organization (PLO) and the establishment of the Palestinian National Authority in the West Bank and Gaza ushered in the Palestinian Central Bureau of Statistics (PCBS), which, with financial and scientific assistance from international organisations, has been able to launch its activities and carry out censuses and other specialised surveys of the Palestinian population under its jurisdiction. Today it is considered by academic researchers to be a reliable source of data about the Palestinian population in the West Bank and Gaza.

As noted in chapter 4's discussion of demography, in contrast to international estimates and those provided by Palestinian and Israeli experts, right-wing Jewish lobby groups contest these findings and provide lower estimates of the Palestinian population in the occupied territories (Hasson 2013; Ilan 2005; Zimmerman and Seid 2004).

Looking at institutions

The contributions of sociology and political science to the study of Palestinians have included analysing the institutional and psychological bases of alienation and national identity (Ghanem 1998, 2001, 2013; Mi'ari 1998; Rouhana 1997), attempts at state formation (Brynen 2000; Jamal 2001), the emergence of civil society and the role of nongovernmental organisations (Hammami 1995; Muslih 1993; Suleiman 1997; Sullivan 1996), the extent of involvement by Palestinian refugees and exiles in the political affairs of their surroundings (Brand 1988; Zureik 1996), and the study of mobilisation in the form of protest and resistance movements (Khawajah 1994; Sayigh 1979; Swedenburg 1990, 1995). Two events have come to epitomise Palestinian resistance to Israeli occupation and in the process have garnered research interests: the first is the uprising, or Intifada, that lasted from 1987 to 1994 (Zureik, Graff, and Ohan 1990–91), and the second is the Al-Aqsa Intifada, which erupted in October 2000 and lasted until 2005. No fewer than a dozen books had been published by the middle of the 1990s in an attempt to analyse the causes of the First Intifada (Mishal and Aharoni 1994; Nassar and Heacock 1990; Peretz 1990), and the second uprising triggered additional scholarly attention from Palestinian (Ajluni 2003; Hanieh 2002), Israeli (Institute for International Security Studies 2010), and Western writers (G. Robinson 2010).

Human rights, legal rights, and conflict resolution

Related to the causes of violence are research efforts directed at understanding the correlates of suicide bombing. There are those who have sought the causes of Middle Eastern and Palestinian violence in strictly cultural and religious terms (Karsh 2006; Pipes 2002) and those who have challenged these explanations by positing a causal relationship between Israeli state repression and suicide bombing (Brym and Araj 2006, 2008). Working within the tradition of Franz Fanon, Charles Lee (2009) examines Palestinian suicide bombing from a philosophical, collectivist perspective. He argues that current positivist approaches to understanding terrorism posit a lopsided question that seeks the causes of terrorism in the behaviour of the perpetrator of the act. He argues for an approach that examines the behaviour of states toward the disenfranchised and colonised people as a factor that contributes to violent resistance.

The work of the political philosopher Giorgio Agamben (1998) on states of exception, "bare life," and the *homo sacer* has prompted scholars to apply his perspective to the study of Palestinian refugees, about whom he had little to say (see Agamben 2000). Maissa Youssef (2007) provides an interesting departure from the legal approach by studying Palestinian refugees in their confrontation with Israel. She argues that although the Palestinians lost diplomatically as a result of the Oslo agreement, where asymmetrical power relations favoured Israel, the "materiality" of Palestinian bodies, exemplified in the biopolitics of the weak (see chapter 4, and R. Kana'neh 2002), presented Israel with a dilemma that could not be resolved by creating two states or expelling the Palestinians from their homeland. Until the refugee issue is resolved satisfactorily, the existence of the refugees, even outside the state, ultimately unsettles and perforates the undefined borders of Israel, a point that was noted by Agamben (1995) in his passing comments on Palestinian refugees. In an article that resonates with Youssef's, Ruba Salih (2013) explores the relevance of Hannah Arendt's claim that refugees constitute the avant-garde of their people and discusses Agamben's notion of "bare life" as applied to the stateless Palestinian refugees. Salih contends that the refugees' subaltern voices act to destabilise the nation-state and call for a reconfiguration of the state-society relations in which democratic, rather than territorial, politics predominate.

As a result of the spread of violence and denial of self-determination, issues of human rights, citizenship rights, and international legality have become increasingly salient and are dealt with by international relations experts, lawyers, sociologists, and sociolegal scholars (Akram 2002; Akram and Rempel 2004; Butenschon, Hassassian, and Davis 1997; Be'er and Abdel-Jawad 1994; Jeffries 2012; Kimmerling 2002; Kretzmer 1990; Pacheco 2001; Ron 1997; Shehadeh 1985; Takkenberg 1998).

The study of conflict resolution, a hybrid specialty combining political science, social psychology, and international relations, has frequently used the Middle East conflict, particularly its Israeli-Palestinian dimension, as a site to test ideas about conflict resolution that are primarily advanced by political psychologists and, to a certain extent, by sociobiologists (Burton and Sandole 1986; Collings 1988). In workshops that are organised specifically to facilitate various encounters between Jewish and Arab elites and quasi-official actors, third-party expert intervention is being deployed to test the utility of interventionist research in conflict resolution (Kelman 1998). The results of these simulations have produced mixed results at best, with serious doubt being cast on their efficacy in resolving ethno-national conflicts. They have mostly served to confer legitimacy on the position of the stronger party – in this case, Israel (Abu-Nimer 1999; Rabinowitz 2001a).

Deconstructing Palestine's history

Traditionally, the historical approach has been dominated by linear, chronological studies of Palestine and Palestinian leadership during various phases of the national struggle throughout the past century. The doyen of modern Palestinian historiography and its encounter with Zionism is Walid Khalidi, whose work over a long academic and research career includes three seminal books, *From Haven to Conquest* (1971), *Before Their Diaspora* (1984), and *All That Remains* (1992). The three books were published by the Institute of Palestine Studies, which he co-founded in 1963. The institute, with offices in Beirut, Washington, DC, and Ramallah, has an active book-publishing program, in addition to three journals: the *Journal of Palestine Studies*, its Arabic-language equivalent publication *Majallat al-Dirasat al-Filastiniyah*, and *Jerusalem Quarterly*. It is worth citing Khalidi's (1988) seminal paper on Plan Dalet of the Haganah, in which he disclosed for the first time the Zionist intentions to expel and depopulate Palestine of its Arab inhabitants as a prelude to establishing the State of Israel.

Historical research on Palestine has benefited from cross-fertilisation with the social sciences and other disciplines in the humanities. A welcome correction to the traditional, linear historical approach has been provided by combining the evolving subaltern research on Palestine (Abu-Manneh 2006; Swedenburg 1995) with studies of social and political history (Farsoun and Zacharia 1997; Kimmerling and Migdal 1993; Tamari 2009), including demography (I. Abu-Lughod 1971; Courbage 1999, 2012; Fargues 2000; Kossaifi 1980; Scholch 1985), population count, land/tenure, and urbanisation (Bisharat 1994; Doumani 1994; Levine 1999), identity formation (R. Khalidi 1997), and social structure of the peasantry (Carmi and Rosenfeld 1974). These works point to significant efforts aimed at deconstructing Palestine's historical narrative, thus challenging the once-dominant versions of Palestinian history, which were originally contributed by mainstream Western and Israeli scholars. The deconstruction of this history has become a major undertaking of Palestinian and other critical scholars working in a variety of disciplines, such as oral history, political science, anthropology, and sociology (S. Kana'neh 1991; W. Khalidi 1992; Masalha 1992). It is worth noting that the Palestinian narrative is having an impact on the once-dominant Western and Zionist narratives, as evident from the debate surrounding post-Zionism (Abdel-Jawad 1996).[2] Overall, however, the recorded history of Palestine, like all colonial histories, remains largely that of either its elite stratum or those who ruled the country at one time or another. At best, one can say that Palestinian history is now a contested intellectual terrain. Yet the application of the comparative approach to the study of Palestine lags behind. Palestine is viewed mostly as a unique case study, even though comparisons with regions that experienced anticolonial struggles such as South Africa promise to be useful (Mitchell, Prakash, and Shohat 2003).

Economics-based studies

Economists have researched Palestinians in their various locales and statuses, and at various points in time, to understand their place in the economy of the host society and the Middle East region generally. In the aftermath of the Oslo agreement, they turned their attention to examining the economic viability of a Palestinian state in the West Bank and Gaza (Abed 1988; Diwan and Shaban 1999; Fisher, Rodrick, and Tuma 1994; Naqib 1995). Since then, a younger generation of economists has questioned the feasibility of such a state in light of Israeli policies of expanding settlements and confiscating Palestinian land. The critical work of Raja Khalidi and Sobhi Samour (2011), Sara Roy (2000, 2007, 2009, 2011), and Leila Farsakh (2005a, 2005b, 2008) on the political economy of the West Bank and Gaza is notable in this regard. These views are shared by Virginia Tilley's (2005, 2009) and Ian Scobbie's (2009) analyses of the consequences of Israeli colonialism in the West Bank for both the economic and the legal rights of the Palestinian population. These outcomes are explored in more depth in a report by the Human Sciences Research Council of South Africa (2009), to which Scobbie was a contributor.

Documenting the "living conditions"

Due to the perpetual state of crisis faced by Palestinians in the West Bank and Gaza, as well as by those living in refugee camps across the Middle East, social scientists and policymakers have turned their attention to examining the "living conditions," demography, and incidence of poverty in Palestinian communities, with a special focus on the refugees. To a large extent, since the early 1990s, quantitative and statistical interests in researching Palestine and the Palestinians have been driven by the launching of the Oslo peace process. Reflecting this development, research interests have emanated from official Palestinian institutions (Palestinian Authority 1998) and from international organisations such as the United Nations Office of the Special Coordinator for the Middle East Peace Process (UNSCO 2011), the World Bank (2013), and the Swiss Agency (2002) for Development and Cooperation (SDC) – all of which have written or sponsored reports, with the SDC also mounting periodic surveys to assess the deteriorating living conditions of Palestinians in the West Bank and Gaza (Bocco, Brunner, and Rabah 2001a, 2001b; Bocco et al. 2001). "The Living Conditions of the Palestine Refugees Registered with UNRWA in Jordan, Lebanon, the Syrian Arab Republic, the Gaza Strip and the West Bank" (Lapeyre et al. 2011) reports the results of extensive surveys carried out in 2005 among Palestinian refugees in their primary locations in the Middle East.

On account of Norway's responsibility under the Oslo agreement to gather data on the humanitarian and living conditions of the Palestinians, the Norwegian nongovernmental organisation Fafo (n.d.), which conducts applied social research, played a leading role during the early days of the Oslo process by launching the first reliable field surveys among Palestinian refugees and non-refugee communities. In due course, Fafo's dual role of conducting social research on behalf of the Norwegian government and providing a venue for Israeli-Palestinian negotiations was subjected to a critical assessment (Zureik 1993).

Although the quality of the data is uneven, it has been possible to draw a composite picture of Palestinian economic life, both past and present, with projections for the future. Whereas most of the above studies follow mainstream economic and social science approaches, the quasi-Marxist field of political economy has been deployed to understand both the historical and contemporary economic position of Palestinians (Hilal 1974; Roy 2000; Shafir 1989), their claim to the land and other economic resources within historical Palestine (Zureik 1979), and the development of labour-market segmentation strategies as they are shaped by colonial practices (I. Abu-Lughod 1971) and by discriminatory state policies (Bernstein 1998; Sa'di 1995; Semyonov and Lewin-Epstein 1994; Yaish 2001).

Public opinion

Fafo (2011) has introduced a research program to assess the "mood" of the Palestinians by regularly commissioning public opinion surveys. Two Palestinian organisations with a longstanding record in public opinion polling are Near East Consulting (n.d.) and the more established Palestinian Center for Policy and Survey Research (n.d.). In the case of the latter, its director, Khalil Shikaki, has become a sought-after commentator on the situation in the West Bank and Gaza. His organisation collaborates with Israeli institutions in mounting joint Palestinian-Israeli polls (Shamir and Shikaki 2010).

Public opinion research about the Middle East conflict in Israel began in the past decade to incorporate the Palestinian minority into national Jewish samples, an example being the omnibus surveys carried out by the Tami Steinmetz Center for Peace Research at Tel Aviv University (n.d.). Surveys dealing with democratic attitudes are carried out annually by the Guttman Center at the Israel Democracy Institute (n.d.) and by the Macro Center for Political Economics (n.d.). The latter has released a large study on the attitudes of youth that contains a chapter on Palestinian youth in Israel (Yahia-Younis 2010).

In addition to political surveys, Israeli public opinion studies, such as those conducted by the Israel Central Bureau of Statistics, have begun to address the use of the Internet and its impact on society (ICBS 2002), and the Israel Internet Association (2011) has commissioned a survey on computer ownership and Internet use among Jews and Arabs. The Palestinian Central Bureau of Statistics (PCBS 2000, 2004, 2006, 2011a) has published the results of a series of national surveys dealing with computer and Internet use in the West Bank and Gaza. The use of social networks in Israel has been examined in a Google-sponsored survey by Yuval Dror and Saar Gershon (2012) that included Arab respondents.

The geography of Palestine

Geographers have joined the study of Palestinians and Palestine by juxtaposing competing claims pertaining to land ownership, access to natural resources such as water, and population policies reflected in containment, exclusionary practices, and residential segregation (Falah 1996; Khamaisi 1999, 2011; Yacobi 2004b; Yiftachel 1998). Some of those contributing to the discussion have drawn creatively upon cognate disciplines in the social sciences to highlight that frontier, place, and space as analytic concepts in both the physical and social sense are useful for understanding methods of social control and national conflicts. These studies are important to understanding state construction in Palestine (Zureik 2001).

Geographers and urban planners as well have contributed in important ways to theorising and analysing the militarisation of cities in conflict zones and urban localities. Three major contributors to the study of urbicide caused by Israeli militarism are Stephen Graham (2003, 2010), Derek Gregory (2004, 2007), and Eyal Weizman (2005, 2006, 2007). Kanishka Goonewardena and Stefan Kipfer (2006) bring together the work of geographers and other theorists to demonstrate the treatment of the city, urban slums, and refugee camps in postcolonial settings and war zones, including Palestine. The use of geography as an instrument of propaganda in Israeli schools is meticulously discussed by Norit Peled-Elhanan (2012).

Research on education

The study of education has always occupied a prominent place in Palestinian research and is closely associated with nation building. The seminal work of Abdul Tibawi (1956) on Palestinian education during the British Mandate period remains a crucial reference in this regard. Early on, the sociology of Arab education in Israel received substantial attention from researchers (Al-Haj 1995; Mar'i 1978) and was one of the areas to witness an early surge in research activities. A theoretical-empirical treatment of Palestinian education under various political and administrative regimes has been carried out by Andre Mazawi (1994, 1995, 1996, 1998) and others (e.g., Y. Shavit 1990). With a focus on Arab education within Israel, Human Rights Watch (2001) in New York has produced an extensive report on the impact of discriminatory state policies on Arab education within Israel. Probably the most thorough treatment of planning for Palestinian higher educational needs in the diaspora was carried out in the late 1970s under the auspices of the United Nations Educational, Scientific, and Cultural Organization (UNESCO). With a view to establishing a Palestine Open University that would cater to Palestinian refugee communities in the Middle East, UNESCO (1980) commissioned a group of experts to prepare a blueprint of an infrastructural and pedagogical nature for such an institution. Israel's invasion of Lebanon in 1982 put a stop to the project's implementation. Still, the demographic and educational data gathered by researchers working on the project hold tremendous historical value.

Science and society

Although the relationship between science, society, and economic development has been singled out as important, this is an area in which critical work on science and society has been wanting in the context of both the Arab world generally and Palestine in particular. An exception in this regard is the work of Antoine Zahlan (1980, 1997), a leading researcher in this area who pioneered the social- and policy-oriented study of science in the Arab world by demonstrating its inferior status relative to other newly developing societies and Israel. A younger generation of Palestinian scholars has embarked on researching the relationship between classroom teaching methods and a deficiency in Palestinian science education (Hashweh 1996; Wahbeh 2003). Nascent research on the place of information and communication technology in Middle Eastern societal development is beginning to make itself felt in writings about Palestinian society. As shown in chapter 6, this is particularly true with regard to the role of the Internet. In 2000, sociologist Sari Hanafi (2008) carried out an innovative study of Palestinian high-level manpower residing mainly in the West who returned to the West Bank and Gaza following the Oslo agreement. He assessed two programs designed to attract Palestinian high-level manpower to contribute to national developments of the West Bank and Gaza. One program, under the auspices of the United Nations Development Programme, is referred to as the Transfer of Knowledge Through Expatriate Nationals (TOKTEN). The other program, Palestinian Scientists and Technologists Abroad (PALESTA), now dormant, is an Internet-based network among Palestinian professionals and the Palestinian territories. Research on use of the Internet and its associated technologies of social media, as pointed out below, is proving to be highly relevant to understanding modes of resistance and connectivity among Palestinian communities who are prohibited from travelling and connecting with other Palestinians.

Studies of gender, social control, and life under duress

Psychologists (Baker 1992), medical sociologists (Giacaman 1988; Giacaman, Rabaia, and Nguyen-Gillham 2010; Giacaman et al. 2007, 2011), as well as feminists and others (Abdo 1991; Cervenak 1984; Haj 1992; Hasso 1998; Sa'ar and Yahia-Younis 2008; Sabbagh 1989) have made significant contributions to the analysis of Palestinian life under duress. Studies of social control and Palestinian experience with the criminal justice system in Israel (S. Cohen 1989, 1991, 1993; Korn 2000; Rattner and Fishman 1998; Zureik 1988; Zureik, Moughrabi, and Sacco 1993), the impact of political violence and its post-traumatic effects on youth and society at large (Khamis 1993a, 1993b, 2000, 2008, 2012a, 2012b; Punamaki and Joustie 1998; Punamaki and Puhakka 1997), family violence (Haj-Yahia 2000, 2001, 2011; Haj-Yahia, Leshem, and Guterman 2011; Shalhoub-Kevorkian 1997a, 1997b, 2004, 2006, 2012a, 2012b), and public health are some of the areas where inroads have been made, particularly among the Palestinians in the occupied Palestinian territories (OPT) and refugee camps (Batniji 2012). Of note here are the extensive and pioneering writings of Muhammad Haj-Yahia and Nadera Shalhoub-Kevorkian on mental health, wife abuse, and domestic violence in Palestinian society.

A thorough treatment of refugees and subaltern Palestinian life under occupation regarding education, health, mobility, and other methods of control and surveillance is provided in a study by Nadia Abu-Zahra and Adah Kay (2013). With a similar subaltern focus, a series of sociological and anthropological case studies on everyday life in Palestine has creatively explored immobility, closure, and time use

(Abourahme 2011; A. Brown 2004; Harker 2009, 2011; R.J. Smith 2011; Wick 2011). Liminality, the ability to shuttle between contrasting worlds of experience, lies at the heart of these studies that attempt to decode the ways that the colonised and the marginalised cope and make sense of their everyday life (see Ghanim 2006; and Said 1996). Resistance receives special attention from Sophie Richter-Devroe (2010, 2012, 2013).

International interest in state creation

A state in the making, Palestine has attracted the attention of national and international research efforts. In conjunction with the implementation of the Oslo agreement between the PLO and Israel, various international agencies were involved in commissioning periodic studies of the West Bank and Gaza. These included the World Bank, European Union, United States Agency for International Development, and various specialised agencies of the United Nations, such as the International Labour Organization, United Nations Development Programme, United Nations Conference on Trade and Development, World Health Organization, United Nations Children's Fund, and the United Nations Office of the Special Coordinator for the Middle East Peace Process, which regularly issues reports on the economy of Palestine.

It is fair to say that these studies, numerous as they are, did not translate on the ground into any meaningful blueprint for state building and empowerment of the Palestinians. On the contrary, even though in 2012 member states overwhelmingly endorsed a non-member status for Palestine in the United Nations General Assembly, some Western countries, led by the United States and Canada, objected to this decision, and the Israeli reaction has been a punitive obstruction of the establishment of a viable Palestinian state through the continued expansion of settlements.

The impasse in which the project of state building in conflict zones finds itself has led some to argue for a research perspective that incorporates nonstate actors. Ron Smith (2011, 317) questions the efficacy of top-down, state-centric studies that portray asymmetric conflicts as occurring "between equal sovereigns," describing the OPT as "a regime of graduated sovereignty, [in which] freedoms of individuals are mediated by the uneven support and repression of the state."

Social movements and the role of media

The rise of radical movements in the Middle East espousing religious ideologies has received substantial press and media coverage, particularly since the attack of 11 September 2001 on the United States. Academic research is no exception. In the early 1980s, Nels Johnson had already published a phenomenological study titled *Islam and the Politics of Meaning in Palestinian Nationalism* (1982). The Hamas movement, too, has been the focus of research by Israelis (Mishal and Sela 2000), Palestinians (Abu Amr 1994; Harub 2000; Tamimi 2007), and westerners

(Gunning 2008; Jensen 2009; Milton-Edwards 1999; Nusse 1998; Roy 2011; Shanzer 2008). It is telling that these works deal exclusively with Islamic fundamentalism, whereas Jewish fundamentalism has received substantially less attention, two exceptions being the work of Ian Lustick (1988) and that of Israel Shahak and Norton Mezvinsky (1999, 2004).

Although the role of social media in shaping the Middle East political landscape came into prominence in the context of revolutionary movements that swept the Arab world in 2011 under the label of the so-called "Arab Spring," the use of online computer communications, the Internet, social media, and electronic networking is not new to the Palestinian experience. Early in the 1990s, the Palestinians embarked on the use of the Internet and online communications, making a significant contribution to our understanding of the role of nongovernmental organisations in political mobilisation (Aouragh 2011a, 2011b; Rohozinski and Collings 2008; Zureik 2006). The use of these technologies has made it possible for Palestinians in their dispersal to connect with one another and overcome restrictions on mobility and the crossing of borders. However, similar to the experience of other Arab compatriots, the Palestinians, as users of the Internet and its associated technologies, are also subject to control – foremost by Israel, which has sole authority over the allocation of electromagnetic spectrums in the OPT, as stipulated in the Oslo agreement, and on more than one occasion has embarked on physically destroying and blocking the operations of Palestinian Internet service providers (Shachtman 2002). The issue of electronic communications is explored in more detail in chapter 6.

This study's contribution

From a theoretical and methodological angle, the contribution of this study is its reconciliation of the colonialism model with a Foucauldian perspective on issues of biopolitics, territory, and state security. As others have demonstrated with regard to other colonial and postcolonial regions (Crampton and Elden 2007; Kelly 2004; Legg 2007), it is possible to examine state racism, dispossession, demography, and biopolitics – core issues that have defined the relationship between the Palestinians and the Zionist settlers for more than a century. Largely inspired by Foucault's work, I deploy surveillance-based control as an organising concept with which to examine population containment, territorial dispossession, and state security and racism. A start along these lines is apparent in several studies (Parsons and Salter 2008; Zureik 2001; Zureik, Lyon, and Abu-Laban 2011), although this is not to deny that as a core concept control was present in the early writings on Israel/Palestine, such as the pioneering works of Sabri Jiryis (1973) and Ian Lustick (1980).

Refugees

Of the crucial issues facing Palestinians, the future of the refugees remains central to resolving the impasse between Israel and the Palestinians. It is thus not surprising to see a markedly increased scholarly and political interest in their fate. Two sets of multilingual bibliographies following the Madrid Middle East Peace Conference, covering the years 1992 to 1999, list close to 1,500 references in Arabic, English, French, and Hebrew dealing with Palestinian refugees. Two-thirds of these references are in English, and about one-fifth are in Hebrew. The overwhelming majority of the Hebrew citations were published between 1995 and 1999, when it finally became apparent that sooner or later the refugee issue would have to be dealt with in the so-called "peace process." The remaining references are divided evenly between the Arabic and French languages, with around 7 per cent of the total allocated to each (Endresen and Zureik 1995; Zureik 2000; Zureik and Mazawi 2000). A more up-to-date bibliographic database and resource centre focused on Palestinian refugees, hosted by Bir Zeit University's Forced Migration and Refugee Unit, includes in excess of 300 references published since 2000 that deal with the Palestinian refugees – mainly books in Arabic and English, with a few in Hebrew. The Refugee Studies Centre at Oxford University houses close to 40,000 references on refugees, including Palestinian refugees. A useful online resource on Palestinian refugees that has been in existence for nearly three decades is McGill University's Palestinian Refugee Research Net (n.d.).

Palestinian and other Arab contributions

Among writings from a Palestinian vantage point, the earliest studies of note on Palestinian refugees are those by Sami Hadawi, a previous tax assessor of the British Mandate government in Palestine, who later worked with the United Nations Conciliation Commission for Palestine in New York. His books *Palestine: Loss of Heritage* (1963) and *Bitter Harvest: Palestine, 1914–1967* (1967) constituted the first detailed public account of destroyed and confiscated refugee property, to be followed in the late 1980s by *Palestinian Rights and Losses in 1948* (1988). The latter includes a section on valuation of material and non-material losses incurred by Palestinian refugees, written by the Lebanese economist Atef Kubursi. In the early 1960s, through the Institute for Palestine Studies, Halim Barakat and Peter Dodd, two sociologists at the American University of Beirut, published a well-known study of Palestinian refugees titled *River without Bridges* (1968). Basem Sirhan, a Palestinian sociologist, very early on wrote an often-cited article titled "Palestinian Refugee Camp Life in Lebanon" (1975). The noted demographer Janet Abu-Lughod (1980) authored one of the early studies to tackle in a systematic way the demography of the Palestinian people by paying special attention to the debate over the numbers and locations of Palestinian refugees resulting from the 1948 and 1967 wars. With a research activity that spans nearly forty years, anthropologist Rosemary Sayigh single-handedly initiated ethnographic studies of Palestinian refugees, using the camps in Lebanon as her research site. She published several well-known articles in the 1960s and 1970s, and these culminated in her well-known book *The Palestinians: From Peasants to Revolutionaries* (1979). Salim Tamari (1996) and I (Zureik 1996) published two "primers" on Palestinian refugees to coincide with the Refugee Working Group talks of the early 1990s, in which we both participated.

A key figure in documenting Palestinian refugee life prior to dispersal is Salman Abu-Sitta (1999, 2005), who meticulously compiled statistical and geographic data on the destroyed villages. Among the younger generation, Ruba Salih (2013) has looked at refugee "bare life" and resistance, Sari Hanafi, Jad Cha'aban, and Karlin Seyfert (2012) have studied poverty among Palestinian refugees in Lebanon, Asem Khalil (2011) has carried out legal analysis of Palestinian economic rights in the Arab countries, Nasser Abourahme (2011) has undertaken a sophisticated analysis of how Palestinians resist and how they negotiate their everyday life between the camp and the checkpoint, Rami Khouri (2009) has highlighted the UNRWA's performance, Randa Farah (2009) has surveyed the attitudes of UNRWA employees toward the organisation, Oroub El-Abed (2009) has turned her attention to the predicament of Palestinian refugees in Egypt, and Ibrahim Hejoj (2007) has detailed poverty in two Palestinian refugee camps in Jordan.

An interesting development in advocacy research, particularly among nongovernmental organisations, is the sprouting of organisations dedicated to researching the refugees' right of return. A special mention should be made of BADIL (n.d.) on the West Bank, which is a research resource centre with close links to the refugee communities. It publishes documentary and advocacy studies on the refugees' right of return. The Shaml Center in Ramallah, established in 1994 but now defunct, focused on citizenship and refugee rights. Al-Haq (n.d.), a legal and human rights organisation founded in 1979 in Ramallah, has a long history of researching Palestinian rights and providing legal advice to Palestinians under occupation. Finally, Al-Awda (n.d.), the Palestine Right to Return Coalition, which has branches worldwide, is dedicated to mobilising Palestinian communities in the diaspora through public education and commemoration of key Palestinian historical events.

Israeli contributions

When the Palestinians and Israelis met in July 2013 in Washington, DC, to negotiate the dispute between them, Israel was on record as denying any culpability in the expulsion and prevention of the return of Palestinian refugees (Shenhav 2012, 68–74). Even if Israel was aware of its role in the creation of the refugee problem, as declassified documents show (Ariel 2013), the top echelons of the government under David Ben-Gurion's leadership shut the door on any repatriation of refugees and made sure that none would trickle back to their homes. The main concern was and remains how to maintain a Jewish numerical majority in Palestine and reap the benefits of seized Arab property. The scant Israeli academic interest in Palestinian refugees at the time should not obscure the fusion between scholarship and commitment to Zionism among mainstream Israeli writers (see Pappé 2009). Anthropologist Dan Rabinowitz (1998) has published an assessment in Hebrew of how Israeli and non-Israeli anthropologists studied the Arab minority. He comments critically on Israeli scholarship's treatment of the Palestinian minority, including Palestinian refugees, and points out its adoption of theoretical and ideological perspectives anchored in functionalism and Zionist ideology. He has returned to the theme of ethnography and the study of Palestine and the Palestinians in a collaboration with Palestinian anthropologist Khaled Furani (Furani and Rabinowitz 2011). Although their study deals with the links between the Biblical research and Palestine, going back to the nineteenth century during the onslaught of British imperialism in the Middle East, the connection between Christianity, Zionism, and the establishment of the State of Israel is left opaque, a lacuna addressed by Lodewijk van Oord (2008, 2011), who has studied Christian- and Western-inspired propaganda efforts in support of the Zionist project in Palestine at the expense of the local Arab population.

One of the early Israeli researchers on Palestinian refugees was anthropologist Emmanuel Marx (1991, 1992), once at Tel Aviv University, who took advantage of his position in the Israeli military to access Palestinian refugees subjects for research. Subsequent to the Israeli occupation of the West Bank and Gaza in 1967, he coauthored, with Yoram Ben-Porath, *Some Sociological and Economic Aspects of Refugee Camps on the West Bank* (Ben-Porath and Marx 1971) for the Rand Corporation. The two authors, with Shimon Shamir, later published *A Refugee Camp on a Mountain Ridge* (1974) in Hebrew, under the auspices of the Shiloah Institute at Tel Aviv University. In 1976 Moshe Efrat published *The Palestinian Refugees: An Economic and Social Study, 1949–1974* in Hebrew through the Horowitz Institute of Tel-Aviv University. In 1981 Avi Plascov wrote *The Palestinian Refugees in Jordan*, and in the mid-1980s the Israeli government published *Will They Be Refugees Forever? Description of Conditions and Suggestions for a Solution* (Aner 1994). Israeli interest in Palestinian refugees has also been reflected in the writings of Israeli legal researchers. In 1986 Ruth Lapidoth of the Hebrew University published a legal argument against implementing the right of return by Palestinian refugees. This article became a standard reference for official and quasi-official Israeli positions on denying Palestinian refugees the right to return to their homes. In 1987, a few years before the Madrid Conference, Benny Morris became the first Israeli historian to address in a serious and detailed manner the question of Palestinian refugees in *The Birth of the Palestinian Refugee Problem, 1947–1949*. Morris ushered into Israeli scholarship what became known later as revisionist or post-Zionist history. Even though he had confirmed in his earlier work Palestinians' claims that they were largely driven from their homes, this did not mean that he regretted what had happened, as was revealed in a newspaperinterview seventeen years later in which he supported ethnic cleansing and the expulsion of Palestinian refugees (in A. Shavit 2004). The taboo is gradually being lifted on the role of the fledgling Israeli state in the expulsion of the Palestinians. Testimony by Amnon Neumann, a soldier in the Palmach from 1947 to 1948, is revealing for its frankness in describing the role of Zionism and how the Palestinians were driven from their villages in the south of the country, how their homes were destroyed, and how if necessary those who attempted to return to their land were killed. The interview was arranged by the Israeli nongovernmental organisation Zochrot (n.d.) as part of its efforts to educate the Jewish public about the causes of the Nakba. When asked to explain why it was necessary to perpetrate these acts that culminated in the Nakba, Amnon Neumann (2011) replied:

This is the first time in a history of thousands of years that these villages are gone. We did not enter the villages to stay there but to expel them. We burnt their houses ... They deserve to remain on their land, as they did for 5000 years before ... It is more interesting to know what were the reasons for this Nakba. Why historically they were never expelled, but we did expel them? All because of the Zionist ideology. This is very clear. We came to inherit the land. Who do you inherit it from? If the land is empty you inherit it from no one. The land was not empty, then we inherited it. I saw this was a deliberate deception of the Zionist movement. And they [the Zionists] did this successfully – a major success.

In the 1990s more Israeli researchers began to turn their attention to the issue of Palestinian refugees. In 1994 Shlomo Gazit, a reserve general in the Israeli army who was coordinator of Israeli government operations in the administered territories, published one of the first policy studies following the Oslo process on how to deal with the refugee compensation issue. In 1997 Maya Rosenfeld wrote a doctoral thesis for the Hebrew University titled "The Way of Life, the Division of Labour and the Social Roles of Palestinian Refugee Families: The Case of Dheisheh Refugee Camp," which eventually appeared as a book (M. Rosenfeld 2004). In 2000, under the auspices of the Institute for Israeli Arab Studies in Jerusalem, Hillel Cohen published, in Hebrew, his master's thesis on the internal Palestinian refugees, who were displaced from their homes in 1948 but remained in what became Israel, titled *The Present Absentees: The Palestinian Refugees in Israel since 1948*. In 2000 Efrat Ben-Ze'ev, an anthropologist affiliated with the Truman Institute at the Hebrew University, wrote her doctoral thesis at Oxford University on Palestinian refugees. Also in 2001 Ilan Pappé published an article on Theodore Katz's controversial Galilee village case study of a Palestinian refugee exodus, which Katz had submitted as a master's thesis at Haifa University in 1988. Although there has been an upsurge in Israeli press and media coverage of the Palestinian refugee issue, the overwhelming majority of these articles remain adamantly opposed to the Palestinian refugee right of return, but the fact that the issue is being discussed is a marked departure from the past (see Halevi 2010).

Western contributions

Among Western writers, Don Peretz, with close ties to Israel at one point, was one of the first to take up the issue, publishing in 1958 his book-length study *Israel and the Palestine Arabs*, which included substantial discussion of Palestinian refugees. In 1988 Laurie Brand, a key researcher on the Middle East, published *Palestinians in the Arab World: Institution Building and the Search for a State*. This was followed by a series of articles on Palestinian-Arab relations. Two well-known articles from the late 1970s and early 1980s that deal with the political-legal aspects of Palestinian refugees were written by Kurt René Radley (1978) and David Forsyth (1983). Immediately before the Madrid Conference, even the Centre for International

Research at the US Bureau of the Census published a demographic study titled *Palestinian Population Projections for 16 Countries of the World, 1990–2010* (Kinsella 1991). In 2003 Helena Lindholm Schulz, in cooperation with Julienne Hammer, published *The Palestinian Diaspora: Formation of Identities and Politics of Homeland*. A seasoned researcher on Palestinian refugees in the area of policy analysis is political scientist Rex Brynen (Brynen and El-Rifai 2007, 2012) of McGill University, who manages the refugee online database referred to earlier (Palestinian Refugee Research Net n.d.).

A new generation of Western scholars, mainly from anthropology, sociology, geography, and culture and media studies, continues to make significant contributions to the study of Palestinian refugees and life in general under occupation. Sophie Richter-Devroe (2013) has conducted ethnographic studies of Palestinian narratives of the right of return, Caitlin Ryan (2012) has turned her attention to the study of resistance to corporeal punishment among Palestinian women, Jane Young (2012) has explored "Zionist carceral practice," drawing upon biopolitics in the works of Foucault and Agamben, Livia Wick (2011) has analysed the uses of time and space in the context of occupation, Karine Hamilton (2011) has undertaken a critical study of how Israel developed a "moral economy of violence" that dehumanises Arabs and Palestinians to justify its military conduct, Ron Smith (2011) has addressed immobility through what he calls "graduated incarceration," Charles Lee (2009) has extended Franz Fanon's writings on the anticolonial struggle in his analysis of Palestinian suicide bombing as "a deathly form of citizenship," and Allison Brown (2004) has dealt with movement restrictions. Anthropologist Ilana Feldman (2007, 2008, 2012a, 2012b) and culture, media, and technology researcher Helga Tawil-Souri (2011, 2012a, 2012b, 2012c, 2013a, 2013b) have published an impressive list of works on Palestinian refugees and occupation.

It should be pointed out that an intellectual hazard accompanying international applied social science's invasion of the study of Palestinians, particularly in the post-Oslo period, has been "uncritical acceptance of empiricist social science tailored to meet the needs of funding agencies," further the "careers of individual researchers," and adhere to the objectives of international policymakers (Hammami and Tamari 1997, 278; see also Tamari 1994). It is fair to say that with a population of approximately 12 million people worldwide, the Palestinians have attracted more than their share of attention from academic circles, policymakers, governmental agencies, international agencies, nongovernmental organisations, political activists, and the media. It is no exaggeration to say that an entire intellectual industry revolving around the Palestinians has sprung up in various Western think-tanks and academic institutions. This makes it more difficult to reach firm conclusions, let alone consensus, about the state of research on the Palestinians. If knowledge is power, as the popular adage goes, it is not difficult to find a correlation between the source of knowledge about Palestinians, as it is propagated in the marketplace of ideas, on the one hand, and the implications of this knowledge for policymaking, influencing public opinion, and analysing the century-old Israeli-Palestinian conflict, on the other. As Edward Said (1978, 1993) has demonstrated in his seminal work, knowledge and interest are highly intertwined at the levels of theory and practice. As will be apparent throughout this study, research on Palestine and Palestinians presents a case in point.

Theory and method
Colonialism and the politics of visibility/invisibility

Until quite recently, the dominant academic literature on Palestine in both Israel and the West has been notable for the near absence of recognition by mainstream scholars that the Israeli project in Palestine in its pre-1948 and post-1967 manifestations is one form of nineteenth-century settler colonialism. An early exception to this is the work of the late Ibrahim Abu-Lughod (1971) in what has become a social science reference book on Palestine. The thrust of this study is to flesh out the arguments against the colonialism thesis and demonstrate that at the apex of the colonial model is a thorough system of control that, in the name of state security, has relied on violence in its various forms, racism, strict patterns of population control, and claims to natural resources such as land and water.

The use of colonialism as an analytic concept for understanding the Israeli-Palestinian conflict has been confined to Palestinian scholars and a minority of critical social theorists – both Israeli and Western. Even so, this is a rather new development whose origin dates back to the middle of the 1990s. At the forefront of Israeli writers who have challenged the Zionist interpretation of Israeli history is Ilan Pappé (2006, 2011), previously of the History Department at Haifa University, who now teaches at the University of Exeter in England. Another Israeli academic in the field is Ronit Lentin of the University of Dublin whose edited book, *Thinking Palestine* (2008b), brought together a group of academics from various disciplines to critically explore the situation of the Palestinians under Israeli control from the point of biopolitics, racism, and the state of exception. Further contributions by Honaida Ghanim (2008) and Pappé (2008) have provided important correctives to applying the work of Giorgio Agamben on the state of exception to the Palestinians. Criticism of Israel's colonial occupation of the West Bank has been provided by Rafael Reuveny (2008b), a previous Israeli officer who teaches in the United States, and by Neve Gordon (2008), a political scientist who teaches at Ben-Gurion University.

Among Palestinian writers, it is worth mentioning the work of Nadim Rouhana and Sabbagh-Khoury (2011) and an earlier work by Rouhana (2006), a Palestinian academic from Israel who teaches in the United States. Among Western writers, the work of the noted Australian anthropologist Patrick Wolfe (2006, 2007) stands out as important in terms of its comparative nature and depth of analysis. And Lorenzo Veracini, another Australian academic and a colleague of Wolfe, has made a welcome contribution to the debate over Israel's colonial experiment with his book *Israel and Settler Society* (2006).

Throughout these works, however, the concept of *surveillance* as such does not figure as part of the colonial edifice that Israel constructed to control the Palestinians. Control (military, political, and economic) was the operative concept. As demonstrated in a conference and subsequent edited collection (Zureik, Lyon, and Abu-Laban 2011) that addressed the relationship between colonialism and surveillance in Israel/Palestine, a detailed understanding of state control mechanisms requires decoding what Foucault (1982) calls the "microphysics of power" so as to understand how discipline is exercised on the body and consciousness of the subject population. State surveillance of memory among the Palestinian population is one such example of disciplining, and acts such as celebrating key dates in Palestinian history have been designated by law in the Israeli Knesset as subversive and illegal (Mada al-Carmel 2010b). The destructive surveillance practices used by Israel in the West Bank and Gaza through the use of checkpoints, identity cards, biometric technologies, and restricted mobility provide fertile research ground for examining the Israeli surveillance panoplies (Tawil-Souri 2012a, 2012b). By examining declassified documents, researchers have uncovered in detail the bureaucratic and informal surveillance methods used by the state and its agencies in controlling the Palestinian population during the first two decades of the state's existence (Sa'di 2011, 2013). It is a system that resembles the Stasi spy system used in eastern Europe during the height of Soviet domination.

Whereas in advanced industrial societies surveillance strives to enhance the visibility of subjects through electronic and other means (Haggerty and Ericson 2006), in the colonial context surveillance has a bifurcated function. While it ensures that the lives of the colonised are closely monitored, it also aims to enhance their *invisibility* through various means, such as, in the case of North America, the creation of reserves and, in the case of the Palestinians, the adoption of racialised zoning laws that keep the coloniser and colonised separate, as well as the erection of physical obstacles and walls to remove the colonised from view (Khalili 2010b; Weizman 2007).

The quantitative-qualitative divide

Interest in ethnographic research occupies a central place in the diverse methodologies encountered in the postpositivist era. The thrust of ethnographic research in general, in the words of Paul Willis (2000, 109), is to understand the relation between three elements: "creative meaning-making in sensuous practices; the forms, i.e. what the symbolic resources used for meaning-making are and how they are used; the social, i.e. the formed and forming relation to the main structural relations, necessities and conflicts of society." Thus ethnography is the analysis of meaning-making as a cultural production of everyday practices, and as such its focus is the creative use (implicitly and explicitly) by agents of symbolic and material repertoires to comprehend and decode the world around them, cope with it, and understand it as a creative endeavour. From a standard positivist angle, the problems with ethnography, and all qualitative work for that matter, are measurement, validity of the data collected, and generalisability of the conclusions reached. A rather different criticism of ethnography comes from the postmodern camp and centres on the authorial problematic of the text. This view is encapsulated by Willis's (2000, 113) "postmodern and poststructuralist critique of ethnographic methods as constituting rather than reflecting their subject matter." The postmodern critique of ethnography questions the finality and authoritative nature of the text and its stability in meaning. The emphasis on difference and juxtaposition in postmodern writings is taken to mean that in the study of culture the line separating the global from the local is becoming blurred. The global is not out there but is increasingly becoming part of the local (Marcus 1995, 566).

Despite the criticisms and limitations of ethnography, which focuses on the everyday experiences of actors, anthropologists have been able to use it to draw our attention to the way human agency resists, copes with, and constructs social order in the midst of adverse circumstances (L. Abu-Lughod 1993). This way of studying Palestinians "from the bottom up," so to speak, gives voice to marginal groups in society and resonates with much of what comes out of cultural studies generally (Peteet 1994b, 1997; Sayigh 1977, 1979; Sirhan 1975, 2005; Suleiman 1997, 2010; Swedenburg 1990, 1995). For this reason, ethnographic studies stand out for their contribution to understanding Palestinian refugee life.

With regard to quantitative research, the most noticeable surge in the use of attitudinal surveys and other kinds of applied research techniques occurred after the occupation of the West Bank and Gaza by Israel in 1967, particularly after the signing of the Oslo agreement between Israel and the Palestinians in September 1993. Although some research is carried out by independent researchers and academics, the bulk of such quantitative research is interest-laden and funded either by international organisations or donor countries, both of which have a vested need to gather such statistics for policy purposes. Included in this surge of quantitative research is the gathering of public opinion data in the West Bank and Gaza intended to gauge Palestinian public opinion with regard to various facets of the Middle East peace process. Here is how Rema Hammami and Salim Tamari (1997, 278) describe the connection between survey research and policymaking in the aftermath of the Palestinian-Israeli peace agreements in 1992 and 1993: "The impetus for these surveys at this time was described by one [Palestinian] pollster as an attempt to provide the Palestinian negotiating team, as well as the PLO in Tunis, with a sense of the community's 'red line'; that is, what issues could and could not be compromised on."

A glaring example of this policy-oriented research was aptly highlighted by the *New York Times* in 1993 when, immediately after the signing of the Oslo agreement between the PLO and Israel, the newspaper pointed out that the Norwegian nongovernmental organisation Fafo was, as it remains, intimately involved in survey research on Palestinians on behalf of the Norwegian and other governments, while at the same time facilitating secret negotiations between the two sides – an instance of securing "peace through survey research" (Cronin 1993; see also Zureik 1993).

Foucault, power, and Palestine

Official discourse such as government reports, commissions of inquiry (Shenhav and Gabay 2001), and censuses are but a few of several means for ensuring state legitimacy (Ashforth 1990; Zureik 2001). Equally relevant in the construction of state hegemony are the writings of social scientists, intellectuals, and media commentators, as demonstrated by Edward Herman and Noam Chomsky (1988) and by Said (1978, 1981). Until recently, the focus of critical research has been on decoding and deconstructing elite discourse. But understanding resistance and counterhegemony is not only a function of decoding and deconstructing discourse of the powerful; as James C. Scott (1987) demonstrates in his studies of peasant rebellions in Malaysia, resistance is also linked to revealing "unrecorded" histories as experienced by the less powerful – those in whose name intellectuals and governments speak. Ethnographic studies and oral histories have played a major role in giving voice and agency to marginal groups in society. This practice has assumed special significance in the case of accounts describing the world of Palestinian refugees and those living in exile and under Israeli occupation.

Analysis of power and resistance is crucial in assessing systems of control. The deployment of power has been analysed by Michel Foucault in terms of subjectivity, administrative practices, and knowledge production. As mentioned in the Introduction, this study discusses population, territory, and control using a Foucauldian perspective, and here Foucault's work on power, in spite of its shortcomings, pointed out below, remains critical to examining the issues raised in this study. What distinguishes Foucault's work is the shift from viewing the state as the main carrier of power to considering the "microphysics of power" reflected in the day-to-day disciplinary measures of population control – whether it is the workplace, checkpoint, school, family, or hospital. It is customary to remark that Foucault's important analysis of normalising the self (i.e., the ways that individuals unwittingly discipline themselves by acting on their bodies and thoughts) falls short of addressing the role of resistance by agency (Giddens 1981, 172; Said 1982, 63–64). For Foucault's defenders, this deficiency may have been true of Foucault's earlier work, where, according to Colin Gordon (1991, 4), he "seemed to give the impression of certain uses of power as having an almost absolute capability to tame and subject individuals." It is certainly not true of his subsequent work on governmentality and the use that he makes of "biopolitics" and the "strategic reversibility" of "power relations" (ibid.). Power here is conceived of in its "productive" capacity. It is precisely because of its capillary forms, whereby governmentality involves in minute detail the intimate aspects of people's lives (e.g., body, sexuality, and reproductive ability), that it renders multiple locations of power visible, thus making it possible to design counterstrategies. According to Foucault (1978, 95–96), "Resistance is integral to power. The existence of power relationships depends on a multiplicity of points of resistance which are present everywhere in the power network. Resistances are the old terms in relations of power: they are inscribed in the latter as irreducible opposite."

Although Foucault acknowledged (non-sovereign) power and resistance, critics are right in pointing out that he did not take full cognisance of agency's reaction to and interpretation of power, let alone modes of resistance. Foucault's analysis "misses any relation between power and resistance. Specifically, it misses any antagonistic relation in which the means of power take shape against resistance" (Macdonnell 1986, 121). Julie Peteet (1994b, 33) makes a similar point by noting that "Foucault's view of the body as a text, as a site of inscription and exhibition by dominant forces, shows little concern with people's responses to having their bodies appropriated and designated as sites of inscription." If ethnographers have provided a methodology for delving into subjectification as a way of revealing the effects of power relations, social theorists have articulated a theory of resistance. With regard to the latter, the work of Anthony Giddens on structuration stands out as an important contribution in this respect. According to Giddens's (1984, 162) structuration, "the dualism of the 'individual' and 'society' is reconceptualized as the duality of agency and structure." Structuration theory portrays human beings as knowledgeable agents who are capable of acting upon and reproducing social systems across space and time through the deployment of an array of material and non-material resources. According to Giddens, "in the production/reproduction of interaction, agents draw upon corresponding elements of social systems: signification (meaning), domination (power) and legitimation (sanction)" (ibid., 19). Giddens's conception of agency is premised on the ability of human agents to make choices and intervene in the course of events by making a difference. As he says, agency implies "that a person could have done otherwise" and that "an agent who has no option whatsoever is no longer an agent" (in J. Thompson 1989, 73). The knowledgeability of agents refers to what actors believe or know about the context of their actions and those of others, including the reservoir of knowledge, tacit as well as explicit (discursive), that actors rely upon in the production and reproduction of structures (Giddens 1984, 375). Actions in which agents engage can be rationalised (i.e., supported by explanations if the need arises) or reflexively monitored (i.e., part of "the flow of activity" in the sense that action does not consist "of discrete acts involving an aggregate of intentions, but a continuous process" (ibid., 376). Structure refers to the "rules and resources recursively implicated in the reproduction of social systems" (ibid., 377). The resources (material, symbolic, and legal) at the agency's disposal can be both enabling and disabling. In Giddens's words, "structuration theory is based on the proposition that structure is always both enabling and constraining, in virtue of the inherent relation between structure and agency (and agency and power)" (ibid., 169). Social reproduction, which is contingent upon practices carried out in the context of "time-space distanciation," is a key element in Giddens's structuration theory. The more differentiated a society, the higher it is on the time-space continuum, as seen with modern, industrial societies. Tribal and traditional societies are low on the distanciation scale because of co-presence and face-to-face communication.

Giddens rejects the proposition that power is a thing "out there" that is unidirectional and flows in a causal manner from an "objective" source to a subject. Thus power is not a zero-sum game but is "the means of getting things done, very definitely enablement as well as constraint" (Giddens 1984, 175). Notwithstanding Foucault's relational treatment of power and indeed the similarity of the two authors in their depiction of power, Giddens rejects Foucault's analogy of the "microphysics of power" or the "capillary of power." In place of the ubiquitous and dualistic conception of power, Giddens substitutes the "dialectic of control," which refers to "the two-way character of the distributive aspect of power" and denotes "how the less powerful manage resources in such a way as to exert control over the more powerful in established power relations" (ibid., 374). The concept of resistance is explicit in his portrayal of agency and structure.

Whereas from the Foucauldian perspective subjectification is achieved through governmentality (i.e., by disciplining the population through noncoercive means), the Palestinian population in the West Bank and Gaza, which lives under colonial rule, is subjected to routine coercive practices in which violence as a spectacle is very much in evidence. In commenting on Foucault's treatment of power, Diane Macdonnell (1986, 121) appropriately notes that Foucault's conception of power "does little to help us consider how power is at work in the deadly forces of physical repression, especially the army and the police." Criminologist Stanley Cohen (1991) remarks that the Israeli secret service has been engaged in applying psychological and physical pressure to extract confessions from Palestinian prisoners since the early 1970s. A landmark government commission headed by Israeli Supreme Court judge Moshe Landau sanctioned the use of violence and recommended in its report that when "nonviolent psychological pressure" fails to extract information from detainees, "exertion of a moderate amount of physical pressure cannot be avoided" (in ibid., 25). Although the Israeli Supreme Court finally ruled that the use of torture against prisoners is illegal, Israel's army continues to use torture to this day, as evident from press coverage (Hockstader 2001), testimonies of Israeli soldiers (Manekin et al. 2010), and reports by human rights organisations, such as Amnesty International (2001) and the Israeli organisation B'Tselem (1998). More will be said about the use of state violence in chapter 5.

The past decade or so has seen tremendous interest in the application of the Foucauldian framework to the analysis of marginal groups (refugees, slum dwellers, and shantytowns) – those who according to Foucault have been relegated to biopolitical abandonment. At the centre of the debate is how to account for the co-existence in modernity of "large destructive structures and institutions oriented toward the care of individual life" (Foucault 1988, in Selmeczi 2009, 519). With a focus on territory, violence, and the body, direct application of Foucault to the Palestinian case has been carried out by Lisa Bhungalia (2012), Michael Dahan (2012), Gary Fields (2010), Adam Ramadan (2009), Caitlin Ryan (2012), Ron Smith (2011), Livia Wick (2011), Jane Young (2012), and myself (Zureik 2001).

The constructivist perspective

I now turn my attention to the role of scientific discourse, showing how science is "translated" in order to accomplish political ends. I have chosen to deal with three innovative studies involving the Palestine conflict whose frame of reference in a broad sense is the constructivist approach familiar to students working in the sociology of science. The utility of this approach is that it enables the researcher to examine scientific controversies and contested knowledge claims without privileging one belief system over another. Unlike positivism, the constructivist approach subjects scientific knowledge claims to symmetric social analysis. By taking various belief systems into account, it enables the researcher to find out how scientific closures are attained (Martin and Richards 1995).

If knowledge is power, as the adage has it, practice is the process by which knowledge is translated into power. In her stimulating work on "archaeological practice," Nadia Abu El-Haj (1998, 2002) borrows from constructivist approaches to the social study of science – as elaborated by, among others, Bruno Latour (1987) and Michel Callon (1995) – in order to argue for the need to go beyond the familiar discourse analysis, which focuses on "science as culture":

> In order to account for such processes of translation – to illustrate the practices and contexts through which knowledge actually becomes power – we cannot focus on discourse alone. In the case of archaeology we need to move beyond the scholarly debates in which archeologists engage and the stories of past and present that archaeologists tell. If science is practice-based, we must pay attention to the work of excavating the land and producing material culture. The objects of the scholarly quest (be they smaller artifactual remains or larger architectural structures) are as significant as are the texts, the interpretations, and the historical narratives that archaeologists create. (Abu El-Haj 1998, 179–80)

In examining the relationship between archaeology and nationalism, Abu El-Haj uses for her case study the excavations carried out by Israeli archaeologists to reconstruct the Jewish Quarter in Jerusalem's old city. She shows how the production of material culture by Israeli archaeologists succeeded in demarcating the porous boundaries between the four main quarters in the old city (Muslim, Christian, Armenian, and Jewish) and how "the (embodied) history and historicity created through the work of archaeology situate the Jewish nation's claim to the city in a historical trajectory separate from that of the rest of the city's inhabitants" (Abu El-Haj 1998, 180). Knowledge is "translated" into power through practice and the bringing together of a constellation of human and nonhuman factors comprised of "embodied skills, experimental devices, and systems of statements," the so-called "actants," in Callon's (1995, 59) terminology. More recently, Abu El-Haj (2012) has turned her attention to an equally daunting task, namely that of investigating the genealogy of the Jews by highlighting the relationship between genetic science, race, and politics.

Using the same constructivist approach, Samer Alatout (1999, ch. 2) has analysed the role of scientific knowledge in the debate between the Zionist movement in Palestine and the British Mandate government in the 1930s and 1940s concerning the availability of water as a resource, which figures prominently in determining the absorptive capacity of the country. Furthermore, he uses the case study to contribute to the state-society debate and argue against a state-centred approach to understanding the process of nation building. The emergence of the nation-state is better understood not solely as the outcome of a decision-making process by political elites but also as a "co-production" involving the translation of several actors' discourses (political and non-political) into practice.

By focusing on water as a strategic resource in the contest over Palestine, Alatout (1999, ch. 2) shows how in the early 1930s the Zionists appealed to a specific type of scientific knowledge – namely geophysics, which relies on the deductive and speculative method, rather than geology, which is based on actual testing of water availability – in order to support their claim of an abundance of water for land irrigation and to justify further Jewish immigration to Palestine. This approach was employed at a time when the political discourse centred on a "Jewish homeland" rather than a sovereign "state." Alatout shows that a shift in Zionist use of scientific discourse occurred between the late 1930s and early 1940s. This shift coincided with the evolving political environment in Palestine, where the concept of a "Jewish homeland," as articulated by the British government in the Balfour Declaration two decades earlier, was being translated in Zionist thinking into the concept of a "Jewish state." The shift in the use of scientific knowledge from geophysics to geology thus coincided with a shift in the scope of projected water needs from the local (homeland) to the national (nation-state). It was the interplay between scientific knowledge and political events that gave rise to what Alatout calls "co-production" of the Jewish state:

> The shift in favour of perceiving Palestine's water resources in terms of one national, geo-hydrological system enabled the perception of Palestine as a national space. More significantly, however, is the fact that perceptions of the national space extended as much, and followed closely, the perceived hydrological mapping of Palestine. What water experts constructed as the water system of Palestine had direct effects on what was imagined as the boundaries of the nation-state itself. (Ibid., 11–12)

A final example that belongs to this genre is the work of Anat Leibler and Daniel Breslau, who have analysed the role of the Israeli Central Bureau of Statistics (ICBS) in constructing the citizen category in the early days of the Israeli state (Leibler 1999; Leibler and Breslau 2005). This population construction was the outcome of a convergence between government policy and scientific practice. More importantly, the use of ethnic markers to count people was instrumental in ethnicising citizenship and creating a stratum of displaced Palestinians, the so-called "present absentees," who remained in the country, lost their land, and are unable to this day to return to their homes (Zureik 2001).

One of the first tasks undertaken by Israel after declaring statehood in 1948 was to conduct a complete census count of every individual present within its self-declared borders. Faced with a need to provide precise counting of both the Jewish and Arab populations immediately after the state was declared and in the aftermath of the 1948 war, the ICBS's director advised the government to impose a curfew on the population so that people could be counted *in situ*. Those who were not present in their homes were counted as absent and did not appear in the census registry. This was subsequently taken by the government to mean that individuals absent from their residence during census taking, even if they stayed elsewhere in the country, could not return to their towns and villages and reclaim their property. This was applied to the Arab but not Jewish population. Roughly 32,000 Israeli Arabs, 20 per cent of the original Arab population that remained in Israel after the 1948 war, were classified as "present absentees" at the time of the first census, and their number now, more than fifty years later, is in excess of 250,000. Up to this day, they have been prevented from returning to their homes. Notwithstanding claims of separation between scientific and political agencies, this is how Liebler (1999, 20) describes the alliance between the government and the ICBS in creating the new category of "present absentee" Arab citizens:

> This separation, so adamantly upheld by Professor Bachi [first director of the ICBS], was able to "whitewash" one of the major results of the first census, which with its attendant curfew became one of the mechanisms that permitted the state to appropriate Arab-owned land and property. Under conditions of curfew, only those found at home could be registered. However, because of the intensive battles fought at the time, a substantial proportion of the Arab population was not home. Nevertheless, perhaps for this very reason, orders were given that those absent from their homes would not be registered as citizens and that their ownership of goods, property and land was not to be recognized. The statistical category of "absentee property owners" – Arab residents whose property rights were abrogated – was born (this category would receive legal recognition a number of years later).

The problem of order

The numerous debates over the origins of ethnic and nationalist conflicts, also subsumed under the "problem of order," have a venerable tradition in social theory. The problem of order has been a central concern of theorists, from Aristotle, Thomas Hobbes, and John Locke to Jean-Jacques Rousseau, Emile Durkheim, and Talcott Parsons, not to mention more recent writers spanning a wide spectrum in the social and behavioural sciences, international relations, sociobiology, psychology, social psychiatry, and history (Wrong 1994). I do not intend to dwell on these debates in any detail here. My purpose is limited to examining two specific approaches in current thinking about the Palestinian-Israeli conflict. The first approach is identified with the psychologically based conflict-resolution perspective and what is called the "co-existence" literature; the second draws upon the human rights literature and transnationalism.

Attempts to understand ethno-nationalist conflicts by linking them to identity and personal security as universal human needs have been undertaken by psychologically oriented writers such as John Burton, a key figure in the World Society School of international relations, and his associate Herbert Kelman. The basis of Burton's approach is a generic-cum-genetic theory positing that all conflicts over territory are a disguised manifestation of deprivations of universal human needs of a psychological nature. Burton's position is encapsulated in the following:

> At the superficial level of personal, cultural and national differences of behaviours and interests, conflicts are win-lose. It is upon revelation of the ultimate goals – the universal, ontological, and even genetic goals of individual and group identity and development – that the problem may be defined more accurately ... The individual operates through an identity group, a primordial attachment, and will use all means available, regardless of social consequences[,] in the pursuit of these needs. (Burton and Sandole 1986, in Collings 1988, 49–50)

Ethno-nationalist conflicts over territory are usually depicted as zero-sum encounters and for this reason tend to be protracted, whereas conflicts involving identity and security can be tackled through negotiations with the aid of a third-party intervention that highlights the realisation of common values and the related positive outcomes for the parties in conflict. Since these are universal values shared by all, including parties to a conflict, Burton and those following his lead argue that face-to-face encounter facilitates self-disclosure of thwarted needs, reduces peoples' insecurities, and helps to resolve the conflict. For the conflict to become manageable, the political is thus reduced to the personal. In Herbert Kelman's (1998, 9–11) words, carefully organised workshop encounters in conflict resolution help "to develop de-escalatory language" that challenges the "demonic" and "monolithic image of the enemy." Territorial conflicts, according to John Burton and Dennis Sandole (1986), are psychologically rooted more in concern for security and identity needs than in concern for concrete attainment of objective reality, such as the acquisition of territory. Kelman, a political psychologist himself, who was active for close to a quarter-century in arranging workshops for Israeli-Palestinian encounters as a vehicle for conflict resolution, subscribes to the same theoretical foundations as Burton, but he does not cast his argument in the same biologically determinist mode. Kelman (1998, 9) expresses the social-psychological assumptions of the "interactive problem solving approach" by remarking that "the satisfaction of the needs of both parties – the needs of human individuals as articulated through their core identity groups – is the ultimate criterion for a mutually satisfactory resolution of their conflict"; consequently, "unfulfilled needs, especially for identity and security, and existential fears ... typically drive the conflict and create barriers to its resolution." However, by depoliticising the conflict and effecting "a shift in emphasis from power politics to mutual responsiveness" (ibid., 11), Kelman's approach suffers from the same shortcomings as Burton's, namely that he downplays the historical and structural components of the conflict and pays lip service to, but ignores, the consequences of the asymmetrical power relationships that characterise such encounters. In their critique of the logical and conceptual foundations of the Burtonian "generic needs" theory, Kevin Avruch and Peter Black (1987) ask, "Where do these needs come from? And why do those particular needs and not others? From what theory are they deduced? Seemingly it is a compound of geneticism, sociobiology and stimulus-response behaviourism. Each is insufficient: together they make a jumble" (in Collings 1988, 33).

In a related work, Avruch (1998) considers national culture as a mediating factor that ought to be incorporated as a corrective to the Burtonian scheme of conflict resolution. The call for cultural sensitivity on the part of Avruch, although it compensates for the determinist-cum-genetic approach of Burton, falls short of dealing with asymmetrical power relations among protagonists. Knowing a lot about your adversary's cultural repertoire can be a two-edged sword. It can help you to better understand your opponent, and if you are the stronger of the two, it can also allow you to use this knowledge to extract more concessions from the other party. Knowledge becomes a tool in the will to power. It is not that Avruch is unaware of asymmetrical power relations. He clearly is, but he argues that culture is an important instrument for decoding power and rendering it meaningful to culturally disparate groups. He asks rhetorically, "What is a blow? How does one know when a blow is about to be delivered or has been delivered? And will blows to the head have the same social (as opposed to physiological – in origin) effects for all heads at all times?" (ibid., 53-54). Short of one being totally unconscious before and after the blow, it does not seem to be all that onerous a task to interpret the meaning of a blow and feel the pain inflicted by it. To say that "power cross-culturally projected is doubly constituted: once in its projection and another in its reception" (ibid., 54) is to treat power as a matter of interpretation and meaning. In other words, it is all in the eyes of the beholder. There does not seem to be any critical realist assessment of power and means to counter it. Actually, in none of these approaches is resistance as a plausible mode of action contemplated. By the same consideration, issues of justice are submerged and obfuscated under the premise that the personal is political and that all one has to do is reduce the world of politics to interpersonal contact.

With regard to the conflict between Israelis and Palestinians, Deirdre Collings (1988, 58) asks rhetorically, "is it enough to suggest that the conflict is not over objective conflict of interest (land) but is over identity needs which have been denied?" The route that Collings takes in answering the question, without denying the importance of identity formation at the individual and group levels, is to view identity formation as a historical process governed by circumstances of mobilisation specific to the group in question. Thus the Burtonian claim that "the Palestinians are rebelling because their identity needs are frustrated," says Collings, works "to cast

Palestinian identity as something which is mystically engraved deep in the Palestinian psyche and which drives these people to their group identity. Further, this explanation circumvents the entire historical process through which identity was forged at the group level" (ibid., 68). In rejecting the primordialist-cum-biological approach inherent in Burton's model, she also rejects the purely situationalist approach. In discussing the debate over primordialist versus situationalist explanations, she rejects the either/or approach to understanding conflict and posits self-esteem as a historical, social construct in order to circumvent generic-cum-genetic essentialist assumptions and the primordialist-situationalist dichotomy (ibid., 66–68).

In an assessment of the encounter experiments held between Palestinians and Israeli Jews, anthropologist Dan Rabinowitz (2001a, 78) has reached pessimistic conclusions concerning the efficacy of the so-called "co-existence field" in fostering Arab-Jewish understanding:

> ... politicized, asymmetric, embedded in larger power balances, the co-existence field's hidden agenda does not sustain the claim that liberal attempts to break barriers between individuals serve as even-handed, neutral mechanisms and work equally for all concerned. It is the failure to acknowledge these dynamics that might turn a generally benevolent, perhaps naïve, project into a mechanism that reifies inequality and actively withholds real change.

An equally critical assessment is echoed by Amr Sabet, who directs his attention to the larger picture of negotiations between Israel and the Arabs. He points out that the politics of negotiations, built as they are on asymmetrical power relations, ultimately demand that the Arab side, being the weaker party, direct its goals away from substantive issues of justice, rights, and entitlements in order to focus on resolving the conflict through cost-benefit analysis. Sabet (1998, 8) goes so far as to suggest, based on "historical experience," that in cases "when basic entitlements are at stake against overwhelming odds, *less* rationality fares better than more rationality" (emphasis in original). He gives examples from the Vietnam War and Finland's conflict with the former Soviet Union to demonstrate the power of "passion" in overcoming a Western rationality matrix. The same could be said of the conflict between Hezbollah and Israel, in which by Western standards the "irrational" behaviour of Hezbollah eventually compelled Israel to withdraw from Lebanon, which is why Israel will oppose at any cost the attempt by Palestinian groups, such as Hamas, to shift the paradigm of conflict from a Western-based one guided by the Oslo agreement to one in which notions of justice and self-determination are paramount.

A wide-ranging examination of the co-existence field has been carried out by Mohammed Abu-Nimer (1999), who concentrates on assessing the outcome of such encounters between Arab and Jewish citizens of Israel. His conclusions are consistent with those summarised above in that he sees these programs as part of a "control" and "co-optation" system designed to make "Zionism more palatable for Palestinians" (ibid., 153).

The central role Max Weber assigns to the nation-state in respect of monopolising the means of violence (in its various forms) is worth expanding upon, for it allows us to examine instances when the state transgresses its administrative role vis-à-vis the citizenry and justifies its use of violence by labelling as "deviant" those activities that are essentially political in nature but deemed threatening to its legitimacy. Here the literature on human rights and transnationalism is helpful (Bisharat 1989, 2005; Bisharat et al. 2009). Violations of human rights by the state are fuelled by the "culture of denial," which Stanley Cohen explains with the aid of theories borrowed from psychoanalysis, cognitive psychology, bystander theory, and motivational accounts. With the death of so-called "meta" or grand narratives of Marxism and liberalism, Cohen (1993, 99) hopes for a future when "human rights will become the normative political language" and the criminalising power of the state will be checked.

Writing within a similar tradition, Lisa Hajjar discusses the national and international expansion of "cause lawyering" on behalf of human rights and efforts at democratisation. Cause lawyering, according to Hajjar (1997, 474), "implies agency, motivation, social identification, political relations and goals . . . The study of cause lawyering, then, involves analysis of the contours of resistance through the medium of law within a given field of hegemonic relations."

Thus, if the state has monopoly over the use of legitimate means of violence, it is no longer true that such a prerogative goes unchecked. The state is being increasingly subjected to norms and pressures emanating from internal and external sources, the so-called "world polity," comprised of auditors representing human rights organisations, international agencies of one kind or another, and nongovernmental bodies. This is not to imply that the nation-state is about to succumb to these pressures but rather that it increasingly finds itself needing to reaffirm its legitimacy as a member of the world polity. The need for legitimacy results in modifications of state policies in response to criticisms involving human rights violations. As James Ron (1997, 282) points out: "The world polity and nation-states thus coexist in an uneasy relationship. Rather than viewing them as distinct entities engaged in a battle for control, we should see them as two fractions of a fluid and interactive process, in which each fraction helps to construct and legitimate the other."

By using Israel's treatment of Palestinian detainees during the First Intifada from 1987 to 1993 as a case study, Ron shows how, under pressure from the world polity, the interrogation measures used by the Israeli state shifted from the spectacle of torture and punishment to that of discipline in the Foucauldian sense. The utility of the "world polity" paradigm is that it opens a window of opportunity and allows marginal groups and populations, who are targets of state violence, to air their grievances. That these populations are marginal places them in a position of disadvantage in terms of effecting a change in the policies of the central government, even when these governments are of the liberal-democratic variety. As Ron puts it:

> In recent decades an increasingly dense world polity has offered an indirect form of representation and transparency for marginalized populations, provided they are able to take advantage of the opportunity. Though world

polity structures are an imperfect alternative to the typical mechanisms of protection offered to full-fledged citizens in democratic states, by using international human rights bodies and human rights discourse as platforms for global lobbying, targeted populations can generate pressure on otherwise indifferent security forces and regimes. Global lobbying by Palestinians in the West Bank and Gaza is a prime example of this method of gaining international protection. (Ibid., 290–91)

One can extrapolate from this discussion by referring to a similar phenomenon in which the Palestinian National Authority (PNA) has been subjected by the world polity to criticisms for violating human rights of the Palestinian population in the West Bank and Gaza. The interesting thing to note here is that, unlike Israel, the PNA has not managed to effect a shift in its "legitimate use of means of violence" against target populations in its midst. "Torture as spectacle" is very much in evidence in the practice of the Palestinian criminal justice system, as several human rights reports testify (B'Tselem 1995). No doubt, this is due to the lack of "experience" by the PNA; gradually, if begrudgingly, it too will have to respond to international criticism and make the transition from torture to discipline. What is ominous, in the case of the Palestinians, is that state building proceeds with little cognisance at the institutional level of the need to protect human rights. No mention was made of human rights protection in the various agreements concluded under the Oslo umbrella (see Harlow 1996, 161). The president of the PNA, Yasser Arafat, when he died, had not signed into legislation the package of basic laws passed by the Palestinian Legislative Council (Council on Foreign Relations 1999). Palestinian lawyers in the occupied territories have gone on strike to protest the continued lack of an attorney general to replace the one who resigned, and the PNA is contemplating a law that severely limits, if not bans, nongovernmental organisations that monitor human rights violations, including those of the PNA (Hass 1999a, 1999b). Al-Haq (n.d.), a Palestinian legal and human rights advocacy organisation, has criticised on several occasions the conduct of the Palestinian National Authority and its security forces in its treatment of Palestinian citizens.

National identities are no longer subject to the constraints of space, time, and national politics. International mobility and the widespread use of communications technology have not only brought people into closer contact with each other by transcending geographical boundaries but have also created, in John Urry's (2000, 78) term, a "hybridity" between agency and communication technology, giving rise to "co-agency" (see also Faist 1998). Others go even further and suggest that computer networks ought to be considered a form of social capital. Sara Ferlander and Duncan Timms (2001, 51–52) hypothesise "that the use of local nets will lead to an increase in association, support and trust that provide the foundation for collaboration, common identity and social capital in the community."

The revival of subgroup national identities is being greatly facilitated by the application of information and communication technology in which time and space are compressed. "E-mail nationalism," argues Benedict Anderson (1994a), is made possible through the emergence of worldwide computer networks that link diasporic, immigrant, and refugee communities to the homeland. Although not limited to fundamentalist causes, this "long-distance nationalism" is exerting pressure on the nation-state and exacerbating simmering ethnic conflicts. It is not surprising to read accounts of Middle Eastern cyberwars (Sher 2000) between Israelis and Palestinians. Palestinians in the West Bank and Gaza may lag behind Israel in Internet connections, at 14 per cent and 30 per cent respectively, but Palestinian use of the Internet is on the increase (PCPSR 1999; Segan 1999). Equally significant is the use by Palestinian refugee communities of the Internet to establish connections among the various refugee camps scattered in the Middle East. Across Borders, an internet project that was first established in the Dheisheh camp in the West Bank, received substantial press coverage for its efforts to link children, in particular, from several camps that are not accessible to each other for political and geographic reasons. In the words of the project director, "we need Palestinian refugees to communicate directly between themselves, unmediated by other interests" (in Usher 1999). This experiment in making use of the convergence between computers and telecommunications equipment is singled out by Edward Said (1999) as a form of resistance by which Palestinians assert collective memory and share experience in the face of spatial obstacles. Chapter 6 explores the role of the Internet in Palestinian society.

Globalism, transnationalism, and the network society

The mushrooming literature on migrant and refugee communities is replete with concepts borrowed from sociology, geography, anthropology, cultural studies, and literary criticism. Concepts such as place, space, globalism, and transnationalism have become part of the discourse on displaced people and refugees. To begin with, I will deal with the work of Anthony Giddens, whose main concern is with the role of modernity in shaping individual experience in Western societies. To the extent that he comments on changes taking place in the developing countries, these changes are perceived as part of global transformations sweeping the world in late modernity. He locates three such changes: globalisation, detraditionalisation, and social reflexivity (Giddens 1995, 2–4). Globalisation is not only confined to the economic sphere or the emergence of world systems, as is customarily alluded to in the debates about modernity, but also implicates the "very texture of everyday life." Due mainly to developments in the means of communication, globalisation structures intimacy and identity; it "invades local contexts of action but does not destroy them; on the contrary, new forms of local cultural autonomy, the demand for local cultural identity and self-expression, are causally bound up with globalization processes" (ibid., 3). In another context, Giddens (1991, 21) remarks that the "concept of globalization is best understood as expressing fundamental aspects of time-space distanciation. Globalization concerns the intersection of presence and absence, the interlacing of social events and social relations 'at a distance' with local contextualities." This theme concerning the articulation of the global and local, dubbed by some as "glocalization" (see Robertson 1995), is explored in greater detail below in a discussion of Arjun Appadurai's (1996) concepts of locality and "modernity at large." Detraditionalisation is associated with what Giddens (1995) calls "reflexive modernization," an aspect of late modernity, which is distinguished from earlier "simple modernization" of the nineteenth and early twentieth centuries. Although during the early phase of modernisation, tradition fused with modernity and reflexive modernisation:

> ... traditions in many circumstances become reinvigorated and actively defended. This is the very origin of fundamentalism, a phenomenon which does not have a long history. Fundamentalism can be defined as tradition defended in the traditional way – against the backdrop, however, of a globalising cosmopolitan world which increasingly asks for reasons. The "reason" of tradition differs from that of discourse. Traditions, of course, can be defended discursively; but the whole point of tradition is that it contains a "performative notion" of truth, a ritual notion of truth. Truth is exemplified in the performance of the traditional practices and symbols. (Ibid., 3)

Finally, social reflexivity is a feature of global communication and is a consequence of living in a detraditionalised social order where "everyone must confront, and deal with, multiple sources of information and knowledge, including fragmented and contested knowledge claims" (Giddens 1995, 3). The self becomes "a reflexive project" in "high modernity." The dialectical relationship between the local and global is associated with risk and ontological insecurity. Because of the convergence in time and space, "for the first time in human history, 'self' and 'society' are interrelated in a global milieu" (Giddens 1991, 32). This observation has important consequences for discussion of migrants, refugees, and displaced people generally.

Anthropologist Arjun Appadurai shares with Giddens the dialectical view both of agency and structure and of the local and the global. "There is growing evidence," says Appadurai (1996, 7), "that the consumption of the mass media throughout the world provokes resistance, irony, selectivity, and, in general, *agency*" (emphasis in original). Appadurai introduces several concepts useful for this study's purpose. First, he makes a distinction between fantasy and imagination. The former is individualistic and associated with the seductive aspects of the media and their numbing effect on the public – a relic of the mass society discourse captured in the motto the "media are the opiate of the masses." Imagination, on the other hand, is collective and has the potential to trigger action. In the age of electronic media, imagination in its collective form "creates ideas of neighbourhood and nationhood, of moral economies and unjust rule, of higher wages and foreign labour prospects. Imagination today is a staging ground for action, and not only for escape" (ibid.). Second, these electronic forms of communication give rise to what Appadurai calls "solidalities," by which he means communities that exist transnationally yet share with each other a field of imagination that fuels collective action. These are communities with the potential to transform from "communities in themselves" to "communities for themselves" (ibid.). Third, with so many "deterritorialised" people on the move, numbering in the tens of millions, from immigrants, guest workers, and refugees to exiles and asylum seekers, it is inescapable that the business of imagination should take on special significance in the context of electronically mediated communication, where the imagination is no longer thought of as the prerogative of "the special, expressive space of art, myth, and ritual, [but] has now become a part of the quotidian mental work of ordinary people in many societies" (ibid., 5). The site of everyday life of ordinary people is impacted more than ever before by imagination of a collective kind. Groups on the move bring to bear different sets of expectations, setting in motion "diasporas of hope, diasporas of terror, and diasporas of despair":

> Many more people than ever before seem to imagine routinely the possibility that they or their children will live and work in places other than where they were born: this is the wellspring of increased rates of migration at every level of social, national, and global life. Others are dragged into new settings, as the refugee camps of Thailand, Ethiopia, Tamil Nadu, and Palestine remind us. (Ibid., 6)

Fourth, unlike the project of modernisation, with its familiar meganarrative of development, economic productivity, and efficiency, we are witnessing "an experiential engagement with modernity," says Appadurai, that makes possible the development of "subversive" micronarratives expressed in the new vernacular of globalisation and gives rise to subaltern oppositionary groups of various kinds. The convergence of "electronic mass mediation and transnational mobilization has broken the monopoly of autonomous nation-states over the project of modernization" (Appadurai 1996, 10). A key element in Appadurai's work is the notion that "globalization is not the story of cultural homogenization" (ibid., 11). Globalisation is mediated by agency to produce differing interpretations of modernity, which are contextualised in specific local conditions. At the core of his relational theory of change (in contrast to a monocausal theory) is the notion of rupture, which "takes media and migration as its two major, and interconnected, diacritics and explores their joint effect on the work of the imagination, as a constitutive feature of late modernity" (ibid., 3). These "modern subjectivities" are characterised by instabilities resulting from the juxtaposition of migration and the "flow of mass-mediated images, scripts, and sensations" (ibid., 4). With international migration and globalisation on the increase, Appadurai argues, it is not valid anymore to think of culture as isomorphic with space. Ulrich Beck (2000, 26–27) makes a similar point in outlining the features of what he calls the "second modernity":

> In the paradigm of the second modernity, then, a question mark is placed over the inner consistency of a social construction made up of anthropological constants and functional imperatives of the first modernity. A territorially fixed image of the social, which has for two centuries captivated and inspired the political, cultural and scientific imagination, is in the course of breaking up.

Corresponding to global capitalism is a process of cultural and political globalization which transcends territoriality as the ordering principle of society (and as the ordering principle of cultural knowledge upon which familiar images of the self and the world are based).

According to Julie Peteet (1995, 173), "for the Palestinians," notwithstanding the shifting nature of borders and territoriality, "there is an isomorphism between space and place," which explains the desire to return to the homeland. Appadurai (1996, 13), who is not exclusively concerned with refugees, whereas Peteet is, prefers instead to highlight *difference* as the basis for understanding group identity and mobilisation: "I suggest that we regard as cultural only those differences that either express, or set the groundwork for, the mobilization of group identities." To the extent that culture is used to designate a group identity, it refers to the "consciousness of these attributes (material, linguistic, or territorial) and their naturalization as essential to group identity" (ibid.). Through several iterations, Appadurai proceeds from rejecting culture as a static entity, to conceiving of it as a process and dimension of difference that forms the basis of group identity, to considering naturalisation of difference as central to the mobilisation of group identity, and finally to advancing culturalism as a specific outcome of late modernity and an essential ingredient in the transformation of group difference into a social movement pitched at the level of the nation-state. In his words, "Culturalism is the form that cultural differences tend to take in the era of mass mediation, migration, and globalization" (ibid., 16). Appadurai goes through this exercise in order to refute the thesis that primordial ties lie at the basis of ethnic identity and to posit in its place a theory that explains ethnic conflict through reference to culturalism and ethnic mobilisation:

> What appears to be a worldwide rebirth of ethnic nationalisms and separatisms is not really what journalists and pundits all too frequently refer to as "tribalism," implying old histories, local rivalries and deep hatreds. Rather, the ethnic violence we see in many places is part of a wider transformation that is suggested by the term *culturalism* . . . [which] is frequently associated with extraterritorial histories and memories, sometimes with refugee status and exile, and almost always with struggles for recognition from existing nation-states or from various transnational bodies. (Ibid., 15)

Thomas Faist (1998, 217) goes beyond globalisation and introduces the concept of transnationalism: "Whereas global processes are largely decentered from specific nation-state territories and take place in a world context . . . transnational processes are anchored in and span two or more nation-states, involving actors from the spheres of both state and civil society." For Faist, space is used in a manner that differs from its traditional usage by geographers and anthropologists. In a transnational sense, space refers not only to a territory's physical features "but also to larger opportunity structures, the social life and the subjective images, values and meanings that the specific and limited space represents to migrants. Space thus differs from place in that it encompasses or spans various territorial locations" (ibid.). Whereas in its traditional usage space referred to geographical location, with place meaning space and culture, in its transnational usage space incorporates culture and global networks: "Transnational social spaces are combinations of social and symbolic ties, positions in networks and organizations, and networks of organizations that can be found in at least two geographically and internationally distinct places" (ibid., 216). In terms that resonate with Pierre Bourdieu's (1977) concept of "habitus," social spaces involve social capital as defined in terms of access to and membership in networks, groups, and organisations, human capital as reflected in educational and occupational qualifications, and economic capital. It is these ties that facilitate further accumulation in the form of economic, human, and social capital. The problem with resources that make up social capital is that they are locally situated, which makes it difficult for refugee and migrant communities to transfer this capital to other localities. For transnational communities to be communities in Ferdinand Tönnies's (1963) meaning of the term *Gemeinschaft*, time and space have to be bound "through exchange, reciprocity and solidarity to achieve a high degree of social cohesion, and a common repertoire of symbolic and collective representations" (Faist 1998, 221). Transnational communities are based on triadic relations involving the refugee and migrant communities, the host country, and the sending country. Transnational communities are either diasporic or exiled. Faist defines "diaspora" as a group that "has suffered some kind of traumatic event which leads to the dispersal of its members, and there is a vision and remembrance of lost or imagined homeland still to be established, often accompanied by a refusal of the receiving society to fully recognize the cultural distinctiveness of the immigrants" (ibid., 222).

Transnational communities are diasporic if they "develop some significant social and symbolic ties to the receiving country"; otherwise, they are considered to be exiled (ibid., 222).

Notwithstanding the popularity of the concept of diaspora, there is no agreement about its analytic utility. As seen by Floya Anthias (1998), current usage of diaspora implies "homogenization" and "unity" of the group in question, a unity that is based on attribution to a place of origin, with all that this entails in terms of primordialism and the overlooking of differences based on gender, class, generation, and political affiliation. These factors have been alluded to above in reference to the Palestinian refugee experience, based on class, generation, and gender. Thus "[t]he idea of diaspora tends to homogenize the population referred to at the transnational level," instead of recognising that "the diaspora is constituted as much in *difference and division* as it is in *commonality and solidarity*" (ibid., 564, emphasis in original). For example, just as the locations of diasporic men and women in the class structure of the receiving society are different, so too are positions of men and women within the diasporic group itself. By defining diaspora on the basis of territorial origin, one ignores the racialised experiences of diasporic groups in their countries of settlement and the equally important role played by the sending nation-state in sustaining ethnicity as a marker of its diasporic members. Given these crosscutting positionings, Anthias questions the claims that diasporic groups, because of their loyalty to a homeland, have the potential to destabilise or weaken the nation-state of their host society. The concerns of second-generation émigrés or refugees need not reflect the concerns of their parents as defined in terms of the politics back home: "The political activities of migrants may be dominated by reference to homeland struggles, although those of their children may be more likely to be focused around issues of exclusion in the country of settlement, or may reconstruct ethnic fundamentalist projects as modes of resistance" (ibid., 570).

The above theoretical discussion provides us with several openings for the study of Palestinians. First, it allows us to conceptualise Palestinian society extraterritorially in recognition that its membership is not coterminous with nation-state boundaries. Second, the convergence between time and space makes it possible to think of society as a web or network of individuals and groups dispersed globally. Third, the duality of structuration permits us to examine discursively and institutionally agency's actions in which power is conceptualised through the dialectic of control (i.e., power from above and from below). This has implications for resistance and control. Fourth, the production of identity is both subjective and objective. It is subjective in terms of the meanings one attaches to group membership and objective as it is shaped by state policies in their various discursive and representational forms.

Sari Hanafi's work on transnationalism, identity, and the Palestinian refugee camp experience stands out as an important contribution to the sociology of the Palestinians. Hanafi makes full, productive use of the works of Agamben and Foucault on the state of exception, security, and governmentality. In a series of studies of Palestinian refugee camps in Lebanon and Syria, he demonstrates that, contra Foucault, governmentality is pursued to further discriminate against Palestinians, not to integrate them and guarantee their security. The camps are "treated as spaces of exception and experimental laboratories for control and surveillance" (Hanafi 2010, 30). His analysis of the Nahr el-Bared camp in northern Lebanon leads him to conclude that the governance of the refugees is premised on the concept of "community policing," according to which the Lebanese state controls the camps, and that its measures do not go beyond providing the refugees with "bare life" (see also Salih 2013). Not so in the case of the camps in Syria prior to the latter's ongoing civil war. Although the state controls the appointment of directors and committees of the camps and has instituted an elaborate system of camp governance, unlike in Lebanon, the camps are not perceived as a threat to the security of the state. In the absence of a modicum of governance to regulate the lives of the camp inhabitants, "alternative forms of governmentalities" have emerged to control the behaviour of the camp residents. Here Islamism stands out as a technology of the soul: "Islamism, as articulated by Hamas, literally as a science of the soul, has transformed the way many Palestinians, especially young men, construct their sense of self. It has brought to the forefront the idea that an "economy of morals" can order societies in the absence of traditional hierarchies" (Hanafi and Long 2010, 153).

As pointed out above, the concept of diaspora is problematic if it rests on a homogenous conception of the refugee or immigrant community residing outside its traditional homeland. In examining the data stored in an electronic network designed to involve Palestinian scientists and technologists living outside Palestine in building the nation, Hanafi (2008, 155) notes that although there was enthusiasm for the idea, it did not translate into a return to the homeland:

> The *homeland* is no longer synonymous only with Intifada and political alienation, but also with job opportunities, scientific and technological development, specialist conferences, and so on. Palestinian identity has moved beyond a completely territorialized framework. One can be a Palestinian abroad, connecting with and aiding the development of the *homeland* in cyberspace. (Emphasis in original)

Conclusion

The overall purpose of this chapter has been twofold. First, it has exposed the reader to the scope and variety of social research on Palestinian society in its various statuses and locations. The sheer volume of research on Palestinians, a segment of which has been alluded to here, and the thematic review carried out, particularly with regard to Palestinian refugees, demonstrate the importance of knowledge production as a process in dealing with conflict situations. Second, by providing a series of examples, this chapter has situated the study of Palestine and Palestinian society in the context of recent theoretical and methodological advances in social science that span colonialism, Foucauldian treatment of power, constructivism, the problem of order in explicating the nature of violence in ethnically divided regions, and transnationalism. In using the constructivist approach, the study puts forward a new way of looking at how state building involves co-production efforts in which the institutions of science are mobilised to achieve colonial political ends. The translation of scientific discourse outside the institutions of science, made possible through an alliance between the political and scientific, has led to serious ramifications for population policies and state construction.

Finally, the chapter has examined mounting interest in the potential of human rights and transnationalism to affect state policies and mobilise refugee communities. Notwithstanding the criticism of globalisation by third world scholars and nongovernmental organisations, transnational networks have opened spaces for minorities and marginal groups in society to engage in resistance. The use of cause lawyering has proven effective in publicising mistreatment of marginal groups who have no recourse to redressing their grievances through the apparatuses of the nation-state. By the same token, globalisation has brought about important technological changes in the area of computer networking, which has facilitated communication and exchange of information among refugee communities that are scattered in various geopolitical spaces and are disconnected from each other.

This empowerment and resistance by marginal groups through a combination of technology-people networks should introduce an important corrective to the traditional sociological conception of agency. It is the hybridity between technology and people, referred to in the language of constructivism as "actants," that compels us to rethink our conception of agency as solely human and instead use "co-agency" to designate this hybridity.

Notes

This chapter draws upon Elia Zureik, "Theoretical and Methodological Considerations for the Study of Palestinian Society," *Comparative Studies of South Asia, Africa and the Middle East* 23, 1–2 (2003): 3–13; and Elia Zureik, *Palestinian Refugees and the Peace Process* (Washington, DC: Institute for Palestine Studies, 1996).

1 The debate surrounding Arab-Jewish population balance is a contentious one, as the discussion in chapter 4 demonstrates.
2 The debate over post-Zionism has become a familiar staple in Israeli academic discourse, pitting "old" against "new" historians, with particular reference to the impact of Israel's creation on Palestinian society (Livneh 2001). The leading participants in this debate among the old, mainstream historians are Karsh (2000) and Shapira (1995), and on the critical side among the new historians are the early Morris (1987), Rogan and Shlaim (2001), and Pappé (1999), to name a few. Arab attitudes toward the post-Zionist debate are explored by al-Haroub (2001).

2
ZIONISM AND COLONIALISM

> There is an unmistakable coincidence between the experiences of Arab Palestinians at the hands of Zionism and the experiences of those black, yellow, and brown people who were described as inferior and subhuman by nineteenth-century imperialists. (Said 1979, 22)

> This [Israel] is not a society of "spider webs" or of rootless individuals who came to gain control of a land that does not belong to them under the aegis of colonialism and imperialism. (Gavison 2011b)

The above statements by the late Palestinian scholar Edward Said and the Israeli legal scholar Ruth Gavison convey drastically contrasting views of Zionism's mission in Palestine. In the former, Said sees a connection between Zionism and colonialism; in the latter, Gavison, an ardent defender of Zionism, vehemently rejects any association between it and colonialism. The following discussion elaborates upon the contours of settler colonialism and the debate surrounding its manifestation in the Zionist project in Palestine.

Specifically, the chapter addresses the contours of colonialism, the debate surrounding the nature of the Israeli state, the logic of Zionism, the place of Theodore Herzl in Zionist historiography, breaching the Zionist consensus, language's role in hegemony, dehumanisation, and state securitisation.

The contours of colonialism

As a concept, colonialism has traversed an intellectual terrain that is fraught with controversy. Four decades ago, sociologist Ronald Horvath (1972) dissected imperialism and colonialism along three axes of domination aimed at control of territory and the management of people. The axes produce a matrix of six ideal types that extend from extermination to assimilation, with relative social equilibrium in between. Horvath identifies no fewer than eleven classifications involving intra- and intergroup differentiations; domestic forms of colonialism; informal, semi-, and neocolonialism; and administrative colonialism interwoven with elements of class and cast. The problematic cell among his ideal types is that of so-called "relative equilibrium," which involves neither assimilation nor extermination. He cites apartheid South Africa as an example of this type. One can hardly regard such a regime, especially at the time Horvath published his article, as constituting relative equilibrium between settlers and indigenous people, given that apartheid policies were in full force in South Africa. Colonialism can exist only in a state of tension with the indigenous population; it cannot be otherwise unless dismantled.

Although on moral grounds colonialism is loathed for its exploitative and dominating nature, some see in colonialism a silver lining for its having brought to colonised people elements of modernisation and indeed civilisation. As we shall see, this is clearly the stance adopted by liberal Zionists (in contrast to revisionist Zionists) in justifying their settler brand of colonising Palestine (see Sa'di 1997). Colonialism and apartheid are closely related (Bakan and Abu-Laban 2010), although in the case of Israel there are important distinctions between the two. Whereas the South African white settlers implemented colonial policies of segregation and discrimination to exploit territory and black labour, the Zionists aimed at exploiting space and territory in the first instance without relying on Arab labour to build their settler state. As Patrick Wolfe (2006) puts it, the Zionists sought the elimination of the Palestinians through transfer and expulsion without necessarily seeking their cheap labour. In his comparison of apartheid South Africa and Israeli policies in the occupied Palestinian territories (OPT), Daryl Glaser (2010) locates close moral and structural similarities between the two regimes. According to Richard Falk (2010, 3), the United Nations rapporteur for human rights, whose remarks were directed at the situation in the OPT: "Colonialism constitutes a repudiation of the essential rights of territorial integrity and self-determination, and apartheid has come to be formally treated as a crime against humanity . . . The entrenching of colonialist and apartheid features of the Israeli occupation has been a cumulative process."

Historian D.K. Fieldhouse, a key researcher on colonialism and imperialism, makes a distinction between colonialism and colonisation – both of which are a product of imperial expansion and empire building and as such impact the values and social structure of the colonised regions. He reserves "colonialism" for a more thorough domination and control of a settled region, whereas "colonisation" refers to the reproduction of European forms of settler society in new territory that is alleged to be unpopulated: "colonialism means exploitation by the foreign society and its agents who occupied the dependency to serve their own interests, not that of the subject population" (Fieldhouse 1981, 4–7). In writing about British colonialism in the Middle East, Fieldhouse makes a further distinction between what he calls "colonies of occupation" and "colonies of settlement." The first term identifies those colonies that are intended to provide the coloniser with strategic and economic benefits.

The second refers to colonies such as Canada and Australia that were intended for settlement. In the context of the Middle East, "Palestine fitted neither," according to Fieldhouse (2006, 117). Yet he notes that, similar to the British in Australia and New Zealand, the Zionist settlers controlled Palestine's modern economy, had a higher standard of living than the indigenous population, early on adopted policies of separation from the native population, and eventually, on the eve of establishing the state, engaged in what he admits to be "ethnic cleansing."

Settler colonialism is distinguished from classical imperial undertakings (Elkins and Pedersen 2005). The latter are carried out militarily to reap economic benefits and secure spheres of influence without necessarily settling the territories, whereas settler colonialism involves the actual occupation and permanent settlement of a country or territory, such as occurred in Australia, New Zealand, South Africa, and the Americas, among other places. In most cases, a mother country provides protection and sponsorship. These large-scale projects of settler colonialism have involved the displacement, subjugation, and at times extermination of the indigenous population, which has been reduced from a majority to a minority – if not in numbers, at least in terms of power relations. But colonialism (or more appropriately, imperialism) can also involve occupying the territory militarily and administratively without settling the country. India under British rule is a prime example. In some cases, colonialism represents a hybrid of military occupation and settlement. French settler colonialism in Algeria was an example, until the French were forced out of Algeria after a bloody war. Israel's occupation and settlement of the Palestinian territories in 1967 is another hybrid example.

Patrick Wolfe (2007; 2008, 123), who has a keen interest in the human rights consequences of colonialism and its genocidal tendencies, uses colonisation and colonialism interchangeably, while stressing that, rather than considering it an event, settler colonialism is best understood as a "structure" and a process that stretches over time, involving the movement of people from one country to another for the purpose of establishing a settler society fashioned after the country of origin – mainly European. Implicit in the colonialism-colonisation duality is the assumption that colonisation is less deleterious in its impact on the colonised region. Here, as noted above and based on Fieldhouse's work, the colonisers settle areas that are not occupied by the indigenous population. In fact, for some, colonisation could have a beneficial economic impact on the colonised, as argued for example by Zionist ideologists and settlers in the late nineteenth and early twentieth centuries – a claim that has been repeated to this day.[1] In contrast to colonialism, colonisation projects a benign, if not positive, view of settlement activity that cloaks the distinction between coloniser and colonised in the neutral language of "separate and equal," while claiming that the intention is not to displace or dominate the native population but to live with its members side-by-side yet separately. This approach, reflected in Israel's pronouncements and settlement policies in the OPT, and prior to that in Israel proper, is used to justify wholesale confiscation of Arab land, racialisation of the native population, and spatial segregation of the coloniser from the colonised. As this study will demonstrate, whether in terms of ideology or outcome, it would be difficult to accept a neat separation between colonialism and colonisation. The settling by a colonising group in new territory is bound to involve imposition and control of the native population in one form or another, regardless of whether the settler group has formal links with a foreign metropolis. Thus "settler colonialism" is a more appropriate label for describing the case at hand. The study will show that the main consequence of settler colonialism is its infringement on the political, social, and economic rights, particularly citizenship rights, of the Palestinian population in Israel proper as well as in the OPT. Ultimately, however, colonialism has to rely on some form of sponsorship or proxy protection, which Zionist settlers eventually made full use of in Mandate Palestine and later in Israel.

The connection between settler colonialism and genocide is gaining ground in human rights research. Inspired by the seminal work of Polish legal scholar Raphael Lemkin (1944) in the aftermath of the Second World War, researchers like Wolfe, who is cited above, and others (Lloyd 2012; Moses 2008; Rashed and Short 2012; Shaw 2010) took the conceptual apparatus of genocide advocated by Lemkin in his analysis of Nazi war crimes and applied it to an examination of the situation of settler colonialism in Palestine.

Within the colonialism model, it is possible to further identify internal or domestic colonialism, which refers to the exploitation by a dominant settler group (and its descendants) of indigenous people who are co-residents of a geopolitical entity in a postcolonial state, as seen for example in South Africa, Northern Ireland (Hechter 1975), and Israel/Palestine. David Lyon (2011) has discussed the applicability of the "internal colonialism" model to Israel/Palestine. He argues that internal colonialism distinguishes between citizen and subject. Israel's control of the West Bank constitutes a form of internal colonialism since the West Bank's Palestinian residents are subjects who are territorially controlled by Israel but lack citizenship rights. I have argued elsewhere that the Palestinians in Israel, although formally citizens of the state, are also internally colonised by a political regime that curtails their access to resources (mainly land, education, and housing but also jobs) and their exercise of full citizenship rights (Zureik 1979).[2]

Finally, there is neocolonialism, which, with recourse to neoliberalism and free market doctrines, relies on bilateral relationships between states and the use of supranational organisations such as the International Monetary Fund, World Bank, and other such bodies to restructure the policies, culture, and internal economies of weaker (mainly postcolonial) states without physically and militarily occupying them. Present-day rhetoric surrounding globalisation conceals a new form of neocolonialism that has become widespread since the latter part of the twentieth century (Fraser 2013; Harvey 2005; Lyon 2010).

The structural and comparative approaches to understanding colonialism discussed above are supplemented by Yehouda Shenhav's (2002) "phenomenology of colonialism," by which he means the way colonial reality is perceived and experienced by those living within its domain, be they colonisers or colonised. This experiential and subjective aspect of colonial reality was thoroughly investigated by Frantz Fanon in his writings on French colonialism in Algeria, notably in his classic work, *The Wretched of the Earth* (1967). As this study will show, understanding Israeli state racism requires delving into the subjective aspects of racial practices as they unfold in a colonial context. This study will also explore the contours of racism in Israeli society and shed light on the background of Israeli educator Nurit Peled's (2006, 1) observation that "Israel's children are educated within an uncompromisingly racist discourse, [a] racist discourse that does not stop at checkpoints, but governs all human relations in this country" (see also N. Peled 2010). In contrast to individual and group racisms, which are amply demonstrated in public opinion polls in Israel, this study argues that *state* racism and its biopolitical governmentality reinforce individual and group forms of racism – one feeds into the other.

What state Israel?

> Like the European colonists in North America, Africa and Australasia with whom they often identified, Zionism's luminaries believed that their rights to Palestine exceeded those of its "natives." Although the movement's leadership could not deny that the land was full of people, it portrayed Palestinians as "a mixture of races and types," a "multitude" distinguished not by their shared history or national character but by their inferior "human quality."
> (S. Robinson 2013, 13)

The above statement by Shira Robinson stands in stark contrast to mainstream social science literature, which remains committed to depicting Israel as a "pioneering" and "settler-immigrant society" that is essentially multicultural and democratic (Eisenstadt 1967), if not, as the adage goes, "the only democracy in the Middle East" with no connection to Europe's settler-colonial ventures.[3]

Some consider Zionism to be an offshoot of so-called diaspora nationalism (A. Smith 1995). This is the case, as some Zionists admit, despite Zionism's development under the shadow of "formal and informal European imperialism," during which key Zionist leaders such as Theodore Herzl and Chaim Weizmann laboured but initially failed to "convince European leaders that Jews would form the white settler group in the country, considered as the ideal collaborator group serving the interests of imperialist-colonialist powers, such as in Australia, New Zealand, Rhodesia and Algeria" (Golan 2001, 141).

My purpose in this section is to tease out the various strands that fall within the colonial approach to describing Israel. Among those who are willing to entertain a colonial perspective (including a minority of Israeli writers), the Israeli state is associated with a variety of labels.[4] Gershon Shafir and Yoav Peled (2002, 1) describe Israeli society in terms of the articulation of three "contradictory" goals: colonialism, ethno-nationalism, and democracy. Horat Peled and Yoav Peled (2011, 117) assert unequivocally that the Zionist project in its 1948 and 1967 manifestations constitutes *one* colonial undertaking: "We believe that the colonial nature of the Zionist enterprise has been persuasively demonstrated in the scholarly literature and needs to be faced without subterfuge. Such recognition would provide a coherent conceptual framework in which to comprehend the State of Israel and the occupied territories as one political entity."

Oren Yiftachel (2000, 736) echoes the "necessity" argument when referring to Israel's pre-1948 settler colonialism as "colonialism of ethnic survival," the post-1948 period as "internal colonialism," and the post-1967 period as "external colonialism."

Ronit Lentin (2008a) characterises Israel as a "racial state" rather than an "ethnocracy," "ethnic democracy," "settler-colonial society," or even "racist state." Her definition of state racialism owes more to Etienne Balibar (1991) and David Theo Goldberg (2008) than to Michel Foucault's (2003) "state racism," according to which the state needs to defend itself against internal and external threats by targeting specific groups that pose a numerical risk and threaten state sovereignty. State racialism is based on cultural and ethnic markers rather than on biological reasoning or colour as a signifier of race. Ultimately, "racial states are surveillance states, policing populations and constructing 'docile bodies'" (Lentin 2008a).

Ronen Shamir (2000), who observes the effective use by Jewish colonisation officials of the infrastructure provided by the Mandate government, designates the British-Zionist dynamics of Mandate Palestine as "dual-colonialism," arguing that the country's Jewish population "was active in the concrete material practices of colonization," whereas the British authorities "provided the political, legal and administrative colonial umbrella" (in Forman and Kedar 2003, 499; see also R. Shamir 2002).[5] It is accurate to say that the label "colonialism," if it is invoked at all by Israeli writers, is usually used in reference to Israeli policies in the OPT. Policy analyst Rafael Reuveny's (2008b) detailed account of Israel's colonialist project in the West Bank triggered a heated exchange with political scientist Ira Sharansky (2008) of the Hebrew University, another staunch defender of mainstream Zionism.[6]

Ann Laura Stoler (2010a), in contrast, is more emphatic in her conclusion: "If democracy is defined, as Hannah Arendt did, by 'the right to have rights' for an entire population within the state's jurisdiction, the Israeli state cannot be considered a democratic one." And in a perceptive article, Palestinian historian Walid Khalidi (2009, 30-31) describes Israel as a *"Reconquista"* state whose settler colonial conduct resembles that of Spain and Portugal in the Iberian Peninsula during the fifteenth century:

> In this same fundamental way, Zionism was on the offensive – a *Reconquista* from the very start. As in the Iberian case, there was never any serious thought about what to do with the "usurpers" or "strangers" on the land – they were simply obstacles to its forward march. Partnership was never a possibility because what was at issue was an exclusive primordial, unchallengeable, indeed divine right.

The debate over the nature of Israel has come a long way since, to quote Abba Eban, Israel was largely described as "a light unto the nations" (in Neff 2003, 43). The engagement by anthropologist Nadia Abu El-Haj with the work of David Theo Goldberg is just one example. In commenting on Goldberg's notion of "racial Palestinianization" and his idea that Israel is a *neoliberal*, colonial state, Abu El-Haj (2010, 29) argues that Israel is best seen as "Janus-faced": "It is a regime that manoeuvres between and speaks in the name of different modalities in relation to shifting forms of capital, shifting global political imaginaries and shifting oppositional struggles – 'threats' – on the ground." Goldberg is credited with having elevated the discussion of race beyond the usual focus on what passes as the study of race relations in liberal societies that are occupied with issues of whiteness, colour blindness, and discrimination. In addition to occupation and the expansion of settlements, Goldberg (2009, 126) argues that the dehumanised position of the Palestinians in Israeli discourse is what underlies the concept of "racial Palestinianization":

> Racial Palestinianization is thus a conceit about contemporary conditions in terms of a projected past conceived in terms of the politics of the present. The Palestinian is a Philistine, with Philistine values, interests, and desires, a primitive sense of never having evolved beyond ancient whims, drives, capriciousness, viciousness, and the irresponsible impulses to which they give rise. The Palestinian is driven by nothing but unprovoked hate and anger, incapable of a higher order of values, of deeper causation, of responsibility as a product of free choice.

Goldberg (2008, 39) concludes that "racial Palestinianization is today among the most repressive, the most subjugating and degrading, the most deadly forms of racial targeting, branding and rationalization." The Palestinians are not simply identified as a different racial group or category but are also "a despised and demonic racial group" (ibid., 42). Drawing upon Foucault, Goldberg notes that "State sovereignty defends itself above all else so as to secure the group, its ethnoraciality, to protect its purity, perpetuity, and power, for which it takes itself to exist and which it seeks to represent" (ibid., 28).

Although Abu El-Haj (2010, 29) endorses Goldberg's characterisation of Israeli racism, she departs from seeing it as "born again racism" that places "racial Palestinianization within a historical trajectory that never happened in the Israeli state." Whereas the Palestinians have not been given the authority to narrate their history, the Israelis, according to Goldberg (2008), have successfully mounted a "counter historical narrative" by gaining world acceptance as a sovereign nation, even though this was accomplished at the expense of the Palestinian narrative. Israel's founding and indeed the ideologies that moulded Zionism were premised on colonial racism "from the get-go" (Abu El-Haj 2010, 32). But above all, it is the consequence of Israel's being a colonial settler state that must be recognised first. What follows from this recognition, states Abu El-Haj, is the question of why – as with all other colonised people – the Palestinians should acquiesce to the Israeli state's existence and not question its legitimacy. Finally, Abu El-Haj questions Goldberg's reference to Israel as a neoliberal state. Being a colonial state, Israel is heavily involved in the expansion and subsidising of settlements. Such heavy state involvement negates any characterisation of Israeli rule in the OPT (or in Israel proper) as neoliberal. She concludes by saying that although the Israeli state through its military apparatus protects the settlers, it "invests in the destruction of the infrastructures, the livelihoods, the lives of Palestinian under its control. This is the 'necropolitical disciplining' of an ever active and interventionist colonial state" (ibid., 40).

Notwithstanding the labelling of Israel as "a colonial-settler society" (Y. Peled 2007, 96; see also Massad 2006, 13–31; and Wolfe 2006, n35), discussions of colonialism tend to generalise its common characteristics regardless of where it takes place; there is the danger of overlooking colonialism's specific features that are geographically and historically contingent. For some, Israeli settler colonialism of the West Bank for more than half a century has gradually evolved to differentiate it from other familiar forms of classical colonialism. As argued by Ariel Handel (2009), colonisation of the West Bank is less a matter of managing the population through a Foucauldian framework of biopolitics and more a matter of controlling the resources (i.e., land, water, and airspace) while *neglecting* the population, or as expressed by anthropologist Ted Swedenburg (1995, 59–60) about Zionism in general, "What seems distinctive about Zionist colonialism is that, most often, altruism is expressed toward the land rather than toward the indigenous population living on it." The practice of spatial separation between the coloniser and colonised in the context of the West Bank, with ramifications for the population, is also discussed by Neve Gordon (2008, xix):

> For many years, I maintain, the occupation operated according to the colonization principle, by which I mean the attempt to administer the lives of the people and normalize the colonization, while exploiting the territory's resources (in this case land, water, and labour). Over time, a series of structural contradictions undermined the principle and gave way in the mid-1990s to another guiding principle, namely, the separation principle. By *separation* I mean the abandonment of efforts to administer the lives of the colonized population (except for the people living in the seam zones or going through the checkpoints), while insisting on the continued exploitation of nonhuman resources (land and water). The lack of interest in or indifference to the lives of the colonized population that is characteristic of the separation principle accounts for the recent surge in lethal violence. (Emphasis in original)

This surface indifference (or better, neglect) of the population is not to be confused with an attitude of live and let live that some see as an outcome of Israeli state neoliberalism – although, as pointed out above, the nature of this neoliberalism is contested in light of Israel's being a colonial settler state. The colonial neglect, if it could be labelled as such, is well thought out, meticulously planned, and engineered in such a way as to stifle Palestinian society and cause maximum havoc in the normal lives of the native Palestinian population by using what Wolfe (2007, 329) aptly refers to as "Zionism's practical logic." As a policy, separation is but one aspect of the so-called "neglect," but is not to be confused with any benign design. It is actually a form of creeping apartheid, as Gordon (2008) sees it.

It can be argued that Foucault's theoretical framework is more relevant to the position of the Palestinian citizens of Israel than it is to Israel's colonial policies in the OPT. Even with regard to the former, Israel's engagements with governmentality in order to "normalize" the status of its Palestinian minority are of a circumscribed scope and, unlike those exercised vis-à-vis the Jewish population, are not intended to normalise the Palestinians through inclusion and participation in the social body. Although disciplinary surveillance power is a cornerstone of Israel's treatment of all its citizens, expected docility is the order of the day only for the Palestinian minority. In drastic contrast, the situation in the West Bank is in line with what Gordon (2008) and Handel (2009) describe. Israel acts as a *sovereign* colonial power in the OPT that is not accountable for its actions to those it rules over.

An interesting deviation from the colonial model is provided by architect and urban planner Eyal Weizman, a critic of what he acknowledges to be Israel's brutal treatment of the native Palestinian population in the West Bank. In rejecting colonialism as an applicable model, Weizman argues that Israel's control of the Palestinians should be viewed in the first instance in terms of spatial configuration (Weizman and Kastrissianakis 2007). Basically, he claims that colonialism, as a grand historical design, does not account for the methods of daily contestation over space as exercised by Palestinians and other international actors such as nongovernmental organisations in confronting occupation, that it gives too much attention to the role of state ideology (Zionism), and that it does not explain the "many fissures" in Israeli hegemonic control of the Palestinians. Yet, as pointed out in this study, since space and territory are central to colonialism in its various forms, why not acknowledge the colonial features of Israel's control methods? I am not convinced that Weizman's concerns cannot be addressed through the prism of colonialism as demonstrated in this discussion. After all, what *motivates* the actions of the Israeli state if not the straightjacket of Zionist ideology, which has been honed for over a century as a means of controlling and dispossessing the Palestinians? However, as will be shown later, Weizman's approach, since it focuses on the details of control, is quite useful in assessing the nature of colonial surveillance, without losing sight of the forest (colonialism) for the trees (daily contestations).

The claim that a state is democratic does not rule out an association between colonialism and democracy. So-called "European democratic states" were colonial in the first instance, as was the American experience from the mid-nineteenth century onward (McCoy 2009). As Gordon (2010) shows, colonialism has been espoused by several democratic regimes that exercise colonial dominion over others. Although he does not subscribe to the notion that Israel is a democracy, Gordon demonstrates that its venture in the OPT is typical of colonial-democratic regimes, the above qualifications notwithstanding. A similar point is made by Mark Duffield

(2007, 228), who goes back to John Stuart Mill in locating the rationale for foreign aid in imperialist designs by well-to-do nations that domestically espouse liberal values and externally act as "practitioners of empire" (see also Hall 2005). In a more general way, historian Tony Judt has warned against the aggressive tendencies of democracy. "The war in Iraq illustrates," he says, "that a democracy, and particularly an armed democracy, is very easily led into war – so long as it is told stories of the kind that are compatible with its self-image" (Judt and Snyder 2012, 307).

My intention is not to spill more ink in discussing the debate over whether Israel is or is not a colonial society;[7] it is important for this discussion to shed light on why I (and an increasing number of other writers) think Zionism's original settlement policies dating back to the late nineteenth and early twentieth centuries exhibit features that are consonant with those of European-inspired colonial regimes (see Abu-Manneh 2006). As Glenn Bowman (2011) concludes, it is the ideational manifestation in the shape of Herzlian settler Zionism and its association with European colonialism that continue to inform the nature of Israeli policies and treatment of the Palestinians in historical Palestine.

The logic of Zionism

> ... political ideas like Zionism need to be examined historically in two ways: (1) genealogically, in order that their provenance, their kinship and descent, their affiliation both with other ideas and with political institutions may be demonstrated; (2) as practical systems for accumulation (of power, land, ideological legitimacy) and displacement (of people, other ideas, prior legitimacy). (Said 1979, 11)

> "Dunam po, vedunam sham" (A quarter-acre here, a quarter-acre there) (Hebrew expression)

In the derogatory language of Chaim Weizmann, the first president of Israel, the Zionist project in Palestine was to be consolidated step-by-step by means of piecemeal acquisition, or "another acre, another goat," as Edward Said has remarked (in Collins 2004), in spite of Palestinian opposition. In the face of miniscule ownership of land through voluntary purchases from land owners, Zionist colonisation in Mandate Palestine and eventually Israel and the OPT proceeded by shadowy practices (Blau 2012), or stealth,[8] by intimidation, and by sheer force (Eldar 2011). The process of dispossession extended to the confiscation and destruction of built-up areas such as homes and entire villages in 1948 and underscored attempts to erase the Palestinian presence in the country. This policy is an integral part of Israel's ongoing attempts to deplete Arab Jerusalem of its population. By its own admission, the Israeli government has revoked the residency rights of a quarter-million Arab residents of Jerusalem and its surroundings since 1967, many of whom are professionals, workers, and students returning from their studies abroad (Eldar 2012b; Hasson 2009). And as revealed in several publicised court cases related to property ownership in East Jerusalem, such dispossessions involve fraudulent transactions (Hasson 2012) whereby Palestinians in economic hardship are enticed to sell property to third parties under dubious circumstances and incomprehensible legal language only to discover later that the intended owner was an Israeli Jewish buyer or, in most cases, either a Zionist institution such as the Jewish National Fund or settlers themselves, a practice that ensures permanent alienation of the land from its original Arab owners. In 2013 a fraudulent property transfer in the West Bank near the city of Ramallah involving a Jewish religious institute that resulted in the eviction of Palestinians from their homes came to light. In this particular case, the Jerusalem District Court confirmed the fraudulent nature of the transaction and ordered the removal of the institute from the illegally occupied Palestinian home (Levinson 2013, 2014). In a previous 2012 case, the settlers presented falsified documents as proof of a recent land transaction, even though the Palestinian owner had been dead since 2011 (Levinson 2012b), and in a related move the Ministry of Defense, which ostensibly controls the land it occupied in 1967, is about to implement a new land registry that bypasses the familiar Ottoman *tabu* registry; the change is intended to give the settlers the right to enter their names in the new registry as proof of ownership. By closing the new registry to Palestinian land owners, Israel has in effect denied them the right of appeal, which is based on the Ottoman registry (Levinson 2012a).

The Zionist project can be best described as a cumulative, colonial enterprise that has continued unabated since its inception (Eldar 2011; Margalit 2006a, 2006b, 2010). Early Zionist settlement of Palestine, starting in the late nineteenth century and continuing throughout the first half of the twentieth century, under Turkish and then British rule, was shaped and ideologically inspired by European colonialism, even though no mother country or metropolis existed to speak of. As will be shown later, this latter circumstance does not vitiate considering Zionism from the outset as a settler colonial movement. Because of the small number of settlers and early unsuccessful attempts at colonising Palestine in the late nineteenth century under the aegis of the Baron de Rothschild, military occupation was not contemplated as a feasible option. Eventually, in the wake of the Balfour Declaration of 1917,[9] there was British-Zionist collusion, which led John Strawson (2002, 377) to comment that "Jewish nationalism develop[ed] in the womb of British colonialism." In the words of Israeli legal experts Geremy Forman and Alexandre Kedar (2003, 497), "thus, at the onset of British rule, official documents attested to an Imperial policy of Jewish colonization, facilitating immigration, land acquisition, settlement, development, and elements of sovereignty. In addition to perceived mutual interests, the British-Zionist relationship was based on a discourse of development and modernization."

Among the early academic writers on Palestine, Forman and Kedar have explored in a series of papers the implications of colonial law in Palestine for Arab-Jewish relations. Although they note the contradictory nature of colonial law and the loopholes it contains that at times enable colonised people to fight for their rights, ultimately the "[l]aw served as both an instrument of domination and a weapon of the weak, albeit most of the time more successfully as the former than as the latter" (ibid., 516).

Among liberal Zionists, Professor Ruth Gavison occupies a central place in arguing for the compatibility of Israel's being simultaneously Jewish and democratic. In a speech she gave in the United States to a legal audience in 2011, she stressed that this compatibility can be accomplished *only* if the Jews remain a stable majority; otherwise, the state would be unstable and degenerate into dictatorship (Gavison 2011a). It is not clear why dictatorship is the only outcome of a multiethnic or binational state, unless Gavison assumes that the Arabs are not ready for democracy, as suggested by her efforts to differentiate Israel from other multiethnic states that are dictatorships and mired in conflict – especially neighbouring Middle Eastern states.

According to Gavison (2011a), it is irrelevant that the overwhelming majority of the Palestinians living in what became Israel were "expelled, ran away, fled"; the main "fact is that they *left*" (emphasis added). Thus the circumstances surrounding the dispersal of the Palestinians are obliterated so as not to admit the overwhelming historical evidence, in no small measure attested to by Israeli researchers, that they were mainly expelled by the fledgling Israeli state and are therefore entitled under international law and a United Nations resolution to petition for return. Not addressing this fact allows Gavison to sidestep both the role played by Israel in creating the refugee problem and its moral responsibility and culpability. More importantly, Gavison falls back on the Zionist-demographic mantra in favour of perpetual Jewish numerical dominance (as a guarantor of democracy) to justify barring the refugees from ever exercising their right of return. She seems to be oblivious to the fact that, based on a spate of bills that have been passed or are being considered by the Knesset, Israel is sliding gradually into authoritarianism to the detriment of the Palestinian population, which is the main target of these bills, but before long the Jewish population will be affected as well (see Association of Civil Rights in Israel 2012c).

Theodore Herzl: a Zionist icon!

It is significant, as pointed out earlier, that key Zionist leaders (unsuccessfully) sought sponsorship from the ailing Ottoman Empire as early as 1896, when Theodore Herzl (1896, 148–49), the ideologist of political Zionism, advocated the following:

> If his Majesty the Sultan were to give us Palestine, we could undertake the responsibility of putting the finances of Turkey completely in order. To Europe we would represent a part of the barrier against Asia; we would serve as the outpost of civilization against barbarism. As a neutral state we would remain allied to all of Europe, which in turn would have to guarantee our existence.

He went on to say, "For Europe we shall form a part of the dike confronting Asia, and serve as the harbinger of culture against barbarism" (in Golan 2001, 143).

Herzl is lionised by the leading Israeli academics, such as political scientist Shlomo Avineri, and he occupies a special place beyond that of being a theoretician and visionary of modern Zionism. It was his "actions" and organisational skills "that changed Jewish history," declared Avineri (2010a) at a conference devoted to Herzl (see also Avineri 2009). The product of liberal bourgeois European society, Herzl popularised his views in the utopian novel *Altneuland* (The Old New Land), originally published in German in 1902. In his writings about Herzl, Avineri (2002) attaches importance to the novel, which he interprets as proof of Herzl's political tolerance, awareness of the Arab presence in the country, and promise to grant the Arabs equal rights and opportunities to participate in the elections in a future Jewish state. Avineri considers these views, which he had already expounded upon three decades earlier in *The Making of Modern Zionism* (1981), to be a refutation of the claim that Zionism is in any way associated with colonialism or racism.[10] In fact, he, like other mainstream Israeli intellectuals, considers Zionism a "revolutionary" movement. As shown below, it was D.K. Fieldhouse, among others, who saw a common thread running through Herzl's vision at the turn of the twentieth century and the unfolding of exclusionary Zionist ideology in the creation of the State of Israel. The view of the Zionist leadership in 1948 "remained that of Herzl: there must be a Zionist state and, as [Prime Minister David] Ben-Gurion saw it, there would be no room in it for non-Jews. The events of 1948 demonstrated that ethnic cleansing, not collaboration, was the Zionist strategy" (Fieldhouse 2006, 345). It would be difficult to accept mainstream Zionist interpretations of Herzl's benevolent stance in the face of his often-cited statement in his 1895 diary about the price to be paid by the local Palestinian population for Zionist colonisation:

> We must expropriate gently the private property on the estates assigned to us. We shall try to spirit the penniless population across the border by procuring employment for it in the transit countries, while denying it employment in our own country. The property owners will come over to our side. Both the process of expropriation and the removal of the poor must be carried out discreetly and circumspectly. The property owners may believe that they are cheating us, selling to us at more than [the land is] worth. But nothing will be sold back to them. (In Penslar 2005, 67)

Forty-five years ago, while riding a wave of fame as a scholar of Karl Marx's exegeses, Avineri addressed the treatment of colonialism by Marx in newspaper reports that appeared in the *New York Daily Tribune* from 1852 to 1862. In the introduction to the edited volume of these reports, Avineri (1968) argued that Marx's writings on Asiatic societies explained the backwardness of these societies in terms of their dominant and static Asiatic mode of production.[11] This became a constant theme in Avineri's comments on the Arab Middle East, including the confrontation between Israel and the Palestinians. Israel is presented as a modern society whose social structure is dynamic and is in no way affected by its colonialist nature (Avineri 1972). The transformative role of colonialism as depicted by Marx, according to

Avineri, is absent in the Arab–Islamic Middle East. This is due in large measure to its indirect form of rule. Thus indirect colonial rule hampered the development of the European-style capitalist mode of production and its attendant class conflict, while leaving primordial and authoritarian rule in place, with local elites being the main beneficiary. The postcolonial Arab world is a continuation of traditional societies in which the "modern" army replaced the old autocracies. Sociologist Bryan Turner (1976–77), among others, has criticised Avineri's explanation of the contrast between the Arab world and Israel. In the case of the latter, he points out that at its inception Israel's development was aided by a sizeable inflow of capital from the outside – a feature that has remained true to this day – and that Israel's class formation was facilitated by ethnic segregation and displacement of the native Arab population. With regard to the Arab world, Turner suggests that a better analogy is Britain's colonisation of Northern Ireland and Palestine: "Just as Marx noted a 'stunting effect' in Britain's conflict with Ireland, so one might find a stunted development in the Middle East under the dual impact of British and Israeli colonization" (ibid., 406). Turner further argues that to appreciate the impact of European colonialism of the Middle East, one must not start with the twentieth century but should examine European penetration of the area (i.e., Palestine, Syria, and Lebanon) by the British and French, which dates back to the nineteenth century, when an economic dependence between the Middle East and Europe was created.

Historians who are wedded to the Zionist project go to great lengths to contextualise Herzl's racist opinion as a product of the general climate of nineteenth-century imperial Europe and, in one particular case, as an outcome of a "manic fit" from which Herzl suffered at the time he wrote these entries in his diary (Penslar 2005, 71). If the Zionist idea of population transfer, described by Walid Khalidi (1993) and other commentators (Masalha 1992; Pappé 2003) as so intrinsic to the Zionist project, is indeed or mainly the product of Herzl's manic fits and psychological condition, how does one explain the detailed plans that Herzl drew up in 1901, with complete disregard for the welfare of the native Palestinian population, for establishing the Jewish-Ottoman Land Company (W. Khalidi 1993), which in many ways mirrored the Dutch East India Company and the British East India Company? Although Herzl's colonial company failed to materialise, its spirit lives on in the institutional structure of key national Zionist organisations, particularly the Jewish National Fund, where, in line with Herzl's proposed charter, Jewish property is communally Jewish, state-owned, and expected to remain Jewish in perpetuity. At the present time, more than 90 per cent of the land in Israel is Jewish-owned (Forman and Kedar 2003), a complete reversal of land ownership patterns in 1948, when Jewish ownership extended to no more than 5 to 7 per cent of the land (Jiryis 1977).

An example of a strident Zionist reading of Herzl is given by Israeli geographer Arnon Golan (2001, 140), who, in dismissing Marxist scholarship regarding the nature of imperialism and its relevance to Palestine, has pronounced that "Zionism was not imperialist or colonialist in nature, but a national liberation movement that developed in eastern and central Europe, in conjunction with other national liberation movements in these regions." In the same breath, he sees fit to describe the Zionist project in Palestine as "a form of non-formal colonialism that flourished under a formal imperial regime." What constitutes "non-formal colonialism?" one might ask. Basically, it is argued that lacking a formal colonial metropole to provide economic and military backing, the Zionists relied on themselves through their technology, knowledge, and capital, while collaborating with the British for the mutual good of both. Among the benefits of such collaboration, Golan mentions British willingness to allow Jewish immigration into Palestine, which contributed largely to an increase in the Jewish population from a mere 10 per cent at the time Britain issued the Balfour Declaration in 1917 to close to 30 per cent on the eve of British withdrawal from Palestine in the late 1940s. Another feature of so-called "non-formal colonialism" is the pattern of Zionist urbanisation in Palestine that grew independently of its Arab counterpart. The Zionist pattern had the "settler" model, whereas the Arab one reflected the "colonial" model. More importantly, according to Golan, "the Jewish [urban] system did not come to dominate the Arab, which remained the political, economic and cultural centre of the Palestinian Arab population" (ibid., 138). According to him, the Jewish and Arab urban systems developed separately under the tutelage of "non-formal colonialism." Thus, according to this logic, if the two sectors are separate, they are separate and different but not necessarily separate and unequal. This portrayal of Zionist settler colonialism as benign and not dependent on so-called formal British imperialism had a corollary, namely that, according to Golan, "from the late 1930s until the termination of the Mandatory government in 1948, the British government in Palestine tended to support the Arab side" (ibid., 141). Contrast this view with that of Israeli historian Haim Gerber (2003), who argues that on several levels the British favoured the Zionists, such as in education, military cooperation, and "cruel" repression of the Arab population. On a different front, support for this position is provided by John Knight (2011), who critically examines the dominant claim made in Palestine historiography that the British police were hostile to the Jewish community or did not do enough to protect it. He shows that, on the contrary, the police and military were instrumental in furthering the Balfour Declaration by training, arming, and recruiting Jewish supernumeraries to put down the Arab Revolt of 1936–39. Specifically, Knight highlights the role of Orde Wingate, described in the annals of Zionism as a "radical believer in Zionism," which "he adopted as his religion" (in Knight 2011, 533). Sent to Palestine in 1936 as an intelligence officer, Wingate eventually took upon himself the task of leading so-called "Special Night Squads," referred to by others as "Jewish murder gangs" (ibid., 534), to fight against the native Arab population.

The claim that urban-economic development of the Arab and Jewish sectors was separate, equal, or just different is standard in Zionist scholarship on Israel's project of settler colonialism. Yet there is contrary empirical evidence to demonstrate that urban Jewish development in Palestine took place at the *expense* of its Arab counterpart, be it in the acquisition of land or in the closure of the labour market to Arab workers in the prestate period, not to mention access to capital.

As Haim Yacobi (2004a, 2004b, 2008), Mark Levine (2005), and Zachary Lockman (1996) demonstrate, the lopsided and dependent urban relationship in so-called "mixed cities" continues to this day. Israeli geographer Yacobi (2008) observes:

> The term "mixed cities" is often perceived as pertaining to an idyllic image of a shared urban space. But it is a misleading idiom, as it hides from the Israeli public the extent of segregation and poverty experienced by Arab citizens living in cities such as Acre, Lod, Haifa and Ramle, where they constitute between 20 and 30 percent of the population . . . This status is not coincidental, evolutional or neutral: It is the product of intentional policy, mostly implicit but occasionally explicit, operating according to ethnonational logic. Its main objective has and continues to be the demographic dominance of the Jewish majority over the Arab minority in the mixed cities.

As a matter of fact, a recent museum exhibit in Tel Aviv focused precisely on the issue of urbanisation in the Arab sector and its relationship to the Zionist project. It was intended to "highlight the injustice against the Palestinian populace in Israel in 1948 and Israel today" with the purpose of reaching "those who are not prepared to view Israeli urbanization from an exclusively Zionist viewpoint" (Yahav 2013). The ultimate test of the Zionist project should be its actual developments on the ground, which belie the ideological claims of Zionism and its defenders, a point emphasised by Benjamin Beit-Hallahmi, Ilan Pappé, and others, as shown below.

To critics, notably historian Gabriel Piterberg, who admonishes Avineri for his "veneer of liberalism," there is nothing further from the truth regarding the standard Zionist narrative. Herzl's statements demonstrate that the "settlers' nationalism [is] intended to create a Jewish state in a territory inhabited by non-white natives" (Piterberg 2008, 10), while affirming Herzl's "belief that having a successful colonial European-like venture in the East was the ultimate path to admission into the West" (ibid., 19). A variant of Avineri's position is expressed by fellow political scientist Ze'ev Sternhell (2010, 111), who argues in a critical review of Piterberg's book that settler Zionism in Mandate Palestine and its consequence for the indigenous Palestinian population must be seen as a *necessity* dictated by historical circumstances and the experience in Europe following the Second World War, when the Jews "had no place to go."[12] Furthermore, for this and other reasons, Zionism cannot be viewed as a form of colonialism. Sternhell (2008), a fierce opponent of settlements in the OPT who almost paid with his life at the hands of Jewish settler terrorists, made an exception and labelled the *settlements* a form of "Zionist colonialism." However, the argument of necessity cannot convincingly explain the systematic dispossession of the native Palestinian minority in Israel and the continued widespread discrimination against its members. As Sternhell and others must know by now, the 1948 expulsion of the majority of the Palestinian population was largely a premeditated act instigated to cleanse the country of its Arab inhabitants.

The argument of historical necessity is also invoked by legal scholar Chaim Gans (2008), with the added stipulation that Zionism (and its fulfilment in the shape of Israel) must acknowledge its responsibility in the creation of the Palestinian refugee problem, although this does not imply that the refugees can exercise their right of return.

The task of reconciling Herzl's seemingly contradictory views is carried out by philosopher M.A. Khalidi (2001) and reiterated by Piterberg (2008, 39–40). Basically, Khalidi argues that Herzl's novel *Altneuland* was a public relations tract aimed at a European audience in the hope of gaining favour with Europe's political establishments. According to Khalidi (2001, 61), "the novel was not conceived as a work aimed primarily at the Jews, but as a work of persuasion aimed at a non-Jewish European audience." The token Arab in the novel is a character by the name of Raschid Bey, who, in Khalidi's words, was a "fawning Oriental" who ingratiated himself in praising Zionist colonisation of Palestine as benefiting the native Arab population (ibid., 58, 61). As shown above, in proposing creation of the Jewish-Ottoman Land Company to colonise Palestine and Syria, Herzl took his cues from other colonial ventures such as the British East India Company of the nineteenth century. The charter of Herzl's company provided detailed plans for land acquisition and resettlement of the Palestinians outside their country; such details were absent from *Altneuland*.

Socioeconomic integration of the native population was never considered a serious option in mainstream Zionist thought – notwithstanding efforts toward this end by Brit-Shalom, a splinter binationalist Jewish group that was active in the 1930s. Indeed, other fleeting attempts at Arab-Jewish so-called "labour union integration" saw Jewish nationalism trump sporadic calls for Arab-Jewish working-class solidarity. In the words of Gershon Shafir and Yoav Peled (2002, 37), "the most distinguishing characteristic of the Jewish Labour Movement in Palestine was that it was not a labour movement at all. Rather it was a colonial movement in which the workers' interest remained secondary to the exigencies of settlement" (see also Shafir 1996). Commenting on Shafir's (1989) conclusion that the foundations of the Israeli state must be understood in terms of what happened prior to 1914 with the establishment of exclusive Jewish settlements and labour closure, Fieldhouse (2006, 127) adds that ultimately the Balfour Declaration is what made the Zionist project possible. Extrapolating to more than a half-century later, one can safely claim that if not for Western support, particularly from the United States, Israel would not have been able to carry out its illegal policies and enjoy immunity from international law regarding its discriminatory treatment of the Palestinians. Equally important, Lockman (2012) demonstrates in a critical, yet appreciative, article that, in analysing the modalities of the Zionist project in Palestine, Shafir (1989) does not give due consideration to the role of violence in the Zionist project of displacing and expelling the Palestinian population – which made the creation of Israel possible.

There is no shortage of celebratory writings about Zionism, even though the critical perspective, which is constantly attacked as anti-Semitic, is gaining ground and becoming increasingly heard in academic circles. Two books in particular demonstrate the pitfalls of adopting an idealist rendition of Zionism. Eyal Chowers (2012, 13) provides a philosophical perspective for understanding the Zionist project in Palestine as "a unique national movement," with its systems of thought and modes of action, and Boaz Neumann (2011, 40) focuses on the role of *desire* as a "primal, existential condition" behind the Jewish colonisation of Palestine in the early part of the twentieth century. Both books are infused with a sense of (social) idealism – the belief that reality is basically a mental construct and exists independently of its surroundings, which in this case is the reality of Palestine and the fact that it was already inhabited by another people when Israel was created. The analysis in both books draws upon the Jewish intellectual experience in Europe and later Palestine, with no reference to comparative studies of settler societies. The Palestinians are absent in voice and action. This omission is intentional, as the authors admit.

Chowers (2012, 11) examines the philosophical foundations of Zionism and claims that his approach departs "from the prevalent theories and vocabularies typically used to examine" Zionism; it also differs from the approaches taken by the critics who seek a connection between Zionism and colonialism and those who sympathise with the movement's ideology. He first tackles the conception of time in Zionist discourse and argues that it represents a rejection of Immanuel Kant's teleological, linear conception of time and progress as key elements of modernity. By conceiving "fragmented" and "semicyclical" time as the basis for "temporal imaginations," he concludes that time opens vistas for conversation between "distant moments and the grounding of identity in concrete images and events" (ibid., 11) and that fragmented time makes possible for the individual and community the recovery of memory and receptivity to the past. In his book's second chapter, Chowers introduces the key concept of "sundered history," which in my estimation has a postmodern ring to it, by providing a "picture of history as shapeless, devoid of binding meta-narratives or underlying structures" (ibid., 15). "Building" is taken as a "prime" metaphor that refers to building the nation and building the environment. The Zionists in Palestine embarked on moulding space as a means to affirm their rootedness and consolidate their sense of community. Even though the Palestinian Arabs constituted an overwhelming majority in the early twentieth century, in no way did this lead to reassessing the totality and morality of the Zionist project. Yet this prime preoccupation with building and the honing of skills, which for all intents and purposes are the hallmarks of colonial activity in general, was accomplished at the expense of developing the language and skills needed for democratic politics.

Boaz Neumann (2011, 2) claims that by focusing on "Zionist desire for the Land of Israel," he too has embarked on an unexplored aspect of Zionism, making his study unlike others that deal with politics, history, religion, or even psychology. Neumann conceives of desire as an "existential" attribute that is revealed in the writings of the early-twentieth-century settlers, referred to in Zionist parlance as "pioneers." But these were a special kind of pioneer, we are told. They did not come to Palestine to "blaze a trail" or "conquer" new territory, as other so-called "pioneers" have done, say in North America, Africa, and other places. They were the pioneers of "building," "construction," and "redemption." This is not pioneerism that one associates with colonialism. He does point out that although these pioneers constituted a tiny minority – 13 per cent – of the settlers, they formed the nucleus of the settler elite strata and eventually the backbone of Israel's military establishment.

The research for Neumann's (2011) book was carried out during the Second Intifada in 2000. In the preface, he is clear about his task: it is an exploration of *Jewish* desire for the land. As someone who does not speak Arabic, he leaves it for the Palestinians to provide the narrative about their desire for the land. This is a questionable symmetry, although no doubt Neumann means to be fair-minded in calling for both sides to tell their stories. In the eyes of the Palestinians, they are called upon to reveal why they desire the land on par with the new colonists, as though the fact of living continuously in Palestine for more than a thousand years is not sufficient proof of their attachment to the land. One does not have to be proficient in Arabic to understand the meaning of the iconic image of Palestinian refugees who were expelled from their homes in 1948 yet for more than sixty years continued to cling to the keys of their expropriated abodes in Palestine. The *land* of Palestine is a perennial theme in Palestinian history and literature – Arabic and foreign. The Palestinians saw no need to sing the praises of Palestine, a country that is their natural habitat and taken for granted, until they were displaced and felt the encroachment of the Zionist project on their land.

Throughout his book, Neumann (2011, 52) describes the settlers' desire for the land in mystical, metaphorical, even erotic terms: "the Zionist narrative of many *halutzim* [pioneers] is a story of falling in love romantically, even sexually, with the Land of Israel." Desire for the land becomes constitutive of the settlers' being. But how does desire come about? Is it innate? Is desire a social construct, as the anthropologist Ann Laura Stoler (1995) reminds us in her writings about colonialism? Neumann outlines several psychological approaches to the study of desire, all of which he rejects since they are based on the Freudian formulation of the unconscious, in which desire is linked to parental relationship and transference of needs. He settles on the following based on his reading of *Anti-Oedipus: Capitalism and Schizophrenia* (2009) by Gilles Deleuze and Félix Guattari:

> What Deleuze and Guattari do is purge desire of its essence and meaning. For desire knows only to crave, to produce. It is pure energy, a fluidity that knows no origins (i.e., derives from no needs) or destinations (i.e., makes no demands) and is not essentially connected to any particular body. And this is how I understand the desire of the *halutzim* for the Land of Israel. (B. Neumann 2011, 30)

It is worth noting that Deleuze's views of the Zionist settlement in Palestine are revealing and, one might add, at variance with Neumann's views. In a 1982 interview, reprinted in 1998, Deleuze said of the Palestinian encounter with Zionism:

> There are two very different movements within capitalism. Now it's a matter of taking a people on their own territory and making them work, exploiting them, in order to accumulate a surplus: that's what's ordinarily called a colony. Now, on the contrary, it's a matter of emptying a territory of its people in order to make a leap forward, even if it means making them

into a workforce elsewhere. The history of Zionism and Israel, like that of America, happened that second way: how to make an empty space, how to throw out a people? (Deleuze and Sanbar 1998, 27)

In addition to propounding his free-floating conception of desire, Neumann (2011, 40) goes on to say tautologically that desire exists because it reproduces itself: "Desire, then, only desires." Moreover, "the *halutzim* chose the Land of Israel because it chose them" (ibid., 41). He continues to state his case in this tautological vein by essentially closing off the debate about the morality and appropriateness of the whole Zionist project. This is definitely a different perspective on Zionism, but is it credible? And what does it tell us about the travails of those on the receiving end of Zionism, such as the Palestinians? It does not explore the social basis of desire. Why is it that some desire and others do not? Why is the language of desire loaded with derogatory descriptions of the native Palestinian population? In a chapter titled "Dissolving Boundaries," Neumann proceeds to dissolve the boundaries between flesh, blood, sweat, and bodily fluids, on the one hand, and the soil of the land, on the other, thus obliterating boundaries between human agency and nature. Even the act of digging a well is riddled with sexual innuendos. The pioneers "saw removing earth as another way to become intimate with and penetrate the Land" (ibid.).

The emergence of political Zionism and Jewish nationalism as a late-nineteenth-century phenomenon is examined by both Chowers (2012) and Neumann (2011) with no appreciation for the "standpoint of its [Palestinian] victims," to quote the title of an article by Edward Said (1979), in which he avers that:

> ... one of the enduring attributes of self-serving idealism, however, is the notion that ideas are just ideas and that they exist only in the realm of ideas. The tendency to view ideas as pertaining only to a world of abstractions increases among people for whom an idea is essentially perfect, good, uncontaminated by human desires or will. (Ibid., 10–11)

Said goes on to note that:

> ... effective political ideas like Zionism need to be examined historically in two ways: (1) genealogically in order that their provenance, their kinship and descent, their affiliation both with other ideas and with political institutions may be demonstrated; (2) as practical systems for accumulation (of power, land, ideological legitimacy) and displacement (of people, other ideas, prior legitimacy). (Ibid., 11)

The absence of any dialectical synthesis between the reality of Palestine and its confrontation with Zionism is a major lacuna. Zionism is presented as self-contained and isolated from its surroundings, with its origins, although European in their inspiration, remaining purely Jewish in their manifestation. Here, it is worth noting an observation by Gershon Shafir, an Israeli himself and a student of early Zionism in Palestine, that captures the relevance of colonialism to understanding the Zionist idea. He notes that in their attempts to escape European persecution, Jewish settlers in Palestine "could escape Europe, but not rid themselves of it" (Shafir 2005, 41).

Breaching the consensus

> The Israeli-Arab conflict has as its core the efforts of the Zionist settlers to create an exclusivist Jewish society in Palestine and the resistance, first of the native Arab population, and later of states, Arab and other, to this colonization project . . . The social, national and state-building processes of Israel are seen by the Arabs as processes of destruction, dispersion and destructuration of Palestinian-Arab society. (Ehrlich 1987, 122)

Avishai Ehrlich's comment is in stark contrast to the routine claims made by Israel and its supporters that the Arab-Israeli conflict is basically a conflict between states and that the Palestine issue is a tangential component of it. The dominant Zionist attitude toward the Palestinians is best reflected in the words of Golda Meir, who more than three decades ago brazenly declared, "there is no such a thing as a Palestinian people," a statement that has been roundly criticised (in *Economist* 2008). Israeli authors who acknowledge the colonial character of Israel's occupation of the Palestinian territories since 1967 describe it as different from what had transpired in Israel proper since 1948; the post-1948 project is viewed implicitly or explicitly as noncolonial in essence and as having turned colonial inadvertently or "accidentally" after 1967, as in Gershom Gorenberg's work (2006). Overall – except by a few writers, as shown below – the Zionist project is still largely seen in its historical context as noncolonial, if not liberatory, and any deviations from the liberation model are seen as aberrations caused by historical necessity. Although the unfoldings of the Zionist project in historical Palestine in 1948 and 1967, comprising Israel and the occupied territories, had different histories and trajectories, in both instances expulsion, seizure of land, and displacement of the indigenous population – all of which are settler colonialism's hallmarks – were Zionism's common features.

Whereas historically it has been Palestinian, other Arab, and Western Marxist writers who have analysed Israel since its inception from the perspective of colonialism (Kayyali 1981; Rodinson 1973), in the past few decades several mainstream writers, including Israeli ones, have breached the once-dominant consensus about the nature of Israel as advanced by Israeli and Western social scientists by situatingits formation in the context of colonialism and the ensuing conflict with the indigenous Palestinian population. Executing this intellectual reconstruction has not been easy. It was once considered "slanderous," as sociologist Uri Ram (1993, 330) remarks, to associate Zionism in scholarly discourse with colonialism. Or, as expressed more forcefully by historian Ilan Pappé (2003, 81), who suffered personally and professionally as a result of his critical perspective on Zionism, "any reference to Zionism as colonialism is tantamount in the Israeli political discourse to treason and self-hatred" (see also Pappé 2014).

Through their writings, Jewish political activists and academics with leftist leanings contributed as early as the 1970s to laying the foundations for a critical Jewish perspective on Israeli society that slowly but eventually made its impact felt in the wider academy. I drew upon the writings of this group more than three decades ago in my book *The Palestinians in Israel: A Study in Internal Colonialism* (Zureik 1979), and there is no need to repeat my discussion of that body of work here in full. Uri Ram (1993, 1995) addressed both in a review article and in a subsequent book the intellectual history behind the colonisation framework in Israeli sociology. The immediate discussion that follows is a brief overview of efforts by a handful of Israeli writers who fall within this genre. One of the earliest among this group was Uri Davis, an anti-Zionist member of the defunct Trotskyite Matzpen group, who early on exposed the workings of the Jewish National Fund as a colonial instrument for dispossessing the native Palestinians of their land and who applied the label "apartheid" to describe Israel's treatment of the Palestinians long before it was in use (U. Davis 2003; U. Davis, Mack, and Yuval-Davis 1975). Simha Flapan, once an active member of the defunct left-of-centre Mapam Party, was also one of the early writers to address the impact of Zionism on the indigenous population. It is important to note that Flapan (1979), who acknowledged that the Palestinian struggle constituted a "national movement," did not construe Zionism as a colonial project and was not anti-Zionist himself. Rather, as he stated, it was the ascendancy of militarism[13] and the "disintegration" of what he regarded as universal and progressive values within Zionism that had to be rectified if peace with the Palestinians was to be achieved (ibid., 13). Another Israeli writer who has provided a thorough discussion of Zionism and its colonialist orientations is psychologist Benjamin Beit-Hallahmi, who outright associates Israel throughout its history with colonialism. In his book, *Original Sins: Reflections on the History of Zionism and Israel* (1992), Beit-Hallahmi makes the point that even if the intentions of the Zionist settlers were not colonialist from the outset, Zionism – like settler movements elsewhere – cannot be regarded as anything other than settler colonialism given the way that it unfolded in Palestine. Although the Zionist project did not have a mother country to sponsor it, and was not driven by a search for markets and access to raw material, its sponsorship by colonial powers such as Britain, France, and the United States in successive historical periods gave the Zionists the needed impetus to proceed with little serious consideration of the aspirations and opposition of the indigenous population, which was perceived as a "surplus population" (ibid.). Beit-Hallahmi further notes that "creating Jewish sovereignty in Palestine was only possible at their [the Palestinians'] expense. They had to be eliminated, pushed away or dispossessed" (ibid., 82). Whether or not Zionism was intentionally colonial by design is a moot question, since all settler colonialisms end up dispossessing the natives.

Around the same time, three central figures in this critical school, who are thus identified with the label "post-Zionism,"[14] emerged on the academic scene: sociologist

Gershon Shafir, historian Ilan Pappé, and sociologist Baruch Kimmerling. In *Land, Labour and the Origins of the Israeli-Palestinian Conflict, 1882–1914*, Shafir (1989, xi) remarks, "I came to the conclusion that, during most of its history, Israeli society is best understood not through the existing inward-looking interpretations but rather in terms of the broader context of Israeli-Palestinian relations."[15] This relationship is to be understood by considering the "appropriateness of the model of European colonization for the Israeli case [which] is due to some structural similarities" (ibid., 10). Shafir also remarks:

> ... at the outset, Zionism was a variety of Eastern European nationalism, that is, an ethnic movement in search of a state. But at the end of the journey it may be seen more fruitfully as a late instance of European overseas expansion, which had been taking place from the sixteenth through the early twentieth centuries. (Ibid., 8)

In Shafir's (1989) materialist[16] (in contrast to idealist) perspective, the crux of the initial Zionist colonisation of Palestine was the issue of land and labour, as well as the question of how to implement colonisation without exploiting the native population. None of these issues – land, labour, or population – were resolved by the Zionist project without ethnic separation, exploitation, and eventually outright dispossession and cleansing of the Palestinians.

Ilan Pappé, the most prolific of these post-Zionist Israeli writers, has contributed a series of books that offer a critical assessment of the historical origins of the Arab-Israeli conflict as portrayed in mainstream Israeli historiography; throughout his writings, he has kept his focus on the Palestinian component of the conflict. Pappé rejects the claim of Zionist historiography that the Jewish settlement in Palestine was motivated mainly by nationalism and socialism. It is methodologically incorrect, argues Pappé (1988), to assume a causal link between the ideologies, intentions, and writings of the settlers, on the one hand, and what actually unfolded on the ground, on the other. As he correctly sees it, the Zionist venture was driven from its early inception by colonialism and eventually by ethnic cleansing. In a comparative analysis of Zionist settlement and other Christian missionary movements in Africa, Pappé shows that the ideological manifestations of these groups, which were influenced by European colonialism under the banners of idealism and progress, belied actual developments that resulted in the exploitation and dispossession of the native population (ibid.; see also Pappé 2011).

At the time of his death in 2007, the sociologist Baruch Kimmerling had achieved a prominent position as a scholar and public intellectual. He is well known for his scathing criticism of Ariel Sharon as the main architect of Israeli colonial policies in the occupied territories, which included waging "politicide" against the Palestinians (Kimmerling 2003). His analysis of Zionism and the situation in Israel proper is rather different. In his book with Joel Migdal, *Palestinians: The Making of a People* (Kimmerling and Migdal 1993), there is no place for colonialism as an organising principle for explaining the historical confrontation between Zionism and the Palestinians. The book is a chronological rendition of the emergence of Palestinian nationalism, with heavy emphasis on primordialism and internal factionalism. What made it refreshing for many readers was that it was written by Israeli mainstream academics. Jan Selby's (2005, 108) overview of post-Zionist writings captures the central weakness of Kimmerling's approach:

> He sees Zionism as "a uniquely nonprofit and noneconomic settler movement" driven exclusively by nationalist sentiment, the result being that he ends up saying nothing either about the world-systemic colonial system within which the Zionist movement took shape, or about the political economy of settlement within Ottoman and British Mandate Palestine.

Sociologist Gil Eyal (2006, 33–61) offers a nuanced yet sympathetic interpretation of Zionism, although he admits that as an ideology Zionism is imbued with Orientalist rhetoric, a view that is shared by Israeli historian Haim Gerber (2003), referred to earlier. In commenting on the works of Said, Shafir, and others, Eyal points out that settler Zionism embodied diverse, even contradictory, attitudes toward the Arab population of Palestine – fascination and disgust, superiority and admiration. Although Eyal does not deny the colonialist attitudes of Zionist writers starting with Theodore Herzl, he claims that these attitudes were motivated by the needs of Zionist settlers to distance themselves from the "primitive" culture of the native "Oriental" population (both Arabs and Jews of Middle Eastern origin) and to establish a separate identity that was also dissociated from the European stigmatising of the Jews. I argue that attempts by Eyal and others, such as Derek Penslar (2007),[17] to present Zionism as a hybrid of multifaceted sentiments, including anticolonial sentiments vis-à-vis Europe, do not negate the fact that, except for among a minority of binationalists who were marginalised and sidelined, Zionism's ultimate objective has always been to colonise the land, ensure a substantial Jewish majority – with land dispossession and Arab population transfer being concrete alternatives – and, in the face of Arab opposition, build a society separated from its Arab neighbours by what the revisionist Vladimir Jabotinsky has called an "iron wall." In contrast to other Zionist apologists, Jabotinsky does not shy away from admitting that the Palestinians are a nation and calling the Zionist project a colonial effort that is sustainable only through the use of naked force to counter Arab opposition:

> Zionist colonization, even the most restricted, must either be terminated or carried out in defiance of the will of the native population. This colonization can, therefore, continue and develop only under the protection of a force independent of the local population – an iron wall which the native population cannot break through. This is, *in toto*, our policy towards the Arabs. To formulate it any other way would only be hypocrisy. (In Sa'di 2010, 47; see also Lustick 2008)

Up to now, Israel has remained uncommitted to acknowledging its role in what anthropologist Danny Rabinowitz (2000) has called "the original sin" that resulted in the 1948 destruction of the Palestinian community, on whose remnants Israel was created.

In presenting his critical interpretation of mainstream Israeli writings, historian Gabriel Piterberg (2008, 62) argues that Zionism's colonialist character and its "foundational myth" are manifested along three "fundamentals of hegemonic settler narratives":

> . . . the alleged uniqueness of the Jewish nation in its relentless search for sovereignty in the biblically endowed homeland; the privileging of the consciousness of Zionist settlers at the expense of the colonized, and at the expense of the results of colonization by the settlers rather than their intentions; and the denial of the fact that the presence of the Palestinian Arabs on the land destined for colonization was the single most significant factor that determined the shape taken by the settlers' nation.

In tandem with persistent attempts to erase the Palestinian narrative about historical connection to the country, Israeli politicians at the highest level have engaged in distorting and outright concealing the Palestinian presence in the country. Ongoing research by doctoral student Shay Hazkani (2013) has shown that by withholding archival material from researchers, the Israeli censor continues to conceal the true nature of events following the 1948 onslaught against the Palestinian civil population and its expulsion: "Under the leadership of Prime Minister David Ben-Gurion, top Middle East scholars in the Civil Service were assigned the task of providing evidence supporting Israel's position – which was that, rather than being expelled in 1948, the Palestinians had fled of their own volition."

Discourse and power

The language of obfuscation

> Political language – and with variations this is true of all political parties, from Conservatives to Anarchists – is designed to make lies sound truthful and murder respectable. (Orwell 1946, 139)

> "When I use a word," Humpty Dumpty said in a rather scornful tone, "it means just what I choose it to mean – neither more nor less."
> "The question is," said Alice, "whether you can make words mean so many different things."
> "The question is," said Humpty Dumpty, "which is to be master – that's all." (Lewis Carroll, *Alice's Adventures in Wonderland*, in Peteet 2005, 153)

Raymond Williams's (1976) notion of "key words" allows Robert Home (2003, 298) to note that, "through their rhetorical and hegemonic weight," such words "offer prisms through which colonial and postcolonial state objectives can be seen. They offer shifting and alternative meanings, deployed for different, sometimes hidden, objectives by different interests."[18] Home analyses four key words that were used to describe the British and Zionist plans for colonising Palestine: "settlement," "transfer," "partition," and "absenteeism." These became tools in dispossessing Palestinians of their land. They were used as a mechanism to override a traditional and communal land tenure system in favour of privatisation: "These four keywords, with their shifting interpretations, sustained in the Mandate period an assault by the modernizing colonial state upon the communal land tenure systems of the Palestinian village (where two-thirds of the Palestinian population lived), preparing the way for the massive land confiscations by the successor Israeli state" (Ibid., 301).

The word "settlement," Home points out, had two special meanings in British colonial discourse. First, article 6 of the League of Nations' *Palestine Mandate* stated that the British "shall facilitate Jewish immigration under suitable conditions and shall encourage . . . *close settlement* by Jews on the land, including State lands and waste lands not required for public purposes" (in Forman and Kedar 2003, 496–97, emphasis added). "Close settlement" referred to intensive agriculture by means of large-scale agricultural settlements. The second meaning referred to the use of cadastral maps to fix land locations and titles, thus privatising land ownership and leaving it to the courts to adjudicate legal transactions. This process set the stage for the Zionists to eventually approach individual owners for the purpose of land purchase.

"Transfer," the second term examined by Home, also had double connotations. First, it was concerned with land transfers: "With only registered transactions recognized by the courts, it provided the legal framework for purchase of land. Within a decade, the scale of transfers to Jews, and the accompanying evictions of Palestinian agricultural tenants, were revealing the contradictions in the Mandate, and making the British uneasy" (Home 2003, 299). The same procedure was followed by Israel after 1948 in the aftermath of the expulsion and flight of the Palestinians and again after 1967 in the West Bank. In due course, the second meaning of "transfer" referred to the Palestinian population's transfer: "After 1948 the keyword transfer acquired a different and more sinister meaning, associated with a potential policy of systematic physical expulsion of the Palestinians from the state of Israel" (ibid.).

With regard to "partition," Home notes that this third key word, as it appeared in the Ottoman land code, implied something quite different from that acquired under the British Mandate. Under the Ottoman code, partition allowed

> . . . jointly owned village land to be periodically reallocated. Land might be held in uneconomic sizes and shapes, with inherited shares of an estate expressed in fractions of no real value; periodic land readjustment could be achieved through application by two-thirds of the owners of shares in undivided land, and was recorded in a formal partition schedule. (Home 2003, 299)

Thus the onslaught against communal land ownership was made possible by defining "partition" politically to mean territorial division between Arabs and Jews.

Finally, "absenteeism," Home's fourth key word, had double connotations. First, it referred to land owners who under the British system and later Israel were defined as forfeiting ownership due to their absence from the country and/or because the land remained idle for a minimum period of time. Whereas under the Ottoman system such land would be held in state trust, and original owners of *miri* land had up to ninety years to restore ownership, the Zionists operated under a different interpretation of the land code, for once the state or the Jewish National Fund assumed ownership, such land remained Jewish in perpetuity. Absentee owners increased significantly after the 1948 expulsion. Refugee property was at one point controlled by a military governor and was administered by the so-called "custodian of absentee property." Here too this meant that property was not held in trust by the state, as the original British Emergency Regulations stipulated, after which the Israeli system was set up, but would be transferred to Jewish owners and permanently alienated from its original Palestinian owners.

The association between power and knowledge, emphasised by Edward Said (1978) with a special reference to colonialism's dominant discourse, is apparent in Israel's continuing attempts to erase the colonial past and depict the present as free of any connection between Palestine (its landscape, culture, and continuous Arab presence) and its Arab-Islamic heritage (see N. Gordon 2002; and Piterberg 2001). What makes the task of colonialism all the more feasible is that it rests on asymmetrical power relations in which the coloniser utilises its technology, know-how, superior economy, and military power to impose a way of seeing and describing the colony that naturalises its actions and discourse toward the colonised. In discussing colonial discourse, Julie Peteet (2005, 153–54) notes that words "are more than simple reflections of reality, referencing a moral grammar that underwrites and reproduces power." In this way, colonial language delegitimises Palestinian claims and stifles voices of dissent in opposition to the Zionist project. In analysing the naming of events, places, and actions in the Israeli-Palestinian conflict, Peteet is cognisant of the power of words:

> Words are extraordinarily important for the way they embody ideological significance and circulate moral attributes. In other words, in a conflict setting the words chosen from a vast lexicon to describe events, actions, peoples, places and social phenomena reverberate with, uphold or contest power. They constitute moral worlds and the humanity of participants and thus, ultimately, the distribution of rights. (Ibid., 154)

She demonstrates how binary terminology is deployed in public discourse about the conflict: the 1948 Nakba for the Palestinians versus independence for the Zionists, resistance versus terrorism, civilised world versus evil world of terror and darkness, murder and assassination versus legitimate state-targeted killings, and so on.

In the wake of the Oslo agreement, Israel seems to have stepped up its use of what Peteet (2009) calls "discursive subterfuge" to conceal its true colonial intentions in dealing with the Palestinians. For example, as settlements continued to expand, the seemingly neutral term *hipardut* or *hafrada* ("separation" in Hebrew), enunciated by Yitzhak Rabin in 1995 (Massad 2010), was used to describe the official policy promoted by successive Israeli governments in the occupied territories (see BADIL 2009). From 2001 to 2009, during Ariel Sharon's and Ehud Olmert's successive tenures as prime minister, *hipardut* mutated into *hitnatkut* (severance of contact or relationship) and was eventually transformed into *hitkansut* (ingathering, converging, or becoming inward-looking) (Cook 2006). *Hitkansut*, which was borrowed from Jewish spiritual teachings, served the ideological underpinning of the right-wing Kadima Party's unilateral policies in the occupied territories and, contrary to claims by its critics, was presented as a form of Jewish self-reflection that was not intended to denigrate the Other (Philologos 2006).

Eyal Chowers (2012), whose work was discussed earlier, addresses the role and revival of the Hebrew language by contrasting two national figures, the poet Chaim Bialik and the essayist Ahad Ha'am. Both are considered key cultural nationalists who viewed language as a tool of spiritual revival. Among researchers of *Palestinian* history, Asher Ginsberg (whose pen name is Ahad Ha'am) is well known for a letter he wrote after a visit to Palestine in the closing decade of the nineteenth century in which he warned against accepting the Zionist idea that the land was empty and that its Arab inhabitants were primitive and backward. Bialik, in contrast, viewed the Hebrew language as a means of coping with Biblical *tohu* (chaos, formlessness). Language's "foremost reason for existence is to cover up formlessness in a pile of words and metaphors, descriptions and conventions. Language engulfs humans in a world of meanings they have developed in order to deny Tohu, or the abyss" (ibid., 197–98). Chowers describes the consequences of concealing uncomfortable truths through language by way of an example from the actions of David Ben-Gurion, an admirer of Bialik. Ben-Gurion struck a committee in 1949 to suggest replacement names for Arab localities whose inhabitants had been driven out of Palestine in 1947–48. Of the 533 new names suggested by the committee, "only eight Arabic names were transliterated untouched" (ibid., 301). Thus language was put in the service of historical and national erasure of the Palestinians. In his discussion of contemporary Israeli politics, Chowers makes passing reference to the political use of language in the context of the Israeli-Arab conflict, as seen for example in the censoring of any reference to the Nakba in Israeli school textbooks. He attributes the concealing aspects of the Hebrew language to the conflict with the Arabs. It is not clear, however, whether the Hebrew language would have revealed the truth about reality if there had been no such conflict.

Taking examples from contemporary events, Chowers (2012) provides a quick summary of how language has been used by Israeli officials and the military to convey messages other than the real intention of the enunciators. The 1982 Israeli attack on Lebanon was officially dubbed *melhemet shalom hagalil*, meaning "war for the safety/peace of the Galilee, thereby turning the meaning of the highly potent word *shalom* on its head" (ibid., 202). He goes on to say:

> The term *hisul memokad*, which can be translated as "focused liquidation" – a kind of marriage between the detached surgical term *memukad* and the

language of commercial sales – is in fact "targeted assassination"; the word *hisuf* (an old twist on the word *lahsof*) means the act of revealing or exposing something, but is used by the army to signify a military action in which the orchards, gardens, buildings, fences, and so on of Palestinians are removed for "security reasons." (Ibid.)

Michael Sfard (2012), an Israeli human rights lawyer, demonstrates how the corruption of the Hebrew language by the Israeli military and bureaucracy constitutes a form of Orwellian "double-speak":

> ... extrajudicial executions have become "targeted assassinations." Torture has been dubbed "moderate physical pressure." Expulsion to Gaza has been renamed "assigning a place of residence." The theft of privately owned land has become "declaring the land state-owned." Collective punishment is "leveraging civilians"; and collective punishment by blockade is a "siege," "closure" or "separation" ... The occupation addresses its subjects not in words, but in deed. It is not a language designed for dialogue, but for an extended speech in which the speaker acts and the listener is acted upon. This is the lingua franca common among Palestinians and Israeli soldiers.

This linguistic turn revived another dimension of the debate, namely the growing comparison of Israeli policies in the occupied territories with those of South Africa's previous apartheid regime. For those subscribing to the apartheid label, its most visible manifestation in the occupied territories is the so-called "separation wall," the building of settlements and roads for exclusive Jewish use, and a whole host of other concrete policies that will be discussed below. As pointed out in a report by the Human Sciences Research Council of South Africa (2009), in many respects the Israeli form of separation resembles, and some would argue is worse than, the once-practised system of South African "apartheid," which in the Afrikaner language also means "separation" (Dugard 2003). Although, as expected, this semantic equivalence is rejected outright by Zionists across the ideological spectrum, the slide into an apartheid regime is nevertheless highlighted by Daniel Blatman (2011), head of the Institute for Contemporary Jewry at the Hebrew University. He sees an apartheid state that is reminiscent of the old South Africa developing in Israel as a result of "the tsunami of racist laws" enacted by the Knesset. He specifically cites the Acceptance Committee Law, according to which localities are entitled to vote on accepting or rejecting newcomers (meaning Arabs); the Nakba Law, which authorises the state to withhold funding for education and for culture programs from local councils that celebrate the Nakba, and the Citizenship Law, which strips citizenship from those who are convicted of espionage or treason. In Blatman's view, the aim of these legislations "is the gradual establishment of an apartheid state in Israel, and the future separation on a racial basis of Jews and non Jews" (ibid.). Indeed, the South African government officially condemned the "forced

78 Zionism and colonialism

removal" of Palestinians from East Jerusalem to make room for Jewish settlers and compared this action to what transpired during the apartheid regime in South Africa (Ahren 2009).

A word of caution is sounded by Julie Peteet (2009), who argues for a "strategic" use of the label "apartheid" in the Israeli-Palestinian context, inasmuch as the analogy with South Africa's old apartheid system is valid on several counts: Israel sets limits on the free mobility of the Palestinian population, it controls the land and other natural resources such as water, it uses the pass system and repressive policies to counter opposition to military rule, it fosters economic dependency, it has implemented a dual legal system – one part governing the native Palestinians and the other being for exclusive use by Jewish settlers – it privileges the settlers (e.g., in the Law of Return), and as the coloniser, it has exclusive control of the security apparatus.

Peteet's (2009) warning against accepting the apartheid analogy *in toto* is pragmatic and based on the following considerations. First, the injection of race language in denouncing Israeli methods of occupation will not illicit international support on the scale of South Africa due mainly to the Jewish historical experience of discrimination and racism, not to mention the Holocaust. Peteet may be onto something here, except that the debate over domestic Jewish racism is now voiced in Israel itself (Bar'el 2014; Shenhav and Yona 2008), where all along public opinion data on attitudes toward the Arab population have overwhelmingly demonstrated a high level of racism and endorsement of discrimination – significantly among Jewish youth (Kashti 2010; Zelikovich 2010). Furthermore, racism in Israel is not confined to surveys of fleeting public attitudes but permeates the institutional structure of the state, such as the Knesset and government policies (Mada al-Carmel 2010a; Rabinowitz, Ghanem, and Yiftachel 2000; Roffe-Ofir 2010; Weiler-Polak 2009). According to reports on civil rights in Israel, the level of discrimination and racism shown toward the Palestinian citizens of Israel has risen substantially in the past few years (e.g., see ACRI 2009, 2012c), and in all likelihood it will continue to rise in the presence of a far-right government, some of whose ministers publicly espouse racist attitudes toward Palestinian citizens of the state. A study by Israeli psychologists has revealed a high level of self-victimisation and delegitimisation of Palestinians (Bar-Tal and Teichman 2005). Violations of civil rights do not stop at the doorsteps of the homes where Palestinians live in Israel. These attitudes toward civil rights will eventually engulf the Jewish sector as well, although admittedly they will take a different form and have lower intensity. David Landau (2010), in the face of personal and physical attacks on those whom he considers to be liberal Israeli Jews, has warned that "Israel has slid almost inadvertently a long way down the slope that leads to McCarthyism and racism." The charge of protofascism is now voiced more frequently in Israel (N. Gordon 2010). Blatman (2011) sees a direct link between anti-Arab racism and laws enacted by the Knesset:[19]

> Israeli racism, whose natural "hothouse" is the colonialist project in the territories, has long since spilled into Israel society and has been legitimized in the series of laws recently passed in the Knesset. Only people who avoid looking at the broad historical context of such a process [he refers to Nazi laws and apartheid South Africa] are still able to believe it is possible to stop the emergence of an Israeli apartheid state without getting rid of the colonialist-racist grip on the territories.

As expected, there will be those old-guard liberal Zionists of the left who take issue with this characterisation, echoing Shlomo Avineri's (2010b) view that "Israel is the opposite of fascist" and that, like other democracies, it merely has marginal extremists who tarnish its image. Avineri comments that these racist tendencies directed at non-Jews are being fought in the public arena and so far have not been translated into laws depriving non-Jewish Israeli citizens of democratic rights. In replying to Avineri, Arnon Golan (2010) points out that what is talked about is the gradual slide into a fascist political culture and that its proponents are not marginal figures but include government ministers, government-salaried rabbis, and the leadership of several right-wing parties. The belated cry against pronouncements such as those by rabbis against renting homes to non-Jews or against Jews marrying non-Jews is nothing short of a mild rebuke. It is unlikely that these rabbis will be dismissed from their position or prosecuted.

To return to Peteet's (2009) comments, it seems that more, not less, *public* discussion of racism in Israel is called for so as to publicise its widespread use and make the analogy with apartheid more tangible and credible, as has been done by Daryl Glaser (2010). Second, according to Peteet, unlike South Africa, Israel has never enunciated an explicit policy of discrimination against the Palestinian population that is written in law, although one could quarrel with this stance in light of Knesset legislations aimed at criminalising any mention of the Nakba and other related discriminatory legislations that target the Palestinians of Israel.[20] It is thus, according to Peteet, difficult for the public to seize on what appears to be camouflaged policies of racism. Third, the demographic comparison is lopsided since, in the case of Israel, the Jews comprise a majority (a slim one, mind you, if we consider the Arab-Jewish population balance west of the Jordan river), compared to South Africa's whites, who amounted to no more than 17 per cent of the population at the height of the apartheid regime. Peteet (ibid.) concludes by noting that "it may be time to develop a new language." She is correct to say that "apartheid" cannot thoroughly explain Zionist ideology or Israeli practices. It can simply offer broad points of comparison, a framing by an already powerful concept. Yet the Afrikaans term, as noted above, does have a Hebrew counterpart in the term *hafrada*, meaning separation, or putting distance between oneself and others – in this case, the Palestinians. In Hebrew, the wall is often referred to as the "*hafrada* barrier." As we have seen, however, a new language is indeed being introduced, superseding the *hafrada* slogan, but this language is being deployed by Israeli policymakers to justify Israeli policies. It is high time for critical scholars to address the issue. This does not mean that the argument of separation is irrelevant. According to Aluf Benn (2010), the success of Ariel Sharon's separation policies has the advantage of removing the Palestinians from the sight of the Israeli public. Commitment to the idea that "they" (the Palestinians) are there and that "we" (the Jews) are here ensures that there is little knowledge among the Jewish public about what is happening in Gaza and the West Bank and hence little acknowledgement of responsibility. Finally, Peteet (2009) is correct, however, in pointing out that the Palestinians face a formidable obstacle in confronting Israel's effective use of the current buzz words "terrorists" and "security" to justify its policies toward the Palestinians. To a very large extent, the international community has accepted Israel's rationale.

The language and logic of security

> The barrier that Israel is presently constructing within the territory of the West Bank ... goes by the name of "Seam Zone," "Security Fence," or "Wall." The word "annexation" is avoided as it is too accurate a description and too concerned about the need to obfuscate the truth ... the fact must be faced that what we are presently witnessing in the West Bank is a visible and clear act of territorial annexation under the guise of security ... Annexation of this kind goes by another name in international law: conquest. (Dugard 2003, 6–8)

> The logic of security has become the most authoritative prism through which to refract difference so as to stratify subaltern groups. (Bletcher 2005, 731)

Semantic analysis of political discourse has occupied international relations experts since the early part of the twentieth century, when the field of communication and mass media assumed a central role in the analysis of political and social life. As quantitative analysis and eventually computerisation progressed, there was a need to understand actors' utterances and weigh the meaning of words by developing semantic coding methods that made it possible to determine the affective and neutral tone of one's utterances and communication patterns. In Canada, political scientist Ole Holsti (1969) pioneered the technique of content analysis of large texts by developing a coding method and computerised dictionary to translate the meaning of key words into quantitative measures. Psychologists developed the concept of the semantic differential to assign quantitative values to attitudes and manipulate these values in sophisticated analysis that made it possible to determine correlations and causality.

As the popularity of qualitative research grew, content analysis techniques were developed for application in qualitative research as well so as to establish connections and communication patterns among the studied groups and individuals. A plethora of software is available to researchers in the humanities for this purpose.

The authors dealt with below rely on a much more straightforward, interpretative analysis of language to show that, in the context of the Israeli-Palestinian conflict, media and public discourse tap stereotypes that are framed in a specific cultural-temporal context and are reinforced by the power positions of the protagonists. This is a key distinction between content and discourse analysis. For Joseph Massad (2010), it is a problem not of word usage as such but of "translation" using the Zionist lexicon to describe facts on the ground. Thus for Zionism, colonisation goes hand-in-hand with peace, and any resistance to colonisation is translated into a declaration of war: "*Colonialism is Peace, Anti-Colonialism is War*" (ibid., emphasis in original). Similar translation problems occur with reference to sovereignty and security. Israeli human rights lawyer David Kretzmer (1990, 137) points out in mild language that Zionist (dis)possession of Palestinian land is defined in terms of collective security, even though this results in discriminatory practices and dispossession of the Palestinians: "The perception of Jewish ownership of land and settlement as essential mechanisms of maintaining the security of the Jewish collective means that security measures which restrict basic liberties of Arab citizens may be employed to facilitate them."

There is nothing new here since colonial history has always linked security claims to appropriation of land from the native population. This is the cornerstone of colonialism, of which Zionism is but one late example. Thus, in the name of security, Israel has launched numerous and disproportionate targeted killings of the Palestinians in the occupied territories and in the refugee camps in neighbouring countries such as Lebanon. Under the current right-wing Israeli government, the security argument is increasingly advanced to justify human rights violations targeting Palestinian citizens in Israel. Amira Hass (2006) poignantly comments that when it comes to the Palestinians, Israel acts in "the name of security, but not for its sake." Palestinian legal scholar Samera Esmeir (2004, 3) points out that issues pertaining to "[d]emography, Arab-owned lands, Arab Palestinians moving and crossing borders, political dissent, certain forms of knowledge, speech, memory and the relationship to the past" become security concerns.

Hillel Cohen (2004) singles out the chilling effect of the security argument on the dissemination of information. He argues that the General Security Service, or Shin Bet, has successfully managed to curtail research on its activities in the name of state security.

A germane example of language analysis of security claims is provided by Yonathan Mendel, who shows that when it comes to discussions of security, there is almost unanimous agreement among Israeli media outlets to refrain from critical assessment of the military establishment and to take its word at face value. This is made possible through the exercise of voluntary self-discipline by the media, which as Mendel (2008) comments, makes the "practice [of journalism] all the more dangerous" (see also Sfard 2012). As portrayed in the media, the Israeli military is "forced to fight" and react to Palestinian violence but never initiates it, even though, as Mendel points out, the Israeli army had killed 4,485 Palestinians in the previous seven years, most of whom were civilians. References to apartheid, *Palestinian* citizens of Israel, Bantustans, ethnic cleansing, the Nakaba, racism, and so on are taboo in the Israeli context. By content analysing three major Israeli newspapers a decade ago, Neve Gordon (2004) examined the role of the Israeli press in legitimating and rationalising extrajudicial killings of Palestinians. Three-quarters of Israelis polled supported the policy of extrajudicial killings, even though 45 per cent believed that these executions increased Palestinian violence and only 22 per cent said that assassinations would deter Palestinian violence. Gordon concludes that, by ignoring the context and background of Palestinian violence and instead presenting it as a by-product of an irrational and violent culture, the newspapers legitimised government actions. Rarely do we see Israeli journalists actually interview family members of those who commit suicide bombing so as to understand the circumstances that led to such acts. Academic research on suicide bombing in Palestine has established a causal relationship between state repression and suicide bombing (Brym and Araj 2006, 2008). The campaign to vilify Arab citizens in order to delegitimise their right to engage in lawful protest is revealed in semistructured interviews with Arab leaders and journalists, as well as in content analysis of two major Hebrew newspapers' coverage of the Land Day protests that are organised annually to commemorate the confiscation of Arab land in 1976 and the killings of six Arab citizens by the police. By drawing upon a stereotypical interpretation of Arab culture as basically violent, the findings show a systematic exaggeration by the press of the violent intent of Arab protest, which usually takes place with little evidence of violence. Collective Arab behaviour is depicted as a threat to public security. When it comes to introducing changes in the socioeconomic and political position of the Arab minority, the press, the authors conclude, "serves as one of the primary agents preventing such changes by constantly denigrating this population" (Wolfsfeld, Avraham, and Aburaiya 2000, 129).

It must be stated that although Israel has used the "state security" argument to its fullest in order to trample on human rights and dispossess Palestinians, the argument is not unique to Israel, as demonstrated by events following the attack of 11 September 2001 on the United States. In the name of security, Western states, particularly the United States under President Barack Obama, have increased their surveillance of American citizens, with a special focus on Muslims and Arabs, and adopted measures that infringe on human rights (Webb 2007).

Security is not always about security, as a report of Israeli practices at the country's largest border crossing at Ben-Gurion Airport shows. According to a former airport employee, the checks at the airport have expanded and are now designed to confront the "geopolitical situation of the region." Searches and lengthy interrogations, which lead to unnecessary delays, are intended to prevent activists and pro-Palestinian groups from visiting the OPT. They range "from volunteer work to non-violent demonstrations or protest actions that pose no security threat to Israelis" (Greenberg 2012; see also Vilnai 2014).

Who articulates the logic of security, and how is it conveyed to a target audience? Is security defined through the speech act, as the Copenhagen School claims, or is it defined in conjunction with other forms of communication such as televisual media? How to appraise its success or failure, and how to estimate its cost from the human rights perspective? Above all, should an existential security threat be accepted at face value because it has been enunciated by official decision makers? These are important questions that cannot be addressed in their entirety here.

Although research about securitisation has received new impetus since 11 September 2001, it had already been introduced in the "security" literature more than a decade earlier by Barry Buzan and colleagues at the Copenhagen School. Even though securitisation claims invariably involve surveillance, this literature eschews linking surveillance to framing the issue of securitisation and, in turn, to privacy violations and human rights. Buzan and Waever (2003, 491) define securitisation as "the discursive process through which an intersubjective understanding is constructed within a political community to treat something as an existential threat to a valued referent object, and to enable a call for urgent and exceptional measures to deal with the threat." Securitisation defined this way is a form of *discourse* designed to draw attention to an existential threat. Furthermore, Buzan defines the concept of "macro-securitisation" in the following way:

> By "macro-securitisation" I mean a securitisation aimed at, and up to a point succeeding, in framing security issues, agendas and relationships on a system-wide basis. Macro-securitisations are based on universalist constructions of threats and/or referent objects... A macro-securitisation can be about a shared fate, where the referent object is staged in universalist terms (e.g. the planetary environment, human civilization), or about a widespread sharing of the same threat even though the specific referent objects are mainly at state and societal level (e.g. terrorism, disease). (In Mekerishvili 2008)

In the words of Waever (1995, 55):

> What then is security? With the help of language theory, we can regard "security" as a speech act. In this usage, security is not of interest as a sign that refers to something more real; the utterance itself is the act. By saying it, something is done (as in betting, giving a promise, naming a ship). By uttering "security" a state representative moves a particular development into a specific area, and thereby claims a special right to use whatever means are necessary to block it.

Assessment of the securitisation field that concerns itself with issues of societal identity has raised questions about its constructivist thrust, which is anchored in an analysis of speech acts (following the works of philosophers John Austin and John Searle), to the neglect of other forms of communication (M. Williams 2003). Moreover, the Copenhagen School posits that language goes beyond shaping our perception of reality by treating language as self-referential and equating speech claims with reality itself. The main task of the speech act, according to the securitisation school, is to bring about consensus between the audience and the "securitising actor." In his criticism of the speech act approach adopted by the Copenhagen School, Thierry Balzacq (2005, 181) echoes Ludwig Wittgenstein's words: "in this scheme, there is no security problem except through the language game." To move away from a universalist, subjectivist frame of reference in the analysis of securitisation, Balzacq's criticism advances a "pragmatic," strategic framework that contextualises securitisation in terms of the power position of the enunciator of security claims, the social identity of the "securitising actor," and the nature of the intended audience, while allowing for the presence of oppositional groups that could provide alternative security claims.

What is peculiar about the linguistic turn in the securitisation research is its neglect of the rich literature on power, language, and hegemony, in the tradition of Edward Herman and Noam Chomsky's (1988) work on how societal consensus is manufactured.

As pointed out above, the literature on security does not make clear the connection between state securitisation and surveillance, on the one hand, and the human consequences of the convergence of securitisation and surveillance, on the other. More pronounced is the absence of what Pavel Baev and J. Peter Burgess (2002, 125) call, in the context of the rhetoric over the "war on terror" and with reference to the Israeli-Palestinian encounter, the practice of state "terrorization of the political other." Although at one time there were attempts by some governments (such as Canada's) to introduce human security in order to complement state and military security, the weight of the state and its monopoly over the means of violence rendered human rights security concerns subservient to state security (Zureik and Hindle 2004). The stress on state security continues to exact a high human toll through ethnic cleansing and the drive toward population homogenisation in various parts of the world. According to some, the upshot of this is that securitisation policies by the nation-state accomplished the opposite of their original intentions by perpetuating conflict and undermining state security (Mulaj 2007). Michael Williams (2003, 525) explains:

> At the heart of these issues is the question of whether a theory so closely tied to speech for its explanatory and ethical position is capable of addressing the dynamics of security in a world where political communication is increasingly bound with images and in which televisual communication is an essential element of communicative action.

Drawing upon the Habermasian notion of "communicative action" as a means to enhance democratic practice in the public debate about security issues, Williams points out that the Copenhagen School's theory of securitisation remains very much tied to discourse analysis of speech acts and is yet to address how communicative action through images and electronic media impacts an audience in a cultural and social context located outside a space of interaction between the speech actor and the target audience. The Palestinian population is usually bracketed outside such discourse, which is mainly carried out between a Jewish speech actor and the Jewish audience. The intention is to exclude Palestinians from taking part in the public debate about existential security issues as they are defined by Israeli-Jewish policymakers. As a matter of fact, there is a complete disconnect between the Jewish and Arab public regarding what constitutes the public good and security issues.

Security and the state of exception

> ... the tradition of the oppressed teaches us that "the state of emergency" in which we live is not the exception but the rule. We must attain to a conception of history that is in keeping with this insight. (Benjamin 1999, 257)

It is not surprising, however, that there is a great deal of interest in the applicability of Giorgio Agamben's (1998, 2005) "state of exception" framework to Israel. In the course of attempting this alignment, several criticisms have been voiced. One criticism of Agamben's work is that he presents a passive, totalising view of the oppressed. Nowhere do we see the colonised reacting in voice or in action to their subjugated existence (Lentin 2008b, 1–22; see also Jamal and Sandor 2010). A related cautionary note is sounded by Eyal Weizman, who questions the applicability of Agamben's binary framework regarding the state of exception and argues that characterising the West Bank and Gaza, indeed Israel itself, as primarily in a state of exception potentially obscures the complex assemblages of actors involved in contesting methods of social control, including surveillance practices (Weizman and Kastrissianakis 2007). This becomes even more apparent in discussions of patterns of resistance to surveillance. Furthermore, Agamben's work lacks any reference to "gender violence," particularly the role of women and how they are targeted for systemic violence in national conflict situations (Lentin 2006, 3).

Ilan Pappé provides a different and more encompassing criticism of the applicability of Agamben's framework to Israel. This critical assessment of Agamben is shared by Abigail Bakan and Yasmeen Abu-Laban (2010; see also Ghanim and Shalhat 2011; and Lentin 2008b). Pappé (2008) argues that Israel is not in a state of exception but a "state of oppression" as far as the indigenous Palestinian population is concerned. He labels this the "state of the Mukhabarat" ("intelligence state" in Arabic), echoing the characterisation by the late Israeli philosopher Yeshayahu Leibowitz, who called Israel the "Shin Bet state" (in Levy 2011). Following Agamben's argument, to say that Israel is in a state of exception is to subscribe to the notion that it was once a democracy for all of its citizens but has gradually become undemocratic. Three conditions characterise a state of exception: "changes in sovereignty, amendments of constitutions and transformations on the ground, based on new legislation or delegislation" (Pappé 2008, 155). According to Pappé, none of these prevail in the case of Israel.

With regard to the first point, Pappé points out that there has been no real transition in power from the legislature to the executive, as was the case in Germany's state of exception with the rise of Adolf Hitler. In its treatment of the Palestinians, "The state rests on its power to oppress – regardless of whether the power lies with the government or the parliament" (ibid., 156). The distinction between the sovereign (executive) and parliament is meaningless in the case of Israel, as far as the Palestinian *homo sacer* is concerned (Pappé 2005). The "bare life" of the Palestinians is disconnected from any transition and slide into undemocratic practices. The majority Jewish population is not affected by any changes in sovereignty or by the presence of Palestinian "bare life." Furthermore, Jewish citizens of Israel "are disinterested in this debate, since we [Jews] accept the state's racist ideological infrastructure and trust it to disallow any legal or real parallels between 'us' and 'them,' the oppressed Palestinians" (Pappé 2008, 156).

The second requirement for a state of exception to exist is that the citizenry must be unaware of the diminution in the system of checks and balances governing the functioning of government. In the case of Israel, Pappé (2008, 157) argues, "the Israeli state of oppression [of Palestinians] is noticed, acknowledged and welcomed by its Jewish citizens who leave it in the hands of the political elite to vacillate between *de facto* and *de jure* acknowledgement." Only when the dilution of the system of checks and balances begins to affect the Jewish majority does Agamben's model of the state of exception become relevant to the Israeli case.

Finally, according to Pappé, the overarching Zionist framework of the state was designed from the outset to dispossess and oppress the Palestinians. Thus the model of the state of exception fails in its applicability to the Israeli case due to the fact that, being a colonial state from its inception, Israel embodied certain laws and rules that *sui generis* are antidemocratic in their impact on the Palestinian population. Prime examples of this are the Emergency Regulations, which date back to the time of the British Mandate and are still on the books, and the Israeli Law of Return. Here, Pappé (2008, 159) concludes that Israel is an exception to the state of exception:

> The integration of these abuses of power, law and sovereignty into the ideology of a colonizing regime is beyond Agamben's discursive and analytical framework. And these elements that are basically racist and colonialist and not the outcome of a collapsing republic or democracy are far more sustainable as facts of life. They remain so pervasive in the lives of citizens not because of laws, their interpretation or even their abuse, but because of the way the State of Israel came into being, and due to an element that is totally absent from the paradigm of the state of exception: the hegemony of the security apparatuses.

The language and process of dehumanisation

The language of dehumanisation is not confined to the Palestinian-Israeli conflict. Events in Iraq following the US invasion of 2003, most notably prisoner treatment at the hands of American interrogators in the Abu Ghraib prison, involved a familiar torture practice where culture, religion, and ethnicity figured prominently in shaping the attitudes of American prison officials.[21] As a matter of fact, the Abu

Ghraib model has been referred to in describing instances where Israeli soldiers have behaved in a similar manner toward Palestinian prisoners (*Haaretz* 2008). Dehumanising Palestinians in the occupied territories is a frequent practice among members of the ruling establishment and, to a very large extent, among the public at large. Data revealed in numerous public opinion polls, discussed in chapter 5, show that the attitudes of the Jewish public – young and old – to the issues of the citizenship and human rights of the Palestinian citizens of Israel are tainted with racism. In the words of Neve Gordon (2004, 319):

> ... the Palestinians are frequently presented as the bad guys: they are immoral evil beings who do not really care about the value of human life; they are the provokers, aggressors, assailants and terrorists, who are driven by emotions, irrational and fanatic aspirations. Israelis, on the other hand, are often portrayed as moral beings; human life is of great value to them, they merely react in order to defend and secure life, they are the victims who are driven by rational calculations and whose major aim is to protect life.

That the law is rarely applied in criminal situations involving Arab victims and state agents is proof that the exception is the rule. For example, a policeman who shot and killed an Arab citizen protesting in 2006 was eventually sentenced to thirty months of imprisonment – and this was an exception. The Musawa Centre for Arab Rights in Israel, which keeps track of such incidents, has reported forty-five cases where the police shot Arab civilians that were not officially investigated (Khoury 2010). Since the mass protests of October 2000, there has been only one case in which a policeman or soldier has been criminally indicted. In spite of the fact that thirteen Palestinian citizens of Israel were killed during the demonstrations, no indictments were ever filed against any of the policemen involved, and all the cases were closed by the attorney general. Worse still, none of the mild recommendations of the Or Commission (2003) concerning ways to close the gaps between Jews and Arabs in many different realms of life in Israel were ever implemented by the government (Dalal 2003; Y. Peled 2005). As expected, the situation is no different when the victims are Palestinians from the territories. Here is how journalist Avi Issacharoff (2009) describes the ethnically bifurcated structure of the Israeli criminal justice system:

> Experience – and statistics – show that Israeli law enforcement is remarkably lax when it comes to tackling violence against Palestinians ... The (justifiably – original) prevailing feeling among Palestinians in the West Bank is that their blood is of no consequence. It's hard to find a Palestinian today who will make an effort to approach the Israeli police about a settler assault, unless Israeli human-rights groups help him. The way Palestinians in the territories see it, Israeli law is enforced only if Jews are harmed, while incidents in which Palestinians are murdered, beaten or otherwise wounded are treated cursorily at best – and more often, are ignored entirely.[22]

It is not uncommon to come across unpolished racist statements by Israeli leaders. According to Robert Fisk (2005, 507), in August 2000 Prime Minister Ehud Barak called the Palestinians "crocodiles." One-time Israeli chief of staff Moshe Yalon described them as a "cancerous manifestation" and equated the military action in the occupied territories with "chemotherapy." In March 2001, the Israeli tourism minister at the time, the late Rehavem Ze'evi, called Yasser Arafat a "scorpion." Rafael Eytan, a former Israeli chief of staff, referred to the Palestinians as "cockroaches in a bottle." Menachem Begin called them "two-legged beasts." A decade ago, the Shas Party's spiritual leader, who suggested that God should send the Palestinian "ants" to hell, also called them "serpents." Updating these labels with reference to more recent accounts reveals that in August 2010 the same Sephardic chief rabbi, Yosef Oveida (2010), pronounced that "God should strike" the Palestinians "with a plague." Dan Schueftan, a professor at Tel Aviv University, was quoted in the *Maariv* newspaper in October 2009 as having said that "the Arabs are the biggest failure in the history of the human race. There's nothing under the sun that's more screwed up than the Palestinians" (Leibovitz-Dar 2009). Journalist Amira Hass (2010a) captures the logic of Israeli justice when it comes to Arab victims at the hands of the state's agents:

> If anyone in the world had called Israel an "abscess," we would have generated a wave of protests, and learned scholars of anti-Semitism would lecture about the vocabulary that the Nazis borrowed from pathology and microbiology (the same holds for Mahmoud Ahmadinejad). But when a deputy prime minister of Israel and a member of the Labor Party used a clinical metaphor to talk about the Gaza Strip this week ("Gaza is an abscess, troublesome pus" in original), no one got upset. We are always allowed to do what others are not.

Speaking before the United Nations General Assembly in September 2011, Prime Minister Benjamin Netanyahu reiterated that the Jewishness of the Israeli state, where 20 per cent of the citizens are not Jewish, must be acknowledged by the Palestinians as a prerequisite for peace (IMFA 2011). In a Knesset speech on the eve of his visit to the United States, Netanyahu stated the same conditions as a prelude to negotiations with the Palestinians (Bronner 2011). Avigdor Lieberman, Israel's foreign minister at the time, declared at the United Nations in New York in October 2010 that "without recognition of Israel as the nation-state of the Jewish people and refugees," there would be no peace with the Palestinians (IMFA 2010). The implication of this stance is clear: it rules out the return of any Palestinian refugees to their homes in Israel, and it robs non-Jewish citizens of the state of their universal rights.[23]

The Palestinians constitute what the Italian philosopher Giorgio Agamben (1998) calls *homo sacer*, according to which the universal laws of humanity do not apply to them. For Israel, the Palestinians, particularly those who reside in the

OPT, deserve to exist in conditions of "bare life." Their minimal existence is tolerated but not enhanced. Invariably, the law is suspended when it comes to rectifying Palestinian grievances. Israel is usually quick to cite "national security" as justification for its lethal actions. Life for its Palestinian citizens is in a perpetual state of emergency because exception to the universal application of the law is the rule. As a colonial state, Israel is best viewed through a racialised prism given that ethnicity and race govern the treatment of its citizens. As shown in chapter 4, the discourse of biopolitics (i.e., demography and population management) and settlements in Israel are logical expressions of Zionism, and they will continue to be its cornerstone until Israel achieves its objective of getting rid of as many of its Palestinians as possible through either expulsion or so-called "population and territorial exchanges."

At best, the Palestinians in Israel are treated as a "suspect community" that must be closely surveilled by the state's various institutions and the Jewish public. The Zionist project remains in full throttle; in line with what the founders of the state dreamed of, current and future leadership will not rest until the Palestinian presence in Israel is significantly reduced.

Conclusion

This chapter has traced Zionist perceptions of the Palestinians and the land on which they live, showing that although there have been diversions and nuanced interpretations of Zionism on the part of Zionist spokespersons and their supporters, a constant core has remained, which continues to typify attitudes toward the Palestinians, whether they are citizens of Israel or reside in the occupied territories: a focus on effecting population management and territorial control so as to ensure perpetual Jewish dominance in historical Palestine. As is the case with colonial projects in general, territorial exchange and land confiscation as well as population displacement or outright expulsion have been entertained and at crucial times practised by the Zionist leadership of various political shades. With ethnic cleansing in place, these methods reached a crescendo on the eve of the state's establishment in 1948, and they are now being voiced and practised with regard to the West Bank.

I have argued that although these attitudes reflect a specific Zionist ideology that is being increasingly couched in the language of security, land redemption, and religious invocations, the project is basically secular and is rooted in the colonial character of the Zionist movement and its manifestation in Israel in 1948 and subsequent expansion through settlement activities in 1967. For this experiment to succeed, there must be a sustained discourse that dehumanises the native Palestinian population. The language of securitisation has been used in a blanket fashion to justify the suspension of basic human rights for the Palestinians. Through an examination of language use, this chapter has demonstrated the ideological basis of the discourse that shaped (and continues to inform) the attitude of the Israeli state toward the Palestinians.

Notes

1 An example of the distinction is made by Eliezer Ben-Rafael (2004, 313) when he says, "in fact, Zionism is better described as colonization than as colonialism. Colonization denotes a new population that establishes itself in a given environment, eventually, to the disadvantage of a local population, and builds a society of its own. By no standard is this pattern more moral than colonialism, but the distinction itself is of crucial importance."
2 Highly relevant in this context is the work of Yoav Peled (1992), who describes Palestinian citizenship in Israel as a passive form of ethno-liberalism, in contrast to an Israeli-Jewish republican form of citizenship that is based on active participation in defining the public good. Fifteen years later, Peled (2007) argued that Israel's Palestinian minority had experienced further erosion in citizenship rights. According to Adi Ophir (2007, 126), the Palestinians living in Israel constitute "impaired citizens," and other writers refer to them as a "trapped minority" (see Rabinowitz 2001b). A critique of the latter concept is provided by Henry Rosenfeld (2002).
3 For a contrary view of democracy and colonialism in the Israeli experience, see Neve Gordon (2010). Thomas Abowd (2007, 999–1000) accurately describes the state of social science research on Israel:

> But as one explores the politics of residential space in this urban center [Jerusalem], it is difficult to avoid another phenomenon, one that has no less defined the relationship between Palestinians and Israelis over the last several decades — namely, the persistence of colonialism . . . contrary to dominant ways of representing this national conflict, Jerusalem is a colonized space at the heart of a colonial struggle. By examining Israeli authority as *colonial* authority, I seek to challenge the bulk of the scholarly literature on the Israeli-Palestinian conflict that, nearly without exception, denies or is silent about this terrain's colonial present. (Emphasis in original)

4 In addition to being called a "democracy," Israel's political system has been described using a plethora of labels, including "ethnic democracy" (Smooha 2009), "ethnocracy" (Yiftachel 2006), and "partial democracy" (Elstein 2011).
5 For a nuanced discussion of whether Zionism is colonialist, see Forman and Kedar (2003).
6 Sharansky offers familiar criticism of those who describe Israeli policies in the occupied territories as colonialist. He charges that the Palestinians have come under the sway of "aggressive Islam" and have missed opportunities presented to them by Israel (Sharansky 2008, 290), to which Reuveny (2008a, 294) replies:

> "[T]he ascendance of an aggressive form of Islam," Sharkansky writes, "make[s] it difficult, if not impossible, for Palestinians to accept anything Israel is likely to offer." This statement begs the question, what is Israel actually offering that the Palestinians reject? Perhaps the ongoing settlement expansion since 1967, numerous Israeli checkpoints, blockades of Palestinian areas, curfews, and demolition of Palestinian houses? Perhaps the ongoing confiscation of more than 50 percent of the land on the West Bank, much smaller Palestinian water allocations per capita than those given to Jewish settlers, roads closed to Palestinian traffic, or the separation barrier that Israel builds around but inside the West Bank, which the International Court of Justice in the Hague has ruled illegal? Other colonial rulers who faced revolts have taken similar actions.

7 Essentially, those mainstream researchers who acknowledge the colonial character of Israeli society, including those who are identified with the liberal wing of Israeli writers, tend to limit the applicability of the colonial model to the period following the Six-Day

War in 1967 and the establishment of settlements in the occupied Palestinian territories. For an exception to this, see Shafir (2003).

8 An example of using stealth methods to obliterate Palestinian refugee property is provided by Aron Shai (2006, 93) in his discussion of how more than a hundred Palestinian villages in the "Northern region" alone were "leveled" and "removed" from the landscape between 1965 and 1969 upon the orders of David Ben-Gurion and in collaboration with the Israel Archaeological Survey Society, the Jewish National Fund, the Israel Land Administration, and several ministries:

> The plan was to conduct the operation quietly, without too much fuss. It was clear to all that if large numbers of villages were demolished all at once, there would be a public outcry. The plan was to "level" an area stretching from the Galilee panhandle southward; to include every hill, mound, and hut, so that the land would be "clean." As one interviewee said, this would prevent Arab villagers from claiming one day: "that is my tree. This was my village." This interviewee also stated that if there had been abandoned Jewish villages, they would also have been razed, since the goal was to clear the land.

9 In 1919 Lord Balfour spoke in unambiguous language and with typical British imperial arrogance: "The Great Powers are committed to Zionism. And Zionism, be it right or wrong, good or bad, is rooted in age-long traditions, in present needs, in future hopes, of far profounder import than the desires and prejudices of the 700,000 Arabs who now inhabit that ancient land" (in W. Khalidi 2014, 1).

10 Avineri does not miss an opportunity to lash out at those who espouse critical views of mainstream Zionism. In a newspaper article he opined that "Post-Zionism does not exist," insisting that those who advocate it are bent on "total denial of the Zionist project and of the very legitimacy of the existence of the State of Israel as a Jewish nation-state" (Avineri 2007). Avineri was taken to task by, among others, Meron Benvenisti, former deputy mayor of Jerusalem, for supporting the 1982 Israeli invasion and occupation of parts of Lebanon, including West Beirut. In an open letter, Benvenisti (1982) described Avineri's character in justifying the war:

> I am disturbed not by your appearance and talk, but by the syndrome contained in it. I consider this to be a sign of adapting and [being] willing to serve any regime ... This kind of valueless adaptation is characteristic of intellectuals and political movements in societies that have lost their ideological conscience, and is now spreading among us. Your contribution to this deterioration here is not smaller than that of those who deliberately cause the process of the increase in extremism. In this you expect the reward of the just while doing what the wicked do.

11 For a fuller treatment of the debate surrounding the Asiatic mode of production and its applicability to the Arab state, see Zureik (1981).

12 In a scathing opinion piece, Zeev Sternhell (2014) departs somewhat from his previous views and from the Zionist mainstream's position regarding the Palestinians, which he interprets both in Israel and in the occupied territories as being governed by Jewish history and nationalism rather than being based on humanist values that recognise the rights of the Palestinians to self-determination. According to him, this historical position is shared by the right, left, and centre.

13 Among the noted critics of Israeli policies is the well-known Polish-Jewish sociologist and philosopher Zygmunt Bauman, who lives in Britain. In an interview for the Polish weekly *Politiku*, he compares the West Bank wall to the Warsaw Ghetto walls, criticises

Israeli militarism, and accuses Israel of being "terrified of peace" and of "taking advantage of the Holocaust to legitimize unconscionable acts" against the Palestinians (in Frister 2011).
14 For a comprehensive discussion of the debate surrounding post-Zionism, see Silberstein (1999, 2002).
15 More recently, Neve Gordon (2008, xix) has adopted a strikingly similar position: "I firmly believe that one cannot understand the current disputes informing the Israeli-Palestinian conflict without taking into account the ethnic cleansing that took place during and after the 1948 war."
16 For an interesting and thorough analysis of Shafir's book, see Zachary Lockman (2012), who argues that although Shafir made an important contribution to highlighting the materialist basis of Zionism – in contrast to the dominant idealist notion, which equated early Zionism with socialism – Shafir's analysis fell short of acknowledging the *violent* nature of the Zionist experiment and its impact on dispossessing the native Palestinian population.
17 Although Penslar's (2007, 91) chapter, "Is Zionism a Colonial Movement?", acknowledges that "colonial elements were present as well in the treatment of Israel's Arab minority and state confiscation of its land," the thrust of his chapter is ideational, without considering the important materialist issues of land, labour and capital, and violence – the main ingredients of colonialism in the pursuit of nation building. The chapter is an exposé of what he sees as Zionism's cultural uniqueness and its anticolonial reaction to Europe. When present, the colonial attitudes of Western Zionists, he contends, were directed at Mizrahi Jews, not the Arab population. He does not see a thread connecting early and late Zionist policies toward the Arab population, whether in Israel proper or the occupied territories, particularly as the latter involves continuing land seizure and population control.
18 Shifts are apparent beyond the variable ideological meanings of key words. Using the constructivist approach in the context of social science, Samer Alatout (1999, ch. 2) has analysed the role of scientific knowledge in the 1930s and 1940s in the debate between the Zionist movement in Palestine and the British Mandate concerning the availability of water, which figures prominently in determining the absorptive capacity of the country. Furthermore, he uses the case study to contribute to the state-society debate and argue against a state-centred approach to understanding the process of nation building. The emergence of the nation-state is better understood not solely as the outcome of a decision-making process by political elites but also as a "co-production" involving the translation of several actors' discourses (political and nonpolitical) into practice.

Focusing on water as a strategic resource in the contest over Palestine, Alatout (1999, ch. 2) shows how in the early 1930s the Zionists appealed to a specific type of scientific knowledge – namely geophysics, which relies on the deductive and speculative method, rather than geology, which is based on actual testing of water availability – in order to support their claim for the abundance of water for land irrigation and justify further Jewish immigration to Palestine. This occurred at a time when the political discourse centred on a "Jewish homeland," in contrast to a sovereign state. Alatout shows that a shift in Zionist use of scientific discourse occurred between the late 1930s and early 1940s. This shift coincided with the evolving political environment in Palestine, where the concept of a "Jewish homeland," as articulated in the Balfour Declaration, issued by the British government two decades earlier, was being translated by Zionist thinking into a "Jewish state." The shift in the use of scientific knowledge from geophysics to geology thus coincided with a shift in the projected water needs from local (homeland) to national (nation-state). It was the interplay between scientific knowledge and political events that gave rise to what Alatout (2014, 317) calls "the imagined boundaries of the nation-state":

The shift in favour of perceiving Palestine's water resources in terms of one national geo-hydrological system enabled and solidified the perception of Palestine as a national space. More significantly, however, perceptions of the national space extended as much as, and followed closely, the perceived hydrological mapping of Palestine. What water experts constructed as a geohydrological system of Palestine had direct effects on what was imagined as the boundaries of the nation-state itself.

19 Blatman (2011) refers to three such specific laws: "The Tsunami of racist laws passed by the Knesset in recent months is also being explained by reasoned and worthy arguments: the right of small communities to preserve their own character (the Acceptance Law); the state's right to prevent hostile use of funds it allocates to education and culture (the Nakba Law); and the right to deny citizenship to persons convicted of espionage or treason (the Citizenship Law)."

20 Demography, which will be dealt with in chapter 5, lies at the heart of Israeli legal measures ostensibly aimed at the Palestinian population. Hamoked, an Israeli nongovernmental organisation active in defending individual rights, reports that in 2008 the Ministry of Interior stripped 4,577 Arab East Jerusalemites of their residency status, which is twenty-one times the average number of the previous forty years. The rationale for this action was that these were individuals who had travelled outside Jerusalem to work, study, or visit for an extended period of time. In the words of the executive director of Hamoked, "The Interior Ministry operation in 2008 is just part of a general policy whose goal is to restrict the size of the Palestinian population and maintain a Jewish majority in Jerusalem. The Palestinians are natives of this city, not Johnny-come-lately" (in Hasson 2009).

Mada al-Carmel (2011), a Palestinian nongovernmental organisation in Haifa, has made available online a thorough report on passed and pending Israeli legislations that have direct bearing on the Palestinians within Israel. It notes that what has been worrying human rights organisations is the marathon of the past few years, since the radical right ascended to power, in which Israeli legislators have embarked on lobbying for and enacting the passage of a series of bills aimed at curtailing and eroding the individual rights of Palestinians. On 22 March 2011, the Knesset completed its second and third readings of a bill commonly identified as the "Nakba Bill," which empowers the finance minister to withhold financial support from associations, organisations, or local councils that commemorate the Palestinian Nakba on Israel's Independence Day.

Other laws that the report details and that are worth mentioning include the Citizenship and Entry Law, which was amended in 2005 but originally passed in 2003. This law privileges Jewish immigration and bans family unification of Palestinians whose members live on both sides of the Green Line. Of course, the Law of Return, which gives any Jew in the world the automatic right to immigrate to Israel, is another longstanding law that privileges the settling of Jews in Israel. Arabic, once an official language with status equal to that of Hebrew, is under attack by attempts to reduce its status to that of a secondary official language. The Loyalty Oath Law makes it possible to strip individuals of their citizenship for alleged "disloyalty" to the state. On 29 March 2011, the Knesset approved the amendment to the Citizenship Law in its third reading, permitting revocation of the citizenship of anyone convicted on charges of "terrorism," espionage, or any other act that harms state sovereignty. On 22 March 2011, the Knesset passed the third reading of the amendment to the Communal Societies Law, according to which anyone who wishes to reside in a small town in the Naqab and Galilee areas that contains fewer than four hundred families must be admitted by an "Admissions Committee" formed by residents of the town, a representative from the Jewish Agency, or a representative from the World Zionist Organization. Additionally, the law authorises the aforementioned committees to reject any candidates who are not deemed "socially suitable" or who could harm the community's "cultural fabric." These and other such laws are opposed by human rights organisations both in and outside Israel.

21 It is significant that through its experience in the OPT, Israel contributed to the training of Americans in their Iraq campaign, including the treatment of prisoners. At the ideological level, anthropologist Raphael Patai's book, *The Arab Mind* (1973), became the bible for acquainting the American military with Arab culture. Arab culture was represented as backward and rigid. I responded at great length to Patai's work more than three-and-a-half decades ago (Zureik 1979, 82–86). Basically, Patai, an Israeli who was trained at the Hebrew University, sees a peculiar Arab personality distinguished by specific mental attitudes as the bases for the conflict with the West. For more recent discussions of Patai's work with regard to the role of language in Iraq, see Hersh (2004), Lagouranis (2008), and Rajiva (2005).

22 A similar point is made by journalist Yossi Melman (2011).

23 For a more thorough treatment of the insistence by Israel that, as a condition for resuming the negotiations and reaching some sort of an agreement, the Palestinians must acknowledge Israel as a Jewish state, see Bishara (2011), Ghanim and Shalhat (2011), Jabareen (2011), and Zreik (2011).

3
COLONIALISM AS SURVEILLANCE

> One of the most powerful strategies of imperial dominance is that of surveillance, or observation, because it implies a viewer with an elevated vantage point, it suggests the power to process and understand that which is seen, and it objectifies and interpellates the colonized subject in a way that fixes its identity in relation to the surveyor. (Ashcroft, Griffiths, and Tiffin 1998, 226)

The gaze metaphor in surveillance studies owes its origin to Jacques Lacan's "mirror stage" theory, in which "the gaze corresponds to the grande-autre," or the process of Othering, whereby the coloniser's self-affirmation and identity construction are configured on the basis of stigmatising and denigrating the identity of the Other, the colonised. In this process, "the identification, objectification and subjection of the subject are simultaneously enacted: the imperial gaze defines the identity of the subject, objectifies it within the identifying system of power relations and confirms its subalternity and powerlessness" (Ashcroft, Griffiths, and Tiffin 1998, 226). Although Othering is a convenient way of propping up one's ego and power, it is inherently fragile: it must be constantly fed by the illusory inferiority of the Other — and is thus constantly at risk of being discredited. A key feature of surveillance in colonised regions is its racialisation of the "native." As noted by Alex Lubin (2008, 674), who locates Orientalist discourse underpinning the rationale for erecting a wall on the border of the United States and Mexico and for the Israeli occupation wall in the West Bank, "Racialization is always relational and comparative, establishing a clear order of right and wrong, strong and weak, civilized and savage." Yasmeen Abu-Laban and Abigail Bakan (2011) demonstrate that what distinguishes surveillance in Israel/Palestine is its racialised context and the asymmetric power relations between the coloniser and colonised.

Academic research by social scientists and legal scholars about surveillance and security in Western countries has grown remarkably in the past couple of decades, particularly since the attack of 11 September 2001 on the United States. Yet, among key social science writers on modes of surveillance, states of exception, and securitization, empirical research on colonial and postcolonial regimes – notably in the Middle East – is underrepresented. This is peculiar since surveillance and the state of exception, in which the law is framed and suspended for the purpose of ruling indigenous populations and territory, is a common feature of both colonial and postcolonial zones experiencing ethno-national conflicts. Before surveillance became a topic of interest to social science, studies of colonial situations bearing on the central role of surveillance came mainly from the humanities: historians, anthropologists, and more recently media and culture studies scholars. As the discussion below demonstrates, the insights of these researchers provide an important point of departure for this study.

Colonial and postcolonial surveillance

> Such scientific racial classifications and racist evaluation of colonized populations [which were based, among other things, on biometric considerations] effectively functioned to legitimate colonial occupation and the acts of colonial genocide perpetrated by the colonizers against Indigenous peoples.
> (Pugliese 2010, 39)

Two features are central to colonial surveillance studies as essential instruments of ruling and state formation: the quotidian everyday context of people watching people and the formal aspect of colonial policies that are embodied in bureaucratic, enumerative, and legal measures that are aimed at controlling the territory by classifying and categorising the population through what Martha Kaplan (1995) calls "panopticism." Thus, in his masterful work on India, C.A. Bayly (1996) shows how the gathering of information in colonial India involved not only census and survey data about the population and territory but also information gathered through informal surveillance by astrologers, physicians, marriage brokers, and holy men. Categorisation and enumeration of the population in precolonial India were carried out by local elites and subsequently modified and implemented by the British for the purposes of ruling and taxation. From the mid-eighteenth century onward, the British cultivated "colonial knowledge" that was embedded in a corpus of Orientalist tropes. The stereotyping of the Other in Orientalist discourse, inasmuch as it is a basic staple of colonial knowledge,[1] should not obscure the fact that, as Bayly shows, it is not always successful and triggers resistance by the colonised. Indeed, India's resistance to British rule shows how the colonised successfully used the same tools of information dissemination that were applied by the coloniser to control them, notably the print media. As Martha Kaplan (1995, 93) remarks, "Clearly, the power of colonized people to articulate their own projects, to challenge colonial discourses, and to make their own histories constrains the projects of colonizers and – sometimes – remakes the panopticon into a constraint on its constructors."

David Spurr (1993) lists twelve discursive modes by which colonial rhetoric constructs the Other. These start with surveillance and extend through appropriation, aestheticisation, classification, debasement, and negation to eventually end with resistance. Spurr's list is not all that different from the one provided by Bernard Cohn (1996), who analyses colonial knowledge through six "modalities": historiographic, observational/travel, survey, enumerative, museological, and surveillance.

Surveillance is not a one-way activity. Mary Louise Pratt (1991, 6) takes into account the co-presence of the coloniser and the colonised in a dialectical fashion in the context of the "contact zone," which she defines as "the space of colonial encounters, the space in which peoples geographically and historically separated come into contact with each other and establish ongoing relations, usually involving conditions of coercion, radical inequality, and intractable conflict." She argues for the need to understand how the coloniser and colonised are co-constituted through these encounters. This observation has direct relevance to understanding how encounters between Israeli state agents (i.e., soldiers, police, and bureaucrats) and Palestinians are co-constituted, albeit in a situation of asymmetrical power relations – be it at the checkpoint, at the airport terminal, in everyday movement, or in routine contact with the elaborate bureaucratic apparatus of the state and its military. As this chapter will demonstrate, ethnographic studies prove to be powerful research instruments in highlighting the carceral experience of Palestinians under occupation (R.J. Smith 2011).

Quantification and categorisation as discursive forms of surveillance

> To divide, deploy, schematize, tabulate, index, and record everything in sight (and out of sight) . . . are the features of Orientalist projections. (Said 1978, 86)

As pointed out above, Kaplan (1995) considers the use of questionnaires, censuses, maps, records, and reports by colonial regimes to be tools of surveillance. As a matter of fact, Kaplan provides evidence from the British rule in India to question Michel Foucault's (1977) claim regarding the unique association between modernity and panopticism in Europe, a point that will be explored below. Benedict Anderson (1994b, 169–70) views census construction in Dutch colonial Indonesia as a form of "feverish imagining" that relied primarily on the "logic of quantification" and "identity categorization" as means of controlling the population.

As declassified official documents become available to researchers, it is possible to piece together the surveillance methods used by colonial regimes in ruling over their colonies, as demonstrated in Martin Thomas's (2008) study of Britain and France as they embarked on expanding their colonial domains in North Africa and the Middle East between the two world wars, and in Alfred McCoy's (2009) in-depth historic analysis of the development of the "surveillance state" in the Philippines following its occupation by the United States in 1898. In both cases, the imperial powers introduced surveillance as a key institutional mechanism for ruling colonised regions and, in doing so, resorted to technical and nontechnical forms of surveillance. The historical studies of surveillance in colonial societies demonstrate the eventual spillover, or "boomerang," effect – to quote Foucault (2003) – of such practices and their deployment in the home countries, as shown by McCoy (2009). The colony becomes a laboratory for developing and testing surveillance technologies for home use and marketing purposes. This is clearly the case with Israel, whose military officialdom and technologists do not miss an opportunity to tout the fact that their surveillance and control technologies have proven successful in putting down Palestinian opposition to its colonial practices, as demonstrated in *The Lab* (2013), an Israeli documentary film directed by Yotam Feldman (Maoz 2013; see also Cook 2013). The documentary shows how retired government officials and Israeli officers who have become weapons manufactures and military-industrial entrepreneurs go to great lengths to explain how they have profited worldwide from marketing their war technologies on account of their success in fighting the Palestinians in the West Bank and Gaza.

It is significant that the basic tools of surveillance as we know them today (i.e., fingerprinting, census taking, mapmaking, and profiling), which include the forerunners of present-day biometrics, were refined and implemented in colonial settings (Pugliese 2010), notably by the Dutch in South East Asia, the French in Africa, and the British in India and North America (on the latter, see Hannah 2000, 175–76; and K. Smith 2010). In *Colonising Egypt* (1988, 35), Timothy Mitchell remarks:

> Foucault's analyses are focussed on France and northern Europe. Perhaps the focus has tended to obscure the colonising nature of disciplinary power. Yet the panopticon, the model institution whose geometric order and generalised surveillance serve as a motif for this kind of power, was a colonial invention. The panoptic principle was devised on Europe's colonial frontier with the Ottoman Empire, and examples of the panopticon were built for the most part not in northern Europe, but in places like colonial India.

For the British, Simon Cole (2002, 63, 75) explains, fingerprinting was "viewed as a tool for colonial governance," and "the system of fingerprinting identification actually emerged in the colonies rather than in England." Proponents of fingerprinting as a method of surveillance and sorting of the population into "deviants" and "normal" groups were led in the nineteenth century by Francis Galton, the British eugenicist and advocate of social Darwinism. It is no coincidence that the impetus for the British to further develop a scientific method of population classification by means of identity cards occurred in the wake of the 1858 Sepoy Mutiny, in which Hindu and Muslim conscripts rebelled against the British East India Company (Sengoopta 2003).[2]

Methods of surveillance and control are also transferred from one colonial setting to another (Sinclair and Williams 2007) and from the colony to the home country. Taking their cues from the experience in India, the British introduced identity cards in Palestine during the Arab Revolt of 1936-39 as part of their campaign to stave off Palestinian opposition to colonial rule and illegal Zionist immigration (H. Cohen 2011). With a focus on Palestine, Laleh Khalili (2010a, 415) explores the "horizontal circuits through which colonial policing or 'security' practices have been transmitted across time or from one location to another, with Palestine as either a point of origin or an intermediary node of transmission." In a more recent work, Khalili explores the development of counterinsurgency measures by the British in Mandate Palestine and their subsequent adaptation by Israel. Central to these measures and their refinement by Israel were the expropriation of land, application of curfews, restrictions on mobility through the deployment of permit regimes and checkpoints, expulsion, and collective punishment. Khalili (2013, 185) mentions one main difference between Israeli and other colonial counterinsurgency tactics, such as those adopted by the United States in the Philippines or the French in Algeria: "Although Israeli settler colonialism is predicated on expulsion, carceral methods are used throughout the Occupied Palestinian Territories (OPT) via encirclement and enclavization of vast terrains." The occupation wall is considered the main instrument for containing the Palestinian population. Khalili reminds us that the British used similar techniques and carceral mechanisms to cope with the Arab Revolt, including watchtowers and security fences, and that they hired a Zionist construction company and Jewish personnel to build these fences. Israel has adopted a similar carceral practice in the occupied territories (J. Young 2012).

Glenn Bowman uses encystation and entombment as metaphors to describe the effects of the wall's encirclement of the Palestinian populations in the towns of Bethlehem, Qalqilya, and Tulkarem, which are cut off from the rest of Palestine. He points out that the objective is to put the Palestinians beyond the sight and reach of the Israeli-Jewish population and to ensure that the newly built system of bypass roads will be for exclusive Jewish settler use. The encirclement of the Palestinians has put the "surrounding social body at risk" (Bowman 2003, 129). The wall itself has resulted in the expropriation of 10 per cent of Palestinian lands. Bearing in mind that the West Bank and Gaza constituted 28 per cent of the area of Mandate Palestine, land expropriation for roads, the wall, and above all new settlements, is expected to reduce the size of the Palestinian enclaves to no more that 45 per cent of the area of the West Bank, which is almost 15 per cent of the area of historical Palestine. The larger effect of quarantining the Palestinians is to make life socially and economically unbearable and to cause their emigration, mainly to Jordan. At one time, this was Prime Minister Ariel Sharon's preferred transfer solution, in line with his often-quoted statement that "Jordan is Palestine." In an interesting paper, instead of viewing the conflict in symmetrical fashion as involving state and nonstate elite actors, Ron Smith (2011) challenges the state-centric definition of the conflict and directs his attention to the Palestinian subaltern experience in coping with Israeli-imposed "graduated incarceration" in the OPT.

The biopolitical is understood from the bottom up and in terms of "microgeographies" involving the daily lives of the colonised.

According to historian Martin Thomas (2008, 46):

> ... statistics on crime levels among distinct community, extensive record keeping about individual suspects, and the use of paramilitary "special forces" to deal with the outbreak of political violence or to break colonial strikes were all practices familiar in British India before World War I. All were adopted by the Palestine Police in the 1920s, whose Criminal Record Office and Fingerprint Bureau both drew on profiling techniques developed in India.

The Promise (2011), a television drama by British director Peter Kosminsky that caused protests in Israel, draws parallels between current-day Israeli policies of house demolitions and practices by the British during their presence in Palestine (R. Kupfer 2012).

Keeping records, or "ruling by records," as Richard Saumarez Smith (1996) calls it, is a cornerstone of colonialism, as it is of any modern administrative body. Anthropologist Talal Asad (1994, 76) singles out the importance of statistics for colonial rule by noting that "from the latter part of the nineteenth century on, statistics became increasingly important in the European empires." The important distinction in the case of colonialism is that the *classification criteria* of land, population, and other forms of recordkeeping have serious implications for governing and dispossessing indigenous populations. This point is demonstrated by anthropologist Arjun Appadurai in his discussion of the difference between the British census in India and the one used in the home country. First, the stress on race and ethnicity characterised the British efforts in India, in contrast to the British home census, which in its early days emphasised geographical distribution and social class. Second, unlike in India, the British home census was tied to citizenship, electoral politics, and representation. Third, whereas the British home census sought to identify marginal and problematic groups (the poor, criminals, etc.) in society, the Indian census made no such distinction. It blanketed the entire population for the purpose of control as though the entire population were problematic and deviant (Appadurai 1993, 317–18; see also Major 1999). What is at issue here is the constructivist power of social statistics. With words reminiscent of sociologist Anthony Giddens's (1987) notion of the "double hermeneutic," according to which theories and concepts about society feed back into society and constitute the very phenomena that these theories purport to study, philosopher Ian Hacking (2002, 11) captures the significance of scientific categorisation and its "looping effect" on the behaviour of individuals:

> There can be strong interactions. What was known about people classified in a certain way may become false because people so classified have changed in virtue of how they have been classified, what they believe about themselves,

or because of how they have been treated as so classified. There is what I call a "looping effect."

This is what Hacking (1999) calls the power of statistics to "make up" people. Thus, from the perspective of surveillance as well as administration, counting people is not an objective, neutral exercise that leaves things unchanged. Both who does the counting and how people are counted and their identity categorised in censuses have ramifications for biopolitics and governance, as will be discussed in more detail in chapter 4. In commenting on Hacking's work, Ann Laura Stoler (2010b, 8) remarks that "the power of categories rests in their capacity to impose the realities they ostensibly only describe. Classification here is not a benign cultural act but a potent political one."

Bernard Cohn (1987) looks at the processes of census construction used by the British in India in implementing imperial policy. He shows how "objectification" and quantification of the population were achieved in India by means of categorisation, standardisation, and classification, with elements of race and caste being based on Western notions of class structure, and above all by imposing a racial hierarchy on the caste system, which derived mainly from Western notions about "race sentiment" or purity of races. It is important to note, however, that local and communal precolonial conditions play an important role in maintaining traditional values. In the words of Sumit Guha (2003, 162), "community structures of feeling and communication survived into the colonial era, and used the colonial public sphere to assert their claims."

In violating the ethical rules governing modern censuses, statistics have their "darker side," as for example when governments target specific vulnerable groups, usually on the basis of race and ethnicity, for close observation and monitoring that lead to human rights abuses (Seltzer and Anderson 2001). The Nazi regime, with the aid of the IBM Corporation, performed targeted enumeration in the early part of the twentieth century to identify Jewish German citizens for the purpose of locating and eventually exterminating the group (Black 2001). But population targeting is one side of a sinister coin. Reverse targeting is another practice of census (un)taking. Since in modern nation-states censuses are associated with citizenship rights, the exclusion of certain groups from enumeration has negative consequences, such as the denial of citizenship rights and their associated social benefits. As demonstrated by Anat Leibler (2011), in the case of the first Israeli census in 1948, calculated plans to exclude some of the remaining Palestinian citizens from being counted had serious ramifications for failing to document their citizenship, such as the denial of access to their homes and property. To this day, they are referred to as the "present absentees" (present in the country but absent for census purposes) and their descendants continue to reside in unrecognised localities with no access to their original homes. It is significant to note that the snap census Israel carried out after it occupied the West Bank and Gaza in 1967 repeated the 1948 process by undercounting the resident population of the occupied territories and denying the right of return to Palestinian residents who were absent from their abodes for study, work, travel, or other reasons when the census was undertaken (Loewenstein 2006). In the words of a report by Human Rights Watch (2012, 17–18) in New York:

> Among the Palestinians whom the 1967 Israeli census did not register were Palestinians from the West Bank and Gaza who were displaced during the fighting in 1967 and had not returned by the time of the census, as well as Palestinians who were residing abroad at the time for work, study, or any other reason . . . The 1967 conflict displaced at least 270,000 Palestinians from the West Bank and Gaza. Other estimates are significantly higher: for example, the UN Relief and Works Agency for Palestine Refugees (UNRWA) estimated that the 1967 conflict displaced about 390,000 Palestinians from the occupied Palestinian territory.

One should not lose sight of the fact that, as Christine Zacharia (1996) and Kevin Wilkins (2004) note in commenting on Palestine, the census has the potential to mobilise marginal and dispossessed populations into actions of resistance. Some claim that in a more general sense the rise of the modern nation-state in the West is associated with the use of the census not exclusively as a surveillance tool to punish deviants but also as a means to provide citizens with social benefits (Higgs 2001).

In his work on Mandate Palestine, Michael Fischbach (2011, 298) captures the constructivist nature of colonial recordkeeping for governance:

> Data such as population censuses, tax lists, land records, survey maps, and so forth, do not merely dispassionately represent a world – in this case, a population that the state governs – that is "out there" in a pristine, positivistic sense. The processes of sorting, categorizing, and describing help create the very population that is being observed and recorded. This represents not merely the need for simplicity dictated by bureaucratic need, but also the wider "imaginings" about the nature of society.

As pointed out above, the constructivist aspect of surveillance takes on special meaning in colonial and postcolonial regimes. The recording of census data involves interpretation and identity construction, according to which censuses and other population data are grouped, sorted, and labelled in ways that reflect the administrative needs of those in power. However, Fischbach notes, the British were not able to rule by records alone and had to rely on "local knowledge" and the appointment of village leaders who facilitated the collection of population and land ownership data. Fischbach further asks, "beyond the obvious degree to which data and information helped Britain rule Palestine, did such surveillance transform the basic nature of Arab life in Palestine as a result?" His answer is that "the record would suggest that they did not, not because of any weakness in the transformative power of the data, but because of Palestinian resistance to the Mandate itself and the Zionist project, and because the British need to work with the Palestinians in implementing certain policies forced them to temper their outside, unilateral decision making" (ibid., 306–7).

With regard to the United States and Canada respectively, Matthew Hannah (2000) and Keith Smith (2010) discuss how colonial surveillance in nineteenth century North America facilitated the appropriation of native territory, the creation of the reserve system, and the stifling of opposition to the settlers. In both studies, the authors draw upon a Foucauldian framework to demonstrate how surveillance was accomplished by means of recordkeeping, deployment of informers and bureaucrats, missionaries, enforcement of alien, Western-based legal systems, and the adoption of disciplining techniques that included policing, schooling, Christian proselytising, and above all the reserve system itself. Smith accords a special place to liberalism as an ideology that justified the treatment of the native population as an inferior group in terms of values, rationality, and claims to the land. Hannah, in contrast, extends this focus by linking governmentality, or the regulation of the social body, in colonial situations to surveillance and spatial knowledge through mapping and enumeration. Although governmentality is premised on noncoercive "benign rule,"[3] it nevertheless contains a "colonial" structure. His point is that the metropolitan and colonial concerns share similar features, the most important of which are rule from a distance and collection of information, such as in census taking and mapping of national territory, "without seeking the consent of the people." Hannah does admit, however, that historical analysis of colonisation and the administration of colonies can benefit from understanding regulatory policies and the extent to which they are different in colonial and noncolonial situations.

Yael Berda (2013) singles out surveillance in the colonial state as signifying a shift from controlling the territory to managing the population. The creation of a dual legal system, one for the coloniser and another for the colonised, as is the case with the West Bank and Gaza, becomes a defining feature of the colonial administration (see also Shenhav and Berda 2009).

Maps as instruments of colonial power

> The map thus plays an important role in the ruling class tendency to erase from historical memory the violence and bloodshed out of which the state was born. Map, territory and power become mutually implicated in one another, as the map encourages a primordialist thesis about the autochthonous state, depoliticizing and ideologically mystifying the original violence through which the state and its territory were shaped. (Neocleous 2003, 421–22)

Mark Neocleous's observation that maps embody ideological assumptions that reflect power relations among contesting parties is supported by other writers, notably the eminent geographer John Harley (1988), who views maps as texts to be subjected to discourse analysis, and Mark Monmonier (1991), who warns that "maps lie" while at the same time performing a surveillance function. According to Harley (1988, 301), "Maps are preeminently a language of power, not of protest" (see also Crampton 2001). Although this is largely true, it is important not to lose sight of the dialectics of power relations, as revealed in the Palestinian case, to be discussed below.

A key disadvantage of the Arabs in their struggle against the Zionist colonisation of Palestine is Israel's access to financial resources, weapons, and manpower skilled in the use of technology, including mapmaking. As several writers have pointed out, the Zionist focus on territorial control resulted in an obsession with mapmaking and the mastery of cartography for military and colonising purposes. Efrat Ben-Ze'ev (2011) shows how the British role was essential in training the fledgling Israeli army and providing it with cartographic and mapmaking knowledge that was brought to bear in 1948 in capturing Arab territory and eventually driving the Palestinian population out of the country. The Arabs of Palestine, largely a peasant and illiterate society at the time, could not muster such corresponding resources, including the contacts the Zionists had forged with the British in Palestine. Of particular interest here is the way Zionist strategists utilised British cartographic knowledge and resources to acquire maps about Palestine (stolen in some cases) and to learn the art of mapmaking (Ben-Ze'ev 2009). A key Zionist organisation that compiled maps of Palestine and comprehensive lists of Palestinian villages and landholdings for military and settlement purposes was Shai, the intelligence arm of the Haganah. The data compiled were instrumental during the 1948 war and the ensuing mass expulsion of Palestinians; after the establishment of the state, the information was utilised to provide demographic data on the Palestinians remaining in Israel, who were then subjected to nearly two decades of military rule (H. Cohen 2008). Rona Sela's (2011) investigative report about the Haganah's aerial surveillance and spying activities in the 1940s demonstrates that they were instrumental in preparing the so-called "village files" as a prelude to the ethnic cleansing of Palestine in 1948. These files, which included maps, aerial photographs, textual surveys, and socioeconomic data about the villages, were meant to serve military and intelligence purposes. The Jewish National Fund, the key organisation in charge of Zionist colonisation in Palestine, produced propaganda maps of Mandate Palestine for settlement purposes (Bar-Gal 2003). After 1948, including the post-1967 period, map production was overtly tied to the expansion of settlements in the OPT. Political parties and various nongovernmental organisations produced ideologically based versions of current and future maps of the OPT with different border designations (Leuenberger and Schnell 2010).

The cartographic erasure and destruction of more than four hundred villages from Palestine's landscape following the flight and expulsion of their Arab inhabitants was a major undertaking of Zionist institutions such as the Israel Land Administration, the Jewish National Fund, and the Israel Archaeological Survey Society (see Shai 2006). In considering the Israeli-Palestinian case, Yair Wallach (2011, 359–61) views maps as constructions involving inscriptions, practices, narratives, and performances in which "[t]he meaning of the map is therefore not inherent but rather dependent on its discursive context"; yet he questions the value of "'counter-mapping' as a tool of resistance." In considering Palestinian and

Israeli use and production of maps, Wallach argues for a "de-territorialized" reading of political maps as "empty signifiers." Maps are texts that are invested with multiple meanings, emotions, and values. Although this is true at one level, even if detached from reality, Wallach presents the various readings of a map as acts of co-equals and neglects to take into account the element of power as a determining factor in the use of maps, as though maps had only symbolic and emotional value. Palestinians no doubt continue to press their case and use maps as a testimony to combat Zionist settlement expansion and erasure of their history, yet they lack the power to apply map reading in any concrete situation, such as political negotiations, even though the map could be considered a mobilising element in nationalist discourse, as asserted by Wallach. In contrast, Ariel Handel (2009) captures the essence of the argument concerning power and maps by distinguishing between the use value and the absolute value of maps. Absolute value is the measured distance between two points, whereas use value refers to the experience endured in travelling a specified distance, such as the time spent in going from one point to another. As shown in the discussion of time below, use value is crucial and is determined by political and military criteria:

> These maps present concretely Israel's expansion at the expense of the Palestinians, and their importance is clear. Nevertheless, this manner of mapping has a few weaknesses and is even more remarkable in light of the state of affairs in the OPT today. First, these maps assume that both sides – Palestinian and Israeli – share the same space. This is a problematic assumption, which will be discussed below. Second, underlying the maps is the assumption that the conflict is a zero-sum game in which every piece of land taken from one side is added to the balance of the other. That assumption – which makes it possible to portray areas in the map as "Israeli" or "Palestinian" and to mark clear boundaries distinguishing one from another – causes confusion by creating an imaginary system between the two sides. These weaknesses derive from the fact that the maps present the *absolute value* of space instead of its *use value*. (Ibid., 180, emphasis in original)

Digital technology has enabled the disenfranchised Palestinians to react by producing and disseminating counterversions of Palestine's maps that contain detailed historical data collected by the British on property ownership, population enumeration, and village statistics. This counter-mapping makes it possible to identify the extent of the destruction of Palestinian villages and the confiscation of Arab land (Abu-Sitta 2005; ARIJ 2009). A review essay on Palestine atlases has provided other examples of countermapping initiatives, this time by non-Palestinian geographers (Tawil-Souri 2012b).

In an examination of village life in pre-1948 Palestine as portrayed by Palestinian refugees in memorial books, anthropologist Rochelle Davis (2007, 62) shows that the maps represent the shared ideals of the community and are anchored in nationalist discourse about displacement, loss of land, and destruction of places:

"Through these accounts, the places and names take on meanings beyond their roles as just location markers; instead they become signifiers and ideographs of a specific past embodied in the name, and embedded in their social construction and transmission."

Maps are also powerful tools of indoctrination and hegemony in a more fundamental way; they are used to project a past and describe a present so as to inculcate the young in the values of the dominant group. In *Palestine in Israeli School Books* (2012), Israeli educator Nurit Peled-Elhanan explores the role of the education system in socialising young Israelis into a Zionist territorial identity through propaganda, in which maps occupy a central place. By performing multimodal semiotic and textual analysis of maps, pictures, and images printed in geography textbooks used in middle and high schools, she is able to show the peripheral place and the "cartographic exclusion" of the Palestinians in the history and landscape of Palestine and later Israel both pre- and post-1967. The map structures our view of reality, it is a form of hyperreality, or, as put by Jean Baudrillard (1994, 1), "the territory no longer precedes the map, nor survives it. It is nevertheless the map that precedes the territory – precession of simulacra – that engenders the territory." Current maps of Palestine in Israeli schools impersonalise the Palestinians, Judaise and de-Arabise the country through changes to the topography and the names of places on the maps, and adopt a narrative of progress for the Jews and stagnation for the Arabs. Peled-Elhanan (2012) argues that a form of Jewish "elite racism" is apparent in the discourse of these maps. She correctly points out that such racism is neither unique nor new to Israel. An analysis of pre-1948 Jewish textbooks in Palestine has revealed a similar view of the Palestinians (Bar-Gal 1994). Public opinion polls and case studies of Israeli Jews dating back to the 1980s, if not earlier, are cited by Peled-Elhanan in support of her argument. A psychological study of Israeli Jewish adolescents' attitudes toward the Palestinians has demonstrated the prevalence at an early age of an "infrastructure set of beliefs" that "focus on delegitimization of the outgroup – a process by which members of the outgroup are morally derogated and considered of less existential value than ingroup members" (Hammack et al. 2011, 152). Strong feelings of delegitimisation are correlated with high levels of individual and collective fear. As shown in the next section, racism, fear, and surveillance are interrelated. Under the current Israeli right-wing government, teachers in selected public schools receive bonuses if, according to one report, they impart the *correct* values to students, which clearly advantages Jewish schools, particularly religious Zionist schools, and disadvantages Arab schools (Kashti 2013a). Citing new research, Or Kashti (2013b) argues that under the current education ministry, the tendency is to "perpetuate intolerance" among Jewish students. An assessment of the Ministry of Education's plans to introduce civics in school textbooks is provided by Halleli Pinson of Haifa University, who questions the textbooks' emphasis on ethnic identification and culture at the expense of structural factors having to do with discrimination and exclusion. "Not only is this approach not liberal," Pinson says, "but one wonders whether it is even consistent with a democratic regime" (in Skop 2013).

Fear as justification for surveillance

> The real burden of the new urban fear – the part that is not hallucinatory or hyperbolised – is borne by those who fit the racial profile of white anxiety: Arab and Muslim Americans, but also anyone with an unusual head-covering, Middle Eastern passport or unpopular beliefs about Israel. (M. Davis 2001, 48)

> In Israel, the war on the Palestinians, and their creation of knowledge and national narrative, is many decades old, but has been deftly woven by the Israeli political and security elite since 9/11 into the international "war on terror." The Israelis style themselves as the "pioneers" in that "war on terror." (Falah 2007, 588)

As a feature of power, surveillance in everyday life is involved in the constitution of subjectivities at the level of desire, fear, security, trust, and risk – all of which ultimately impact human dignity and individual autonomy. It is broadly accepted that surveillance refers to "the focused, systematic and routine attention to personal details for purposes of influence, management, protection or direction" (Lyon 2007, 14). Personal details usually refer to information of one type or another that nowadays most likely exists in electronic format. The assumption underlying this view of surveillance is that organisations, be they public or private, are engaged foremost in the collection of data for the sake of population management, national security, and financial transactions, among other objectives. In the process, however, there is the danger of privacy violations, as revealed in recent postings on Wikileaks and in the ongoing debate surrounding the involvement of the American National Security Agency in mass surveillance of the American public through exhaustive collection of so-called "metadata."

Privacy and surveillance are usually considered each other's nemesis, or to quote philosopher Lucas Introna, they are "co-constitutive" of each other. This makes privacy a requisite to autonomy, for "without privacy there would be no self" (Introna 1997, 269–70). Joseph Kupfer (1987, 81–82) argues that "privacy contributes to the formation and persistence of autonomous individuals by providing them with control over whether or not their physical and psychological existence becomes part of another's experience. Just this sort of control is necessary for them to think of themselves as self-determining." The assumption is that the greater the surveillance, the lower the risk factor. Greater privacy requires greater trust, but, paradoxically, surveillance is required to produce trust. According to Richard Ericson and Kevin Haggerty (1997, 117), "privacy can expand only with trust, but trust can only expand with surveillance." The contingent relationship between surveillance, trust, privacy, and risk must be underscored. Privacy laws are essential to regulating the protection of personal information and safeguarding against state and other forms of intrusion. These matters become especially problematic in conflict zones where security and risk are correlated in a particular way in the shadow of the state of exception. In Giorgio Agamben's (2002, 2) words, there is a price to be paid by states that are obsessed with security: "security reasoning entails an essential risk. A state which has security as its only task and source of legitimacy is a fragile organism; it can always be provoked by terrorism to turn itself terroristic."

In colonial settings, in contrast, exclusion through restrictions on mobility and access to territory, rather than through inclusion – a process aptly described as "inclusive exclusion" (Ophir, Givoni, and Hanafi 2009) – guides the rationale for surveillance activities (Abu-Zahra and Kay 2013). As a colonial occupying power, Israel is interested less in the management of the population and its well-being (in the Foucauldian sense) than in controlling, excluding, and appropriating the territory in which the population resides. This priority, however, does not minimise the importance that the colonial state attaches to the collection, control, and categorisation of population data. This is how exclusion acquires its inclusive characteristic.

Immediately after the attack of 11 September 2001, fear for personal and national security figured prominently in the debate about the "war on terror." In fact, according to public opinion data in the West, to question the introduction of intrusive surveillance techniques as a deterrent to terrorism was tantamount to compromising state security (E. Smith 2006). In time, the public has moved away from unquestioning acceptance of limitations on personal freedom and privacy in the name of national security. Yet so pervasive has the discourse of security-cum-fear become that, according to Mike Davis (2001, 50), "the globalization of fear became a self-fulfilling prophecy." Israeli writer Seth Freedman points out that the Jewish history of suffering is used callously by the State of Israel to create a permanent "culture of fear" in order to justify its brutal security measures toward the Palestinians. He describes the transformation that he went through after deciding to take a stroll in the Palestinian town of Bethlehem dressed in civilian clothes rather than in a military uniform:

> I gazed casually at the same windows and doors at which I'd previously had to stare, hawk-like, in case a gunman or bomber should burst out and attack our squad. I looked calmly at the same gangs of youths who, when I was in uniform, I'd had to judge in an instant – whether they were benignly intentioned or baying for my blood.
>
> The fear instilled in me by the army all but dissipated once I was simply a tourist strolling through the town. Conversely, the more weaponry and protective gear I carried, the more terrifying the place became which, it dawned on me, was a distillation of Israel's core and eternal paradox – one that has dogged it since the moment the state was created. (Freedman 2008)

As revealed in numerous public opinion polls, prejudice and hatred are cultivated to delegitimise the Palestinians in the eyes of the Israeli-Jewish public. In times of ethnic conflicts, governments are able to rule by capitalising on citizens' fear, and surveillance of all kinds in everyday life is promoted as necessary to reducing fear and risk. The psychological toll of surveillance points to positive correlations between intensive surveillance and feelings of paranoia and psychosis (Kershaw 2008). As Spurgeon Thompson (2002, 100) states, paranoia "is the inevitable result of living with intensive state surveillance." Most commentators agree that surveillance implies intrusiveness into one's private domain and, indeed, personal autonomy and dignity. One has only to recall the depiction of surveillance in George Orwell's novel *Nineteen Eighty-Four* (1949), which has been reinforced in Christian Parenti's *The Soft Cage: Surveillance in America from Slavery to the War on Terror* (2003), and the more recent revelations about massive surveillance of Americans and foreign nationals in the name of state security under the administration of President Barack Obama. It seems that Canada is not all that far behind the United States in tracking the personal information of its citizens through the activities of Communications Security Establishment Canada (Payton 2014).

Israeli rule of the West Bank and Gaza provides an example of the link between fear and constant monitoring by means of identity cards and other bureaucratic measures. When asked what they fear most, many Palestinians cite the loss or confiscation of their identity cards, without which they are under the threat of expulsion or loss of residency rights (see Abu-Zahra 2008a). Thus the identity card acts like a double-edged sword: it facilitates their monitoring, but without it they are liable to be expelled.

Rajaie Batniji, a Palestinian physician at Stanford University, wrote a poignant essay after a trip to visit his family in Gaza. In the essay he echoes Hannah Arendt's (1943) lamentations about statelessness and loss of dignity among refugees. Noting that "Gaza is something of a laboratory for observing an absence of dignity," he writes that violations of dignity include

> ... not being seen or being incompletely seen; being subsumed into a group identity; invasion of personal space (including physical violence); and humiliation ... The constant surveillance from the sky, collective punishment through blockade and isolation, the intrusion into homes and communications, and restrictions on those trying to travel, or marry, or work make it difficult to live a dignified life in Gaza. (Batniji 2012, 466)

Modalities of surveillance: case studies

If colonial surveillance is a strategy of dominance, how is it accomplished? Here, I proceed by listing several key strategies that combine people watching people in a quotidian context with the use of bureaucracy, the military, and a panoply of surveillance technologies. Altogether, I present case studies covering Israel/Palestine in the following areas: the identity problem, the disciplining of memory, racialised time, cloak and dagger operations, colonial bureaucracy, legal discrimination, spatial surveillance, immobility, biometrics and biopolitics, and the boomerang effect.

The ever-present identity conundrum

> Write down!
> I am an Arab
> My identity card number is fifty thousand
> I have eight children
> And the ninth will come after a summer
> Will you be angry? (Darwish 1964)

Written in prison more than fifty years ago, the stanzas in this epigraph are from the well-known poem "Identity Card" by the late Mahmoud Darwish, considered to be the Palestinian national poet. In this poem, Darwish refers to the identity card number to remind the police interrogators that he is a citizen of the country and to protest, as the *New York Times* obituary mildly put it, "Israel's desire to overlook the presence of Arabs on its land" (Bronner 2008). From a sociological perspective, however, the poem captures a more encompassing Palestinian experience of displacement and monitoring both inside and outside Israel. It tells the story of how Palestinians assert their claims of belonging to the land by having large families, by attesting to their continuous majority presence in historical Palestine, and by resisting Israeli policies.

Plans to introduce national identity cards in Western countries have triggered heated debates on the grounds that, in the hands of governments, the cards carrying personal information could become a tool of "ubiquitous surveillance" over people's lives (Bennett and Lyon 2008; Lyon 2008). In colonial and postcolonial countries characterised by histories of foreign occupation and ethnic conflict and cleansing, the use of national identity cards as markers of group membership predates the current debate about privacy violations and identity theft in Western countries. As pointed out earlier in this chapter, several writers have analysed how colonial and postcolonial regimes introduced maps, censuses, statistical records, and identity cards as essential ingredients in the project of ruling.

In Israel mandatory identity cards were introduced in 1949 following the establishment of the state. The ethnic background of citizens comprised the main marker of identification on these cards. Sixty years later, the old identity cards were replaced with biometric ones that will be cross-referenced with existing government databases (Somfalvi 2008). The regime of identity cards in the OPT is drastically different from the one used in Israel. In the West Bank and Gaza, the identity cards are the product of three political environments: Israel's administrative and military rule; the Oslo agreement, which transferred the day-to-day running of the territories to the Palestinian Authority, which issued its own identity cards applicable in zones under its administrative jurisdiction; and the fact that Palestinians living in Israeli-annexed East Jerusalem are governed by a third system according to which Israel issues identity cards to the Arab residents that differ in colour from the those issued to its own population within the 1967 borders. The identity card emerges as the primary surveillance tool. One Israeli writer calculated that Israel utilises in excess of a hundred different types of permits to control the movement of Palestinians in the occupied territories (Levinson 2011).

The comparative study, whether historical or contemporary, of national identity cards is increasingly gaining the attention of researchers (Caplan and Torpey 2001; Lyon 2008). Of relevance here are the works of several writers who have addressed the issue of identity cards in both Israel and the occupied territories, most recently Nadia Abu-Zahra (2008a, 2008b; Abu-Zahra and Kay 2013), Usama Halabi (2011), David Lyon (2011), and Helga Tawil-Souri (2011). Lyon (2011) argues that, generally speaking, the rationale for introducing identity cards is twofold: it lies in the state's need for securitisation, and it guarantees the allocation of rights and duties to citizens. However, in the OPT, identity cards are essential tools in the Israeli matrix of control. They regulate mobility and residency but do not bestow any citizenship rights. For Tawil-Souri (2011, 220), the identity card is an instrument of colonial power: "at every checkpoint exists an under-theorized manifestation of a low-tech, visible, physical and tactile means of power: the ID card." Halabi (2011), who considers the identity card an instrument of surveillance, notes that, although starting in 2002 the nationality designation (i.e., Arab, Jew, or Druze) was removed from the identity cards, other codes have been instituted as ethnic markers. In the case of Israeli citizens, eight coded stars have replaced the old nationality identification. Palestinian residents of East Jerusalem are issued identity cards whose serial number starts with the digits "08," whereas those who reside in the occupied territories are assigned a serial number starting with "09." Identity cards are also issued in different colours: identity cards for East Jerusalem are blue, and for Gaza and the West Bank they are orange (although the Palestinian Authority replaced these with blue covers after the Oslo agreement). A further means of classification concerns those who are of so-called "mixed marriage": the offspring of an East Jerusalemite Palestinian who is married to a nonresident is given a code "086," and as of 2002 the law prohibits family reunification of West Bank and Gaza residents if they marry an Israeli resident and are males under thirty-five or females under twenty-five.

The disciplining of memory

> Memory is one of the few weapons available to those against whom the tide of history has turned. (L. Abu-Lughod and Sa'di 2007, 6)

> A colonization of the mind occurs when your lack of control over your space is naturalized and you cannot imagine, nay believe, anything different. (Jamoul 2004, 584)

In line with the workings of internal colonialism, the Israeli state implemented a major instrument of surveillance during its first two decades by imposing military rule over the Arab sector that was aimed at confiscating Palestinians' land and controlling their mobility. Alina Korn (2000, 168) describes the system of military rule:

112   Colonialism as surveillance

Various methods of political control were elaborated during the period of the military government and were widely used. These were designated to construct a social reality whereby the military government would be perceived as an "all-seeing, all-knowing body," even when its presence was not always evident. In order to realize this panoptic concept, a ramified network of paid agents and informers was operated. In return for the information and services provided, these agents and informers received privileged treatment. The military government awarded special favors to those who cooperated and enacted sanctions as punishment, on those who did not; it employed numerous means of incentives and also pressure, in order to broaden the circle of cooperation.

In addition to the far-reaching consequences of the military government on daily lives, the system of surveillance and its imposition of various restrictions contributed to the criminalisation of Palestinian citizens of Israel. "The means and forms of surveillance that were applied in order to broaden the political control over the Arab population," says Korn (2000, 170), "brought in their wake an over enforcement of the military regulations, and as a result a rise in the convictions rates."

Not unlike the Israeli practice of divide and rule in controlling the West Bank and Gaza, the encompassing edifice of surveillance erected by Israel inside its 1967 borders gave rise to various categories of Arab residents. Korn (2000, 173) describes this segmentation of the Palestinian population:

> The laws that served to expropriate lands from the Arabs, together with the restrictions on their movements, created several categories of Arab residents with different civil status: Arabs who had fled from their homes during the battles to other places within the boundaries of the State of Israel ("refugees"); Arab inhabitants that had been evacuated from their villages against their will, both during and after the war, to other places within Israel ("evacuees"); legal inhabitants or refugees that had returned legally but had lost their rights over their property because they were absent from their place of residence during the population census carried out in 1948 ("present absentees"); refugees who returned to Israel illegally, of whom some were permitted to remain, and others were refused resident permits ("infiltrators").

The lasting psychological effects of surveillance are borne out by Areej Sabbagh-Khoury's (2007) research on the military government's role in Palestinian life. Based on her interviews, she has concluded that, long after the military government had been abolished in 1966, Palestinians continued to be fearful of speaking out against state policies. She remarks that they are like the prisoners in the panopticon: although they do not know whether they are being watched by the guards, they simply assume the worst, refrain from opposition, and largely remain silent.

An example of the process of disciplining memory is illustrated by the late Emile Habibi, a noted Palestinian novelist and one-time member of the Knesset, in

"The Story of the Fish That Understands All Languages." There, Habibi (1974, 151) presents a son's narration of a dialogue between himself and his mother:

> At school you [mother] warned me: be careful in what you say. And when I told you that the teacher is my friend, you whispered as if he could be watching me! And when I heard the story of Tantura [a village near Haifa whose Palestinian population was expelled by Zionist forces in 1948], I cursed them, and you whispered in my ear: be careful in what you say.
> And when I met with my friends to declare a strike, they too told me: be careful in what you say.
> In the morning you [mother] told me that I talk in my sleep, be careful in what you say! And when I hummed tunes in the shower, my father would shout at me: change this tune. The walls have ears, be careful in what you say.[4]

In discussing Israeli attempts to stifle Palestinian commemorations of the Nakba, Tamir Sorek (2011) introduces a useful corrective to the current conception of surveillance. He points out that, as currently conceived, surveillance's main purview is the collection of behavioural and personal data. Such a definition, he argues, is inadequate in accounting for surveillance as a process of memory disciplining and construction at the group level. The crux of his concern is the process of self-disciplining that individuals go through at the level of consciousness to conform to the dictates of the majority and thereby avoid punishment. This is a form of panopticon surveillance in which people are aware that what they say and do may be constantly observed. Whereas at one time the government's secret agents would monitor the Palestinian population, a shift has occurred whereby disciplining the Palestinians is carried out through the "civic gaze" of ordinary people, accompanied by threats from Jewish politicians to punish Palestinian citizens if they continue to commemorate the Nakba. Thus, in stressing self-disciplining in contrast to behaviour and data-based surveillance, it is possible to account for the disciplining of consciousness and memory.

Commemorating the Nakba has drawn criticism from within, so to speak. It is pointed out that in dwelling on the past, Palestinians hamper finding a pragmatic solution to their predicament. The quotation from Lila Abu-Lughod and Ahmad Sa'di at the start of this section refers to memory as an act of resistance by the dispossessed. Anthropologist Ilana Feldman (2006, 40) concurs:

> Critics of Palestinian political positions will often say that the continued focus by Palestinians on their memories of home has obstructed their ability both to cope with the reality of the present and to acquiesce to resolutions to the Israeli-Palestinian conflict that do not involve the right of return. What is overlooked in the critique (among other things) is the extent to which this circulation of memory through refrain has in fact helped to keep the tragic realities of Palestinian history from utterly destroying Palestinian community and political life. If Palestinian experience has not been entirely reduced to

the "bare life" described by Agamben, and if they have not suffered a "loss of the entire social texture," as Arendt saw the plight of refugees, it is in no small part due to the way the refrain of home incorporates both past and present, both territoriality and de-territorialization.

Israeli attempts at subverting public discourse on Palestinian collective memory constitute acts of "memoricide," according to Ilan Pappé (2006) and show no signs of abatement. If one is to chronicle Israeli taboos on what passes as Palestinian memory, one must start with the actual expulsion of the Palestinians and official denial by Israel that it played any role in this act, as though the Palestinians left their country en masse of their own volition or were ordered to leave by neighbouring Arab governments, as advocated by successive Israeli governments over the years. The official and popular success of this denial left any discussion of the Nakba in the twilight zone of induced forgetfulness and indoctrination – forgetfulness that the act did take place and indoctrination (or forced memory) to ensure that future Israeli generations would encounter only the official discourse, particularly the narrative of the state security apparatus (H. Cohen 2004), in the writings of mainstream Israeli scholarship, school textbooks, popular culture, and the media. Eyal Sivan's documentary film *Izkor, Slaves of Memory* (1990) captures the implications of forced and official memory. The film depicts the Israeli public as immersed in commemorating state-sanctioned Jewish events with total disregard for Palestinian suffering. The film revolves around four annual commemorations (Passover, the Holocaust, Fallen Soldiers Day, and Independence Day), which ostensibly, according to Sivan, constitute "a powerful machine for the perpetuation of memory [that] goes over Israeli society like a steamroller" (ibid.). The Holocaust, a second defining catastrophic event in contemporary Jewish experience, is invoked and manipulated to trump any attempts to discuss the Palestinian case or to debate the significance of Palestinian memory surrounding the Nakba. Yosefa Loshitzky (2006) points out that with the aid of museums and public events worldwide, the Holocaust has come to occupy a place in global memory; but, she insists, it becomes pathologised when used to justify acts of brutality against the Palestinians. The Holocaust, in the words of Norman Finkelstein (2001, 6–7), became "an industry" that "was used to justify the criminal acts of the Israeli State and U.S. support for these policies." Loshitzky and others also note that mere mention of the Nakba and criticism of Israeli policies are tantamount to anti-Semitism. Finally, with the backing of its political institutions, the Israeli state has passed legislation that penalises local Palestinian councils by cutting off or reducing their allocations of state funds if they organise memorials to commemorate the Nakba.

For memory to become transformative, it must become collective. This is the theme of Sa'di and Abu-Lughod's edited anthology *Nakba: Palestine, 1948, and the Claims of Memory* (2007). History is the record of the victor's version of events. By relying on oral history as told by the victim, instead of the officially sanctioned archival material, their anthology presents a narrative that counters Zionist claims about what happened in 1948.

Racialised time

> They [the occupation forces] are stealing our time. Everything takes so long! (In Peteet 2008, 15)[5]

> The intended effect of the Israeli military surveillance network, together with the long-practiced strategies it implemented, is to fragment time and space in such a way that it becomes impossible to lead a normal life. (Abujidi 2011, 233)

In the above quotations, Palestinians complain about the impact of the occupation on their use of time. One ontological feature of surveillance that is overlooked in current studies, especially those conducted in colonial settings, is its ability to inject racialism and affect one's mastery and use of time. This is evident in detentions and searches at airports, borders, and checkpoints where monitoring is not carried out strictly in a random fashion and does not affect all people to the same degree. In the case of Palestine, it is mainly carried out to deter certain travellers from visiting the occupied territories, especially foreign residents who sympathise with the Palestinians and those who are of Arab origin (Greenberg 2012). The Association of Civil Rights in Israel (ACRI 2012a) has challenged this practice, arguing that these searches are illegal according to Israeli law, but the domestic security agency Shin Bet has continued its practice of surveillance and seizure of personal material such as computers (Edelman 2013). The enterprising journalist Amira Hass (2012b) has reported the experience of an Arab-American traveller who was interrogated at Ben-Gurion Airport. "Do you feel more Arab or more American?" the interrogator asked, before supplying the following answer: "surely you feel more Arab. Why did you visit Israel more than once? Surely, it is cheaper to visit Canada, Venezuela, etc." The implication is that there must be a secret, illegal reason for visiting the OPT.

Colonisation, anthropologist Julie Peteet (2008, 14) points out, extracts its toll from Palestinians along the two important dimensions of space and time: "Palestinian space shrinks, time slows, and mobility is constrained," whereas the Israeli occupiers have "freedom of movement and expansion through space and control of time."

It is worth pondering the meaning of time in *current* Zionist colonising experience. Political scientist Amal Jamal (2008) introduces the concept of "racialized time" to examine Israel's differential treatment of its Palestinian citizens and those who live in the occupied territories. His point of departure is to argue, through recourse to Martin Heidegger's work, that control over one's time is an essential human requisite; it distinguishes humans from animals. Relegating Palestinians to the margins of society by seizing control of their time, Jamal argues, places them beyond the pale – in what Agamben (2005) calls a "state of exception." The Zionist narrative depicts time as dynamic and eternal in the Jewish experience and as empty, static, and discontinuous in the Palestinian experience. Moreover, Israeli "Jewish time is distinguished from Palestinian time by adopting methods whose objective is to suppress, block, delay or keep still the flow of Palestinian time"

(Jamal 2008, 376). According to Peteet (2008, 14), "in general, colonial regimes tend to fashion the native as occupying a different, timeless and motionless zone, distinct from the settlers' modernity and civilization."

In arguing his case, Jamal (2008) invokes colonial and postcolonial literature (e.g., Frantz Fanon) in which native values are depicted as inferior to those of the coloniser. Israeli control of Palestinian use of time and space is thus legitimised and facilitated by surveillance in the form of closures, checkpoints, the so-called "separation wall," restriction on mobility, and land use. This control was practised in Israel proper at one time, but for the past forty-five years it has been focused more on the occupied territories. Over the years, international and local human rights organisations and the media (not necessarily mainstream media) have documented numerous cases of mistreatment and humiliation of Palestinians at the checkpoints. In addition, Palestinians have been denied the right to seek access to their land, places of employment, and emergency healthcare, with the latter at times resulting in death (UNHRC 2008). As pointed out above, of particular significance is the association of time with space in the colonial context, which Jamal sees as having significant repercussions for the quality of life in a global world dominated by advanced technology. If time is emptied of its human meaning and mobility is methodically restricted, how can the Palestinians take part in the determination of their daily life and benefit from exposure to world cultures? Colonialism maintains the gaps and hierarchies between rulers and ruled in the use and valuation of time.

Cloak-and-dagger operations

Israel has made a name for itself in international politics and diplomacy as the invincible spy state that infiltrates foreign agencies in pursuit of its enemies. Israel has advanced this image as a unique form of state branding. In popular culture such as films and novels and in diplomatic circles, Israel is presented as a model of how to carry out espionage and cloak-and-dagger operations in order to apprehend or assassinate its enemies pre-emptively – and at times mistakenly. The Israeli surveillance system is also a formidable *domestic* spy network aimed primarily at the Palestinians under its control in Israel and the occupied territories, although it does not hesitate to go after Jewish and non-Arab targets if state security is at stake. To make its state surveillance system as efficient as possible, especially during the early decades when it confiscated Palestinian land, Israel created an institutional structure that monitored the Palestinian population bureaucratically with the aid of separate divisions in various government departments and agencies (e.g., education, police, military, statistics bureau, intelligence agencies, and land registration).

A dominant feature of early Israeli surveillance practices was the use of old-fashioned spy networks of people watching people, which were embedded in local Arab communities. As shown below, these networks relied heavily on Palestinian collaborators and informers whose cooperation with Israel was the result more of personal and economic necessity than of any ideological identification with the state. At times of organised dissent and violent opposition to colonial rule, nontechnical surveillance involving people watching people also relied on special undercover units, the so-called *"mista'rivm"* ("Arab pretenders" in Hebrew), to gather information and liquidate individuals deemed dangerous by the state. There was, of course, no recourse to due process. These units were widely used in the West Bank and Gaza during the first (1987–93) and second (2000–04) Palestinian uprisings, and their use continues. On many occasions, starting with the Second Intifada, the actions of these units involved extrajudicial killings of Palestinian activists, which resulted in the death of innocent civilians (Zureik and Vitullo 1992).[6]

The police were compelled to admit their deployment of the *mista'rivm* units, usually used by the Israeli army and the Shin Bet in the occupied territories, to target Arab citizens of the state (Zarchin 2009). This admission prompted Adalah, the Legal Centre for Arab Minority Rights in Israel, to charge "that since the unit was designed explicitly to target Israeli Arab criminals, whereas other police units focus on particular types of crime and not populations, its very existence is liable to encourage discriminatory, racist policing" (in Khoury, Lis, and Kyzer 2009). Arab author and journalist Sayed Kashua (2009) has published an interesting commentary on the conduct of the *mista'rvim* in the form of a parody. Using Hebrew, he tells his Jewish readers (including the *mista'rivm* themselves) that the Arabs are quite aware of undercover agents in their midst who masquerade as native Arabs. The *mista'rvim* are trained to speak in the local dialect and to behave and look like Arabs of days gone by. The irony, Kashua says, is that these transparent and ludicrous performances are a poor imitation, if not a caricature, of present-day Arabs, and it is these performances that give them away in the eyes of the local Arab population.

The use of such undercover methods dates back to the prestate period in the 1940s, if not earlier, when Jewish undercover units operated in Palestine and in neighbouring Arab countries. At the time, the purpose of these special units (the Palmach) of the fledgling Israeli army (the Haganah) was to gather intelligence; to engage in acts of terror and sabotage, if necessary, in order to spread fear and spur Jewish immigration from Arab countries to Palestine, and to counter the activities of Palestinian nationalists who opposed Jewish immigration and the selling of land to Zionist settlers. Initially, local Jews who spoke Arabic and Jews who originated from Arab countries were recruited to these units in the prestate period (Zvika 1986). After 1948, Israel widened its domestic surveillance networks by recruiting Jewish immigrants from Arab countries, in addition to native Palestinian informants and collaborators, to gather information about the political activities of Palestinians; this first applied to Palestinian citizens of Israel and was later extended to residents of the West Bank and Gaza (Novik 2011; Raviv and Melman 2014).

Before 1948, Zionist surveillance activities centred on gathering political intelligence to secure land purchases in Palestine and overcome Palestinian resistance. Eventually, however, both before and after 1948, surveillance was aimed at confronting Palestinian violent opposition and frustrating Palestinian nationalism (H. Cohen 2008). For land acquisitions, the informer's task was to collect information about the availability of land and its location and then to entice landowners to sell to the Zionists. When it became clear that mounting Palestinian opposition to

Zionism could not be contained through political intelligence alone, surveillance tactics were widened: the target became information about Palestinian military organisations and guerrilla activities. At times, this information was shared with the British in Palestine. As part of its opposition to Zionism, Palestinian activists sought to block the flow of information from collaborators to the Zionists through economic boycotts and assassinations of other Palestinians.[7] Assassinations were also carried out by Jews against other Jews (H. Cohen 2011).

In the face of mounting opposition to Zionist colonisation, remarks historian Hillel Cohen (2008, 158), "the Zionists increasingly used manipulation and financial and material inducements to recruit Arabs." When voluntary land sales dried up – not more than 7 per cent of the land in Palestine had been legally sold through various means to the Zionists by 1948 – surveillance methods were developed to locate land-owning Palestinians who were in financial distress. Offers would then be made to these individuals: in exchange for payment of their debts, they would sell their land to the Zionists. It would be an understatement to say that the result of collaboration caused divisions in Palestinian society and weakened its opposition to Zionist settlers.

In a book covering the post-1948 period, Hillel Cohen (2006) demonstrates the continuity in Israeli surveillance practices across the pre- and post-1948 periods. The networks of collaborators, established in the prestate period, were subsequently expanded by adding new recruits – including those who at one time had resisted Israeli policies but found themselves compelled to cooperate in order to secure jobs and other favours from agents of the state. In particular, state surveillance agencies sought the cooperation of Palestinian notables and heads of clans in an effort to discredit the over-whelmingly Arab Communist Party. The Communist Party, in the early decades of the state, mounted an ideological and organisational campaign to mobilise Palestinian citizens in Israel against the dominant Zionist political parties and to expose Israeli policies of land confiscation and the military government. The deep involvement of the state security apparatus in civil society in the Arab sector reveals the extent to which the state manipulated the Arab community. Cohen shows how the domestic intelligence service (Shabak) used collaborators to intervene through threats and promises of favours in order to weaken the Communist Party's hold on Arab voters and strengthen the position of so-called "Arab" political parties affiliated with the main Zionist parties, particularly Mapai, the ruling labour party at the time. Immediately after independence, Israel took measures to prevent, at all costs, Palestinian refugees from returning to their homes. Here too the state's army of collaborators gathered information about what the state called infiltrators, many of whom were killed by the Israeli army, with others being forced to return to the refugee camps.

Colonial bureaucracy

> Who was born and who died and who wants to change address and who wants to get a passport and who wants to go here or there . . . all of this – you have to register . . . in the Civil Administration. One mustn't forget that

> the entire registration of citizens, including in Gaza, is held by Israel. The one who registers the citizens is the one in control . . . Bureaucracy reigns supreme. (Braverman 2011, 283)

The above quotation from an Israeli human rights activist demonstrates the connection between recordkeeping and state power in the Israeli-Palestinian context. This connection remains very much a cornerstone of Israel's system of control to this day. In tandem with the above, the state exercised "intimate" bureaucratic surveillance of education and local elections in the Arab sector. In the former case, employment of Arab teachers was conditional upon approval of the security services.[8] In the latter, the government historically relied on the traditional Arab social structure by appointing heads of loyal clans to deliver votes to Zionist parties and run the affairs of local councils. As Hillel Cohen (2006) points out, monitoring processes run by the security services were opposed by other Zionist parties who competed for Arab votes, such as the left-wing Mapam (United Workers Party). For self-serving reasons, the defunct Mapam exposed the close connection between the security services and the ruling Mapai. It is not uncommon to come across cases where the state's security agencies coerce Palestinians to work as collaborators in return for favours. To this day, media reports reveal cases of Palestinians from the occupied territories who are denied access to medical treatment or release from prison unless they cooperate with the Shabak (Melman 2008; Reuters 2008).

Usama Halabi (2011) and Ahmad Sa'di (2011, 2013) have provided clear examples of the invidious effects of collaboration and surveillance by the Israeli state on the daily lives of Palestinian citizens. People's livelihoods depend on the extent to which they are willing to collaborate with the authorities in collecting information about their fellow community members. This old practice remains in place to this day, as confirmed in newspaper reports. Referring to a checkpoint-monitoring group, Chaim Levinson (2011) says, "the Shin Bet security service uses the permit system to recruit informers. Palestinians whose permit requests are rejected 'for security reasons' are often invited to meet with Shin Bet agents, who offer 'assistance' in obtaining the desired permits in exchange for information." This does not mean that the surveilled individuals are unaware of these activities, as pointed out by Halabi (2011).

Using archival material, Sa'di (2005) traces the role of collaborators in aiding the state in its formative years of selectively incorporating the Palestinian minority through "minimal hegemony." That is, Palestinians would be able to exercise a form of citizenship not predicated on acceptance of the state's national goals as dictated by dominant Zionist ideology as long as the Palestinian minority refrained from actively opposing such an ideology. This observation is in line with Korn's (2000, 167–68) commentary:

> The young State of Israel made no effort to influence or change the attitudes of its Arab citizens (as has been done in relation to the Jewish immigrants that came after the state was established, for example), and made no attempt in

encouraging them to identify with the state. The apparatuses that specialized in dealing with the Arab population and the use of various techniques of control, supervision and manipulation, were designated to ensure "correct political behavior" and different types of obedience, dependence and cooperation.

Sa'di (2011) has methodically traced the evolution of Israel's methods of control of the Palestinian minority since the state came into being. He shows how, failing in the first decade to transfer or encourage the remaining Palestinian minority to emigrate, the state had to devise alternative control methods. These surveillance methods had several dimensions. First, they were bureaucratic and allowed the state to withhold economic and development projects from the Arab sector if its leaders did not cooperate with the state. Sa'di demonstrates that bureaucracy was used as a surveillance mechanism par excellence. It documented and stored detailed information about Palestinians' lives; to a very large extent, it controlled their life chances (employment, education, land ownership, travel, etc.). Second, surveillance led to the ghettoisation of the Arab community by breaking up its spatial contiguity. By confining the Arabs to geographically designated areas, the state was able to implement its projects of land confiscation. Third, by means of "divide and rule," the Arab community was treated not as a single national unit but as one divided into tribes and religious denominations, each of which was treated according to its willingness to cooperate with the state.

It was the sociologist Max Weber who first described bureaucracy as a "legal-rational" means of organisational efficiency and planning in the modern nation-state (see Braverman 2011). He argued that the strength of bureaucracy is the universal application of legal criteria. But Weber also saw bureaucracy as a form of "iron cage" that constrains human potential and creativity. In colonial regimes, bureaucracy deviates fundamentally from Weber's prescriptions of the "legal-rational" model. In the words of Yael Berda, the bureaucracy of occupation in the West Bank and Gaza "operates like the British bureaucracy that managed populations of subjects in the colonies. The colonial model is based on the principle of racial hierarchy, in which there is one legal and organizational system for the ethnic group in power and another for the group that is under their control" (in V. Lee 2012; see also Berda 2012b, 2013). The theme of bureaucracy, race, and imperialism is dealt with by Yehouda Shenhav (2013) along three lines: racialism, moral aloofness, and arbitrariness. Racialism, with its depiction of the colonised as inferior, irrational, and lacking civilization, is the most salient feature of imperial bureaucracy. He contends that the arbitrariness of bureaucracy is reflected in the tendency of its overseers to transcend the rule of law and govern by decrees and states of emergency. Shenhav draws upon the work of Hannah Arendt to point out that the imperial bureaucratic cadre distances itself from the native population on matters of values. According to Arendt, "aloofness became the new attitude of all members of the British services; it was a more dangerous form of governing than despotism and arbitrariness because it did not ever tolerate that last link between the despot and his subjects, which is formed by bribery and gifts" (in ibid., 391). With regard to Israeli colonial occupation of the West Bank, Shenhav further comments, "The coupling of bureaucracy with race is most conspicuous in the Israeli Jewish rule over the Palestinians in the West Bank. It is apparent that the bureaucracy of the Israeli occupation bears close resemblance to the imperial type" (ibid., 394).

Thus bureaucracy becomes a formidable weapon that constrains colonised subjects, along the lines described by the Israeli journalist Amira Hass (2011). She captures the essence of Israel's bureaucratic strangulation of the Palestinians in a language that echoes Zygmunt Bauman's (1989) warnings of bureaucracy's debilitating impact on the human condition:

> A machinery of repression depends not only on guns and torture in cellars. As the Soviet-bloc regimes proved, bureaucracy is central to the system. The same is true with us: Far from the barriers of transparency of a proper democratic society, Israel has created a complex and invisible bureaucracy that completely controls Palestinian freedom of movement, and hence freedom of employment, livelihood and studies, the freedom to fall in love and establish a family, to organize and other basic liberties. (Hass 2011)

The manipulative nature of Israeli bureaucracy in the state's dealings with the Palestinians is captured by Robert Home (2003, 306): "A modern, positivist ideology of law and the state supported the colonists/colonialists in dispossessing the colonized, and trapped the indigenous Palestinians in a world of manipulated bureaucracy worthy of the pages of Kafka and Orwell."

The overarching relationship between the settlers and natives is best characterised as a process of what Harvey (2003) calls "cumulative dispossession" – a play on Karl Marx's concept of "capitalist accumulation" – whereby the coloniser, through recourse to force, bureaucracy, and colonial law, lays claim directly or indirectly to territory and property in general, resulting in internal displacement and large-scale expulsion of the native population (Wolfe 2007, 342). Now, in the age of human rights discourse, it is difficult to embark on large-scale, naked expulsion of the native population; instead, the Israeli case presents ample evidence of gradual economic strangulation, which amounts to invisible or silent transfer of the Palestinian population in order to maintain a Zionist-imposed population and territorial configuration (B'Tselem 2013b; Guego 2006; Zureik 2003). As will be demonstrated in chapter 4, the pursuit of calibrated suffering and necropolitics by Israel has exacted a formidable toll on the Palestinians. This is the crux of national biopolitics in a colonial context.

Sociologist Yael Berda (2012a) has elaborated on the significance of what she calls "mundane" surveillance of Palestinians in the occupied territories. The Oslo agreement created a "phantom sovereignty" by which Israel exercises an "omnipresence" over the daily lives of Palestinians. She astutely points out that a by-product of the Oslo agreement and the division of the occupied territories into zones of control was to augment the old system of human surveillance with a more bureaucratic system based on the "power of classification." Security threat is the organising principle governing the surveillance of Palestinians. Such surveillance is total; although it focuses on the "mundane activities" of the local population, in the process it gathers information "of the deepest kind" about the "very, very daily" lives of Palestinians. The permit system brings the population into daily contact with the bureaucracy of the occupation and enables it to collect extensive information about the private lives of Palestinians; the "gathering of information is done for its [own] sake."

The Israeli Centre for the Defence of the Individual (Hamoked 2013) has carried out a detailed examination of the bureaucratic structure and the permit regime under which Palestinians live, noting that this regime has further reduced their access to 5.9 per cent of the West Bank area between the wall and the Green Line (known as the "seam zone"). Israel has ignored the advisory opinion of the International Court of Justice regarding the illegality of the wall, which is built mostly on private Palestinian land. Hamoked argues that "the permit regime is nothing short of a regime of separation based on nationality, and as such it is a grave breach of international humanitarian law and international human rights law" (ibid., 6). The main feature of the wall and the seam zone is the implementation of draconic bureaucratic measures that are incomprehensible to the local population. According to Hamoked, regulations governing the use of the permit regime "have only been published in Hebrew and since they are extremely complex and written in legal language, they are not readily comprehensible even to Hebrew speakers" (ibid., 10). In any case, these permits are valid for a maximum of two years. Over time, however, there has been a decline in the number of applicants, and the permits issued have become for shorter durations. In its report, Hamoked remarks that "the permit regime remains a discriminatory system which many are unable to navigate successfully, if at all" (ibid., 8). In its assessment of the impact of the regime on access to agricultural land, family relations, and the quality of life in general, Hamoked estimates that upon completion of the wall, around 30,000 Palestinians will have to endure restricted access to their land and villages except by permits that are difficult to obtain (ibid., 9).

Legal discrimination

Legal discrimination refers to laws that specifically target individuals and groups for maltreatment on the basis of their race, ethnicity, gender, or other ascribed attributes without necessarily appearing to be discriminatory, although the case of apartheid in South Africa was an example *par excellence* of discrimination that was written into law and statutes. Self-declared democratic societies are not immune to practising discrimination, even if it is not enshrined in law. Many scholars argue that the Israeli Law of Return is basically a case of legal discrimination because it automatically bestows on individuals of the Jewish faith and their descendants the right to obtain Israeli citizenship but denies this right to the indigenous Palestinian population in its dispersal. This is not the only enshrined law that discriminates against non-Jews. Other instances, such as land ownership laws referred to previously, are intended to dispossess the native Palestinians by stipulating that once the land is Jewish-owned in the form of state land, it shall remain Jewish in perpetuity.

Unwritten, subtle, and informal practices of discrimination endure in many societies, including democratic ones, but Israel has dispensed with subtlety and embarked in the past few years, with the rise of the political right under Prime Minister Benjamin Netanyahu's leadership, on passing a slew of bills in the Knesset that on their face appear to be security-based, nationalistic, and not aimed at any one particular group in society. In reality, these laws disproportionately target the Arab minority, although some have a wider scope and affect individual rights in general. Several nongovernmental organisations in Israel, such as the Arab Association for Human Rights (Mossawa), the Legal Centre for Arab Minority Rights in Israel (Adalah), Mada-al-Carmel (the Arab Centre for Applied Social Research), and the Association of Civil Rights in Israel (ACRI), to name a few, make available online detailed reports on recent Israeli passed and pending legislations that, because of their discriminatory thrust, have direct bearing on the Palestinians in Israel. These and other organisations point out that what has been worrying human rights organisations is the marathon of the past few years in which Israeli legislators have embarked on enacting and lobbying for the passage of a series of bills aimed at curtailing and eroding civil and political rights. I present the highlights of certain significant legislations as they have appeared in the above-mentioned organisations' publications.

In March 2011 the Knesset passed several discriminatory legislations. It completed its second and third readings of a contentious bill commonly identified as the "Nakba Bill." The controversy surrounding commemoration of the Nakba was brought to the fore by the efforts of right-wing politicians in Netanyahu's government. They lobbied for and succeeded in passing legislation that empowers the finance minister to withhold financial support from associations, organisations, and local councils that commemorate the Palestinian Nakba on Israel's Independence Day. In its final version, the bill targets institutions such as local councils and nongovernmental organisations (rather than individuals), which are subject to fiscal penalty.

In March 2011 the Knesset approved the amendment to the Citizenship Law in its third reading, permitting revocation of the citizenship of anyone convicted of "terrorism," espionage, or any other act that harms state sovereignty. During that month, the Knesset also passed the amendment to the Communal Societies Law. According to the law, anyone who wishes to reside in a small town in the Naqab and Galilee areas that contains fewer than 400 families must be admitted by an "Admissions Committee" formed by residents of the town, a representative from the Jewish Agency, or a representative from the World Zionist Organization. The law authorises the aforementioned committees to reject any candidates who are not "socially suitable" or who will harm the community's "cultural fabric." As described by ACRI (2012c), "The bill primarily intends to deny ethnic communities access to Jewish communities set up predominantly on state land." These are examples of several enacted and pending legislations that are, according to ACRI, "anti democratic bills" (ibid.; see also ACRI 2012a, 2012b). It is valid to say that these and other such laws are opposed by human rights organisations in and outside Israel because they are intended to keep Arabs out of homogenous Jewish small towns.

Other laws detailed by Adalah (2012) and worth mentioning in passing include the Citizenship and Entry Law, which was amended in 2005 but originally passed in 2003. This law privileges Jewish immigration and bans unification of Palestinian families whose members live on both sides of the Green Line. It is estimated that 25,000 families are affected by this separation. More recently, in 2014, the Knesset passed a law that favours those who serve in the army, mainly Jews, by granting them preferential treatment in housing, employment, and education (Mossawa 2014; see also ACRI 2013, 20–22).

Finally, a law that is still being considered demands a loyalty oath to confirm the allegiance of non-Jews seeking to obtain official Israeli documents such as an identity card through marriage, immigration, or residency. The Loyalty Oath Law makes it possible to deny or strip individuals of their citizenship for alleged "disloyalty" to the state. This pending law stipulates that Israel is a "Jewish, Zionist and democratic state," something that Palestinian citizens and some secular Jews object to because the law overrides the ethnic and national feelings of one-fifth of the population of Israel (see Adalah 2013). It is significant that these moves are being led by Israel Beiteinu, the party of Avigdor Lieberman, Israel's foreign minister.[9]

Spatial surveillance

A substantial and empirically focused analysis of Israeli monitoring of the Palestinians in the occupied territories using spatiality as the main architecture of surveillance is provided by architect Eyal Weizman. In *Hollow Land: Israel's Architecture of Occupation* (Weizman 2007), which was preceded by *A Civilian Occupation: The Politics of Israeli Architecture* (Segal and Weizman 2003) and by a series of articles on the "politics of verticality" (Weizman 2002), Weizman describes in detail Israel's (civilian and military) control of the movement of people in the West Bank, transformation of the landscape through zoning and the building of Jewish settlements, monopoly over water resources, control of the airspace, and allocation of the electromagnetic spectrum. As he says, these form part of Israel's panoply of surveillance measures, which also encompasses "electronic techniques of demarcation, population control, identity cards, inspection, currency control" (Weizman 2007, 288), among others. What distinguishes the occupation of the West Bank from traditional forms of colonisation, according to Weizman, is not the ideology of occupation itself, which is still driven by a desire to dispossess the Palestinians and suppress their national aspirations, but its implementation, its architectural contours, and the contradictions that arise therein.[10] He points out:

> Settlements are constructed according to a geometric system that unites the effectiveness of sight with spatial order, producing "panoptic fortresses," generating gazes to many different ends. Control – in the overlooking of Arab towns and villages and in the overlooking of main traffic arteries; self-defence – in

the overlooking of the immediate surroundings and approach roads. Settlements could be seen as urban optical devices for surveillance and the exercise of power. (In Yacobi 2004b, 57-58)

Using postmodern idioms – "structured chaos," "improvisation," and "plastic geography" – Weizman (2007) describes the fields in which the various actors are involved in the contest over space. He argues that the co-existence of direct discipline and indirect forms of control no longer fits a theoretical narrative that presupposes an evolution from "disciplinary societies" to "control societies."[11] Although it is prudent to go beyond Michel Foucault's binary framework of power, which juxtaposes the spectacle of the premodern against the disciplinary power of the modern, the colonial and racialised specificity of Palestine (and undoubtedly other colonial and postcolonial settings) calls for yet another amendment to this binary system, as noted by Achille Mbembe (2003, 27): "Late-modern colonial occupation differs in many ways from early-modern occupation, particularly in its combining of the disciplinary, the biopolitical, and the necropolitical. The most accomplished form of necropower is the contemporary colonial occupation of Palestine."[12]

Another example of the intersection of spaciality and surveillance is provided by Haim Yacobi, who deploys Foucault's metaphor to analyse what he calls "urban panopticism" in the city of Lod, an Arab-Jewish mixed city that witnessed a significant Palestinian population expulsion in 1948 and subsequent segregation between the Palestinian and Jewish parts of the city. Segregation is explained as an outcome of urban planning designed to retain power for the majority. According to Yacobi (2004b, 62), "The built environment in Lod cannot be seen as merely a technical division of organizing space. Rather, similar to other cultural representations it expresses, produces and reproduces power relations." The basic premise of this approach is to view the production of space as part of a control project that defines space in accordance with a political agenda.

A third example relates to the process of what Stephen Graham (2003) calls urbicide (i.e., the planned destruction of urban areas, both cities and infrastructure), which refers to urban warfare in the West Bank but is equally applicable to Gaza, where the Palestinians have endured several attacks, particularly those of December 2008, and to the invasions of Lebanon in 1982 and 2006. An important outcome of this research is to demonstrate that military technologies of surveillance are making their way into urban settings, thus blurring the division between civilian and military sectors. However, during times of conflict – whether in Iraq, Afghanistan, or Palestine – third world regions present an "unclean" urban terrain of guerrilla warfare, where regular armies find it difficult to operate. According to Graham, "Palestinian cities are portrayed as potentially impenetrable, unknowable spaces which challenge the three-dimensional gaze of the IDF's [Israel Defence Force's] high-technology surveillance systems and lie beyond much of its heavy-duty weaponry" (ibid., 70).

It is significant that Israel's brutal urban warfare strategies in Palestinian cities and refugee camps, including in Lebanon, have influenced American urban warfare in Iraq. Graham demonstrates the close connection between Israel and the United States in this regard, so much so that during Israel's major incursion in the sprawling West Bank refugee camp of Jenin in 2002, an act that was roundly condemned by international human rights organisations, American military personnel were reported present to observe first-hand Israel's operation. Furthermore, there have been reports that the Israeli military visited the United States to train the Americans and were in Iraq to see the American conduct of urban warfare. Thus, Graham (2011, 135) remarks, the "Israeli military and security experience in addressing these purported imperatives – as the ultimate surveillance-security state – is rapidly being exported around the world." The Israeli impact goes beyond Americans copying Israeli urban warfare tactics to include an ideological component reflected in the "war on terror" campaign of President George W. Bush's administration as well as pre-emptive war and targeted assassinations, which have been condemned by human rights organisations and experts in international law. The upshot of this, according to Graham, has been the "Palestinianization of Iraq," which "involved the various Iraqi insurgencies and militias directly imitating the tactics of Hamas or Hezbollah as well as the US military directly imitating the IDF" (ibid., 137).

Using the city of Nablus as a site for her research, Nurhan Abujidi (2011) explores the physical and sociopolitical structures that form part of Israel's colonisation of the West Bank. The matrix of surveillance involves curfews, regulating the use of public spaces, violating private spaces such as the home, imposed confinement, and temporary and arbitrary occupier's laws. Altogether, these encompassing measures reflect what one author has called an attempt at "colonization of the mind" (Jamoul 2004, 581). Through interviews with Nablus residents, Abujidi describes the development of daily resistance tactics rooted in counterknowledge, commemoration, and schooling.

(Im)mobility

> [The] quintessential Palestinian experience . . . takes place at a border, an airport, a checkpoint: in short at any of those modern barriers where identities are checked and verified. (Khalidi 1997, 1)

Here, historian Rashid Khalidi captures the generalized feeling among Palestinians of being watched and surveilled. Body searches, identity documentation, standing in line for hours awaiting a signal from conscripts in the Israeli army to either proceed or be turned away are emblematic of the checkpoint experience, which is characterised by dehumanisation, lack of sovereignty, and overall limitation on free movement.

Population registration – including the census and the permit regimes governing the movement of people that Israel introduced in the pre- and post-1967 periods in the name of state security – was crafted in such a way as to further spatial control and the expansion of Jewish colonies, restrict mobility, and stunt economic development of the Arab sector (Esmeir 2004). With the wall, checkpoints, fences, watchtowers, and segregation barriers in the background, not to mention the panoply of high-technology surveillance machinery, researchers point out that the permit regime is best viewed as the intersection of carceral (body) control, mobility, and biopolitics (Parsons and Salter 2008; J. Young 2012). One researcher who has explored in depth the implications of the identity card and the permit system as tools of discrimination and denationalisation is anthropologist Nadia Abu-Zahra (2008a, 2008b; Abu-Zahra and Kay 2005, 2013). From 1948 to 1966, Israel imposed military rule on the Arab population in Israel by extending the British Emergency Regulations in Palestine, which remain on the books to this day and are renewed annually. In the name of security, for eighteen years Israel imposed a permit system and curfews on the Palestinians within its 1948 borders while systematically confiscating Arab land. After 1967, the permit system was refined and implemented in the occupied territories in a more thorough fashion.

Permits and identity cards are not new inventions, although they were experimented with and perfected in colonial situations. They are used in times of war and by settler regimes, as seen in apartheid South Africa, in British colonies like Palestine, Egypt, and India, and during the two world wars (Abu-Zahra and Kay 2013). What is unique about the Israeli case is the longevity of the system and the fact that it is accompanied by policies of displacement, spatial segregation, and denationalisation.

In the words of Nadia Abu-Zahra and Adah Kay (2013, 21), "the censuses for 1948 and 1967 were used for denationalization and dispossession." As they point out, the purpose of these censuses was to underregister the Palestinian population, gather information about property ownership, and document the extent of family separation due to expulsion. Furthermore, Israel used the label "infiltrator" to criminalise Palestinian refugees who risked being shot at upon returning to their homes. As part of its surveillance measures, blacklists were established to penalise Palestinians who refused to cooperate with Israel's colonial enterprise as informers or sell their land to the Zionists. The construction of so-called "village files" by the Israeli military served to keep track of land ownership, expulsion of Palestinians, and the social structure of the village. When used in combination, the identity cards, permits, including temporary permits, and restrictions on mobility "made life so difficult for Palestinians that it amounted to 'induced transfer'" (ibid., 5).

Allison Brown deploys a Foucauldian framework to examine productive power in encounters between soldiers and the Palestinian population at the checkpoints. She notes that "observation is in itself a form, perhaps the main form, of resistance" (A. Brown 2004, 516). Cameras that are distributed freely to the local population by the human rights organisation B'Tselem are used to document the abusive behaviour of soldiers at the checkpoints. Like other researchers, Brown notes the random, if not chaotic, nature of the surveillance system: "checkpoints and roadblocks are often unpredictable in terms of the time it will take to pass, and because 'flying' points could be set up at any time" (ibid., 513). The focus on the everyday lives of refugees is a common theme in ethnographic studies of Palestine.

Patterns of resistance that are not acknowledged as such are decoded to reveal how Palestinians negotiate their way through contradictory positioning and liminality. These strategies allow researchers to configure subjectivities instead of situating our understanding of Palestinian refugees in the framework of "recognition and rights." Nasser Abourahme (2011, 455) succinctly states the dilemma facing researches in such settings:

> In other words, people are using the different constitutive nodes of the present – even the checkpoint – to reproduce their lives in ways that do not correspond to anything we might recognize as resistance or anything we can reduce to survivalism. How do we interpret the colonial subject that is neither in revolt nor in open crisis? What kinds of languages of signification do we read, if any, in her/his quotidian practices? How to avoid reading or ascribing intent? Such questions seemingly need to be premised on a more fundamental query: what kind of time is this curious present? And whose temporality are we talking about?

Somewhat critical of ascribing semiotic meaning to understanding resistance, Livia Wick (2011) addresses the intersection of time and space (described in the borrowed neologism *zamkaniyah*) in the context of the West Bank's occupation by Israel. The temporality of space is shaped by a daily routine of occupation in which Palestinians are subjected to endless waiting and detours, whether on the road, at work, or in establishing stable relations – so much so that, as the Israeli journalist Amira Hass (2006) has remarked, it amounts to a "theft of time." Mindful of attempts to romanticise resistance in acts that are not perceived as such by the Palestinians themselves, Wick turns her attention to carceral analysis and the impact of closures and curfews on women in particular. In simple terms, Wick (2011, 28) writes, "instead I examine practices of living, waiting and making do every day in specific political and economic circumstances." She finds an empowering dimension to this existence. Women form alliances locally and across class lines. "Palestine under closure," says Wick:

> ... seems to be transforming gender practices by giving women greater influence in their affinal families, making them responsible for the care of their children with little help from the extended family. The individualized responsibilities allow them to recode their productive and reproductive labour as vital for the continuity of the family and community. (Ibid., 31)

Biometrics as the new biopolitics

As a suspect minority, the Palestinians in Israel look with trepidation at any efforts to expand the system of population monitoring and registration in the name of efficiency. In their eyes, this has the potential to track their movements more thoroughly and store personal information about them in real time. The biometric campaign in Israel was opposed by human rights organisations for fear that it would compromise individual privacy and give governmental bodies wider access to personal information without securing adequate oversight (Kisch 2013; Klinger 2011). Two-thirds of Israeli Jews and Arabs said in a public opinion survey that the biometric information stored by the Ministry of Interior is not immune to leaks and other infringements. However, 57 per cent of Arabs and 42 per cent of Jews agreed to the establishment of the database (Maagar 2009). Unlike European countries, for example, citizens in Israel are not the owners of biometric information about them stored in this database, which one report described as "the most expansive in the Western world" (Wilson 2013). Biometrics, as commentators note, establishes a closer link between the biological and political, forging what is known as the biopolitical (Lebovic and Pinchuk 2010). The driving force behind the biometric legislation in Israel, which became law in 2009 but whose implementation was delayed following a two-year pilot project that started in August 2013, is the argument that it ensures security and protection against theft of personal information.

The criticisms of this initiative cover issues such as reliability of the technology, possible leakages of the stored information to a third party, and failure to explore other technological means for collecting and preserving personal information, but the most serious issue of all, as expressed by human rights organisations and activists, is the unrestricted use and sharing of such a database by various governmental institutions, particularly the police, without a court order. The Israeli Supreme Court has described the biometric legislation as "extreme and harmful" (in Zarchin 2012). Jonathan Klinger (2011) captures the essence of such criticism:

> As we learned from a recently leaked document, the only reason that a biometric database is required was to pass information to the police about the citizens of Israel. This is the reason the police rejected a safer mean[s] of storing biometric information . . . The same police that use violence on the protesters from the right and left, who crush political dissent by Arabs and social activists, now ask for unprecedented authority over Israeli citizens.

The Association for Civil Rights in Israel has mounted a campaign to stop the biometric project, including its pilot project. The association argues:

> . . . the "pilot" was designed so that most of the issues it examined were not at all related to the question of its necessity, but rather to technical aspects that were supposed to be examined anyway. Before the experiment even began, a governmental paper defining the investigation determined that the database is necessary and that there is no point in examining alternatives.
> (ACRI 2012b, 38)

The Supreme Court justices have expressed criticism that "the 'pilot' plan excludes the possibility of genuine investigation" (ibid.). A thorough criticism of the Israeli biometric pilot project is provided by Jonny Silver (2013), who asks citizens not to adopt the project because of potential privacy violations; most importantly, he notes that "the project is designed not to protect your identity but to enable the authorities to spy on individuals" and that "the authority overseeing the project has proven to be unreliable."

In court cases that have resulted in acquittal or discontinuance, biometrics has also been criticised by the European Court of Human Rights on the grounds that it is unconstitutional to keep personal data (e.g., DNA, fingerprints, and cellular phone information). At the core of these concerns is the potential for privacy violation. As Halabi (2011, 212) points out, the Communication Data Law allows the police to collect identification data (i.e., name, national ID number, phone number, and address), location data, subscriber data, and transmission data related to the sender and receiver, "time of sending or receiving, duration and volume of the transmission."

The boomerang effect

> It should never be forgotten that while colonization, with its techniques and its political and juridical weapons, obviously transported European models to other continents, it also had a considerable boomerang effect on the mechanisms of power in the West, and on the apparatuses, institutions, and techniques of power. A whole series of colonial models was brought back to the West, and the result was that the West could practice something resembling colonization, or an internal colonialism, on itself. (Foucault 2003, 103)

It is a common observation that surveillance adopted in monitoring marginal groups and minorities (those perceived as a threat to the state) will eventually be extended to the majority, and in colonial situations, as Foucault remarks in the passage above (see Graham 2012) and as Alfred McCoy (2009) documents with respect to the Philippines, colonial methods of surveillance make their way back to the metropole. Witness, for example, the recent use of surveillance vehicles in the West Bank that were first introduced by the military in a Tel Aviv demonstration on behalf of social justice (Sheizaf 2012). It has not escaped commentators that Arab citizens of the state are targeted by the police for generalised surveillance, even when they join peaceful social justice demonstrations like the one held in Tel Aviv in 2012. But "unlike the directives about Jewish demonstrators, which focus on rioters and anarchists, the section about Arabs does not specify which type of demonstrators police should watch out for, referring only to Arabs in general" (Edelman and Arad 2012). A telling example of the extent of routine, day-to-day surveillance of the Palestinian population is an incident involving beachgoers in Tel Aviv. The Municipality of Tel Aviv employs inspectors to enforce city bylaws and maintain cleanliness of the beaches. These inspectors are not police officers and thus do not have the authority to arrest people. The inspectors spotted what looked like Arab bathers and asked them for their identity cards. It turned out that these were Palestinian men from the occupied territories who had crossed the border without a permit (which is next to impossible to obtain) in search of employment. The inspectors turned the Palestinians over to the police. In the words of an Israeli activist, "Israel has become a nation of informers" (in R. Arad 2012).

Israeli state surveillance is not confined to Palestinian citizens; it touches the lives of the Jewish majority as well, although it takes different forms and is not so bound up with nationalistic considerations (Ilan 2007, 2008a, 2008b, 2009; Michael 2007; Yoaz 2007a, 2007b, 2007c). Until 2004 the Israeli army tapped all outgoing international telephone calls. As reported by Andrew Stevens (2011, 7):

> The concern over expanding the power of police to monitor communication data is not ill-founded. Between 2006 and 2007, wiretapping increased by over 100 per cent in drug investigations and by 172 per cent in the fight against 'organized crime,' according to figures submitted by the police to the Knesset Constitution, Law and Justice Committee. Electronic surveillance overall increased by 22 per cent from 1,128 instances in 2006 to 1,375 in 2007. As a comparison, authorities in the United States conducted a total of 1,839 wiretaps in all of 2006. Israeli courts refused only 11 surveillance requests by the police in 2007. In total, police eavesdropped on 778 suspects and witnesses on 1,205 telephone and cell phone lines.

In 2007 the police reported that there were 1,375 wiretap cases in Israel (Ilan 2008a, 2008b; Levy 2008). What is significant about these data, in addition to the disproportionate wiretapping, compared to the United States, which has a population fifty times larger than that of Israel, is that the courts in Israel almost automatically approve police requests for wiretaps. Of 400 wiretaps analysed in 2006, only 3 were not approved by the courts. This led Privacy International (2007), a nongovernmental watchdog of privacy practices worldwide, to comment that "[al]though the courts are supposed to weigh privacy concerns against law enforcement needs before authorizing wiretaps, authorization is, in practice, almost automatic upon request." By several accounts, "Israel's omniscient ears," as the title of a report in *Le Monde Diplomatique* calls the Urim military base (Hager 2010), make Israel one of the Western countries with the largest listening posts. Situated in the Negev and "hidden until now," this military base "has rows of satellite dishes that covertly intercept phone calls, emails and other communications from the Middle East, Europe, Africa and Asia. Its antennas monitor shipping and would have spied on the aid ships [the Gaza flotilla] in the days before they were seized" in 2009 (ibid.; see also Melman 2010). Two-thirds of the Israeli public endorse the US government's practice of listening in on communications of world leaders, and 90 per cent believe that the United States listens in on Israeli leaders as well. Survey results reveal a lopsided picture, with two-thirds of the Palestinians in Israel being opposed to spying on foreign leaders (IDI 2013).

The so-called "Big Brother Law," approved by the Knesset in 2007, allows the police to set up a database on citizens that contains telephone numbers (including unlisted ones), names of mobile telephone subscribers, serial numbers of mobile phones, and maps of antenna locations. The database has been described as the "biggest database in the West" (Ilan 2007).

In a worldwide ranking of surveillance societies based on thirteen privacy indicators, Privacy International (2007) assigned Israel a score of 2.3 on a scale from 1 (extensive surveillance) to 5 (minimal surveillance). Israel was found to practise maximum surveillance with respect to two of the thirteen indicators: giving police access to personal data and monitoring travel and transborder data flows. No doubt as a result of the attack of 11 September 2001, Privacy International placed the United States, United Kingdom, Spain, and Australia in the same category (ibid.). Since these are aggregate country data, the report does not deal with the differential application of surveillance to specific societal groups such as minorities. However, based on various reports by human rights organisations, there is no doubt that, compared to the Jewish population, the Palestinian minority in Israel is subjected to more intensive forms of surveillance.

Until recently, debates about privacy violations did not rank high on the public agenda in Israel, and even less prominent were concerns over Israeli policies in the OPT that impinge on the privacy of the Palestinian population.

Conclusion

In the twenty-first century, the issues of state and corporate surveillance have become paramount. Revelations about the Obama administration's use of snooping tactics to spy on the telephone conversations of citizens and to collect personal data, as justified by the national security argument, seem to dominate the news. In search of "terrorists," the United States is prepared to bypass the issuing of legal warrants and court procedures in order to cast its surveillance web so that it includes domestic and foreign nationals – both in the United States and overseas. The collection of personal data by parts of the corporate sector, such as the telephone companies, and their willingness to share such data with the Obama administration have added to the fears expressed by human rights groups.

The past two decades have seen an accelerated expansion of overt surveillance practices in warfare. The use of drones in Iraq, Afghanistan, and other parts of the Middle East, such as Yemen, is now acknowledged as a form of targeted assassination through remote control. With the push of a button, soldiers sitting behind their desk thousands of kilometres away from the conflict zone can wreak havoc on unsuspected communities through so-called "collateral damage."

An old hand in the business of surveillance, Israel uses its military power to market its military hardware, particularly drones, as field-tested technology. Palestinians in the occupied territories constitute a laboratory for drone testing that Israel touts in its sales pitch. Like the United States, Israel is immune from international legal sanctions against the use of such lethal weapons.

Surveillance technologies of one kind or another are a constant factor that highlights the workings of colonialism – whether in the sixteenth or the twenty-first century. Resistance to surveillance as it spreads from the colony to the home country is gaining ground. National security arguments are being subjected to scrutiny, and there is more awareness of the role of surveillance in violating human rights. It is accurate to say that such awareness is more evident in the advanced countries, the originators of colonialism. Whether resistance to surveillance will be manifest in the third world remains to be seen.

Notes

1 A good example of the relationship between colonial knowledge and empire management is provided by David Nugent (2010), who covers a period from the late nineteenth century to the turn of the twenty-first century in analysing the role played by social scientists in the home country in furthering American political and economic interests in the face of crises in capitalist accumulation. Social scientists were instrumental in enabling American imperialism to manage its overseas interests without having to physically occupy foreign lands.
2 Postcolonial India is very much occupied with adopting biometrics as a technology of surveillance and classification of the population that will link various institutions of the state apparatus by means of unique identification systems in order to govern the most populace democracy in the world. Arguments of national security loom large in this debate and transcend concerns of efficiency (Jacobsen 2012).
3 Nikolas Rose and Peter Miller (1992, 174) make the point that in the modern nation-state, "power is not so much a matter of imposing constraints upon citizens as of 'making up' citizens capable of bearing a kind of regulated freedom." However, this may not be true in colonised regions, where naked power and coercion are the basic tools of ruling.
4 My translation from the original Arabic.
5 The quotation is from a Palestinian in the West Bank who was interviewed by anthropologist Julie Peteet.
6 The practice of targeted assassination continues to this day and is carried out using sophisticated surveillance technologies such as drones that track down and assassinate Palestinians who appear on Israel's list of wanted people (Whitaker 2004). It is estimated that between 2000 and 2008, Israel assassinated 400 individuals using the extrajudicial technique of targeted killings (N. Gordon 2008).
7 For a discussion of extrajudicial killings of Palestinians by Palestinians in the occupied territories, see Yizhar Be'er and Saleh Abdel-Jawad (1994).
8 It was only in 2005 that the Ministry of Education removed from its midst the Shin Bet operatives who were responsible for screening teachers in the Arab sector for political orientations (Khromchenko 2005), although it is not clear whether the Shin Bet input into hiring and firing Arab teachers has been completely eliminated.
9 Furthermore, the Israeli government has approved a bill that would ban state funding of any nongovernmental organisations involved in events to commemorate the Nakba (Khoury, Zarchin, and Ravid 2009), and the Ministry of Education has banned mention of the Nakba in books used in public schools (Kashti 2009).
10 The central point underlying Weizman's work relates to his notion of contradictions. The relation between state power and Israel's settlement policies and occupation of the West Bank is not to be understood in terms of a one-to-one correspondence, with the

former determining the latter. The relation between space and power "is responding to many and diffused forces and influences; space is the product of conflicting interests" (in Weizman and Kastrissianakis 2007).
11 A similar point is made by Btihaj Ajana (2005, 7), who remarks that "discipline and control are being merged together within the realm of biopolitics through the hybridisation of management techniques and the dispersion of networks of control." This can be seen through the use of CCTV in urban centres and in the surveillance of roads. As part of its privatisation efforts, the Israeli military has devised a new course to train civilians in the use of its surveillance drones, which are marketed worldwide. It is important to point out that there is a close link between the training program, the Israeli military, and the civilian companies chosen to train operators in the use of the drones (Y. Azoulay 2007; Fulghum and Wall 2002). The Israeli military has gone one step further and installed unmanned video-directed machine-gun stations at Gaza checkpoints (*World Tribune* 2008).
12 A similar point is made by Derek Gregory (2004) and, along similar lines, by Honida Ghanim (2008).

4

BIOPOLITICS, EUGENICS, AND POPULATION DISCOURSE

> [The] population is nothing more than what the state takes care of for its own sake. (Foucault 1988, 160)

I pointed out in previous chapters that biopolitics and territory constitute two of the three core elements of any modern nation-state – both of which correspond to a third element, that of state security. Colonial and colonising states exhibit special features pertaining to each of these elements. In this chapter, I examine biopolitics in Zionist discourse in the pre-1948 period and how biopolitical governmentality is exercised by Israel within its 1967 borders and the occupied territories. Although in commenting on the European nation-state, Michel Foucault is correct to single out the shift in the eighteenth century from sovereignty over territory to the disciplining of the population, the factor of colonialism places the debate over biopolitics in a different light. In settler-colonial cases, as with nation-states, it is true that the state's care for the population is self-interested, as Foucault opines in the quotation above, but the rationalities for this self-interest and the modalities of how it affects coloniser and colonised are strikingly different inside Israel and in the occupied territories. In the name of state security, the state pursues a two-pronged policy: in this chapter I examine state policies regarding demography and population management, and in chapter 5 I show how violence and necropolitics emerge as integral components of the state's colonial policy. This is because the Israeli state is already defined in ethno-national terms that preclude its Palestinian citizens from taking part in defining the public good, which as we saw in the previous chapter is being reinforced through the introduction of a slew of legislations in the Israeli Knesset to strengthen the Jewish ethnic character of the state at the expense of Arabs' rights and their national identity. The brutal pursuit of the Palestinians in

Gaza and the West Bank, in the name of security, is a testimony to the fact that biopolitics is not just about letting people live and leaving others to die, but also about the state's conscious efforts to manage the physical and social opposition to its grand colonial schemes.

Biopolitics is not the exclusive prerogative of the state and its ruling apparatus, as per Foucault (2007). It is also worth considering biopolitics from the bottom up, so to speak; to invoke James C. Scott's seminal book *Weapons of the Weak* (1987), for the Palestinians, there is also biopolitics of the weak. How do minorities, the colonised, the disenfranchised, and the poor adopt a policy of resistance and survival that relies on thinking about reproductive strategies? Consider, for example, the following newspaper headline: "Palestinian inmates 'sneak sperm out of jail'" (*Aljazeera* 2013). The story explains that a fertility doctor in a Nablus clinic on the West Bank confirmed that a Palestinian detainee in an Israeli prison smuggled his sperm to his wife, who had a child from the artificial insemination. According to the *New York Times*, the same fertility clinic assisted fifty Palestinian women to conceive by means of *in vitro* fertilisation (Abu Aker and Rudoren 2013). A similar process of artificial insemination involving sperm smuggled from jail was reported in Gaza (Reuters 2014). In *Birthing the Nation: Strategies of Palestinian Women in Israel* (2002), anthropologist Rhoda Kana'aneh provides a nuanced discussion of reproductive strategies in which nationalism, modernisation, and the confrontation with Israel figure prominently. Although family planning is notoriously difficult to implement successfully in more stable societies, Kana'aneh points out that in addition to economics and the well-being of the newly born, the decisions of Palestinian families regarding family size are very much tied to nationalist considerations, even as they aspire to modernise. Here lies the crux of the dilemma: the clash between modernisation and demography. But resistance is not only about reproductive strategies. It is also about confronting the state in its daily brutal pursuits and in its carceral prison policies (J. Young 2012).

This chapter deals with the following: the nineteenth-century debate concerning nation building and population selection, also known as eugenics; Zionism and eugenics; the profile of Arthur Ruppin, an arch Zionist coloniser and a promoter of eugenics in Palestine; population balance as biopolitics; Zionist population discourse; modernisation and demography in a colonial context; population containment as a component of biopolitics, and ideology and public opinion.

From biopolitics to eugenics

Since the eighteenth century, if not earlier, demography has played an important role in population management by the state. Biopolitics assumed importance in state planning as demography and quantitative statistical techniques became prominent tools of social engineering with the ascendancy of positivism in the works of French thinkers August Comte and Henri Saint-Simon in the seventeenth and eighteenth centuries. However, it was through British empiricism of the nineteenth century that social statistics were systematically introduced at the state level in population policy analysis. Correlation and regression analyses owe their debut to Francis Galton and Karl Pearson, who, through their key positions in the eugenics movement in Britain, made use of their positions as statisticians to solve social problems and advocate the manipulation of population selection in accordance with the then popular doctrine of social Darwinism (see MacKenzie 1981).

On the face of it, population statistics assume a neutral stance. They are considered to be objective representations of the social body. This "standard view," as discussed in chapter 3, has been challenged in constructivist studies of science and technology. The underlying assumption of this perspective is that scientific practices are embedded in a social context. The problem is not that data or numbers are fictitious or idiosyncratic inventions of the people who collect them or that they do not represent a tangible reality out there, but rather that the construction of specific categories and the interpretation of data are theory-laden and reflect assumptions by human agents. Consider anthropologist Arjun Appadurai's (1996, 154–55) statement that ethnic conflict and "treachery about group identity" have much to do with "the large-scale identities created, transformed, and reified by modern state apparatuses," of which the census is an integral part. This observation assumes special importance in postcolonial and deeply divided societies. Timothy Mitchell and Roger Owen (1990) remark that when faced with a traditional social order that exhibits multiple loyalties and hybrid identities, as in the colonial Arab world, "the colonial state sought to reconstitute them [identities] as fixed and singular categories by means of its control over certain means of enumeration, such as the holding of a census" (in Zacharia 1996, 40; see also Benedict Anderson 1994b). Equally important, as Christine Zacharia (1996, 3) points out, "the post-colonial state had to reconstruct its national community upon and against the normalized categories constructed through colonialism. Resistant groups . . . are automatically considered 'anti-national' or 'primordial' and targeted demographically to be brought in line with state interests." As documented in the previous chapter's discussion of surveillance and colonialism, the observations of these scholars constitute an important part of a burgeoning study of population, censuses, and maps in settler and colonial regimes (Cohn 1996; Scott 1998). It is with these observations in mind that I turn to tracing the process of population management of Palestinians as it evolved under Israeli control – both in Israel proper and in the West Bank and Gaza.

Regional, national, and international conflicts impact populations differently, and they invariably involve population analysis through head counting and classification, what Ian Hacking (1999) calls "making people up." Population studies have come a long way since the time of Thomas Malthus, who postulated a correlation between population size and food production, arguing that whereas populations increased geometrically, food production did so at an arithmetical rate. If unchecked, population size will in due course outstrip food supply and will thus lead to conflict that will disproportionately impact the poor in society. More than two centuries later, it is clear that Malthus underestimated the power of science and technology in their introduction of birth control methods and in their ability to make food production more efficient.[1] Less than 5 per cent of the labour force in countries like Canada and the United States is employed in agriculture, yet this contingent is able to feed hundreds of millions of people around the world. Ethnic conflict is better understood as a means of ascertaining group identities and securing scarce state resources. There are close to two hundred nation-states worldwide, the overwhelming majority of which can be considered multinational. Very few states can boast of having a pure ethnic composition. With the rise of multiculturalism, the force of ethnic identity is being brought to bear in a direct, and in many instances violent, way upon political representation at the national and regional levels. Writers have isolated a relationship between demography, citizen representation, and violence. According to Monica Toft (2002), under certain conditions differential demographic growth and *biopolitics* (my term, not hers) play a central role in destabilising states and enhancing the prospects of violence in multiethnic societies. Toft, who deals with Israel as one of her case studies, postulates and confirms a set of hypotheses in which she argues with regard to the Arab-Jewish population balance that in the face of demographic differentials, democratic states are more liable to be internally destabilised than authoritarian ones; differential demographic growth will destabilise democratic states if the position of the growing group begins to approach that of the majority; if allocation of state resources is linked to ethnic membership, differential demographic growth will contribute to state destabilisation, and authoritarian states that are exposed to external threats are more likely to be destabilised than democratic states as a result of differential demographic growth.

Zionism and eugenics

> Castrating the mentally ill, encouraging reproduction among families "numbered among the intelligentsia" and limiting the size of "families of [Middle] Eastern origin" and "preventing . . . lives that are lacking in purpose" – these proposals are not from some program of the Third Reich but rather were brought up by key figures in the Zionist establishment of the Land of Israel during the period of the British Mandate. (Traubmann 2004)

Academic studies and popular reports about the role of eugenics in Zionist writings and Israeli state building reveal the deep influence of German eugenics thinking on childrearing and the socialisation practices in pre- and post-1948 Israel (Stoler-Liss 2003), the early Zionist immigration policies, and the mental health profession in the country (Petersen-Overton 2008). This is an area of scholarship that, until the past decade, had been hitherto little explored in Israeli historical research. The ideas of German eugenicists were influential in Zionist circles, according to Etan Bloom (2011) and Rakefet Zalashik (in Y. Feldman 2009), among others. Several writers have highlighted the importance of Jewish racial purity, mental health, and eugenics in the debates about Zionist settlement and Jewish nation building in Palestine dating back to the nineteenth century, while showing how the discussion of eugenics and social Darwinism was greatly influenced by German thinking at the time, with German Jews playing an important part (Falk 1998, 2006; Hirsch 2009; Karpel 2006; Kirsh 2003; Sand 2009; Traubmann 2004).

Sachlav Stoler-List, who wrote her doctoral dissertation on the health services in 1950s Israel, remarks that "Eugenics is considered to be something that only happened in Germany," which "was indeed the most murderous manifestation of eugenics, but in fact it was a movement that attracted many followers. In every place it took on a unique, local aspect. It is interesting to note that both in Germany and in Israel a link was made between eugenics, health and nationalism" (in Traubmann 2004). Upon further investigation, she discovered that eugenics was not a peripheral pursuit but was fostered and encouraged by those who "created and managed the health system in Israel." She explains that Dr Joseph Meir, head of Kupat Holim Clali, the largest public health provider at the time, who occupied a central "position at the very heart of the Zionist medical establishment in the land of Israel in the mid-1930s, brought young mothers the gospel of eugenics, warned them about degeneracy and transmitted the message to them about their obligation and responsibility for bearing only healthy children," and he did not hesitate to advocate the castration of the mentally ill (in ibid.). Although in the late 1930s, with Nazi ideology looming large over Europe, attempts were made to disavow eugenics, and specialists refrained from using the term in health publications, Meir remained committed to the teachings of eugenics. In response to Prime Minister David Ben-Gurion's policy in the 1950s of encouraging large Jewish families through economic rewards, Meir wrote:

> We have no interest in the 10th child or even in the seventh in poor families from the East ... In today's reality we should pray frequently for a second child in a family that is a part of the intelligentsia. The poor classes of the population must not be instructed to have many children, but rather restricted. (In ibid.)

Although Israeli research on eugenics remains largely unacknowledged, I explore below several works that reveal a keen historical interest in the subject. Their authors include Jewish scientists in Palestine who were committed to the Zionist mantras, although Nurit Kirsh (2003) claims that such research and practice in Israel were driven by "unconscious" ideological commitments to the teachings of eugenics.

Discussing the views of historian Rakefet Zalashik, who authored a book about the history of psychiatry in Palestine, Yotam Feldman (2009) comments that in Israel "the eugenics-based concept of 'social engineering' was part of the psychiatric mainstream here from the 1930s through the 1950s." It is common to distinguish between the theory and practice of eugenics in order to argue that the interest in eugenics was mainly scientific, not practical. Yet Zalashik notes that the psychiatrists who came to Palestine in the 1930s were familiar with the science of eugenics from their German training and advocated its application in the colonisation of Palestine (in ibid.). This had direct implication for introducing the concept of race and linking it to aptitude in the classification of Jews, as observed by one practising psychiatrist at the time who described Jews from the Middle East as follows:

> Their consciousness, with its meager content, does not place any special demands on life, and it slavishly submits to the outward conditions, and for this reason, does not enter into confrontation and so gives rise to a relatively very small percentage of functional illnesses in the nervous system and in terms of mental illness in particular. (In ibid.)

Mental health, with its eugenic corollary, was subscribed to by the Zionist movement at the time as an essential aspect of nation building. According to Zalashik:

> The theory was that a healthy nation was needed in order to fulfill the Zionist vision in Israel. There was a powerful economic aspect to this view of things – the idea being to prevent people who were perceived as a burden on society from bringing children into the world. And homosexuals and frigid women also fell into this category. (In ibid.)

Ruppin: a sociologist and eugenicist

A central figure and a key Zionist official in the prestate period who advocated eugenics was Arthur Ruppin. He wrote extensively on Jewish demography, although his demography about Palestine was found by Justin McCarthy (1990) to be wanting for its bias in overestimating Jewish immigration to Palestine. Ruppin was identified in the annals of the Zionist project as the central "colonizer" and "[t]he Father of Jewish/Zionist settlement in Palestine" (Bloom 2011, 2, 8); he headed the Palestine Office of the World Zionist Organization and established the Department for the Sociology of the Jews at the Hebrew University (ibid., 1, 5).

"Throughout his writings, Ruppin explicitly stressed the superiority of the Ashkenazic Jews to the Sephardic and Oriental Jews in terms of intelligence, creativity, mathematical ability, agility, imagination and hygiene," arguing that "with proper eugenic treatment, [they] could become a new, productive Jewish-Yemenite type, capable of serving the new nation that was evolving" (Bloom 2007a, 198, 199). Thus "Ruppin's cultural planning was devised in such a way as to 'purify' the Yemenites through a eugenic process of selection which would ensure the survival only of those capable of performing hard, physical labor" (ibid., 198). Etan Bloom makes the point that Ruppin used statistics as a means for differentiation: "statistics were more than a means of representing ethnicity; they were instrumental in its very construction" (ibid., 199).

More than other commentators, Bloom has provided an in-depth investigation into Ruppin's worldview as a Zionist planner and the main "colonizer" in Palestine. For the present purpose, three main conclusions can be discerned from Bloom's account. First, Ruppin was a key Zionist official of note who effected a shift from ideology to knowledge and science (the so-called "scientification of Zionism") (Bloom 2011, 360) as the main stay of Zionist strategy in nation building (ibid., 70). His science encompassed statistics, demography, and eugenics. Bloom (2007a, 188) describes Ruppin's positivist orientations as follows: "Ruppin's yearning for expert research, as well as his passion for statistics in general, reflected his dream of establishing a society based on knowledge, rather than ideology, faith, or superficial propaganda."

Second, Ruppin was relentless in advocating mental hygiene as the cornerstone of nation building. In his commentary about Germany, he generally "supported the state and its crucial function and gave it the decisive right to intervene in the life of the individual, promoting the idea that social welfare and education had to be combined with a program of eugenics, in which invalids and the mentally ill would be discouraged" (Bloom 2011, 54). Indeed, according to Bloom (2007b, 333), in 1893 Ruppin "felt complete identification with the anti-Semitic parties, and even asked to be accepted by one of them as a 'German patriot.'" Bloom describes how, a decade later, as a result of Ruppin's personal experience with anti-Semitism, he began to identify with Zionism (ibid., 337).

Third, Ruppin expressed awareness of the Arabs of Palestine, arguing at one level that they should not be treated as natives in the colonial sense. Already in 1911 he described the Arabs as an "important political force" (Bloom 2007b, 303). Yet this did not prevent him from adopting what essentially remains the dominant Zionist position of superiority toward the native population, which is built on the tactics of "postponement" and "displacement."

"Ruppin's case," according to Bloom (2007b, 348):

> ... shows how Zionism coincided with the weltanschauung of some Nazi party members and supporters at least until the mid-1930s. Contrary to the common narrative, which dismissed such links as merely "instrumental" or "pragmatic," it reveals how they were based on a number of common assumptions that cannot be ignored when researching the roots of modern Hebrew cultural identity.

As a matter of fact, Nazi spokesmen quoted Ruppin extensively to justify their own eugenic position.

Dafna Hirsch (2009) supports this claim by noting that the Zionist use of eugenics had a dual purpose: it made possible the use of race as a unifying concept in the service of Jewish nationalism, but it also made possible the classification of the Jews as diverse groups consisting of racial hierarchies. Race in this sense acts as a cultural and biological marker. In-group classification, she argues, was most evident among Jewish scientists who settled in Palestine and sought ways to distinguish European from Middle Eastern Jews. This was consistent, she argues, with Ruppin's eugenic position, which "identified race with mental, intellectual and cultural traits" (ibid., 604). Eugenics for Ruppin had direct ramifications for procreation. In his words, which appeared in the second volume of his *Sociology of the Jews* (1935, 77), "eugenic requirements in the choice of marriage partners are becoming popular in Europe. This way Jews with degenerative symptoms are destined to refrain from procreation and the race will continue to be purified" (in Hirsch 2009, 604).

In his discussion of Bloom's findings, historian and journalist Tom Segev (2009) remarks that what is "less known about Ruppin's views is his belief that the realization of Zionism demanded 'racial purity' among the Jews. In part, his views were inspired by the works of anti-Semitic thinkers, including some of the original Nazi ideologists." Segev goes on to note that Ruppin was not only a follower of what later became known as the Nazi eugenic doctrines but "also had an impact on their formulation" (ibid.). According to Nadia Abu El-Haj (2012, 80), Ruppin also forged a connection between "race, science, eugenics, and Jewish nationalism" as part of his efforts to justify Zionist colonisation of Palestine. With race being a main marker of Jewish nationalism, Ruppin believed that a genetically based racial hierarchy existed among the Jews, with the Western Ashkenazi Jews being more biologically and culturally endowed than Middle Eastern Mizrahi Jews. Similarly, he warned against the dilution of the Jewish stock through marriage to non-Jews. Social Darwinism was a doctrine that formed Ruppin's *Weltanschauung* (Piterberg 2008, 82). The function of eugenics, according to him, is to correct for these factors by adopting policies of population selection and weeding out the degenerate and feeble elements of society.

The debate over Zionism and eugenics is not only of historical interest, as reflected in the ongoing discussion of who is a Jew.[2] This discussion has brought to the fore revelations regarding government policies toward non-European Jews and the place of eugenics in regulating Middle Eastern Jews in Israeli society. Two particular cases are worth noting. The first involves the treatment of Ethiopian Jews who immigrated to Israel in 1984 and 1991. At first, official spokespersons rejected the charge of Ethiopian women that, while waiting in transit camps, they were coaxed by Israeli immigration officials to accept inoculation with the long-acting contraceptive drug Depo-Provera; failing to comply would have jeopardised their chance to go to Israel. However, in 2013, it was revealed by Israeli health officials that such policies did actually exist but were discontinued. Commentators have concluded that "the women's testimony could help explain the almost 50% decline over the past 10 years in the birth rate of Israel's Ethiopian community" (Nesher 2012, 2013).

The second case centres on the treatment of Yemenite Jews who were airlifted to Israel in the late 1940s. According to William Pfaff (1997), "It was revealed that hundreds of immigrant children were literally stolen from their Arabic-speaking parents for adoption by parents of European Jewish origin, in an attempt to meld the Yemenite Jews into what then was the European mainstream." Raphael Falk (1998), a professor of eugenics at the Hebrew University, who argues that the Jews do not constitute a biological race based on DNA, has challenged Pfaff's claims by noting that based on first-hand experience, this was not a generalised practice against Yemenite children. Rather, care was taken to safeguard the health of these immigrants, although no doubt there were some cases of abuse. In his reply, Pfaff (1998) quotes statements from the Israeli press, some of which have claimed that "we are dealing with a [Yemenite] population whose primitivism touches the limits . . . They are hardly superior to Arabs, or blacks, or other barbarians." The feeling of superiority reaches the highest levels of Israeli leadership. Pfaff quotes Prime Minister Ben-Gurion, who has remarked with regard to immigrants from Yemen that "the elementary basis of socialization is lacking . . . [The immigrant's] relationship to his wife and children is that of a primitive . . . His physical aptitudes are restricted and he fails to observe even the minimum of hygiene" (ibid., brackets in original).

The academic debate about genetics has spilled over into the conflict between Israel and the Palestinians, with scientific research paying the price this time. Science thrives and advances on controversies. But this is not what happened when a group of geneticists, led by the well-known Spanish researcher Antonio Arnaiz-Villena (2001), published a paper in the *Human Immunology* journal that examined variations in the immune genes among people in the Middle East region. At the outset, the paper, which was "dedicated to all Palestinians and Israelis who are suffering [from] war" (ibid., 889), demonstrated that the Jews are not a genetically distinct group compared to other people in the region and that they and the Palestinians have a common genetic pool. After publishing the peer-reviewed article, the journal's editor wrote to its readers informing them that the paper in its electronic and hardcopy formats would be expunged from the pages of the journal, something rarely done in academic forums. The journal justified its unusual actions not on the basis of scientific merit but on what the editor and some readers of the journal judged to be the presence of an offending reference that the Palestinians in the occupied territories live "with Jewish colonists." It could very well be that the offending aspects of the paper are the conclusions themselves, which are routinely rejected by Israel supporters, including academics, on political grounds. In the words of British geneticist Sir Walter Bodmer, "If the journal did not like the paper, they shouldn't have published it in the first place. Why wait until it has appeared before acting like this?" (in McKie 2001).

Population balance as biopolitics

The moribund Oslo agreement of the so-called "peace process" is by no means the latest document to spell out the biopolitical implications of the conflict between Israel and the Palestinians. It does, however, provide a vivid and recent example of the centrality of population and territory in ethno-national conflicts, and it gives Israel, the dominant party in the Oslo negotiations at the time, surveillance and veto power over population management, airspace, water, and territorial control – using national security as the main rationale for the biopolitical arguments. To this day, the Palestinian Authority is obligated under the Oslo agreement to turn over to Israel on a regular basis data about births and deaths and about any changes in the entry and exit of Palestinian residents of the territories (Human Rights Watch 2012). Since I have dealt with this issue at length elsewhere (Zureik 2001), it is sufficient here to update the argument with more recent discussions and to provide a summary of the main points raised in the study as they relate to population management in a colonial context.

Zionist population discourse

My contention is that demography, as is the case with all colonial-settler regimes, acts as a cornerstone of Zionist attempts to secure a Jewish majority in a land that was overwhelmingly inhabited by an indigenous Arab population at the time of the first Zionist settlement in Palestine in the late nineteenth century. The demographic debate started in earnest even before imperial Britain issued the Balfour Declaration in 1917, which promised a "national home for the Jewish people" in Palestine. The various reports issued by the colonial power in response to Arab and Jewish reactions are a testimony to the competing claims by both sides regarding population, absorptive capacity of the country, and territory (land ownership).

Although demography is now being increasingly framed in terms of Israeli security and an "existential threat," the preoccupation with Arab-Jewish demographic balance has a long genealogy in Zionist discourse about the "Arab question" and what is labelled the "demographic problem," or *ha-ba-'aya ha-demografit* (Lustick 2013). Jewish ethnic dominance is advanced to counter the "existential threat" and is meant to imply that as a state Israel should remain predominantly Jewish – in numbers and in ethos. Thus ethno-nationalism, better described as bionationalism, is now wielded as the main weapon in Israel's biopolitical arsenal. Increasingly, official spokespersons of Israeli governments from the prime minister down call upon the Palestinians to accept the Jewishness of Israel as a condition of any settlement of the conflict, which so far the Palestinians have resisted because it pre-empts any discussion of the Palestinian refugees' right of return and sidesteps the discussion over the rights of the non-Jewish citizens of the state, among whom the Palestinian minority constitutes 20 per cent.

Writing from New York in 1917, David Ben-Gurion informed his readers, in an article titled "On Clarifying the Origin of the Fallahim [sic]," that unlike the Bedouins and urban Arab inhabitants of historical Palestine, the majority of Palestinian peasants who tilled the soil had deep roots in the country, so deep that they could be traced to the same stock as the biblical Jewish population of Palestine. In his words, "In language, customs, traditions, and manners of the modern fallahim [sic] we find many signs which testify to their Hebrew origin" (ibid., 13). Ben-Gurion reached this conclusion at the time of the Balfour Declaration, when the Jews in Palestine did not exceed 10 per cent of the total population. As seen in chapter 2, whereas two decades earlier Theodore Herzl, the father of modern Zionism, had advocated a solution to the demographic problem that relied on "spiriting" the poor Arab population of Palestine across the borders (see Morris 2002),[3] Ben-Gurion saw a possible Jewish genetic link with the Arab peasant population. In one case, the objective was to transfer the majority Arab population out of the country, as Herzl saw fit, and in the other case, the purpose was to deconstruct Palestinian national identity by dissolving the Arab population into a remnant of the ancient Jewish population. Both cases, however, had a common purpose: to eliminate from the country any distinct national Palestinian-Arab presence through land dispossession, population transfer, and redefinition of Palestinian identity. More than a century later it is clear that, although a form of mass expulsion did occur in 1948 with the creation of the refugee problem, the transfer solution has not eliminated Palestinian presence and the Palestinian identity question remains highly problematic for Israel. Attempts remain underway to define the conflict between Arabs and Jews in Palestine in terms of population balance and, in the process, to use the arguments of security-cum-demography to dilute any viable national Palestinian presence – if not physically for the time being, then symbolically and politically.

Ben-Gurion's foray into genealogy did not leave any lasting effects on the population debate in Israel. Ben-Gurion himself abandoned the fleeting search for a common origin among Arabs and Jews and proceeded to play a decisive role in thinning the Arab presence in what became Israel in 1948. As the first prime minister of Israel, he was personally involved in plans to transfer and expel the Palestinians from the territory seized by Israel in 1948, and he approved the campaign to prevent the 800,000 Palestinian refugees, most of whom were villagers, from returning to their homes (Masalha 1992). In 1951, with regard to the 150,000 Palestinians who remained in what became Israel, Ben-Gurion invited expert opinion from the army, intelligence circles, and rabbinical authorities to advise him on the prospects and legality of their possible conversion to Judaism (Benziman and Mansour 1992). Nothing came out of this idea, and the attempt to construct a hybrid ethnic state composed of Jews and Judaised Arabs was thus relegated to a mere footnote in history.

Whether in academic circles or popular parlance, the demography debate is in perpetual motion in Israel. The press is replete with reports and opinion pieces about the danger facing Israel as a result of the Arab-Jewish population balance, which, if the status quo continues, is predicted to tip in favour of the Arab population in less than two decades. The views are echoed by policymakers and academics of all shades. One example is the framing of the demography debate by a major Israeli think-tank, the Interdisciplinary Center Herzliya. At three of its annual conferences, several speakers in high places repeatedly issued warnings about the "demographic danger" facing Israel as a Jewish state and argued for a policy of Arab population containment – within its 1967 borders and from across the Green Line. Archival material dating back to the 1950s shows that Israeli leaders were fully aware of their role in expelling Palestinians and were busy devising schemes to resettle the refugees in neighbouring countries – although Argentina, Brazil, Somalia, Libya, Tunisia, Algeria, Germany, and even Switzerland were cited as possible transfer destinations. In the words of researcher Arik Ariel (2013), "Israel formulated a policy under which the return of the refugees to its territory would not be permitted under any circumstances." With the population balance uppermost in the minds of Israeli leaders, a committee was struck under the chairmanship of Yosef Weitz, a notorious figure in overseeing and implementing the seizure of Arab land as head of the Jewish National Fund at the time. Although the recommendations were not formally adopted, they nevertheless reinforced government guidelines pertaining to the demographic issue, namely that the Arab population should remain at only 15 to 20 per cent of the total, that those Arabs who stayed in the country should be encouraged to emigrate, that "the Arabs' abandonment of their homes should be considered an irrevocable fait accompli and that Israel should support their resettlement elsewhere" (ibid.). With regard to those who remained in the country, Arik quotes Moshe Dayan, who wrote, "The 170,000 Arabs who remain in the country should be treated as though their fate has not yet been sealed. I hope that, in the years ahead, another possibility might arise to implement a transfer of those Arabs from the Land of Israel" (in ibid.). Under pressure from the US government, Israel at one point agreed to take 10 per cent of the refugees, or from 100,000 to 150,000. However, nothing came out of these plans. During the Oslo refugee talks in the early 1990s, the figure of 70,000 was secretly circulated but was never made official, and successive Likud and right-wing Israeli governments continued to reject the return of any Palestinian refugees.

As Palestine was a colonial-settler society, the issue of immigration in and out of its territory remained paramount in planning and policymaking by the Zionist leadership. As will be seen throughout this discussion, not only is Jewish immigration on the decline, as reported by Israeli officials, but the number of Israelis who return after living abroad for two to five years is also on the decline, an indication that the majority of these émigrés are unlikely to return. This may explain the real motives behind Prime Minister Benjamin Netanyahu's call in 2015 for European Jewry to immigrate en masse to Israel. A spokeswoman for the Ministry of Immigration and Absorption has pointed out that by the end of 2003, there were close to 760,000 Israelis living abroad. This marked an increase of 200,000 since the start of the Second Intifada in 2000. The annual number of returnees between 1993 and 1999 ranged from 4,700 to 6,500 annually; following the Second Intifada, the rates declined to 3,956 in 2000, to 3,546 in 2001, and to only 2,771 by October 2003 (in Alon 2003). And from 1990 to 2001, a total of 270,000 Israelis left the country (Alon 2004). More than a decade later, it was estimated by the Israel Census Bureau of Statistics that between 500,000 and 800,000 Israelis lived abroad (in Winer 2012). Further data show that the trend in emigration continues, with estimates of between 700,000 and 1 million Israelis living abroad. It is argued that although conflict with the Palestinians is one of the factors behind emigration, the main reason for emigration is economic, since there are better-paying jobs abroad for skilled people (Maital 2013).

The Arab-Jewish population balance west of the Jordan River is an important part of the debate surrounding withdrawal from the occupied territories. Of the various academic contributors to the debate, geographer Arnon Sofer at Haifa University sounds the loudest alarm bells. In a letter he wrote to Prime Minister Ariel Sharon in early 2002, Sofer urged complete separation of Jews and Palestinians in the occupied territories and Israel. To safeguard the Jewishness of the state, Sofer unsuccessfully advocated the removal of fifty settlements and separation of

Jews from the Arab residents of East Jerusalem. Such separation was needed, he argued, to forestall a "grave demographic" outcome that will mean the "end of the Jewish state of Israel" (in Galili 2002). Although it has lost some ground in recent years, as a solution, separation is not new to Israeli demographic discourse and is not confined to right-wing politicians and intellectuals, among whom Sofer is counted. The idea of separation originally germinated among liberals and the left in Israel's Labor Party (see Yehoshua 2002) and is now subscribed to by adherents of all shades of the political spectrum in Israel, except for the extreme right, which would prefer to expel all the Arabs residing west of the Jordan River.

Sofer was not content to stress only separation of Jews and Palestinians in the occupied territories. He went further and warned the Jewish leadership in Israel that unless something was done demographically, such as encouraging Jews in Israel itself to move to Galilee and the Negev in order "to save" these areas, "in three years time we will need a dictator to do it" (in Ratner 2003).

In their report *Israel: Demography, 2013–2034: Challenges and Chances* (2013), Arnon Sofer and Evgenia Bystrov repeat familiar points made in previous similar reports. They warn against religious Jewish dominance at the expense of secular Israeli Jews, that Israel's reluctance to divest from its settlements in the West Bank is making the two-state solution unattainable, that if things stay as they are, the Jews west of the Jordan river will dwindle in their share of the population from their current 61 per cent (52.2 per cent if Gaza's Arab population is included) to 55.8 per cent (46.6 per cent if Gaza's Arab population is included) by 2034, and that if economic and social reforms are not put in place, Israel will gradually become a third world country.

Demography and modernisation: the dilemma

In 2003 a press release from the Israel Central Bureau of Statistics (ICBS) stated that the population of Israel numbered 6.75 million people. It is important to note that unless it is stated otherwise, official Israeli figures invariably include the Arab populations of both East Jerusalem, which was unilaterally annexed by Israel, and the Golan Heights among the overall population of Israel. Based on this assumption, 5.16 million (76%) are Jews, 1.3 million (19%) are Arabs, and 0.29 million (5%) are non-Jewish immigrants from the former Soviet Union (ICBS 2003). A decade later, on the threshold of 2013, the bureau estimated that the population consisted of 6.323 million (79%) Jews and 1.645 million (21%) Arabs (ICBS 2012). These figures included close to 300,000 Arabs who lived in East Jerusalem and the Golan Heights. The bureau further estimates that by 2020, the "extended" Jewish population, which includes non-Jews from the previous Soviet Union, will reach 6.9 million (77%), based on a maximal scenario of birth rates and immigration, whereas the Arabs will reach 2.1 million (23%) (ICBS 2010). By 2030 the Arabs are expected to reach 2.4 million (24%) (ICBS 2009), thus bypassing the magic figure of 15 to 20 per cent set by Ben-Gurion and faithfully pursued until the present.

A cursory look at the age-group composition of the Arab and Jewish populations confirms the underdeveloped nature of Arab society. It shows that whereas 25 per cent of Jews were below the age of fifteen in 2001, the figure was 41 per cent among the Arab population; if we move the age line upward to include those who are below nineteen years of age, the Arab-Jewish ratio stands at 51 per cent to 34 per cent (ICBS 2002, table 2-60). Nearly a decade later, in 2009, the Arab-Jewish ratio had hardly changed, with 25 per cent of the Jewish population being below the age of fifteen, compared to 38 per cent of the Arab population (ICBS 2009).

Throughout the early years of the state's existence, the population debate was handled piecemeal, but not without an overriding concern to ensure spatial and numerical containment of the Arab population. Although the size of the Arab population increased eightfold, from 150,000 to 1.2 million people, within about half a century, not one new Arab town was built to accommodate their needs. As a result of a series of land confiscations, discriminatory zoning laws, a military government that was imposed on the Arab sector for eighteen years following the establishment of the state, discrimination practices in hiring, low participation rates in the labour force, and a generally depressed level of Arab-sector funding by the government, the quality of Arab life in Israel remains to this day substantially below its Jewish counterpart. Here lies the crux of the Israeli demographic paradox. It is a basic tenet in demography that modernisation and social integration reduce the fertility rate and bring about a smaller family size, thus narrowing the so-called "demographic differential" in ethnically bound states; as shown below, this process is not straightforward and linear. Neither integration of the Arab minority nor modernisation through industrialisation and education of the Arab sector was seriously pursued by the government. This demographic transformation-cum-modernisation principle is yet to be fully borne out in the case of the Arabs in Israel. Even though Israel is considered by international standards to be a modern, industrial society with a gross national product (GNP) per capita of $34,000 (World Bank 2013) that puts it in league with, if not ahead of, some western European countries, this transformation is yet to affect the Arab sector in an appreciable manner. Among Israel's Muslim population, the GNP is half of the Jewish population's. Distorted forms of urbanisation and social class formations have prevented the closing of the demographic differential between Arabs and Jews. This does not mean that there has been no reduction in the Arab fertility rate in Israel. However, this demographic change has not been sufficient to offset the overall gap between Jews and Arabs. This is particularly true if we also consider the demographic differential between Jews and Palestinians in the West Bank and Gaza.

Demographer Sergio DellaPergola, who heads the Institute of Contemporary Jewry at the Hebrew University, is usually considered a moderate when it comes to the demography debate. At one level, DellaPergola situates the demographic dilemma in a wider context that highlights a reduction in immigration to Israel and an increase from 15,000 to 20,000 in the number of Israelis who annually leave Israel (in Lazaroff 2002). At another level, DellaPergola makes one of the more interesting observations about modernisation and fertility, namely that the impact of modernisation will be slow and gradual. In referring to the experience of the Arab population in Israel, DellaPergola points out that in the initial phase of the modernisation process, fertility rates will increase due to improvement in health conditions. However, once modernisation spreads to various aspects of society (through urbanisation, improvement in education, and entry of women into the labour force), he expects to see a decrease in birth rates. According to DellaPergola, "The Jewish majority will serve as a model for the Arab population, albeit through a slow process" (in Sheleg 2004). However, because of the slowness of this process, the proportion of the Arab population will continue to grow, reaching 23 per cent in 2020 and 26 per cent in 2050, when the levels of fertility among Arabs and Jews will level off at the rate of 2.6 children per woman. In addition to the modernisation process, DellaPergola locates the impetus to high birth rates in the ongoing conflict between Arabs and Jews. There is a cyclical process at play here: although national conflict pushes birth rates upward, with the struggle becoming a contest over numbers, birth rates in turn fuel the conflict and keep demography at the centre of the debate.

At one point, the demography debate was joined by Uzi Arad, a veteran chief of the Mossad, Israel's foreign spy agency, who now directs the Institute of Policy and Strategy at the Herzliya centre. Citing Egypt as an example, he goes one step further and argues that international donors should apply pressure on the Palestinian Authority to introduce family planning (U. Arad 2004). In response to this recommendation, Emmanuel Sivan (2004) of the Hebrew University argues that Egypt's drop in fertility did not occur due to external pressure but due to internal factors, such as enlisting the support of religious establishments in the family-planning campaigns. I might add that Iran's drastic drop in fertility can hardly be attributed to outside pressure by donor countries. It is strictly the outcome of internal dynamics.

Two further sets of studies that have a bearing on the modernisation and demography debate are worth noting. The first is by Itzhak Ravid and the second by Yacov Sheinin, both of whom are associated with the Herzliya centre. The two studies were presented at the centre's annual conferences. Ravid (2001) presented his findings first in December 2000 and again in December 2001, highlighting the rather low rates of Palestinian labour force participation in the West Bank and Gaza – as if the occupied territories were normal regions. He estimates that the workforce in Gaza is one-seventh of the population and that in the West Bank it is one-fifth. This is in contrast to 60 per cent among Israeli Jews. Young people under the age of fifteen constitute half the population in the occupied territories. Natural growth in Gaza is 4.4 per cent, and in the West Bank it is 3.4 per cent, compared to 2 per cent in Egypt. Similar to Arad, Ravid presents Turkey, Egypt, and particularly Iran as examples of Muslim countries where government intervention and family-planning campaigns have significantly reduced natural increase. His main point is that the rest of the Arab countries, including the Palestinians, can do the same. Although Ravid acknowledges that the Palestinians have a higher level of education compared to Egypt and Iran, he does not explain why Palestinian natural increase remains high in the midst of almost universal literacy – surely a powerful indicator of modernisation and a contributor to the glaring demographic paradox. He does not explore why the Palestinians, who are known to have exported their skills to the rest of the Arab world since their dispersal in 1948, still remain under Israeli control in a state of underdevelopment that is worse than that of many other third world countries. In Ravid's study and others discussed here, there is no mention of the role of Israeli policies in distorting the modernisation process in the West Bank and Gaza – as well as among the Arabs in Israel. By focusing on fertility rates in isolation, the impression is left that the underdevelopment of the Palestinians is the fault of demography, which is shaped by their culture and religion.

Ravid (2001, 2) applies the same logic in commenting on the Arab population in Israel, stating that "the gap between natural growth rates between Jews and Arabs has no precedent in other Western countries." He compares Orthodox to secular Jews. Due to their large family size, Orthodox Jews have a high rate of natural increase (3.5%) and a low rate of labour force participation (37%). Thus Ravid presents a "heterogeneous" picture of the composition of Israeli society: it is a society that contains secular Jews, Orthodox Jews, Ethiopian Jews, Muslim Arabs, Christian Arabs, Bedouins, Druze, foreign workers, and so-called "illegal" Palestinian residents from the territories, each of whom have their peculiar demographic differential vis-à-vis the secular Jewish population. The way to rectify the situation and maintain the status of a Western nation is for Israel to devise policies to control the natural increase of the Muslim population through family-planning initiatives and further investment in education. Only this tactic will enable Israeli to maintain a GNP per capita that is close to those of its European counterparts and likely to rise further in the future. He argues that, as it now stands, the tax contributions of the secular Jewish society are subsidising the Arab and Haredi sectors, where large-sized families and a low level of labour force participation predominate.

A similar approach is adopted by economist Yacov Sheinin of the Herzliya centre (Sheinin 2003; Sheinin and Shagev 2003). He points out that government transfer payments account for 12 per cent of household income for the majority secular Jewish population, 24 per cent for the Arab population, and 40 per cent for the ultraorthodox Jewish group. He does not explore the reason why the Orthodox Jews, with their 6 per cent share of the population, receive an allowance that is 167 per cent larger than that of Arab citizens, who, according to Sheinin, comprise 19 per cent of the population. He remarks that in the absence of further Jewish immigration, and if the status quo continues, the annual 3 per cent growth rate of Arabs and Haredim will eventually contribute to a 0.5 per cent annual decrease in the overall per capita income. And in terms of population, by 2030 the majority Jewish group will constitute 63 per cent of the population. Sheinin calls for increasing investment in education and halting the importation of foreign workers, whose presence depresses local Arab participation in the labour force. The solution is to "integrate" and "assimilate the minority populations into the majority group" (Sheinin 2003, 2). Similar to other works on Israeli demography, here too the author falls short in prescribing concrete ways for "integrating" the Arab population. After more than a half-century of residential, educational, and occupational segregation, and numerous unfulfilled government promises to improve the status of the Arab sector, what makes authors like Ravid, Sheinin, DellaPergola, and others think that the government is now ready to embark on genuine integration of the Arab minority? Equally important is the extent to which educational expectations are likely to be translated into concrete job placements. It is common knowledge that one of the most serious problems facing the Arab sector is the inability of its qualified and educated university graduates to find jobs that are commensurate with their qualifications (Al-Haj 2003; Mazawi 1995). This is true for both men and women.

The debate surrounding Israeli demography is addressed in two articles by Ian Lustick. Both articles unpack the political dimension of the ethnic construction of population data. One article (Lustick 2013) critiques the drive by right-wing researchers and settlers to come up with numbers that challenge Palestinian and other demographers' estimates regarding what they consider to be an inflated Palestinian population count in the West Bank and Gaza, claiming that the real estimates put the size of the Palestinian population at around 1 million fewer people than the current estimates. A crucial aspect of the battle for numbers centres on the following: first, right-wing researchers count the 300,000 to 350,000 non-Jewish Russian immigrants as part of their Jewish population pool; and second, they do not base their estimates of the Palestinian population on accepted standard demographic methodology, which involves surveying specific groups and extrapolating the overall structure of the population, but instead they rely on voter registration, health registries that include births and deaths, and school registration. These, Lustick claims, do not include Palestinians who are outside the territories for work, study, and visitation, something that is incorporated into the estimates of the Jewish population. Data on home births, a common practice among Palestinians, are not kept by hospital officials and do not appear in the registry. Finally, Palestinians who reside in East Jerusalem, an area that was annexed illegally by Israel, are not part of the minimal counting by the settlers, whereas they are counted by the Palestinian census as residents of the West Bank.

Lustick's (2011) earlier article addresses a perennial topic of discussion in Israel: immigration to and emigration from Israel. He marshals polling data to assess the ideological orientations of Israeli Jews toward emigration and considers critically the data of the Israel Census Bureau of Statistics to shed light on the historic decline in the number of immigrants and the constant increase in the level of emigration. The issues confronting Israel's immigration-emigration dilemma are rooted in several factors. First, as is the case with all immigrants, here too a sizable portion of immigrants from the former Soviet republics emigrated to other places after initially settling in Israel in search of better job opportunities. This also applies to other skilled and professional groups in Israel. Second, the halo hovering over Zionism is being gradually eclipsed as a result of globalisation and the ascendancy of post-Zionism. It is no longer acceptable to speak of *yordim* (emigrants) in pejorative terms as a sign of Zionism's failures. Lustick points out that there are close to 150,000 Israelis who hold Russian passports living in Israel and the Ukraine (ibid.), and I might add that there are 100,000 who hold German passports (Brot 2011). Already in 2006, the US consulate in New York estimated that there were up to 400,000 Israelis living in metropolitan New York. Only 352 had returned to Israel in the previous year. Overall, 800,000 Israelis resided in the United States at the time (in Amit 2006).

Overall, Lustick (2011, 40) claims that between 1990 and 2008, 20,000 Israeli Jews emigrated annually, compared to between 7,000 and 10,000 who returned. At the ideological level, public opinion polls show a weakening in the attachment to Zionism's colonising calls for settling in the country. For example, 45 per cent of those whose parents were born in Israel are not sure that they want to stay in the country. Whereas 87 per cent of religious Jews say that they plan to stay, only 59 per cent of the secular plan to do so (ibid., 49).

It is important to situate the Israeli discourse on demography in the context of what I call the "policies of containment" toward the Arab population and their ideological underpinnings. The next two sections deal with the attitudes of the Israeli leaders toward the Palestinians in Israel and provide a brief summary of relevant Israeli public opinion polls dealing with issues of immigration, citizenship, and equal rights.

Population containment

During the pre-election period in late 2012, Prime Minister Netanyahu's office released figures from the ICBS that showed ominously for Netanyahu, and by implication for the Jewish public, that of the 12 million people under Israel's control who resided between the Jordan River and the Mediterranean, 5.9 million were Jews and 6.1 million were non-Jews (in Eldar 2012a).

To appreciate the significance of this press release, one has to go back and highlight Netanyahu's fears about the Arab presence in the country, which in 2003 had culminated in his advocacy that the Palestinians recognise Israel as a Jewish state as a precondition for reconciliation. In his speech at the Herzliya conference in December of that year, when Netanyahu was finance minister, he made the following widely quoted statement: "If there is a demographic problem, and there is, it is with the Israeli Arabs who will remain Israeli citizens." Based on Netanyahu's speech, the same newspaper reported, "If Israel's Arabs become well integrated and reach 35–40 percent of the population, there will no longer be a Jewish state but a bi-national one. If Arabs remain at 20 percent but relations are tense and violent, this will also harm the state's democratic fabric" (Alon and Benn 2003).

This was not the first time that Netanyahu had made such a claim, and it was not an idiosyncratic, isolated claim. He elaborated on his ideas in the US conservative publication the *Weekly Standard*:

> If Arab inhabitants are wonderfully integrated and their numbers increase to 35–40 percent of the total inhabitants of the state, then the Jewish state will have been abolished, and it will have turned into a binational state. If their

numbers remain at about 20 per cent, as they are today, or fall, but relations are stiff, contentious, and violent, this too will hurt our democratic character. (In Berkowitz 2004)

Netanyahu's words echo those of a leading settler who said, "The truly critical demographic problem is inside the state of Israel" (in I. Harel 2003). Mass transfer of Palestinians across the border to neighbouring countries as a possible solution to the demographic problem has been voiced by several past (e.g., in Sharon's government) and present ministers. These include the foreign minister Avigdor Lieberman, as well as Tzachi Hanegbi, Limor Livnat, and Uzi Landau, to name a few (Zureik 2003). Of course, more recent public calls to transfer Palestinians owe their revival to the late Rehavam Ze'evi, who situated the transfer idea within mainstream Zionist discourse (Shragai 2001).

The prestigious Interdisciplinary Center Herzliya (2001, 7–8) highlights the centrality of demography in the proceedings of its conference on "The Balance of National Strength and Security":

> The fundamental dilemma that Israel faces as a result of demographic statistics and trends among the Palestinians is between a policy of adaptation, political or otherwise, and a policy of containment. The choice between the options depends on the perception of Israel's future political identity and image. The adaptation policy is the one propounded by those who view Israel as a country of all its citizens – adapting its national character, its symbol and institutions to the changing demo-political balance.
>
> Conversely, those who support the preservation of Israel's character as it was when it was founded – a Jewish state for the Jewish nation – and they still constitute a majority among the Jewish population in Israel, are forced to proffer a counter-strategy that will provide an effective response to the aforementioned [demographic] trends.

Of equal importance, the Israeli government has adopted several concrete steps in its biopolitical strategy against the high Arab birth rate. These constitute what I call "micromanagement techniques" that are directed against specific categories of the Arab population. First, under the pretext of security, Israel no longer approves applications for family reunification between couples when one spouse resides in the occupied territories (Benziman 2003). Moreover, unlike other (Jewish) Israeli citizens who marry non-Israelis, Israeli Arabs who marry citizens from neighbouring Arab countries now find it extremely difficult for the non-Israeli spouse to obtain citizenship and residency rights in Israel (Ettinger 2004b). The government has initiated measures to strip such "foreign" spouses of their Israeli citizenship and residency rights. Israeli officials describe these marriages as a covert method of exercising the "right of return" through the "back door" (ibid.). Second, over protests from civil rights organisations, the Knesset passed the "citizenship loyalty" bill in 2011 legalising the stripping of Israeli citizenship from those who "betray their loyalty to the state" (Lis 2011). Third, a special unit has been established in the Ministry of Interior that, with the aid of private detectives, works to track down so-called "illegal" Palestinian residents from the territories living in Israel. This practice has also triggered criticism from the Association of Civil Rights in Israel (Mualem 2002). Fourth, at one point the government reactivated the Israel Council for Demography after several years of hiatus. What triggered reactivation of the council was discussion in the press and by politicians regarding a decline in the Jewish birth rate, an increase in intermarriages between Jews and non-Jews, the high Palestinian birth rate, the presence of illegal residents, and a large non-Jewish contingent among Russian immigrants to Israel. The council, which was founded in 1967 after Israel conquered the West Bank and Gaza, consists of forty members drawn from the professions and includes demographers, educationalists, obstetricians, gynaecologists, jurists, amongst others. The purpose of the council was questioned by critics who accused it of acting to promote an increase in the Jewish birth rate and a decline in the Arab one (Zureik 2003). Gideon Levy (2002) questions the council's rationale: "And how will the gynecologists contribute to this endeavor? Will they make do with proposing methods to increase the Jewish fertility rate and prevent abortions, or will they also suggest techniques to encourage abortions and reduce the birth rate among Arab women?" Finally, right-wing Knesset members of the old Herut Party unsuccessfully proposed a bill that would have provided financial incentives for Palestinian citizens of Israel to emigrate to Arab countries. The Knesset's legal advisor described the bill as discriminatory because it portrayed the state as "encouraging the Jewish population with financial assistance to come to Israel and settle here whereas Arabs, who are citizens of the country, are encouraged by the state to leave" (in Zureik 2003, 625).

Ideological basis

What makes the demography debate ominous is that it strengthens an already existing political and social climate that encourages racist attitudes toward the Arab population. Writing in the *New York Review of Books*, David Shulman (2014) addresses Israeli racism in the context of the latest sustained attacks on Gaza. Usually, the media is replete with discussions about Hamas violence, racism, and its hatred of Israel. Rarely do we see in the Western media a first-hand discussion of Israeli racism toward the Arabs reflected in what Shulman calls the "wave of blood lust and racist violence, verbal and physical, now raging within Israel." He goes on to enumerate a series of horrific incidents by vigilante Jewish groups and lynch mobs against the Arabs in Jerusalem "where the police either stood by or joined in with right-wing thugs."

Those who follow the sociological and psychological research on racism in Israel should not be surprised by these revelations, as I demonstrate below. This is not a new development but has historical roots in Israeli consciousness that date back to the early days of the state, if not to the prestate period. In reviewing public opinion data covering the 1970s, I have highlighted the stereotypical and negative attitudes held by young and old Israeli Jews toward Arab citizens of the state (Zureik 1979, 142–65). Here are some of the salient findings:

- 80 per cent of a Jewish sample believed that Arabs will not reach the level of progress of Jews.
- 90 per cent preferred to see fewer Arabs remain in the country.
- 90 per cent believed that Arabs "understand force only."
- 84 per cent would be bothered if a friend or relative married an Arab.
- 74 per cent were concerned if their children befriended Arabs.
- 54 per cent of Jewish children were taught by Arab teachers.

Nearly two decades ago, a national survey of Israeli Jews supported the idea of transferring Arab citizens to a Palestinian state. The same survey showed that 56 per cent would deprive Arab citizens in Israel of their right to elect a prime minister, and a similar proportion would deny Arabs the right to vote in political referenda. In 2000 another survey showed that 60 per cent of Israeli Jews endorsed the transfer of Arabs outside Israel. In March 2002 46 per cent of Israeli Jews supported the transfer of Palestinians from the occupied territories, and one-third favoured transfer of Israel's Arab citizens. Indirect population transfer of Arab citizens by means of financial incentives was supported by 60 per cent of the Jewish respondents (Zureik 2003). It is not surprising to discover from Sammy Smooha's (2005) national survey of a decade ago (which excluded the Arabs of East Jerusalem) that 55.4 per cent of the Arabs in Israel feared the possibility of transfer and that 70 per cent feared violence directed toward them by the Jewish population. Among the latter, 77 per cent feared violence from the Arab side (Ettinger 2004a).

In an overview of public opinion data on related issues, Nimer Sultany (2003) documents that one-third of Israeli Jews are willing to deny Arab citizens in Israel the right to vote, that close to two-thirds believe Arab citizens have excessive influence over politics, that three-quarters of Israeli Jews in 2000 and 2002 said Arab citizens should not be involved in crucial national decisions, and that in 2002 almost three-quarters opposed Arab parties joining any Israeli government coalition. This was an increase from 46 per cent in 2000 and 67 per cent in 2001. The most relevant data for the present purpose are those pertaining to the transfer of Arab citizens from their homeland. If anything, the data show that over a decade, from 1991 to 2001, the proportion of Israelis who endorsed the transfer of Arab citizens increased from 24 per cent to 31 per cent. And whereas in 2001 49 per cent said that Arabs should be encouraged to leave, in 2002 the figure rose to 60 per cent. Also in 2001 another survey revealed that 62 per cent of the Israeli-Jewish population condoned the proposition that the government should encourage immigration of Arab citizens of Israel. Fifty per cent agreed that land within Israel that is heavily populated by Arabs should be exchanged for land with no Arabs on it that is located in the Palestinian territory. This is the so-called "stationary transfer." Two-thirds of the Jewish public stated that Arab citizens of Israel constituted a danger to state security. In one of the few national surveys that included Arab respondents, 20 per cent of the whole sample supported the idea of transfer. The figure would have been higher if the sample had been confined to Jewish respondents. And when asked by several polling organisations in 2001 and 2002 whether Arab citizens of Israel constituted a danger to the state, between 60 per cent and 72 per cent answered in the affirmative. Not far removed from the above data reported by Sultany are the results of a poll conducted by the Tami Steinmetz Center for Peace Research (2003) at Tel Aviv University. When asked whether they agreed or disagreed with Netanyahu's statement regarding an Arab demographic threat within Israel, 71 per cent of the Jewish respondents answered in the affirmative, and 42 per cent said that it was acceptable for a minister to express this view. When asked whether Jews should have more economic and political rights than Arab citizens, 41 per cent endorsed more economic rights for Jews, and 44 per cent said that Jews were entitled to more political rights. Finally, the same survey revealed that 73 per cent feared the emergence of a binational state if Israel remained in control of the territory west of the Jordan River.

Starting in the middle of the 1970s, Sammy Smooha of Haifa University was one of the early researchers to conduct polls and write about public opinion in Israel taking the Arabs' political attitudes into account. He then conducted a series of identical polls among Arabs and Jews from the 1980s to as recently as 2012 (Smooha 2005, 2010, 2012). The centrepiece of these polls is an index of Jewish-Arab relations that Smooha developed in the early 1980s and included in six surveys conducted between 2002 and 2009. Use of the term "index" is somewhat misleading. As is customary, an index usually implies a measure that combines several items in a survey, whether attitudinal or otherwise, in order to provide an overall picture of a specific phenomenon, such as democracy, authoritarianism, or in this case, relations between Arabs and Jews. This was not done in the series of surveys carried out by Smooha. Instead of constructing a single index or indeed indexes that captured the relations between Arabs and Jews, the author based his conclusions on a large battery of questions. Sixteen separate issues defined the index. They covered integration, stereotypes, alienation, mistrust, deprivation, collective memory, fear of threats, legitimacy of co-existence, regional conflict, regional integration, identity, cultural autonomy, means of struggle encompassing social and violent protests, options for change, and evaluations of relations between Arabs and Jews.

At the crux of Smooha's research over more than three decades is its presentation of an alternative to the idea of radicalisation among the Palestinians in Israel, a thesis advanced in critical writings about Israeli society that describe the experience of Arabs as predominantly one of alienation and disaffection from the Israeli political system and the dominant Jewish majority. Smooha's counterthesis, which he labels the "politicization thesis," is premised on the notion that although the Palestinians in Israel (whom he calls Israeli Arabs) show a great deal of alienation and disaffection from Jewish social and political institutions, there is a discernible trend toward willingness among the Arab population to seek accommodation with the state and the Jewish public, a willingness to participate in parliamentary politics through voting (mainly for Arab parties), and a preference to remain in Israel rather than be annexed by a future Palestinian state if a compromise is reached between Israelis and Palestinians in the occupied territories. According to Smooha (2005, 12):

> The politicization thesis does not overlook the forces distancing Arabs and Jews from each other, which are emphasized by the radicalization thesis, but claims that along with these negative forces, there are also positive ones that soften them, and the outcome is therefore not necessarily crisis and violence as foreseen by the radicalization thesis.

Overall, however, he points out that the findings of his 2004 survey do not confirm unequivocally either of the two theses mentioned by him. Thus it appears to be a matter of the glass being either half empty or half full. As Smooha states:

> The new index of Arab-Jewish relations . . . will not decide which of the two theses is correct, nor will it determine the extent to which Jews live up to their high moral standards vis-à-vis the Arabs, or rule whether the Arabs are fulfilling what is expected of them as citizens. It will, however, produce new data that will challenge public discourse and policy regarding the status of the Arab-Palestinian minority in the Jewish and democratic state. (Ibid., 12–13)

The 2004 survey (Smooha 2005), which I highlight here, was carried out against the background of violent events in 2000 between Arab protesters and the police in which the police shot and killed thirteen Arab citizens and injured more than a hundred. In spite of a special governmental commission of inquiry that was struck to deal with the events – the Or Commission, none of the policemen responsible for the killings were brought to justice. For the present purpose, the relevant findings from the survey, based on a sample of 700 Jews and 700 Arabs, are as follows:

- 42.5 per cent of Jews and 80.3 per cent of Arabs endorsed the proposition that Arab political parties ought to be included in any coalition government.
- 70 per cent of the Arabs had no confidence in Zionist parties.
- More than one-third of Jewish respondents held negative images of Arabs as less intelligent, culturally backward, and not law-abiding.
- 53 per cent of Jews and 25 per cent of Arabs did not entertain having a neighbour from the other group.
- 12 per cent of Arabs felt proud of Israel's achievements.
- Arabs feared severe infringements of their rights (81%), further confiscation of their land (79%), and state (72%) and Jewish (71%) violence.
- Two-thirds of Arabs feared that they would be transferred to a future Palestinian state or annexed by the Palestinian state.

Smooha has a tendency to present Arab and Jewish fears as though they were symmetrical. In terms of power relations, they are qualitatively different. It is one thing when the majority, which has the full backing of the state and its institutions, expresses its fears, and it is another thing when a powerless minority attributes its fears to the hegemonic nature of the Zionist state, which usually sides with the Jewish public. But the contours of the fears go beyond threats of physical violence, as the following results of a 2012 survey show:

- Between 67 per cent and 83 per cent of the Jews said that the high Arab birth rate was aimed at altering the Jewish character of the state.
- When Netanyahu made his incendiary speech about the "Arab demographic problem" by pointing the finger at Palestinian citizens of the state, 71 per cent of the Jewish public approved of this stigmatising of the Arab minority.
- 42 per cent of the Arabs had personally encountered discrimination by Jews and by the state, and 19.4 per cent had suffered from insults and acts of violence.
- 18 per cent of the Jews had suffered from violence emanating from Arabs.
- On the crucial issue of the nature of the state, 80 per cent of Arab respondents endorsed the proposition that as a state Israel had the right to exist where Arabs and Jews lived together.
- But only 13.8 per cent of Arabs endorsed the proposition that Israel had the right to exist as a solely Jewish, Zionist state.
- 72 per cent of the Arab sample agreed that "Israel as a Zionist state in which Arabs and Jews live is racist."
- Whereas 96.5 per cent of the Jewish sample agreed that Israel was justified in its desire to "keep a Jewish majority," only 24 per cent of the Arabs agreed. (Smooha 2012)

It is interesting to note that the debate over a so-called "land swap," where the predominantly Arab Triangle inside Israel would be ceded to a Palestinian state and a corresponding portion of occupied Arab land would be annexed by Israel, hardly involves the affected Arab population. In addition to Sofer, who endorses the land swap, demographer DellaPergola and previous Israeli government minister Efraim Sneh support the idea as long as it is based on the "consent" of the people affected and as long as the transfer does not involve giving up Israeli citizenship. DellaPergola (2001, 28) endorses the principle of land and population exchange in his report of a major study on demography and the Israel-Palestine conflict:

> Some territorial exchanges might be negotiated between Israel and the future Palestinian state. Minor portions of the Palestinian territories now hosting the denser urban concentrations of Jews next to Jerusalem and to Greater Tel Aviv might be exchanged for some of the areas within the current pre-1967 Israeli boundaries now hosting a predominantly Arab population.

However, when asked in a public opinion survey about the so-called "stationary transfer," a meagre 9 per cent of the residents of Umm al-Fahm, the second largest Arab town in Israel, which is at the centre of the swap idea, approved the idea of land and population exchange (Nir 2002).

Conclusion

Meron Benvenisti (2002) has tackled in a simple, yet elegant, manner the bewildering subnational classifications and conceptual schemes that Israeli rulers exercise as part of their project of ruling the minorities in their midst. Writing in the language of constructivism, he points out that the Israeli government and its institutions construct "fictitious identities" for the Arab minority. There are two opposing forces at play here: fear from the minority, which is portrayed as causing an "existential threat" to the majority and as thus deserving to be demonised and gotten rid of, and the calculated attempts by the majority to fragment the minority into, as Benvenisti states, various "small pieces, making it easier to deal with each piece separately, and set them to fight each other." It is not surprising, he notes, to see how the Arabs under Israeli control become "Israeli Arabs," "Druze," "Bedouin," "East Jerusalem Arabs," "refugees," "Muslims," "Christians," "Arabs and others," and "non-Jewish residents of the Golan Heights." An example of how religion is being increasingly used to define citizenship is a law passed in 2015 in the Knesset that distinguishes between Muslim and Christian Arabs under the pretext that this will give the minorities a chance to improve their position in the economy. The Christians alone among the Arab minority are now represented on a public advisory council that was created to ensure equal employment. Critics slammed the bill as an example of "divide and conquer" aimed at the Arab population (Lis 2014).

It is not only Israeli politicians who engage in the game of identity construction of the Other. Sociologist Sammy Smooha for decades has been measuring subjective identification among the Palestinians in Israel, whom he calls the "Israeli Arabs." Over the years, the Palestinian dimension of this identity has increased noticeably. The review of relevant polls in this chapter shows that racism among the Israeli Jewish public is not a new phenomenon. What is remarkable is the stability of these attitudes in their orientations toward the Palestinians.

The role of Zionism has been explored in this chapter along several biopolitical dimensions: colonisation and eugenics with a focus on Arthur Ruppin, population containment, and the relationship between modernisation and demography. Not only Ruppin but also other Zionist colonisers in high places subscribed to social Darwinism in one form or another. German eugenics philosophy was deeply entrenched in the Zionist worldview. It affected attitudes to Arabs and to Jews from Arab countries. In terms of culture and aptitude, they were both assigned an inferior status compared to European Jews. Ruppin, who is hailed as a moderate due to his support for binationalism in Palestine, did not deviate from the main teachings of eugenics.

In the process, this chapter has also tackled the issue of emigration versus immigration. If things remain as they are, with Jewish emigration continuing to outweigh immigration and with the natural rate of increase among the Arab population remaining high, the result will be an increase in the proportion of the Arab share of the population in the near future. National security, not citizenship rights, are woven into issues of population management, so much so that the Israeli state is becoming increasingly defined in opposition to the size of the Arab population and the presence of Arabs in the country. In Zionist discourse, Arab demography constitutes a core element of the "existential threat" facing Israel as a Jewish state.

Finally, this chapter has highlighted the failure to reconcile modernisation theory and demography. Being a colonial-settler state, Israel's policies and public attitudes toward the Arabs have hampered the decline in their birth rate that was universally postulated by demographers. In the absence of genuine government policies that increase employment, education, and industrialisation, the Arab sector in Israel will continue to exhibit third world features.

Notes

1 This is not to deny that climate warming and soil erosion are gradually making food shortage a reality in the context of worldwide population growth, but this sort of argument is different from that advanced by Malthus and his followers.
2 I do not intend to deal with the debate surrounding who is a Jew. The main Zionist argument that the Jews are biologically and genetically homogenous is challenged by Sand (2009), Elhaik (2012), and Abu El-Haj (2012).
3 Some interpret the entry in Herzl's diary about "spiriting" the peasant population across the borders as referring to Argentina (HaCohen and Kimmerling 2005). Although it is true that the entry did not refer specifically to Palestine by name and that Herzl did entertain Latin America as a colonisation project, he did not mention Argentina by name either when proposing to get rid of the peasantry. Even if the entry were contextualised to refer to Argentina, it is equally applicable to the Zionist project in Palestine, if not more so.

5

FROM CALIBRATED SUFFERING TO NECROPOLITICS

"Force is the only thing Arabs understand" is a basic tenet of Israel that underlies its confrontations with the Palestinians and other Arabs. Although not the originator of this Orientalist notion, one-time Israeli anthropologist Raphael Patai gave it currency and scholarly cloak in his book *The Arab Mind* (1973), as the investigative journalist Seymour Hersh discovered when writing about the Abu Ghraib episode in Iraq and his interviews with US military officials. Hersh singles out two themes that emerge from Patai's book, which was roundly criticised by academics but enthusiastically endorsed by the US military and considered to be "the bible of the neocons on Arab behavior": "one, that Arabs only understand force and, two, that the biggest weakness of Arabs is shame and humiliation" (Hersh 2004). Within this shame-humiliation matrix, as shown by the American Abu Ghraib scandal and by the subsequent revelations about Israeli torture and humiliation of Palestinian prisoners (see chapter 2), is the idea that the Arabs are obsessed with things sexual and that homosexuality is the Achilles' heel of all Arabs.

Israeli violence toward the Palestinians is not limited to military campaigns; it extends to civil society and the state's social control agencies, such as the police and domestic spy networks. For example, the Israeli police do not hesitate to engage in brutal behaviour when dealing with Palestinian citizens of Israel, as occurred in October 2000 when thirteen Palestinians were fatally shot by the police and several hundred were injured while demonstrating in sympathy with their brethren in the occupied Palestinian territories (OPT). The first of such blatant, brutal actions by the Israeli police took place in 1976 when six Palestinian citizens, who were protesting government confiscation of Arab land, were also killed by the police and 100 were wounded. In both instances, the police and other security officials who committed these crimes were not charged with murder. Similar attacks, this time by the Israeli army, were carried out in 1953 and 1956 by the notorious military outfit Unit 101 under the command of Ariel Sharon, who in 1953 sent his troops on a murderous mission to the refugee camp of El-Bureig in southern Gaza, where fifty people were massacred (Chomsky 1983, 384), and to the village of Qibya in Jordan, resulting in sixty-nine Arab fatalities (Shlaim 2014). In 1956 the Border Police massacred forty-seven Palestinians from the village of Kafr Kassim (Chomsky 1983, 158). But the most shocking crimes committed on Sharon's watch as commander were the mass killings of more than 2,000 Palestinian refugees and Shiites in Lebanon in the camps of Sabra and Shatila in 1982 at the hands of Israel's protégés the Lebanese Christian Phalange (Goodman 2014).

The discussion below examines the adoption by Israel of new tools of violence that are couched in scientific language to give them legitimacy and protection from scrutiny by international organisations.

The science of calibrated human suffering

> ... the "dialectics of repression" prompted Israeli leaders and their troops to develop innovative methods of non-lethal punishment which promoted Palestinian suffering, while avoiding overly blatant violations of formal procedures. (Ron 2000, 462)

> No prosperity, no development, no humanitarian crisis. (Amos Gilad, in Blau and Feldman 2009)

Sociologist Jim Ron (2000) explores the use of what he calls Israel's "savage restraint" in confronting the first Palestinian uprising in the late 1980s, a practice that Israel has refined over the years and continues to implement in its brutal pursuit of the Palestinians with self-professed scientific rigour. Suffice it to note here that the above quotation by Amos Gilad, a senior Israeli official in the Ministry of Defense who from 2009 to 2010 headed the Coordinator of Government Activities in the Territories (COGAT), embodies the prevalent thinking of the military establishment. He oversaw the implementation of a calibrated combination of repression and restraint as a way of overcoming the concerns expressed about Israel's actions by human rights organisations. With the backing of the United States and other Western governments, Israel has managed to ignore the United Nations' condemnations and circumvent criticism of its actions. Ron claims that these actions explain how Israel has "sunk deep infrastructural roots since the 1967 occupation, hoping to ensure long-term Jewish rule" (ibid., 464). Israel has been careful to vary the methods of dialectical repression in dealing with the Palestinians in the West Bank, compared to in Lebanon, where, in the aftermath of its 1982 invasion, it became apparent that the massacres in the Palestinian refugee camps of Sabra and Shatila by Israel's protégé the Lebanese Christian Phalange were carried out with Israel's full knowledge and complicity. It must be stated, however, that there is a threshold regarding the dialectics of repression. When Israel felt that its power was challenged, it did not hesitate to engage in what amounted to blanket bombing of Lebanon in the summer of 2006, and it mounted savage attacks on West Bank cities in 2002, particularly Nablus and the Jenin refugee camp; it has acted with equally brutal ferocity during its invasions and bombing of Gaza on several occasions, notably in 2008–09, 2011–12, and 2014. None the less, in all of these instances, Israel would have not been able to exercise its power with impunity without some international sanctioning that was provided explicitly or implicitly by various US administrations and European governments.

The core of the argument provided by Ron (2000) more than three decades ago remains true to this day, although with the passage of time Israel has become less concerned with the international repercussions of its actions, as demonstrated in its continuing use of extrajudicial assassinations and military assaults on Gaza at a high civilian cost. After Hamas won the majority of seats in an internationally supervised national Palestinian election in 2007, Israel tightened its grip on the OPT and embarked on a systematic policy of cutting off the flow of funds and drastically reducing the supply of food and other essentials to Gaza – all in the name of security and fighting terror. In 2006 Dov Weissglass, once Israel's point man in advising successive Israeli prime ministers on policy toward the Palestinians, described the choking-off of the food supply and other essential goods to Gaza's population, which numbered 1.2 million people at the time (and would rise to 1.8 million by 2014), as akin to a diet regiment. He quipped cynically, "it is like an appointment with a dietician. The Palestinians will get a lot thinner, but won't die" (in Levy 2006).[1] Nadia Abu El-Haj (2010, 28) refers appropriately to the monitoring of caloric intake as "the calculus of Israel's necropolitical regime." British aid worker Louisa Waugh (2008) has also documented the situation of Palestinians in Gaza:

> The WHO (World Health Organization) produces a drug list of 480 essential items; Gaza's largest hospital, Al-Shifa, is 90 items short, and has less than three months' supply left of another 130. Exports, too, have been drastically curtailed: family-owned strawberry and flower farms have been ruined; due to Israel's naval siege, the annual catch of Gaza's fishermen is less than a sixth of what it was five years ago. The people of the Strip are now one of the most aid-dependent populations on earth.

Successive Israeli attacks, in which hospitals, schools, homes, and shelters were not spared, have substantiated the above grim picture. In its campaign of 2014, Israel bombed the only functioning power plant in Gaza and shelled Gaza's largest medical complex, the Dar Al-Shifa Hospital, as well as residential dwellings with multiple families in them (Amnesty International 2014).

In the context of collective punishment, it is not surprising to come across figures showing that nearly 50 per cent of adult Palestinians in the occupied territories have been arrested at one time or another (Illouz 2013). Jane Young (2012) argues that "Zionist carceral practice" is in essence that of a colonial policy, as distinct from typical law-and-order policing. With 3,000 Israeli military orders in place (ibid., 94), it is no wonder that between 1967 and 2011, 20 per cent of the Palestinian population was incarcerated; among males, it was 40 per cent. In commenting on these and other figures, Young concludes that the West Bank and Gaza are "the most imprisoned society in the world" (ibid., 2). And, referring to the work of Esmail Nashif (2008), a Palestinian scholar on Israeli prisons, she correctly observes that the carceral and brutal policies of the occupation provide a "flipped story of Foucault" in that, "contrary to Foucault the prisoner is not treated individually under the panopticon. He is treated collectively and racially" (J. Young 2012, 21). This lacuna in Michel Foucault's work is not to be construed as a disavowal of his theoretical edifice. Rather, Israel's colonial violence against the Palestinians "aims at elimination, not by the hanging rope or the guillotine but by techniques of gradual elimination of the human – bodily and morally." Thus punishment is intended "not to punish less, but to punish better – to insert the power to punish more deeply into the social body" (ibid.).

Science in the service of suffering

> ... at present, spatial organizations and physical instruments, technical standards, procedures and systems of monitoring have become the means for exercising contemporary violence and for governing the displaced, the enemy and the unwanted. (Weizman 2011, 3–4)

In his book *The Least of All Possible Evils: Humanitarian Violence from Arendt to Gaza* (2011), from which the above quotation comes, Eyal Weizman shows that although Israel's conduct in pre-2014 Gaza was masked by minimal "humanitarian" standards, these standards were in reality intended to justify the "physical and procedural siege mechanisms applied by Israel in Gaza" (ibid., 5). Weizman goes on to note, with an echo of Giorgio Agamben's work, that these standards "operated by calibrating the level of electric current, calories and other necessities to the minimum possible level in an attempt to govern people by reducing them to the limit of bare physical existence" (ibid.). The statement by Amos Gilad cited above does not acknowledge the escalation of the Israeli siege strategy, which has turned deadly on several occasions during successive Israeli invasions of Gaza. The use of grotesque quantitative measurements couched in mathematical equations (see ibid., 14, 85) is intended to camouflage and calibrate Palestinian suffering so as not to cross what COGAT calls the "red line," a threshold beyond which collective death and catastrophe occur. An investigative report by journalists Uri Blau and Yotam Feldman (2009) has looked into the military policy surrounding the siege of Gaza, with special attention to how decisions governing the selective entry of foodstuffs into Gaza are made. This is a siege that has been widely condemned by human rights organisations, as well as by the United Nations and state governments, although the siege continues to have the full backing of the United States and most Western governments. The entry of basic food products is based on calculating the required minimum caloric intake of the population on the basis of age and gender so as not to cause humanitarian disaster. It is a policy that is guided by what Weizman (2011) calls "the least of all possible evils." One is tempted to see the conduct of the Israeli army during its three invasions of Gaza from 2008 to 2014 through the prism of what Hannah Arendt (2006), writing about Adolf Eichmann's conduct during the Holocaust, calls the "banality of evil" – meaning that bureaucratic efficiency, not individual conduct, was to blame.[2] Nevertheless, Weizman concludes, a policy of least evil does not make it a humane policy or humanitarian under international humanitarian law.

The military guidelines that were eventually made available to journalists (but not to the Palestinians in Gaza) state that this is not a human siege but is intended to prevent the entry of non-essential "luxury" food items, which bizarrely include processed hummus and sesame paste. In the absence of written rules, the Palestinians are left in the dark about which food items are allowed and which are not. When queried by journalists, a COGAT official responded that the Palestinians "know what they are allowed to bring," yet a Palestinian responsible for coordinating with the Israelis told journalists, "Even if there are just 10 types of goods, I want to see it in writing." Journalists have discovered that there is a hidden dimension to selective listing and the lifting of prohibitions on food entry. In addition to bribery, which was mentioned by disgruntled Israeli exporters of fruits and vegetables, a former senior official with COGAT commented:

> There was a vague, unclear policy, influenced by the interests of certain groups, by this or that lobby, without any policy that derived from the needs of the population. For example, the fruit growers have a powerful lobby, and this lobby saw to it that on certain days, from 20–25 trucks full of fruit were brought into Gaza. It's not that it arrived there and was thrown out, but if you were to ask a Gazan who lives there, it's not exactly what he needs. What happened was that the Israeli interest took precedence over the needs of the populace. (In Blau and Feldman 2009)

Journalists have also discovered that under this policy, decisions on what to allow into Gaza are governed by a tug-of-war between the Israeli sellers of foodstuffs (fruits, vegetables, meats, etc.), the Ministries of Health and Agriculture, and the military establishment as the enforcer of the policy. The Palestinian Authority and Palestinian merchants who act as middlemen have little influence on the situation. As a matter of fact, Palestinian intermediaries who have questioned the policy have been told in no uncertain terms to cease.

A telling newspaper report by Amira Hass (2010b) is subtitled "Since Hamas took control of Gaza, officials have employed mathematical formulas to monitor goods from aid groups entering the Strip to ensure amount was in line with what Israel permitted." Thus we read about "coefficients" employed to determine Gaza's "breathing space," a term used by COGAT authorities to refer to the number of days remaining until a certain supply runs out, which dictates the entry of allowed quantities. Israeli authorities have defended this use of statistics, stating that they consulted the Ministry of Health and used consumption data based on the Palestinian census.

Hass (2012c) reports that Israeli "security" is at the top of COGAT's list, followed by concerns for public health, whether the product is a luxury item, how it squares with Israel's "legal obligations," if the product could be used for infrastructure and development projects (here Hass reproduces a list of items such as building and raw materials, cloth, needles and thread, cleaning and bathing supplies, books, musical instruments, and processed hummus), and the reaction of the international community. Hass notes that COGAT came up with a figure of 2,279 calories per person as a red-line threshold below which life would be threatened. It is questionable whether this figure was adhered to, given the plethora of health studies and reports attesting to widespread malnutrition and a lack of essential types of food in Gaza, with detrimental effects on the young and other vulnerable groups, such as women and older people (Save the Children and Medical Aid for Palestinians 2012).

As a result of the military's unwillingness to voluntarily release its guidelines on the prohibition against food and other products entering Gaza, Israel's Gisha Legal Center for Freedom of Movement appealed to the Israeli Supreme Court, which compelled the Ministry of Defense to release its policy guidelines. Gisha published a position paper in October 2012 that contains details about the ministry's document titled *Food Consumption in the Gaza Strip – Red Lines*. The Gisha position paper presents interesting revelations about the process of establishing such data. First, the Ministry of Defense denied the existence of any such policy and stated that any documents, including those in draft form, "have never been used as a basis for implementing civilian policy toward the Gaza Strip" (in Gisha 2012, 2). Later, under pressure from the Supreme Court, the military admitted the existence of such guidelines, but Amos Gilad, who at the time was in charge of COGAT, claimed that releasing the details would harm "Israel's security and its international relations" (ibid., 3). When the document explaining the so-called "red lines" was finally released, Gisha (ibid., 5) commented:

> The presentation includes calculations made by the Ministry of Health in order to determine the number of calories and the weight of various basic food items Gaza residents require, according to age and gender. These figures are translated into the number of trucks needed daily and the specifics of their contents, taking into account local production of vegetables, milk and meat.

The overall impact of the food siege policy was evident in both the health and the economic domains. The Gisha paper points out, for example, that the curtailment of egg exports to Gaza adversely affected the poultry industry, while the blocking of access to the Israeli market, on which the Palestinians are highly dependent, reduced production levels in Gaza and contributed to high unemployment. In the words of Gisha (2012, 7):

It appears that the policy of economic warfare achieved its goal, inasmuch as the goal was to cripple Gaza's economy. In the second quarter of 2008, unemployment soared to 72% compared to the second quarter of 2007, just before the closure was tightened, reaching a level of 45.5%. The number of people receiving humanitarian aid rose from 63% in 2006 to 80% by December 2007.

After the siege of Gaza went into full effect, food surveys in 2008 by United Nations organisations such as the Relief and Works Agency (UNRWA 2008), the World Food Programme, and the Food and Agricultural Organization documented the health repercussions on a population that was already reeling from poverty and high unemployment under so-called "normal conditions." Some 70 per cent of Gaza's residents receive food aid from humanitarian organisations. On the eve of Israel's invasion of Gaza in November 2012, poverty and unemployment levels were worsening (UNCTAD 2012). In its August 2012 report, the United Nations mission in Gaza questioned whether Gaza "will be 'a livable place' in 2020," with the gross domestic product in 2011 hovering around $1,165, a further decline from an already low level of $1,397 in 1994 (in Rudoren 2012).

Suicide killings

> It should be noted that the control of the body has always been one major obsession of the colonial mind, a fixation engendered by the recognition of colonialism's outer limits. The Palestinians that annihilate themselves in order to kill must face a condition in which a suicidal determination has become an ontologically available one. (Veracini 2006, 12)

There has been little balanced discussion of state terrorism and the roots of suicide bombing in the popular press, other than to label it as terrorism and attribute it to culture, religion, and general primitive backwardness. Yossi Sarid (2009), a previous justice and foreign minister in the Labor Party government, quoted one of his students in the aftermath of the 2009 attack on Gaza: "If I were a young Palestinian, I would fight the Jews fiercely, even by means of terror. Anyone who says anything different is telling you lies." Sarid reminded his readers that none other than Ehud Barak, when asked by a journalist a decade earlier what he would do if he were born a Palestinian, had replied, "I would join a terror organization."

Contempt for the Palestinians is not confined to officials and faceless public opinion data. It also extends to politicians and Israeli intellectuals who, in the case of one-time leftist historian Benny Morris, wish that ethnic cleansing of the Palestinians had been pursued in 1948. If this path had been followed by Israel to its fullest, Morris (2004) argues, there would be no refugee problem to contend with now. He advances his position as one more example of the price all modern nation-states must pay to secure independence: "Even the great American democracy could not have been created without the annihilation of the Indians." Historian

A. Dirk Moses (2008, 6) regards the position of Morris and others as an example of a "phallic logic": "Commentators shout 'my trauma is bigger than yours' in order to defend or attack the theodicy that the brutal extermination and disappearances of people over the centuries is redeemed by human progress in the form of the Western-dominated global system of nation-states."

The refugee camp

> We the Palestinians are terrorists and therefore anything they do to us is legitimate. We are treated as *homo sacer* – people to whom the laws of the rest of humanity do not apply. (Shehadeh 2003, 95)

According to the United Nations Relief and Works Agency (UNRWA) for refugees, the descendants of the 750,000 Palestinians who were expelled by Israel in 1947–48 and/or fled from their homes in Palestine now number 5 million. They live in fifty-eight camps in Lebanon, Syria, Jordan, Gaza, and the West Bank that are administered by the agency (UNRWA n.d. c). They are frequently the target of mistreatment by the host governments and the local population, although this varies in intensity and frequency from one country to another. The fighting in Syria that began in 2011 has internally displaced more than 50 per cent of the half-million UN-registered Palestinian refugees there. An additional 70,000 have been displaced to Lebanon and Jordan (UNRWA n.d. b).

Although occupation is associated with all kinds of deprivations in daily life, the sixty-six-year-old Palestinian refugee camp is "not simply where Palestinians have been gathered; it is rather the space in which their existence is constantly being reduced to 'bare life'" (A. Azoulay and Ophir 2004). The camp metaphor extends beyond the actual refugee camps. Azmi Bishara (2004) describes the maze of walls, barriers, gates, observation towers, barbed wire, and electrical wires slicing through villages and other inhabited areas of the West Bank as tantamount to the "recreation of the detention camp where the exception becomes the rule . . . and the state of emergency becomes permanent." It is not surprising to see several authors engage with Agamben's work in their discussions of the situation facing Palestinian refugees. For both Agamben and Hannah Arendt before him, the twentieth-century refugee symbolises, on the one hand, the most vulnerable person under the aegis of the nation-state and, on the other (for Arendt 1978, 66), "the vanguard of their peoples – if they kept their identity" (see also Arendt 2007). Arendt argues that the nation-state, which is burdened with nationalism, resulted in the creation of stateless people. It is in this sense that she is critical of the nation and the state and has serious misgivings about Zionism (see Butler 2007, 2012). Arendt's analysis, according to Agamben (1995), invites us "to abandon without misgivings the basic concepts in which we have represented political subjects up to now (man and citizen with their rights, but also the sovereign people, the worker, etc.) and to reconstruct our political philosophy beginning with this unique figure [the refugee]." Refugee camps and refugee-hood epitomise the state of exception in conflict zones.

Here Palestinian refugees live outside juridical law but inside the spaces controlled by the sovereign that controls the law. To quote Agamben (1998, 28), "He who has been banned is not, in fact, simply set outside the law and made indifferent to it, but rather *abandoned* by it, that is, exposed and threatened on the threshold in which life and law, outside and inside, become indistinguishable" (emphasis in original). Thus bare life reflects the objectification and commodification of life where individuals are stripped of their dignity and personhood (Edkins 2008).

This is true not only of life in the West Bank and Gaza, which are controlled and directly monitored by Israel. Palestinian refugees in other places of dispersal, such as Lebanon, Jordan, and Syria – and anywhere else, for that matter – live under close surveillance by the host governments (Human Rights Watch 2010), whether inside camps or outside them, and by the UNRWA for Palestinian refugees. The upshot of this, according to T.J. Demos (2006), who echoes Agamben, is that:

> The nation-state is the very power uniquely authorized to suspend law when it sees fit, creating a state of emergency – that zone of indeterminacy between law and non-law that opens a space for extrajudicial brutality (e.g., torture and executions) – that is now threatening to become the rule. In reality Palestinians already exist in the shadow of the nation-state, precariously inhabiting Israel's seemingly permanent state of exception.

Palestinian refugees have gone through numerous massacres and calamities since they were expelled from their homes in Palestine, all of which have been carried out in the name of state security under the aegis of one nation-state or another. In 2015 Palestinian refugees became caught up in the civil war in Syria, and as a result the Yarmouk refugee camp near Damascus has been savagely attacked and almost emptied of its Palestinian residents. An extreme case of the vulnerability of Palestinian refugees in their bare life came into relief during Israel's invasion of Lebanon in 1982 due to the ensuing Sabra and Shatila refugee camp massacres near Beirut, with the full knowledge and connivance of the occupying Israeli army under the command of Ariel Sharon, commander of Israeli forces in Lebanon at the time.[3] In 2014 Palestinian refugees paid a heavy price for the civil war that was raging in Syria as a result of direct bombardment of the refugee camps.

I keep reminding readers that the shortcoming of Foucault's writings on biopolitics lies in its underdetermination of colonialism, which prevents his analysis from accommodating the intersection between race, gender, population, territory, and governmentality in a colonial context (Venn 2009; Stoler 1995). Robert Young (1995), in a widely cited article, notes that although Foucault did not take colonialism into account in his writings, he did in later years deal with modern racism, which he traced to the middle of the nineteenth century and the rise of eugenics. Biopower became a disciplinary tool in the hands of the state that enabled it to regulate the welfare of the population on behalf of race and class supremacy. Nazism was the culmination of such a "blood" ideology, in which "class, sexuality and race" were held together (ibid., 11). It must be said, however, that Foucault primarily directed his concerns inwardly toward European societies. But in doing so, according to Couze Venn (2009), he downplayed the "constitutive role of colonialism" and European capitalist development in shaping biopolitics. To the extent that Foucault (2003, 103) dealt with colonialism, it was to record its impact on Europe by means of what he called the "boomerang effect":

> At the end of the sixteenth century we have, then, if not the first, at least an early example of the sort of boomerang effect colonial practice can have on the juridico-political structures of the West. It should never be forgotten that while colonization, with its techniques and its political and its juridical weapons, obviously transported European models to other continents, it also had a considerable boomerang effect on the mechanisms of power in the West, and on the apparatuses, institutions and techniques of power. A whole series of colonial models was brought back to the West, and the result was that the West could practice something resembling colonization, or an internal colonialism, on itself.

From disproportionate killings to necropolitics

In a briefing at the start of the name-coded Operation Cast Lead in 2008, a company commander instructed his Israeli soldiers:

> I want aggressiveness – if there's someone suspicious on the upper floor of the house, we will shell it. If we have suspicions about a house, we will take it down . . . There will be no hesitation . . . Nobody will deliberate – let the mistakes be over their lives, not ours. (In Amnesty International 2009, 6)

This section provides an overview of Palestinian and Israeli fatalities since 2000, followed by separate summaries of fatalities in each of the four major campaigns by Israel against the OPT: Operation Defensive Shield in the West Bank from 29 March to 3 May 2002, with special focus on the Jenin refugee camp; Operation Cast Lead from 27 December 2008 to 18 January 2009; Operation Pillar of Defense from 14 to 21 November 2012, and Operation Protective Edge, carried out intermittently from 7 July to 24 August 2014, when a ceasefire was established. It is important to note that there were other campaigns in which Gaza was targeted, such as Operation Summer Rains from June to September 2006, Operation Autumn Clouds in November 2006, and Operation Warm Winter from February to March 2008.

An overview of Arab and Jewish casualties in the south of the country that was compiled by *Haaretz* newspaper starting on 21 April 2001, after the outbreak of the Second Intifada, and that covers two separate Israeli incursions – one from 27 December 2008 to 18 January 2009 and the other from 14 to 21 November 2012 – demonstrates the extent of disproportionate killings. Including the fatalities of the 2014 incursion into Gaza, a total of 6,816 Palestinians and 135 Israelis were killed in the south of the country (Table 5.1). In Operation Protective Edge, 2,100 Palestinians from Gaza and a total of 64 Israeli soldiers and 6 Israeli civilians were killed. Palestinian estimates put the number of buildings destroyed at 10,800, and 50,000 were damaged. Included in these statistics are 277 schools, 270 mosques, and 10 hospitals. Among the fatalities were 500 Palestinian children (Rudoren and Akram 2014). A United Nations assessment of the cost of this war concluded that current figures underestimate the human and material damage. The number of displaced people now stands at 350,000. And a UNICEF official in Gaza said "that if the severe Israeli trade constraints on Gaza were not relaxed, a preliminary analysis showed it could take 18 years to rebuild destroyed housing, furthering the prospect that young Gazans would reach adulthood in deprivation, anger and despair." In particular, this official singled out the severe psychological impact of the war on children, who constitute 50 per cent of Gaza's population (in Gladstone 2014).

Covering a somewhat overlapping period from 29 September 2000 to 30 September 2012, statistics compiled by the Israeli Human rights organisation B'Tselem (2014b), which this time include the West Bank and Gaza, show that 4,660 Palestinians were killed in Gaza and 1,840 in the West Bank, for a total of 6,500 Palestinian casualties in the OPT, in addition to 69 Palestinians who were killed within the Green Line. During the same period, 500 Israeli civilians and 90 army personnel were killed by Palestinians. The statistics for Israeli fatalities in the OPT are 254 civilians and 253 combatants. The number of Palestinians who were killed by other Palestinians was 671. B'Tselem further shows that of the total number of Palestinians killed in the OPT, 1,335 were minors below the age of fifteen. A total of 44 Israeli minors were killed in the OPT and 85 in Israel. Targeted assassinations by Israel killed 259 Palestinians, and an additional 434 Palestinians, so-called "collateral damage," were also "killed during the course of a targeted killing." Of the total Palestinians who were killed by Israel, 3,029 (2,190 in Gaza and 839 in the West Bank) were not involved in hostilities. In Israel 500 Israeli civilians were killed. Excluding the 2014 attack on Gaza, Defense for Children International Palestine (2015) documented the death of 561 children, whereas in 2014 Operation Protective Edge alone claimed the lives of 500 Palestinian children. Between the start of the Second Intifada in September 2000 and April 2013, the number of casualties among Palestinians who were eighteen years of age and younger was 1,373. And the number of child fatalities in Gaza was 1,045, compared to 129 Israeli children who were killed by Palestinians during the same thirteen-year period (Hass 2013).

Operation Defensive Shield, 29 March to 3 May 2002

In the wake of Ariel Sharon's provocative visit to Al-Aqsa Mosque in Jerusalem in 2000, the Palestinians launched their Second Intifada, or Al-Aqsa Intifada, which lasted from September 2000 to February 2005. The period witnessed suicide

TABLE 5.1 Palestinian and Israeli Fatalities in Gaza and Southern Israel, 2001–14

Year	Palestinians killed	Israelis killed
2001	179	1
2002	373	0
2003	370	0
2004	625	7
2005	103	4
2006	525	5
2007	295	2
2008	833	8
2009	1,013	9
2010	71	3
2011	102	11
2012[a]	227	9
2012[b]	174	6
2014[c]	2,100	70
Total	6,816	135

[a] Up to 1 November [b] 14–21 November [c] 8 July to 25 August

Sources: The data up to 1 November 2012 are in Levy (2012); the data for 14–21 November 2012 are in United Nations Human Rights Council (2008); and the data for 2014 are in Rudoren and Akram (2014).

bombings carried out by Palestinians and large-scale attacks by Israel on Palestinian towns, villages, and refugee camps; these resulted in mainly civilian fatalities on both sides: 4,000 Palestinians and around 1,000 Israelis (*BBC News* 2005; Araj and Brym 2011). A United Nations (2002) report described the operation as "[t]he most extensive Israeli military incursions in a decade."

B'Tselem's (2002) report on the operation documented the extent of house demolitions, land confiscation, destruction of agricultural land, curfews, denial of access to medical treatment, and violations of human rights.

The following discussion focuses on the Jenin refugee camp, which Israel attacked in April 2002. During the campaign, it tested new tactics of urban warfare that drew upon postmodern writings.

Postmodern violence

> If until now you were used to move along roads and sidewalks, forget it! From now on we all walk through walls! (Aviv Kochavi to his troops, in Weizman 2007, 199)

Israel's attack from 19 to 28 April 2002 on the densely populated Palestinian refugee camp of 14,000 residents in the West Bank town of Jenin attracted the attention of political and military pundits, who mostly hailed the introduction of new tactics and strategies to counter guerrilla warfare in urban centres. Coming at a time when the United States was embroiled in its first Iraq war, Israel was anxious to provide an example of how to deploy unconventional military strategies in urban guerrilla warfare. To capture the extent of the destruction of life and infrastructure in Jenin, Stephen Graham (2003, 63), a British geographer, uses the term "urbicide" to describe "the deliberate wrecking or killing of the city." According to Graham, the bulldozer, described by an Israeli chief of staff as a "strategic weapon," is one element in the urbicide matrix. And the demolition of houses and cities is carried out so as "to reduce the vulnerability of the growing archipelago of Jewish settlements and highways to Palestinian attack." The strategy of urbicide leads to "the forcible de-modernization of Palestinian society" (ibid., 64). The erection of the Israeli version of the Berlin Wall complements this process and functions to limit population movement, stifle the economy, and deprive Palestinians of access to their land. Altogether, Palestinian society is subjected to cultural, economic, and social strangulation. "Finally," Graham declares, "urbicide by bulldozer is also intricately linked to a maze of discriminatory planning and building regulations, which ensure that virtually all new Palestinian housing is constructed 'illegally' in cramped and poorly serviced conditions. These are then reviled by Israeli politicians as uncivilized nests of terrorism" (ibid., 65).

The tactics deployed during the Jenin incursion saw the application of what Weizman (2006) called "lethal theory." Here again, we encounter Israel's military fascination with and pretension of scientific (philosophical) explanations. Leading the movement to fashion Israel's twenty-first-century army around the concept of postmodernity are retired General Shimon Naveh and current General Aviv Kochavi. With theories borrowed from the writings of well-known postmodern French philosophers, such as Michel Foucault, Gilles Deleuze, and Felix Guattari, the cornerstone of this theory is the need to move away from a centralised, hierarchical structure and toward decentralised urban warfare. As Yotam Feldman (2007) notes:

> Naveh and his pupils took the Deleuze-Guattari theory, which was formulated as a philosophy of resistance and liberation and was influenced by the student revolt in France in 1968 as well as by feminist and anti-nationalist thought, and made it the theoretical underpinning for assassinations, defoliation, home demolitions and wall breaking in homes.

Under the Israelis army's now defunct Operational Theory Research Institute, Naveh set out to disseminate to officers an operational theory of postmodern warfare. When attacking urban centres, such as the refugee camps in Nablus and Jenin, they were told to use "swarming," "walk through walls," and avoid the streets. Walking through walls means literally walking through roofs, living rooms, bedrooms, and corridors to overwhelm Palestinian fighters and avoid exposure to counterattacks in streets and open spaces. Drawing upon his architectural training, Weizman (2007, 186) remarks, "The tactics of 'walking through walls' involved a conception of the city as not just the site, but as the very *medium* of warfare – a flexible, almost liquid matter that is forever contingent and in flux" (emphasis in original). Thus, due to the new teachings of Naveh and Kochavi, during Operation Defensive Shield the "West Bank has become a giant laboratory of urban warfare at the expense of hundreds of civilian lives, property, and infrastructure." The outcome of such innovation in warfare is described by Weizman as "destruction by design" (ibid., 188, 201).

Three case studies

Operation Cast Lead, 27 December 2008 to 18 January 2009

The report by B'Tselem (2011) on Operation Cast Lead states:

> The magnitude of the harm to the local population was unprecedented: 1,391 Palestinians were killed, 759 of whom did not take part in the hostilities. Of these, 318 were minors under age 18. More than 5,300 Palestinians were wounded, 350 of them seriously. Israel also caused enormous damage to residential dwellings, industrial buildings, agriculture and infrastructure for electricity, sanitation, water, and health, which was already on the verge of collapse prior to the operation. According to UN figures, Israel destroyed more than 3,500 residential dwellings and 20,000 people were left homeless.

It is important to note that violence did not cease with the official end of the campaign. B'Tselem states that between 19 January and the start of Operation Protective Edge on 7 July 2014, 486 Palestinians were killed by the Israeli military in Gaza and that 97 were killed in the West Bank, compared to a combined 37 Israeli soldiers and civilians who were killed by Palestinians in the West Bank and Gaza. Among the fatalities were 105 Palestinian women and children, compared to 13 Israelis. And, according to B'Tselem (2014a), these figures do not include "Palestinians who died after Israel delayed their transfer for medical treatment" outside Gaza and the West Bank.

The official Israeli position is that Cast Lead was launched in response to rockets emanating from Gaza into southern Israel. Israel usually focuses on the large number of rockets fired at Israel, although the extent of damage, both in lives and property, is usually small, compared to the destruction heaped on Gaza. It is important, however, to go beyond the stated reasons for Israel's actions in order to identify the other, deeper justifications of this campaign, as well as whether it has a common denominator both with other such campaigns and with Israel's ingrained hatred of the Palestinians.

Operation Pillar of Defense, 14–21 November 2012

Relative to other campaigns, Operation Pillar of Defense in 2012 against Gaza was short, lasting for only one week. Yet the level of killing and destruction was significant, particularly in the second half of the operation. On the Palestinian side, 80 per cent of the uninvolved civilian fatalities were recorded in the last four days of the operation. Thus B'Tselem's (2013a) report "challenges the common perception in the Israeli public and media that the operation was 'surgical' and caused practically no fatalities among uninvolved Palestinian civilians." The United Nations (2013) reports that the number of Palestinians who were killed in Gaza alone was between 177 (Israeli sources) and 189 (Palestinian sources) and that the number of Palestinians who were injured was between 900 (Israeli sources) and 1,526 (Palestinian sources). Israeli fatalities amounted to 4 civilians and 3 soldiers. B'Tselem's (2013a) statistics on the age composition of Palestinian fatalities show that 36 per cent were under the age of eighteen and that 10 per cent were over fifty-five.

Human rights violations were singled out by the United Nations, B'tselem, and Amnesty International, among several human rights organisations. The list of violations included killing bystanders, hampering medical treatment of the injured, and destroying homes and property, which usually resulted in loss of life, as occurred on 18 November 2012 when "an Israeli air strike without prior warning hit a three-storey house belonging to the Al-Dalou family in Al-Nasser neighbourhood, central Gaza City. The airstrike killed 12 people, five of whom were children and four were women. Ten of those killed belonged to one family" (UN 2013, 6). This is one of several cases outlined by the United Nations, whose report attests to how quick Israel was to claim that "people who have relevance to terror activity" were hiding among civilians (ibid., 8). The report further states:

> During the crisis civilian properties other than residences, such as farms and businesses, also sustained damages or were destroyed as a result of IDF attacks. While some of these were the result of direct hits by airstrikes, others were the result of being located next to or close to targeted areas. This again raises questions whether the basic principles of distinction, proportionality, and precautions were fulfilled. The overall loss and damage inflicted on the agricultural sector is estimated at USD 20 million. (Ibid.)

After analysing several cases in which Palestinian civilians were killed or injured, B'Tselem (2013a) reached similar conclusions: the "report raises suspicions that the military violated International Humanitarian Law (IHL). Breaches of two major aspects of IHL are of greatest concern: lack of effective advance notice of an impending attack and an unacceptably broad definition of what constitutes a 'legitimate target.'"

Operation Protective Edge, 7 July to 24 August 2014

On 19 August 2014, two weeks after the conclusion of the incursion into Gaza, the Israel Democracy Institute (IDI 2014) released the results of a public opinion poll showing that 92 per cent of Israeli Jews thought the war was justified and that 45 per cent thought the amount of force used was insufficient. The *Jerusalem*

Post reports that 71 Israelis died and that 842 were treated for mainly shock and minor injuries (Hartman 2014). The BBC, which describes the Gaza war as "the first social media war," reports that 2,104 Palestinians were killed, of whom 1,462 were civilians, including 495 children and 213 women (Hughes 2012). Quoting United Nations figures, *BBC News* (2014) further points out that of the 1.8 million people who inhabit Gaza, 475,000 were left living in emergency shelters or with relatives, that 17,200 homes were destroyed, and that 244 schools were damaged, including schools operated by the United Nations Agency for Refugees.

In a perceptive opinion piece, Raef Zreik, a Palestinian lawyer who is the academic director of the Minerva Humanities Centre at Tel Aviv University, makes two relevant points about Israel's resort to violence. First, Israel invokes Zionism constantly to mobilise world Jewry as a means to achieve its aims of combating anti-Semitism and building a state, but in the process it remains wedded to achieving these goals by creating and sustaining enmity toward others – the Palestinians in particular. Force is used to achieve the latter end. Second, as we saw in chapter 4, there is at the level of Israeli public opinion overwhelming support for measures that largely dehumanise the Palestinian people and for the use of deadly violence against them. In Zreik's (2014) words:

> It's hard to be convinced that the side effects of military action in the form of harm to civilians are seen in Israel as an undesirable goal when the air is full of slogans like "death to the Arabs" and calls to "destroy" and "annihilate" the enemy. But there's every reason to believe – even if there's no proof – that Operation Protective Edge in Gaza this summer [2014] was a war against an entire nation. [See also Hass 2009]

Joel Beinin (2014) is more direct in attributing wide-scale destruction of Palestinian lives and property to a deep-rooted Israeli form of Orientalist racism that triggers hatred and violence against the Palestinians. Thus prior to the 2014 Israeli incursion into Gaza, calls for "death to the Arabs" and other similar racist calls by Jewish mobs and Israeli politicians were heard frequently, not to mention the series of bills passed by the Knesset in 2011 that target Palestinian citizens of Israel.

Conclusion

Because of the Israeli-imposed policies of separation, Palestinians in the West Bank have been reduced to helpless spectators unable to come to the aid of their brethren in Gaza (Kershner 2014). Yet Israel's spokespersons never tire of boasting that its army is "the most moral army in the world" (Keinon 2014). Go tell it to the Palestinians, who have been at the receiving end of the Israeli army's brutality since 1948, if not before. Israel is constantly seeking justifications for its military conduct, and there is no shortage of legal experts (e.g., Asa Kasher, in A. Harel 2009) and other apologists at home (e.g., Henkin 2003) who are prepared to lend support to the practices of the Israeli army. Immediately after the end of the 2008–09 Gaza invasion, which took the lives of 1,400 Palestinians, in contrast to 9 Israelis, Asa Kasher, a philosopher at Tel Aviv University, explained in newspaper interviews the ethical justifications for the conduct of the Israeli army in its confrontation with Palestinian fighters, regardless of the high civilian cost. For Kasher, such conduct, which includes targeted assassinations and large collateral damage, is perfectly moral and justified as long as it is aimed at protecting the lives of Israeli soldiers:

> Sending a soldier there to fight terrorists is justified, but why should I force him to endanger himself much more than that so that the terrorist's neighbor isn't killed? I don't have an answer for that. From the standpoint of the state of Israel, the neighbor is much less important. I owe the soldier more. If it's between the soldier and the terrorist's neighbor, the priority is the soldier. Any country would do the same. (In A. Harel 2009)

Israel describes its violence toward the Palestinians along several dimensions. First, the violence is said to be an act of self-defence. Second, Israel claims to obey international norms governing rules of military engagement by taking special care to avoid harming the civilian population. Third, it frames its fight against the Palestinians as a matter of national survival. Fourth, since the attack of 11 September 2001 on the United States, it has argued in public forums that its fight is part of the global fight against the terrorism engulfing Western countries, a group to which Israel considers itself to belong. Fifth, Israel claims to spearhead a global fight against anti-Semites, a group to which the Palestinian radical factions are said to implicitly, if not explicitly, belong. Finally, Israel does not hesitate to equate criticism of its policies with anti-Semitism.

Books and articles have been written to refute each of the above points. The evidence presented so far clearly casts doubt on Israel's intentions, bearing in mind that its attitude toward the Palestinians germinated during the pre-1948 period in its settler-colonial policies. The basis for Israel's position in debating these points is that it rejects the idea that it is engaged in a form of state terrorism or that through its military actions it is committing war crimes that contribute significantly to the loss of lives and destruction of property; it sees itself as righteous and forced to act the way it does. One here cannot help but recall the words of Golda Meir, who more than five decades ago complained that Israel cannot forgive the Palestinians for compelling it to kill them!

In all cases, Israel rejects or refuses to cooperate with international investigative bodies, as it did in 2014 when the United Nations Human Rights Council appointed an independent commission to investigate allegations of war crimes on both sides of the Gaza war. It is significant that when faced with international pressure like that marshalled by the Human Rights Council, Israel tries to blunt such criticism by appointing its own commissions of inquiry. It is no wonder that human rights organisations in Israel such as B'Tselem (2014a) regard this Israeli government exercise as serving only to rubber stamp the conduct of the military in Gaza.

Notes

1 In an open letter to the British government asking it to withdraw its ambassador from Israel in the wake of the Gaza attack of 2008–09, a prominent group of British Jews cited Weissglass's comment and quoted Matan Vilnai, the Israeli deputy defence minister at the time, who warned that the Palestinians would suffer from "a bigger shoah" (holocaust). The writers of the letter went on to say, "this reminds us of Governor General Hans Frank in Nazi-occupied Poland, who spoke of 'death by hunger'" (in *Guardian* 2009). Adding his voice to the Israeli calls for collective lethal punishments of Palestinians is Mordechai Eliyahu, former Sephardi chief rabbi of Israel, who quoted Jewish scripture in 2007 when calling for blanket bombing of the Palestinians living in Gaza (Wagner 2007). In 2004 former chief of the Israeli army Raphael Eitan, who opposed vacating Palestinian land, remarked that "when we have settled the land, all the Arabs will be able to do about it will be to scurry around like drugged cockroaches in a bottle" (in *BBC News* 2004). In the words of Ilan Pappé (2009):

> ... it is not only in military discourse that Palestinians are dehumanized. A similar process is at work in Jewish civil society in Israel, and it explains the massive support there for the carnage in Gaza. Palestinians have been so dehumanized by Israeli Jews – whether politicians, soldiers or ordinary citizens – that killing them comes naturally, as did expelling them in 1948, or imprisoning them in the Occupied Territories.

There is no shortage of Israeli official pronouncements that show contempt for and dehumanisation of Palestinians. Public opinion is no different, including Israeli youth who regularly demonstrate their high level of racism toward the Palestinians, including those who are citizens of the state. As minister of transport in Ariel Sharon's government in 2003, Avigdor Lieberman, current foreign minister of Israel, offered to provide transport to Palestinian prisoners for the sake of drowning them in the sea rather than releasing them from prison (N. Gordon 2009). For an overview of anti-Arab racism in Israel, see Abunimah (2009).

2 Hannah Arendt's portrayal of Adolf Eichmann as a cog in a ruthless Nazi extermination machine has been seriously challenged by Bettina Stangneth in her book *Eichmann before Jerusalem: The Unexamined Life of a Mass Murderer* (2014), which argues that Eichmann was a wilful participant in and planner of the Holocaust.

3 The Israeli official report, titled *Report of the Commission of Inquiry into the Events of the Refugee Camps in Beirut – 8 February 1983* (IMFA 1983), laid "indirect responsibility" for the Phalange units' ability to enter the camps and massacre hundreds of refugees. The appendix of the report remains classified to this day. For a contrary view that lays the blame squarely on the Israeli government, particularly Ariel Sharon, see MacBride and colleagues (1983).

6
THE INTERNET AND ACTS OF EVERYDAY RESISTANCE

During its early days, the silicon chip offered the possibility that finally the third world would be able to experience economic and social development without having to labour through the industrial phase of heavy mechanisation experienced by Western industrial societies. With an exponential drop in the price of the chip, accompanied by an exponential increase in its storage capacity, the third world could finally see its future path to prosperity materialise through a quick transition from preindustrial to postindustrial ways. Yet most commentators now admit that the preindustrial-postindustrial divide, which has distinguished the developing from the developed world since the nineteenth century, is now being replicated through the emergence of a digital divide separating the third world from advanced countries (Sciadas 2005). The third world remains largely a consumer of Western technology rather than a producer of its own technology. This is primarily the case with information and communication technologies (ICT). Compared to the West, the Arab world and the third world in general lag behind in terms of registration of patents and investment in research and development (Madar Research and Development 2014, 20).

Early on, the presence of the digital divide triggered interest in researching the causes of this divide and ways to overcome it in the hope of lifting the third world out of its economic and technological inferiority by achieving a level of sustainable development (Mansell and Wehn 1998). The study of ICT diffusion in the third world has followed two main approaches or their variations. The first approach focuses on the institutional mechanisms of a country – its infrastructure, wealth, nature of the human capital, and government regulatory policies – as key ingredients in building the information society. This approach characterises a great deal of the basis for the standard diffusion models – in both developed and developing countries. The second approach, less prevalent in the literature but no less important, focuses on the role of the cultural-national framework in facilitating or hindering the adoption of ICT and its deployment in society. Although the two approaches are interrelated, the thrust of the latter approach is to unravel the relationship between values, national culture, and attitudes to technology. In particular, it is argued that the development of democratic and participatory norms at the level of civil society is essential for the successful diffusion of the Internet.

This chapter provides a literature review of the conceptual framework for understanding ICT adoption in the Arab world and the debate surrounding the digital divide; an overview of the rates of diffusion of the Internet and other information and communication technologies in the Arab countries; an examination of historical data and case studies from major Palestinian cities in the West Bank and Gaza, refugee camps, and villages that highlight Palestinian experience with the Internet and Israeli policies toward the Palestinians regarding the Internet and information technology; a discussion of the dialectic of the Internet, and conclusions.

Conceptual framework

Broadly speaking, research on patterns of technology adoption in the Arab world can be divided into two main categories. First, there is policy-oriented research, which to a very large extent is driven by the interests and aid programs of international organisations and donor countries. This is particularly true in the case of Palestine, where national ICT policies remain in their formative stage and where dependence on the outside world in adopting ICT is a dominant feature to this day. Other Arab countries with national ICT policies have tended very much to operate in a top-down fashion, guided by nation-state interests, with varying degrees of attention (depending on the country in question) being paid to public use and modes of access to the technology. Second, at the level of values, the literature reflects the old debate surrounding the relationship between modernisation and traditional value orientations of Arabs. There are those who explain technology transfer and its concomitant problems on the basis of the culture and value system of the region. According to this approach, the receiving region is portrayed as passive and lacking agency. Within this debate, we are beginning to see promising lines of investigation. Rather than divide the list of determining "variables" in a dichotomous fashion, Jon Anderson (2000), who borrows from actor-network theory in the social study of science (see Latour 1987), argues that it is more productive to think of a "dense model of diffusion that includes innovative and creative initiatives as well as more passive responses at the consumer level." Thus it is important to "open this 'technology' variable into its social and cultural components, which include the work habits and organization of the developers, recruitment and support of technologies" (Anderson 2000, 422). Anderson makes the important point that it is not upon the recipients as consumers that we should focus in the early stages of the diffusion of Internet technology; rather, it is the production process that is relevant, namely the nature of the sociotechnical system that surrounds the agents responsible for technological innovations, the processes they adopt to achieve their goals, and the available infrastructure. Here he singles out the role of diasporic groups as agents of change and facilitators of technology transfer and its diffusion. Indeed, in the case of the Palestinians, the prime movers in Internet use during its emergence in the early 1990s were either Western-educated or were able to shuttle between Palestine and the outside world.

A different kind of support for the above argument comes from Mamoun Fandy (2000), who argues that, contrary to the preaching of modernisation theorists, diffusion of ICT in the Arab world has not been accompanied by democratisation. As long as the state continues in one way or another to monopolise ICT, there is little hope that civil society will benefit from ICT. A digital divide continues to characterise the Arab world. This is true regionally as well as within the countries concerned. For example, Fandy points out that it is precisely because the elites, in a place like Saudi Arabia, have at their disposal disproportionate access to ICT that opposition to the regime has not taken the route of democratisation. Instead, and this applies to other parts of the Arab world, there is a technological bias within ICT. For example, why is it that cell phones are diffused in Egypt at a rate four times higher than Internet use? This has to do with trust, he argues. Arab society remains to a very large extent an oral society. Personal contact, through voice and face-to-face exchanges, remains a preferred mode of communication. Relatively speaking, there is a cultural bias against trusting the Internet because of its impersonal nature, compared to the cell phone and prior to that the audio cassette. Thus oppositional groups were initially able to build mass support networks in the Arab world by relying on simple technologies like the cassette long before the Internet was introduced there. But it is clear now, in light of the Arab Spring, which extended from late 2010 to mid-2012, that with the expansion of Internet use and the adoption of various networking technologies, societal engagement and activism are becoming noticeable features of the Arab world.

A case study by Carole Hill and colleagues (1998), whose focus is the cultural influences of ICT penetration, provides support for the argument regarding the role of diasporas in innovation, although without denying the importance of indigenous culture. Based on an interview sample of 270 "knowledge workers" drawn from Jordan, Egypt, Saudi Arabia, Lebanon, and the Sudan, the authors show that those who lived in the United States were more inclined to adopt computers at work than those who did not. Yet this was not accomplished at the expense of collectivist and family values. Many of the interviewees explained that their reluctance to use a computer at home was due to its "foreign" origin, to the fact that it was not based on face-to-face communication, and to its tendency to disrupt family life. The authors conclude by noting that "the preferences in Arab culture for face-to-face dealings mitigate against technology interfaces as does the cultural tendency to build consensus and create family-like environments within organizations" (ibid., 36). A high level of education seems to enable some to override the cultural influences and incorporate outside factors into their orientation to the technology. It is important to note that the authors of this study do not call for either ignoring or modifying Arab culture to accommodate ICT demands:

Culturally appropriate IT design and implementation which considers the differential influence of culture on IT may enhance its transfer. Instead of blaming the workers, or some cultural values, as singular explanations for ITT [information technology transfer] failure, we propose that a combinatory approach, perhaps incorporating the most salient factors of culture in designing transfer processes, might enhance ITT organization/business in Arab society. (Ibid., 37)

Beyond the digital divide concept

No doubt there is a so-called "digital divide" separating the developed from the developing countries. However, the concept itself has come under scrutiny for failing to account for the social factors that contribute to such a divide. Mark Warschauer (2002), with research experience in the Arab world, remarks that the digital divide concept has a technological connotation and can very well imply "digital solutions" to the problem, devoid of considering social and political problems that stand in the way of ICT social inclusion. With regard to the specific circumstances of the Palestinians, Warschauer (2006, 10) singles out the bifurcated outcome of Israeli occupation of the Palestinian territories:

> The occupation and consequent economic hardship and political instability have made diffusion of ICT more difficult by depressing consumer demand for technology and discouraging industry investment. Israeli incursions in populated areas, together with the large number of road blocks and other obstacles to mobility, make the maintenance of any kind of infrastructure difficult; how specifically this affects ICT access and use, and what can be done about it, should be an important component of study. At the same time occupation has motivated the Palestinian people to go online both to overcome problems of physical separation – Palestine from the Diaspora, occupied territories from Jerusalem and Israel, Gaza from the West Bank, and across blockades and road closures throughout the territories – as well as to make their voices heard in the international arena.

Generally speaking, differential access to and use of ICT exist at the levels of race, gender, national origin, disability, and income differentials. In paraphrasing two central writers in the debate over the digital divide and digital access (DiMaggio and Hargittai 2001), Warschauer (2006, 7) notes that although social class and affordability in purchasing computers should not be downplayed, there are other barriers to adopting ICT that go beyond affordability:

> These barriers include differential access to broadband telecommunications; differences in knowledge and skills in using computers, or in attitude toward using them; inadequate online content available for the needs of low-income

citizens, especially in diverse languages; and governmental controls or limitations on unrestricted use of the Internet in many parts of the world.

To move away from a strictly technological or economic model, Warschauer introduces the "literacy" model. Literacy is more than just the skill to read and write; it is "a set of social practices" (ibid., 10). Defined this way, literacy incorporates social context, including gradations and types of skills. In other words, and here he draws upon the work of Brazilian educator Paolo Freire (1994), literacy is not a problem of cognition or the availability of reading material – although of course the material has to be there before reading can take place – or even a problem of culture; rather, literacy is determined by power and politics. Warschauer suggests that effective use of ICT to access, adapt, and create knowledge has a reciprocal relationship with physical resources like computers and telecommunications, digital resources like relevant content in diverse languages, human resources like literacy and education, and social resources like community and institutional support.

Conflict zones exhibit specific features that go beyond the so-called "digital divide" and influence the modes and capabilities of communications. Below, I present the Palestinian situation as a case study of how Israeli occupation and military control of the Palestinian territory have shaped the methods of electronic communication. Following an overview of the extent of ICT diffusion in Palestine, the chapter draws upon my qualitative study of early experiences of Internet use in Palestine, with a special focus on Palestinian youth.

Overview of ICT diffusion

Since the attack of 11 September 2001 on the United States and subsequent threats made by militant groups against the West, tracking Internet usage has become a major undertaking of Western countries, particularly the United States, in their search for the perpetrators of terrorism. The Middle East garners the lion's share of Internet monitoring by foreign governments, and people of Middle Eastern origin who reside outside the Middle East are equally susceptible to surveillance by host governments. During the past two decades, Internet usage has evolved substantially to encompass the proliferating developments and use of social media, surveillance, hacking, and cyberwar.

The "terrorist" emphasis in the media, although important, risks overlooking important features of Internet usage by ordinary Middle Easterners. The Internet is increasingly being used as a networking tool in a region where travel and physical crossing of borders remain onerous undertakings. Although there are stark differences in the rates of Internet diffusion among countries in the Middle East, the overall picture attests to a substantial increase in Internet penetration. According to Internet World Stats (2013a) (Table 6.1), between 2000 and 2013, Middle Eastern countries registered an increase in Internet usage of more than 3,000 per cent. With a combined population of around 231 million people (3 per cent of the world population) and a phenomenal growth rate in Internet usage, these countries account for around

3.7 per cent of global Internet usage. The overall regional average is 45 per cent, which places the Middle East in fifth place globally, slightly above the world average of 39 per cent. As well, there are notable variations among Middle Eastern countries in Internet penetration, from highs of 90 per cent for Bahrain and 88 per cent for Qatar and the United Arab Emirates to lows of 26 per cent for Syria, 20 per cent for Yemen, and 9 per cent for Iraq. Palestine (i.e., the West Bank and Gaza) is situated at the midpoint, with a rate of 54 per cent (Internet World Stats 2013b).

Interregional variations are also apparent when examining the rankings along an ICT index that is based on adding up the number of installed personal computers in a country, the number of Internet users, and the number of mobile and fixed phone lines and then dividing the result by the country's population size; the higher the score, the more successful a country is in building and utilising an information technology infrastructure. Internet use is correlated with national literacy rates. For example, based on data from the International Telecommunications Union, Palestine has the highest literacy rate (94%) and Internet penetration rate (54%) among Arab countries of the Levant and North Africa. However, it ranks twelfth out of a total of eighteen Arab countries on the ICT index. The index is dominated by the oil-rich Gulf States. Clearly, there is a connection between the wealth of a country, the availability of needed infrastructure, and its place on the ICT index (Madar Research and Development 2012, 19–21). In the case of Palestine, there is the added factor that the development of its infrastructure is contingent on Israel's policies and its military occupation of the Palestinian territories.

Palestine

Following the Oslo agreement in 1993, using ICT to spur social and economic developments in the West Bank and Gaza became a main staple of policy recommendations from the World Bank, the International Monetary Fund, the United Nations Development Program, donor countries in the European Union, the United States Agency for International Development, and others. This is understandable bearing in mind that Palestine lacks natural resources and has historically prided itself on its human capital and resourcefulness.

Three main components of ICT indicators are discussed in the next section: the diffusion of telephony (i.e., land-based telephones and cellular telephones), Internet subscription and use, and ownership and use of computers.

Historical data

Rudimentary public opinion surveys in the West Bank and Gaza that were carried out as early as 1998 by the Palestinian Center for Policy and Survey Research (PCPSR) indicated that 27 per cent of Palestinians owned satellite dishes and that 12 per cent owned personal computers. Of those who owned computers, 7 per cent were Internet subscribers, and about 2 per cent had Internet access at work. These preliminary data further revealed that computer ownership and

TABLE 6.1 World Internet Usage and Population Statistics, 31 December 2013

World regions	Population as of 31 Dec. 2013	Users as of 31 Dec. 2000	Users as of 31 Dec. 2013	Penetration (% of pop.)	Growth 2000–13 (%)	Users (%)
Africa	1,125,721,038	4,514,400	240,146,482	21.3	5,319.6	8.6
Asia	3,996,408,007	114,304,000	1,265,143,702	31.7	1,106.8	45.1
Europe	825,802,657	105,096,093	566,261,317	68.6	538.8	20.2
Middle East	231,062,860	3,284,800	103,829,614	44.9	3,160.9	3.7
North America	353,860,227	108,096,800	300,287,577	84.9	277.8	10.7
Latin America/Caribbean	612,279,181	18,068,919	302,006,016	49.3	1,671.4	10.8
Oceania/Australia	36,724,649	7,620,480	24,804,226	67.5	325.5	0.9
World total	7,181,858,619	360,985,492	2,802,478,934	39.0	776.3	100.0

Source: Internet World Stats (2013a).

Internet access were concentrated in large urban centres like East Jerusalem, Gaza City, Hebron, and Ramallah (PCPSR n.d.). A year later, another private survey by the PCPSR reported an increase in ICT ownership and access: 45 per cent of Palestinian homes owned telephones, and 38 per cent owned satellite dishes. Home computer ownership stood at 13 per cent, and Internet subscription was 14 per cent among those who owned computers at home and 5 per cent among those who had computers at work (PCPSR 1999).

Data from a 1999 survey of 7,559 households conducted by the Palestine Census Bureau of Statistics (PCBS), revealed regional, educational, occupational, and gender differences in the distribution of basic ICT indicators. Although the survey did not aim to map ICT distribution in Palestine in any detail, it contained useful information for establishing a benchmark for the evolution of ICT in Palestine. The findings of this first national household survey can be summarised as follows:

- Whereas the north and centre of the West Bank accounted for slightly less than half of the population, between them they garnered close to two-thirds of computer ownership. Gaza, which had one-third of the population, accounted for 14 per cent of computer ownership.
- Three-quarters of computers were found in urban centres, 17 per cent in rural areas, and 7 per cent in all the refugee camps combined.
- Among homes where the head of the household had a professional, technical, or senior civil-service job, 48 per cent owned computers. Such households accounted for about 18 per cent of the general population.
- More than half of all computers were found in homes where the head of the household had a postsecondary education. This figure increased to 75 per cent with the inclusion of homes where the head of the household had a grade 11 or 12 education.
- The proportion of Palestinian households that simultaneously had a personal computer, a phone, and an Internet connection was a meagre 2 per cent. (PCBS 2000)

In 2003 a small-scale study by the nongovernmental organisation Panorama in Ramallah, based on a sample of 800 Palestinian university and secondary school students from the Jenin area, examined Internet usage, presence of computers in the home, computer skills, parental attitudes to ICT, and educational experience with ICT. The highlights of the study give us a glimpse into early experience with computers and the Internet:

- Among young people, 68 per cent had a computer in the home, 28 per cent had an Internet connection, 70 per cent had a satellite dish, and 76 per cent used a cellular phone.
- When asked to rate the quality of the ICT sector in the Jenin area, two-thirds said that it was lower than in all other Palestinian towns, whereas 34 per cent reported that it was at about the same level.

- When asked in a follow-up question to give reasons for the low ranking of Jenin compared to other towns, 47.6 per cent mentioned Israeli occupation, 15.4 per cent cited a weak private sector; 21 per cent mentioned bad infrastructure, and the remaining 16 per cent referred to the community.
- Close to 90 per cent agreed with the statement that the Israeli occupation had increased the importance of the ICT sector.
- The majority agreed that the educational system did not provide adequate training in the use of ICT equipment and that the schools stressed theoretical over practical knowledge with regard to ICT. The majority of these students mentioned individual initiative and self-teaching as the main methods of ICT training.
- Parents saw a negative moral impact as far as ICT was concerned, particularly with regard to women's access to sites on the Internet. Encouragement by parents to use the technology was directed mainly toward males in the family (Panorama 2003).

Table 6.2 provides longitudinal data for Palestine on basic ICT indicators. Apart from ownership of land phone lines, which was reported by one-third to one-half of households, ownership of personal computers in the combined Palestinian territories increased by 500 per cent, availability of the Internet at home increased by 600 per cent, and cell phone use nearly doubled to 218 per cent. If we look at the regional variations, we see that the West Bank and Gaza had similar rates of Internet usage and cell phone and landline ownership but that the West Bank (53%) had a slightly higher rate of household ownership of computers than the West Bank and Gaza (46%). A 2011 PCBS national survey, which consisted of 4,448 households, showed that of those without computers, 49 per cent mentioned the high cost and 27 per cent cited a lack of qualified individuals at home to oversee computer use. Internet use by males was 72 per cent, compared to 66.2 per cent by females. Of the entire sample, 27.2 per cent had an e-mail address, and 47 per cent mentioned experiencing viruses, 9.3 per cent hacking, and 7.3 per cent theft of documents (PCBS 2011a).

As regards the Palestinians in Israel, the Arab-Jewish gap in Internet usage is quite wide. For example, the Israel Central Bureau of Statistics discovered in a 2009 social survey that 69 per cent of the Jewish respondents had access to a computer, compared to 40 per cent of the Arab respondents (ICBS 2009). In a 2008 survey, 30 per cent of the Arab population had access to the Internet, compared to 64 per cent of the Jewish population (Knesset 2010, 2; see also Mesch and Talmud 2011).

Case studies of focus groups

The sample

In 2005 I interviewed 124 young people divided into ten focus groups (Zureik 2006). This was a purposeful sample designed to explore early familiarity of young Palestinians with information and communication technologies, particularly the Internet. The interviewees were chosen from the five major Palestinian cities of Ramallah, Nablus, Gaza City, Bethlehem, and East Jerusalem and from refugee

TABLE 6.2 Basic ICT Indicators in Palestinian Households, 1999, 2004, 2006, and 2011

ICT indicators	Gaza				West Bank				All			
	1999	2004	2006	2011	1999	2004	2006	2011	1999	2004	2006	2011
Household computers (%)	9	25.4	30.8	46.5	11.4	31.5	33.9	53.2	10.8	29.4	32.8	51.4
Household telephone lines (%)	36.5	39.7	45.6	41.6	45.0	44.8	53.5	45.3	42.1	43.0	50.8	40.0
Internet at home (%)	4.7	8.1	16.2	30.0	5.7	10.5	15.7	30.6	5.4	9.7	15.9	32.1
Cell phone use (%)	29.8	64.1	78.6	94.7	51.0	77.6	82.1	95.1	43.7	72.8	81.0	95.7

Source: The data for 1999 are from a survey of 7,559 households in in the West Bank and Gaza conducted by the Palestinian Central Bureau of Statistics (PCBS 2000); and the data for 2004 are in PCBS (2004, table 1); both data sets are based on weighted samples. The data for 2006 are in PCBS (2006), and the data for 2011 are in PCBS (2012).

camps near Ramallah as well as refugee camps in Khan Yunis and Rafah in Gaza. The rural areas were represented by the village of Kufr Al-'Labad near Nablus and by the villages of Al-'Azariyya and Dahiyat Al-Bareed at the outskirts of East Jerusalem.

Of the sample, 41 per cent lived in cities, 35 per cent in refugee camps, and 24 per cent in villages. The sample was evenly divided between males (52%) and females (48%). Of the city dwellers, 72 per cent had a university education, 12 per cent held college diplomas, and 12 per cent were either students or graduates of high schools; 4 per cent were grade 9 graduates. Among refugee camp residents, 58 per cent were university graduates, 14 per cent held college diplomas, and 28 per cent were either students or graduates of high schools. Two-thirds of the entire sample were between the ages of fifteen and twenty-five, around 20 per cent were between the ages of twenty-six and thirty, and the remaining 7 per cent were above the age of thirty-one. The average age of males and females in the sample was 25.3 and 23.2 years respectively.

Cities

Ramallah

Two focus group interviews comprising twenty-nine respondents were held in Ramallah; one group was chosen from the city of Ramallah itself, and the other from the nearby refugee camps of Al-Am'ari, Jalazone, Qalandia, and Um Al-Sharayit. Nine of the refugee camp participants came from Al-Am'ari, four from Jalazone, three from Qalandia, and one from Um Al-Sharayit.

The interviews yielded several interesting findings about computer and Internet usage. Everyone in the two Ramallah focus groups thought that the "computer is a good thing for society." Although three-quarters of city participants had computers at home, compared to less than one-third of refugee camp dwellers, the average time spent on a computer among camp residents, including at Internet cafés and schools, was higher than among city residents: 3.1 versus 2.8 hours per day. A minority of both city dwellers (8.3%) and camp dwellers (20%) said that they had computers at school. Only one high school student from the city reported that she used a computer at school to do school work. This was in contrast to three refugee students who reported using computers at school for this purpose.

Three-quarters of refugee camp respondents said that they visited Internet cafés and centres, compared to one-third of city dwellers. However, substantially higher Internet access at university was reported by city dwellers (41.7%), compared to university students from the camps (6.7%). Of the city dwellers, three indicated that they accessed the Internet from home, compared to four of the seventeen refugee camp dwellers.

Between 80 per cent of camp residents and 90 per cent of city residents indicated that they were aware of computer and Internet security issues. None of the city dwellers thought that sending information over the Internet was secure, compared to 60 per cent of camp refugees. When asked whether their personal information was secure over the Internet, 50 per cent of city dwellers and 87 per cent of camp residents said no. One-third of city residents said that they did not know. When asked whether they thought that their personal information was being monitored, 12.5 per cent of camp dwellers and 16.7 per cent of city residents said yes.

The majority of both groups reported that they were aware of privacy issues on the Internet, and various means of protecting personal information were cited. Respondents from the camps mentioned changing their username once a month; others accessed the Internet in special places that provided firewalls. In some cases, respondents mentioned how hackers had penetrated and accessed their accounts and had then reported to their employers the sites that these respondents regularly visited.

More than 90 per cent of both groups thought that outsiders monitored information traffic over the Internet, and when asked to name who these outsiders were, 50 per cent of city dwellers cited the Israeli government and its security agencies; 20 per cent cited the United States, including the CIA; and 30 per cent mentioned both the United States and Israel. Among camp dwellers, whose responses throughout the survey showed a highly politicised view of the world, 73 per cent cited the Israeli government, and the responses of the remaining 27 per cent were distributed evenly, at 9 per cent each, among the United States, Israel and the United States, and Israel and official Palestinian institutions.

Whereas 75 per cent of city dwellers endorsed the use of the Arabic language as a medium of communication to facilitate access to the Internet, among camp refugees the corresponding figure reached 93.3 per cent. Although many preferred Arabic as the medium of communication over the Internet, they did acknowledge that its use was curtailed by a lack of search engines in Arabic. Those respondents who attended university found it easy to use English.

Several of the city dwellers talked about the use of wireless technology as a means of circumventing obstacles to accessing the Internet. In particular, they saw it as necessary in rural areas not connected to the electricity grid. A couple of city respondents attributed the slow penetration of wireless technology to the monopoly exercised by the Palestine Telecommunications Company.

When asked to rank the Internet in terms of usage priority, work came first, followed by contact with relatives, education, chat, entertainment, news, and finally e-commerce. There was a general consensus among the respondents on the ranking order.

Although the Internet was widely known – if not widely used in those days – special features of Internet usage characterised the situation in Palestine. In the case of the group from Ramallah, Internet users singled out the use of the computer to network with relatives and friends whom they were unable to see. This was particularly true among the refugee community, given its limited means of geographic mobility. Lack of mobility was not confined to the refugees but also affected the Palestinian population as a whole, due to frequent closures and curfews imposed by the Israeli occupation authorities. Both groups stressed how they used the Internet to contact relatives in neighbouring countries or overseas whom they had never seen. Chat rooms and MSN Messenger were singled out as means to re-establish contact with friends whom they had known in school or university but were unable to see face-to-face. The Internet was useful in two other contexts. First, it facilitated efforts to overcome conservative trends in the community that prohibited contact between males and females. This was mentioned by those who lived in the conservative northern West Bank. In one case, a male respondent mentioned that he had met his wife through the Internet. Second, due to frequent closures, universities and colleges in Palestine resorted to the use of the Internet as a means to deliver educational material to students.

Internet cafés occupy a special place in the Internet landscape of Palestine. Many people do not own a computer or cannot afford to subscribe to the Internet; this has made Internet cafés and youth centres, particularly in the camps, popular points of access. The views expressed during the focus group interviews supported the popularity of Internet cafés, particularly among male respondents. In one case, a respondent mentioned how he used the Internet at a café owned by a friend who allowed him to spend up to six hours in the evenings accessing the Internet free of charge. These early encounters with the Internet led several respondents to think seriously about studying information technology at university, which one respondent had done.

In a wide-ranging discussion of the Internet and computers, one female respondent, who subscribed to the Internet, cautioned against "obsessive" use of the Internet for fear that, like television, it could lead to addiction and "mental laziness." She was against home monitoring of computer and Internet by parents and older siblings. Self-reliance and self-guidance were the methods that she relied upon. She was quite aware of the danger of meeting people on the Internet who could introduce themselves under false pretences.

In several cases, the Internet had become an indispensable tool for doing research. There were technical, socioeconomic, and political problems associated with Internet access in Palestine. One respondent indicated that she had been unable to get a leased Internet connection at home due to what she called "overloading" of the phone lines. In contrast, university students had access to large servers on campus that enabled them to download large documents. Some pointed out how e-mail was used to exchange, correct, and edit documents – both at work and in teaching.

One female respondent described how, for a university assignment, she had used her entry into chat rooms to study the phenomenon of meeting friends and meeting future marriage candidates through the Internet. To avoid hackers getting into individual accounts when using credit cards, some respondents opted for buying credit cards with dollar limits, say $100, after which the card expired automatically. In cases where knowledge of English was rather weak, respondents mentioned that the Internet had become a learning source for increasing their English vocabulary. In one case, an employee of the Palestine Census Bureau of Statistics mentioned that he had connected to his workplace in emergency situations by using a satellite card, which enabled him to communicate from a distance, such as from the airport.

The issue of home monitoring of Internet use occupied a central place in the focus group discussion. The views varied from total monitoring by elders, to sporadic monitoring, to establishing a system of trust. One female respondent counselled that it was better to have a reasonable system of supervision and to make the Internet available to all household members on a twenty-four-hour basis; otherwise, members in their early teens would frequent Internet cafés, where there was minimum supervision. The downloading of music and games was common. One respondent mentioned that she worked in a radio station where music was downloaded regularly from the Internet and rebroadcast over the air. It was mentioned that those who lived in Jerusalem could subscribe to a digital subscriber line (DSL), which would allow broadband transmission of data and images. Online purchasing, especially of books, was reported by few respondents. The delay in delivery of the books from Israel to Ramallah did not encourage the use of e-commerce. Although several respondents had attempted to take workshops and courses to improve their skills in specialised programming, the cost was prohibitive to many at $800 per course.

Nablus

Eleven focus group participants, six male and five female, were recruited from Nablus, the largest Palestinian city on the West Bank. They ranged in age from nineteen to twenty-six years old, with an average age of 22.1 years. In addition to endorsing the importance of the computer and the Internet for Palestinian society in general, respondents stressed the need to raise public awareness of these technologies through public campaigns and special policies aimed at absorbing computer science graduates into the labour market so as to prevent "brain drain." Of the participants, five were university students, two were computer professionals (one of whom was unemployed), one was a lawyer, one was a teacher, and one was a white-collar employee. The majority emphasised the importance of personal motivation in developing computer skills, although a minority attributed skill acquisition to the need to strengthen the theoretical base in computer science training.

The average daily use of the computer ranged from two to seven hours. Forty per cent averaged four hours per day on the Internet, and 20 per cent averaged between five and six hours. Seventy per cent indicated that their knowledge of the computer and the Internet was quite good. They considered those who could not use the computer and the Internet to be "illiterate" by current technological standards. Frustration with computer use was due to frequent electrical power cuts, technical failures that resulted in the loss of stored information, viruses that commonly infected floppy disks and then travelled from one machine to another, theft of one's electronic address, a lack of knowledge about whom to contact to solve technical problems during emergencies, traffic overload that hampered access to the Internet, and failures of system programs. In one case, a respondent's inadequate knowledge and frustration had been revealed by an incident in which her computer mouse did not work. She was told by the repair shop technician that there was nothing wrong with the computer and that all she had to do was reset and restart it.

In describing the importance of the computer to Palestinians in general, the respondents gave several reasons that touched on national, personal, and communal interests: furthering one's education, gaining technical skills, and increasing creativity through access to worldwide information. A second cluster of uses for the computer centred on publicising the struggles of Palestinians under Israel's occupation of the West Bank and Gaza and on recruiting international support for Palestine. Third, several respondents cited the Internet as a means to connect Palestinians worldwide.

Ten respondents mentioned using Arabic as the main language of communication over the Internet, although eight said they used English too.

When it came to protection of personal information over the Internet, five respondents were familiar with various means of protecting personal information, such as changing passwords frequently, installing a firewall, ignoring unsolicited e-mails, using antivirus programs, and blocking advertisements. Five respondents had little knowledge of the subject.

E-commerce was not popular on the Internet due to users' lack of trust of the technology. They were wary of giving personal information regarding credit cards, although some respondents mentioned that it was possible to obtain credit cards from banks with a predetermined use value.

In terms of priorities in the use of the computer and the Internet, research came first, followed by work, entertainment, news, contact with others, and finally e-commerce. Home use of the computer was subject to parental authority or to supervision by older siblings.

This group ended the session by offering several recommendations on how to facilitate the diffusion of ICT: organising workshops on how to use the computer and the Internet that are open not just to students of ICT but also to all those who are interested in ICT from a professional angle; providing all schools with computer labs to train their students in ICT; recruitment of ICT students by local employers; development of long-term national and local ICT policies; monitoring Internet use at home because the "Internet is like a double-edged sword"; establishing ICT centres for students to meet and exchange ideas; and preparing students in ICT skills before they start their technical programs in college.

Gaza City

Gaza City is the largest population centre in the occupied Palestinian territories. At the time of the survey in 2005, the population stood at nearly 400,000. Of the fifteen focus group participants, nine were males and six females. Their ages ranged from sixteen to forty years, with nine respondents falling between the ages of sixteen and twenty-four. The average age of the group's members stood at 25.7 years. Five respondents held college diplomas, seven had bachelor degrees, one was a secondary school graduate, and the remaining two were a university student and a secondary school student. Of the thirteen who were employed, five were in the government sector, six in the public sector, and two in the private sector.

In terms of place of employment, three worked for the Palestine Census Bureau of Statistics, one managed an Internet café, another was an inspector in the Ministry of Health, one was a teacher, one worked in sales, one was an accountant, and six were employed by various nongovernmental organisations (NGOs). The majority of the group's members were educated beyond secondary schooling, and all were engaged in white-collar occupations.

There was consensus among the respondents that the computer and the Internet benefited society. Both technologies simplified life and, in particular, made the jobs of professional people easier. The Internet made it possible for people to connect with relatives and friends whom they otherwise were not able to contact. But not all respondents were sanguine about the technology. Some expressed fear that it could lead to computer and Internet addiction, particularly as a result of chatting. Eight of the respondents reported that they spent in excess of twenty hours per week on the computer and the Internet, and an additional three mentioned averaging from eleven to fifteen hours. Several expressed the opinion that Internet use by young people was fraught with moral concerns due to easy access to pornographic sites.

Each respondent had access to at least one computer at home, eleven used a computer at work, and two spent between one and six hours per day using computers at Internet cafés and in women's clubs. Although most participants were heavy users of the computer at home and work, this was not the case for the high school student, who reported using the computer at school for less than one hour per week.

Six of the participants used the Internet at home, five at work, and four in public places. Among those who had Internet at home, the average usage time varied from one and a half to six hours per day, which was similar to the time spent on the Internet at work. With regard to public places, users averaged a half-hour to one hour per day. The high school student in the sample averaged one hour on the Internet at school per week. He was careful not to use it for chatting, due to school monitoring. The university student in the group logged onto the Internet a total of three hours per semester.

Here, too, use of the technology was described as a function of the sociopolitical conditions of Gaza. Because of frequent closures and constant surveillance by Israel, the Internet had become an indispensable tool for students to reach their teachers and for citizens to connect with their relatives in other places. Others reported using the Internet to make friends overseas. Few used the Internet for downloading music or playing games. The engineering student in the sample used the Internet to exchange technical information with other students living in neighbouring countries and in the West.

All of the respondents were aware of privacy risks. One participant referred to personal experience of having his Internet privacy violated. However, they all concurred that there was no privacy protection over the Internet, and they named Israel and the United States as the primary sources of Internet surveillance of Palestinians. Some went as far as to say that Yahoo and Hotmail were practically "Israeli sites."

Arabic was the preferred language of use on the Internet for fourteen of the sample's respondents, although nine said that they used English as well as Arabic, and one respondent mentioned using English more often than Arabic. In descending order, the Internet was used for chatting, work, study, networking, and e-commerce.

Bethlehem

Thirteen participants – seven males and six females – took part in the focus group interviews in Bethlehem (population 29,019). They ranged in age from fifteen to twenty-nine, with an average age of 20.9 years. Four were university graduates, five were university students, one was a secondary school graduate, and the remaining three were in preparatory and high school. Of the five employed people, three worked in the NGO and public sectors, and the remaining two were employed in the private sector.

Time spent on the computer and the Internet varied: the average was ten to twelve hours per week for two respondents, five hours for five respondents, four hours for two respondents, three hours for one respondent, and two hours for two respondents. An average of five hours per week were spent on the computer and the Internet. Of the thirteen respondents, five used the technology for communication, for research, and to search for general information. Two respondents used it for e-mail and work purposes, four for communication and news searches, and the remaining two for e-mail only.

Overall, the respondents thought that the computer and the Internet were beneficial for society, although some cautioned that the "information revolution" could lead to cultural domination by the West. They also said that overindulgence in the use of computers and the Internet could lead to a form of addiction, resulting in negative health consequences and distracting students from their school work. Frustration with the computer was mentioned by most participants. This was attributed to the slowness of the Internet and computers. Viruses were singled out as an important factor in causing frustration in computer use.

Twelve of the participants mentioned that they had at least one personal computer at home. Five stated that they used the computer at work, and four used it at Internet cafés and in social clubs. Unlike the two university students, who had access to computers on campus, none of the high school students said that they had access to computers at school. Ten respondents indicated that they used the Internet at home, three at work, and seven at Internet cafés and in social clubs. Two used the homes and offices of friends to access the Internet, whereas the university students used the Internet at school.

Respondents used computers to access the Internet, type reports for work and school, plan, do computer-assisted design, and gather information. In one or two cases, the computers facilitated access to the Internet for the sake of conducting e-commerce. Overall, participants were satisfied with self-regulating their use of the computer in the workplace and at home. Their Internet usage was wide-ranging and included messaging, phone calls, and transmitting live and still pictures at a reasonable cost. It is interesting to note that use of the Internet for messaging was not confined to contacting acquaintances in faraway places but included communicating with friends and relatives in the West Bank and Gaza, where geographic mobility was limited due to closures and curfews. The respondents estimated that they spent between one to four hours per day on audio and video messaging.

The respondents were familiar with issues of privacy and security in connection with Internet use. However, after some prompting and explanation, one female respondent pointed out that privacy was of great value to her personally, whereas another male participant noted that his work demanded security of information and pointed out that privacy and copyright legislation were nonexistent in the Arab world. They all concurred that personal information was not secure on the Internet. Three mentioned that their personal e-mails had been intercepted and their identities stolen. When asked whether governments targeted and spied on Internet users, the majority agreed that this did happen. However, with regard to the Palestinian Authority, several noted that even if it wished to do this, it lacked the technical and physical means.

The participants singled out Arabic as their preferred language for both computer and Internet use, followed by English, French, and Hebrew. Nine participants mentioned that they were compelled to use English because of the quality of information available on the Internet through English search engines. Two respondents indicated that they were familiar with translation on websites. In descending order, the Internet was used for contacting relatives and friends, work, entertainment, news and political coverage, e-commerce, and education.

Finally, when asked to assess family control of computer and Internet access at home, eight of the respondents said that there was no problem in access, although parents occasionally deterred family members who were still in school from spending too much time on the Internet. Four respondents mentioned that their families had drawn up plans regarding times of computer and Internet use, depending on need and priority. One respondent mentioned that at times he faced problems due to the number of users and the fact that older siblings tended to monopolise computer use. The group indicated that there was no gender or age discrimination in computer use at home.

Villages

Kufr Al-Labad

Located near the city of Tulkarem, Kufr Al-Labad is a village that had around 4,000 inhabitants at the time of the survey. The focus group consisted of eleven participants – six males and five females – whose ages ranged from twenty-one to forty-five years, with an average age of 32.45 years. The respondents were comprised of three teachers, one lawyer, one unemployed electrician who worked as a farmer, one employee of the Ministry of Youth and Sport, one head of a local sports club, one employee of a travel agency, a housewife, and a university student.

Three of the respondents had three years of experience using the computer, three had five to six years of experience, two had "little" experience, one had "medium" experience, and one respondent said that he had more than twenty years of computer experience.

With regard to the Internet, nine had minimal experience, one had been using the Internet for less than a year, and one had seven to eight years of experience. The majority evaluated the computer positively in terms of its research, educational, and networking potential.

The problems faced by participants when using the Internet were, in descending importance, the cost of Internet access, ownership of a computer, dependence of the Internet on the home landline, lack of training in Internet usage, unreliability of electrical supply, and viruses. To solve the overriding problem of cost, several respondents suggested that the Internet cost be reduced and that Internet subscriptions be made available on a fixed basis, the way television licences are paid for.

To cope with security and privacy issues on the Internet, respondents mentioned encryption and the use of secret codes for their passwords. However, they also said that it was always possible for hackers and foreign agents such as Israel to intercept personal e-mail. Other participants were concerned that Internet users did not pay sufficient attention to copyright laws when they downloaded text, music, or videos.

The majority were most comfortable using Arabic on the Internet, although five said that they used both Arabic and English. Only one respondent felt that it was easy to use English, particularly for printing downloaded documents.

In descending order, the reasons given for using the Internet were news, networking with family and friends, chat lines, academic research, general information, and entertainment.

Al-'Azariyya and Dahiyat Al-Bareed

These two villages are situated at the outskirts of East Jerusalem. A total of nineteen respondents were interviewed: nine from Al-'Azariyya (population 17,000) and ten from Dahiyat Al-Bareed (population 25,000). Of the former, six were females and three males. The latter group had six males and five females. The ages varied from fifteen to twenty-four years, with an average age of 17.8 years, in the case of Al-'Azariyya, and from fifteen to nineteen years, with an average age of 18.5 years, in the case of Dahiyat Al-Bareed. In Al-'Azariyya six respondents were university students, two were in preparatory school, and one was employed as a college lecturer. In Dahiyat Al-Bareed the majority were students – six in high school, one in preparatory school, and two in university. One respondent worked as an administrator in a law office.

Time spent using the computer and Internet in the case of Al-'Azariyya was one to three hours per week for four people, one to two hours daily for two people, and three to six hours daily for five people. In the case of Dhahiyat Al-Bareed, the rate was four to five hours daily for six people, one to two hours weekly for two people, and one to two hours daily for three people. The majority of respondents ranked themselves as quite knowledgeable in computer and Internet use. One or two people indicated that they were not regular users of the technology, and one in particular expressed serious reservations about it.

Frustrations with computer use and Internet access were experienced by all participants. These were caused by unsecure Internet connections, unexpected power cuts, high traffic on the Internet, slowness of data transmission, and viruses. One person cited the lack of someone to correspond with on the Internet. They all agreed that the technology had its positive and negative aspects. The outcome depended on the user and the purpose for which the technology was used. Two respondents from Dahiyat Al-Bareed remarked that computers could isolate individuals from their surroundings and, in doing so, could contribute to psychological problems. Cost and an insufficient number of Internet cafés and community centres equipped with the Internet were cited as factors inhibiting Internet access.

The home was at the centre of computer use, although more than one-third of the combined groups mentioned that they had computer access at work as well. A similar proportion used the computer both at home and at Internet cafés. The two university students in the Dahiyat Al-Bareed group had campus access to computers and the Internet. Several in the combined groups knew about data protection and viruses. They also pointed out, without specifying the source, that spying on users did take place on the Internet. Several knew of various programs that were used to protect Internet users from identity theft and unlawful access to their data. Computer use at school was conditional on teachers' supervision. Four respondents in Al-'Azariyyah mentioned that their older brothers monitored computer use at home. Others used passwords to protect files stored on their computer. In Dahiyat Al-Bareed a couple of respondents referred to their mothers as the main decision makers regarding computer and Internet use.

In Dahiyat Al-Bareed, three individuals resorted to English first in accessing the Internet, followed by Arabic, four used Arabic only, two used English only, and the rest used combinations of English and Arabic. Respondents in Al-'Azariyyah said that Arabic was their predominant language, followed by English. Some mentioned that at school the teacher obliged them to use Hebrew.

Suggestions for how to improve access to the Internet and computer included increasing the number of hours when computers were available in schools; organising summer camps to train students in the use of the Internet and computer; lowering the cost of Internet access; mounting a campaign to make the public aware of the importance and benefit of computers and the Internet; increasing the number of Internet service providers; allowing for a system of prior reservation at Internet cafés and increasing the number and location of Internet cafés and community centres; providing publicly accessible terminals in large cities and on main streets, and expanding the telecommunications network and providing a larger number of telephones at a reduced cost.

The refugee experience
West Bank

Although the computer and Internet were used in various capacities among camp residents, what stood out in the interviews was the use of the Internet to connect with other refugee communities. One respondent remarked that she used the Internet in the Women's Center to participate in the "across borders project," which brings Palestinian refugees worldwide in contact with each other. The Internet was used to send pictures as well. She narrated how she took a course to enable her to use the Internet for these purposes. She singled out Lebanon, Gaza, and Hebron as three communities whose refugees had expressed an interest in networking with other refugees.

Not everyone was an Internet or computer enthusiast. One male respondent from the Al-Am'ari camp in Ramallah declared that he was not a "friend" of the computer or Internet and did not intend to become one. When pressed to say why and how he planned to contact relatives and friends who lived outside the camp, he replied that all his relatives and friends were close enough that he could rely on face-to-face contact. Palestinian refugees in Lebanon were on the mind of most refugee respondents in the sample. For example, one respondent mentioned how he used the Internet to collect background data on the refugees in Lebanon, such as their numbers, health conditions, and employment status. It was through his Internet contacts that he had become aware that the refugees in Lebanon were barred by the government from working in seventy occupations.

One male respondent who worked as a programmer mentioned how the Arabic language was not treated "with respect" by search engines. For example, he noted that Google in the early days would translate text from Arabic to French for free, but when the request was from French to Arabic, Google demanded a fee. The discussion revolved around his French-speaking Algerian girlfriend whose Arabic dialect was difficult to understand. Because of language problems, he communicated with her in English. Although most communicated in Arabic, they used the English alphabet phonetically to communicate in Arabic.

As expected, in a politicised environment the issue of using the Internet for political goals was mentioned by several respondents. One male respondent mentioned that he used Internet chat rooms to defend against attacks on Islam and to explain the situation in Palestine/Israel.

The views on monitoring were varied and included those who believed that employers in both the public and private sectors monitored Internet users. Very few were concerned about home monitoring. In one case, a respondent mentioned employers who had monitored their employees upon request from Israeli authorities.

The respondents noted that one appeal of e-commerce was that it was often cheaper to book a hotel room or buy a plane ticket using the Internet. Most respondents were aware that using the Internet was beyond the reach of many people. Many respondents thought that the authorities should pressure the Palestinian

Telecommunications Company – a monopoly – to lower its subscription rate so that Palestinians living in rural and poor areas could afford to get connected.

Khan Yunis

Located in Gaza not far from Gaza City, Khan Yunis (population 47,360 at the time of the interviews) is the second largest refugee camp in the Palestinian territories after the Rafah camp. The focus group consisted of eight males and six females. Respondents varied in age from twenty-one to forty-five years, averaging 28.6 years. Seven of the group members held bachelor degrees, four held college diplomas, and the remaining three were high school graduates. Three were unemployed, one was a business owner, and the rest held jobs in accounting, in teaching, or with NGOs (either paid or volunteer positions).

Most of the respondents were frequent computer users, although three respondents classified themselves as "below average" users. The heavy computer use was due to work circumstances, with several respondents indicating that they used the computer between six to seven hours daily. Computer use at home ranged from two to four hours daily. Four participants indicated that they did not own a computer due to cost. Those who did own a computer shared it with other family members. All but one or two believed that the computer was an essential tool in modern society. The only problem that respondents singled out was the access to "immoral material" over the Internet. At a more general level, one respondent remarked that the computer could be good, bad, or excellent depending on its usage. A couple of respondents mentioned that they used the computer to research and prepare school assignments. Three mentioned that they had taken short courses in how to use the computer.

Discussion of the Internet was wide-ranging. Several respondents used the Internet, or knew of others who used it, to conduct business transactions. In one case, a female respondent mentioned how her husband, who in the past had relied on the postal service to receive product samples from China for sale in the Palestinian territories, now used the Internet to display the samples to customers, thus cutting down turn-around time and cost. Views on the Internet were more stark than views on the computer. Like other focus group participants, the Khan Yunis respondents raised the moral issue of children's use of the Internet. Although the extent varied, all respondents expressed concern about young people's unmonitored exposure to the Internet. In some cases, misuse of the Internet was attributed to lack of know-how. "The Internet is like a spider's web," opined one participant. "It opens horizons in various positive ways, although there is no denying the fact that it has some negative consequences. For example, a collaborator working for Israeli intelligence can use the Internet to deliver useful information to them." He proceeded to say that he knew of a case where Israeli intelligence had penetrated Palestinian servers and provided users with wrong information. The Internet was also monitored by managers of Internet cafés. Another respondent said that between 70 and 90 per cent of Internet traffic was monitored by foreign sources. Overall, respondents concurred that there was no guarantee of privacy over the Internet. In the words of one participant, "it is next to impossible to escape Internet monitoring because it is important for Israel and the USA to monitor the Palestinian people." The view that Israel and the United States monitored Palestinian usage of the Internet was expressed several times over the course of the focus group session: "The conflict between us, the USA and Israel continues, although it is now taking a new turn after the introduction of the Internet. As well, surveillance [of Palestinian users] takes place through the use of satellite technology to disable Palestinian [web]sites."

The Internet was also used to seek out general information, as in the case of a mother who turned to the Internet to find information about her child's illness. Another participant used the Internet to download student applications from European universities. The Internet was singled out as very important for the work of NGOs because it facilitated networking at an effective cost.

Arabic was mentioned as the most frequently used language on both the computer and Internet, although there was no escaping the fact that English was also used on the Internet, mainly because Arabic search engines were not as numerous and because the information available on them was limited. Several respondents pointed out that one needed to know English in order to do proper searches for scientific topics.

Several respondents knew what e-commerce meant, but very few actually used it. One respondent had bought a book through the Internet. Some respondents resorted to the cell phone to send messages, although it was pointed out that this was more expensive than using the Internet. A couple of respondents used the phone over the Internet, which turned out to be the cheapest method, assuming that one had access to the Internet. All participants concurred that price was the main deterrent to using the Internet, and they suggested that Internet access be treated on the basis of licensing fees, the way television sets are licensed.

Rafah

The twelve participants in the Rafah camp (population 57,839 at the time of the interviews) were divided equally between men and women. They ranged in age from twenty-three to forty years, with an average age of 26.9 years. All of the males and three of the females were university graduates; of the three other females, two held college diplomas, and one was a high school graduate. Ten were employed, and two were unemployed. Except for one or two respondents, the majority held government jobs or were employed in the NGO sector. Six of the participants indicated that they owned a computer.

Four respondents used the Internet at home, five at work, two at school, and two in clubs and at Internet cafés. The time spent using the computer was two to seven hours per day at work, two to four hours per day at home, and roughly two hours per day in clubs and at Internet cafés. The computer was used at school by one person who happened to be a teacher, and one university graduate in the sample used the computer for an average of an hour-and-a-half daily to study and prepare reports.

Although the majority described the computer in positive terms, all expressed frustration with its use and that of the Internet due to interruptions of electricity, viruses, or slowness in accessing the Internet. Similar to what was expressed throughout the focus group interviews, these respondents had serious reservations about the security of their files, password, and identity when accessing the Internet. As well, concern was expressed about children accessing pornographic sites on the Internet. Use of chat rooms exposed many participants to unwelcome "intruders." In descending order, the Internet was used for work, chat, study, contacting relatives and friends, browsing for news, and e-commerce. Overall, the Internet was used to browse in media outlets. The respondents who were employed by NGOs and nonprofit organisations underscored the importance of the Internet in networking, disseminating information, and maintaining contact with donors.

Most of the participants acknowledged that there was no privacy on the Internet. Two to three participants mentioned that their private e-mail and password had been intercepted. Others mentioned that their information on the Internet, particularly when engaging in chat, had been compromised. All respondents stressed that the Internet was monitored by Israel and the United States, particularly those who used Hotmail and Yahoo accounts.

Five participants indicated that they used only Arabic on the Internet. Three indicated that Arabic was their primary language but added that they could use English if the need arose. One indicated that he used Arabic and English equally. Only one used English more often than Arabic, and one used both Arabic and Hebrew.

Use of the Internet at home was not prioritised. However, all participants stressed the need for the Internet to be monitored at home. Although they were familiar with using the Internet to buy goods, only one participant had tried to purchase products on the Internet, and this transaction had gone through a local agent. One respondent mentioned that her relatives used the Internet for commercial purposes.

Respondents were familiar with wireless Internet technology. However, this service was not available in Rafah. Others pointed out that Paltel, the private Palestinian carrier, was a monopoly, which made it difficult for competitors to operate in Rafah.

Balata Camp

In addition to my interviews, I accessed the results of an ethnographic study of the Internet carried out from 2003 to 2004 by doctoral student Kole (Konstantin) Kilibarda (2005), who at the time was living in the Balata refugee camp (population 24,000) near Nablus in the north of the West Bank. Individual interviews were conducted with managers or owners of the camp's four Internet service providers and its three main Internet access points, located in Internet cafés, with representatives of five leading community-based organisations that worked in Balata, and with a sample of thirty active Internet users (twenty-five men and five women), who ranged in age from ten to thirty-nine years, the average age being twenty-one years. This demographic profile closely corresponded to the profile of the camp, where most active ICT users were young males.

It is worth pointing out that the Nablus region has a long history of resisting foreign occupiers dating back to the nineteenth-century rule of Mohammad Ali Pasha, the governor of Egypt during the Ottoman period, and to the subsequent British rule in Palestine. Following the outbreak of the Al-Aqsa Intifada in 2000, opposition to occupation resulted in 505 people being killed in the Nablus governorate and 3,018 injured. These included 120 residents of Balata camp who were killed by Israeli soldiers and over 1,000 injured. As will be shown below, this active resistance also informed early Internet use.

Following 1995, when the first Internet connection was established in Balata camp, Internet use grew considerably, first through dial-up home connections and later by means of high-speed connections. It is estimated that by late 2002 approximately 25 per cent of households in Balata camp had computers at home and that 5 to 10 per cent had a high-speed Internet connection. As of September 2004, there were three main Internet cafés still running in the camp, along with two main computer shops. The importance of Internet cafés as a point of access to ICT has been heightened since 2002, when Israel's military operations destroyed the ICT infrastructure of NGOs and community-based organisations in the camp.

In discussing cell phone services, Kilibarda (2005, 10) summarises one interviewee's account of the unfair advantage reaped by Israeli-owned providers:

> Israeli-run cell phone service providers are operating illegally in the West Bank, as they don't fall under licensing agreements regulating telecommunications in the areas ceded to the PA [Palestinian Authority] under the Oslo Accords. This fact underlines the inability of Palestinian governing institutions to adequately regulate the local ICT infrastructure as well as the opportunistic/predatory nature of the economic policies pursued by Israeli corporations in the Occupied Territories.

Kilibarda goes on to say:

> In addition to operating extra-legally, the Israeli operators also enjoy unfair advantage. During the time of this study, Cellcom [an Israeli service provider] was simply "more available" than Jawwal in Balata, which is the reason that most of our interviewees claimed Cellcom was "more popular" than Jawwal. The limitation of Jawwal's service capability was, to a large degree, a direct function of Israeli restrictions imposed on the import of necessary technologies and its refusal to release more spectrum to the Palestinian side. During this author's stay in the camp, Jawwal had to stop issuing SIM cards due to network congestion caused by such restrictions. Jawwal only began issuing SIM cards again in September 2004 once some of these restrictions were lifted. (Ibid., 10–11)

It seems that the cell phone is classified as a security device. Kilibarda (2005, 41) quotes an Israeli with the Samaria Brigade who said that "some units have been given explicit orders to shoot any young men seen using cellular phones, highlighting the perceived 'threat' such a technology poses to the operations of the Israeli military."

Interviewees perceived the Internet as opening opportunities for Palestinians to expand their job horizons, as well as opening opportunities for young Palestinians to lift themselves out of their isolation and enable themselves to emigrate in search of a better future. More than 90 per cent thought that the Internet was important for Palestinians generally, and 43 per cent thought that it was important for the refugee in particular.

When interviewees were asked whether they thought that there was full privacy on chat and e-mail, 77 per cent said that there was no privacy. Here we encounter a theme noted earlier, namely that those who perceive an absence of privacy share the general feeling, as one respondent said, that "Israel didn't leave anything in our lives that isn't monitored. We can't have privacy." Another respondent was just as clear: "Everything is under the control of the Israelis and the Americans." Yet "all interviewees thought that some types of control should be imposed on Internet use" to prevent the young from being exposed to immoral websites (Kilibarda 2005, 21).

Kilibarda (2005, 23–24) makes the point that under the conditions in Palestine, where there are deep cleavages along region, gender, income, education, occupation, and employment, the pattern of ICT diffusion and access has tended to reproduce pre-existing forms of social stratification, including the privileging of Israeli settlers over Palestinians, urban Palestinians over those in the camps and the villages, men over women, the rich over the poor, the employed over the unemployed, and the upwardly mobile and better educated over those with lower educational attainment.

NGOs were particularly targeted by Israeli soldiers in the Balata Camp, resulting in wide destruction, which negatively impacted the NGOs' training programs and their capacity to maintain electronic records and archival material with functioning equipment.

The perception that the Internet can be put in the service of "information warfare" also emerged as a dominant theme in Kilibarda's (2005) interviews. The Internet was seen as a tool to distribute leaflets and posters, as well as to publicise stories of Israeli assassinations and military actions in the camp.

The dialectics of surveillance and resistance

> It is thus the case that technologized surveillance and security increase the vulnerability and insecurities of already marginalized social groups, jeopardizing their welfare and life, but they can also encourage such marginalized groups to use cyberworld devices and tools to resist them. (Shalhoub-Kevorkian 2012a, 56)

Publicised cases involving hacking and government or corporate snooping and surveillance of the private affairs of citizens via the telephone, the Internet, and other mobile technologies by far exceed attempts to harness ICT technology for everyday resistance purposes. However, as Nadera Shalhoub-Kevorkian points out in her study of young Palestinian women from East Jerusalem, the use of the Internet by marginal and oppressed groups is not an insignificant, random practice. From her focus group interviews, it is clear that the Palestinians resort to the Internet as an essential means to communicate with others and to secure information for personal use. Here is how one of her interviewees described the Internet:

> Let me just end by telling you that last week, I watched my cousin's wedding by Skype and was able to join them, at least virtually. In other parts of the world, if you work hard, if you study, if you contemplate your steps, you have a good chance of building a house, traveling and participating in family gatherings. We Palestinians are displaced all over the world, and we here in Jerusalem live in a prison, and I even live with no identity card. My only way to resist Israeli occupation is by using the Internet, studying, sharing, meeting people and developing myself. We in Palestine, and people like me, would die without the Internet. (In Shalhoub-Kevorkian 2012a, 65)

Although Palestinians in general are constantly under the gaze of Israel in one way or another, Palestinian refugees occupy a special place in the surveillance matrix. Virtual mobility has become a tool to overcome geographic and spatial immobility (Federman 2003). In her research on Palestinian use of the Internet in Palestine, Lebanon, and Jordan, Miriyam Aouragh (2011b) demonstrates how the Internet facilitates shared experience and the emergence of refugee collective action across borders by overcoming time limitations, immobility, and spatial isolation. Thus pre-1948 memories of the Nakba are shared by the refugees, now in their fourth generation, regardless of their current location and generation. Memories act as a means for mobilisation. These findings are echoed in Laleh Khalili's research on the cyberculture of Palestinian refugees in Lebanon. Khalili argues against technological determinism and the popular assumption that technology exercises a levelling effect on its users by transcending culture, identity, and geography. She asserts that the popular postmodern notions of decentred information, fluid borders, and multiple identities are not borne out by the Palestinian refugee experience: "I argue, however, that *embodied* identities, *territorialized* spaces, and real-world institutions extend deeply into the realm of cyberspace, and that Palestinian virtual culture has non-virtual roots and histories" (Khalili 2005, 126, emphasis in original).

In her interviews with young people, Khalili shows that Internet coverage of events in the West Bank and Gaza, such as the Al-Aqsa Intifada of 2000, played a major role in keeping Palestinian identity alive at a time when the refugees' identity was under assault to such an extent that young refugees were (unsuccessfully) attempting to adopt the Lebanese identity. Names of places in Palestine are incorporated into cyberspace. Moreover, "the consumers of cyber content create narratives from news items and images that place the Palestinians in the Occupied Territories and those in the camps of Lebanon in the same community of suffering ... [A] Palestinian youth in Lebanon writes, 'our pain is one and the suffering is one'" (Khalili 2005, 131).

Several writers have attributed the surge in Internet usage among Palestinians to geographical isolation caused in no small measure by the occupation and to the Al-Aqsa Intifada; some have argued that the Arab Spring further contributed to a heightened interest in Internet usage (El-Haddad 2003; Kershner 2012). This increase occurred in spite of the fact that in the Internet's early days, when the average monthly income of a Palestinian worker was $300, a monthly subscription cost $25. Undeterred by low income, Palestinian home subscribers to the Internet increased from 5 per cent in 1999 to around 33 per cent in 2012 (Table 6.2; see also Cisneros 2001; and Khoury-Machool 2010).

Along the road to joining the cyberworld, the Palestinians face several obstacles, some of which are technological and others sociopolitical. It is correct to say, however, that the major problems of Palestinians who have limited access to the Internet and advanced connectivity are rooted in the political circumstances of their daily lives. For example, on more than one occasion, under the guise of security, the Israeli forces have engaged in wanton destruction of the offices and equipment of Palestinian Internet service providers (Palestinian Human Rights Monitor Group 2002; Shachtman 2002); the Palestinians lack any control over allocation of the wireless spectrum, a fact that impoverishes their technological autonomy and hampers the use of global positioning systems and other mobile technologies (Baboun 2013); Israel limits Palestinians to outdated second-generation technology (Gilbert 2013; Kuttab 2013), or what one commentator aptly calls the "cell phone dark ages" (Lynfield 2013), it prevents Palestinian Internet service providers from accessing up-to-date fourth-generation wireless technology, and it even severely restricts access to the older third-generation platforms – all of which are essential for the smartphone and are available to Israeli users (Davison 2013). The refusal by Israel to allocate cellular frequencies to Palestinian service providers as part of its technological monopoly has forced Palestinian consumers to resort to the Israeli telecommunications market, with huge windfall profits being reaped by Israeli companies (Bryant 2013; Hass 2007; Mozgovaya 2011), and as noted by Ashnel Pfeffer (2012), the digital siege is not limited to the West Bank: "all of Gaza's telephone networks and Internet servers go through Israel; every phone conversation and e-mail is routed through Israel's territory and from there sent on through underwater fiber optic cables to the rest of the world."

As evidence of its attempts to spare Palestinian lives, Israel does not hesitate to mention the recorded messages, or so-called "roof knocks," that it sends to Palestinians whose homes and neighbourhoods are about to be bombed. These phone numbers are gathered by Israeli intelligence, and although the targeted Palestinians are given five minutes to vacate their homes, it is not clear where they are supposed to vacate to since Gaza's high-density housing leaves no room for escape. The warning messages cannot absolve Israel of blame for its actions.

A report in the *Washington Post* during the war of August 2014 discussed the connection between Israel's surveillance methods and the state of the Palestinian telecommunication sector:

> How could the IDF [Israeli Defense Forces] so easily access telecommunications in the Gaza Strip, knowing exactly whom to call at each residence? It's incredibly simple. While the telecommunication companies that operate in Gaza, such as the Palestinian Telecommunication Group (PalTel), are owned and operated by Palestinians, they are routed through servers based in Israel. These servers are easy for Israel's intelligence community to access and can provide an important resource for the IDF. (Taylor 2014)

Close monitoring and intrusive surveillance are bound to produce reactions and even countersurveillance. This is basically the meaning of the dialectics of control, and the situation in Palestine is no exception. The Israeli human rights organisation B'Tselem has provided Palestinian youth on the West Bank with cameras to record the abuses by Israeli forces. This form of citizen journalism has resulted in wide-scale publicity of human rights violations by Israel (Hass 2012a; Mackey 2011). By the same token, it has become apparent that the Middle East conflict is not immune to cyberwar. During military incursions, the Palestinians and their supporters have engaged in retaliatory cyberattacks against Israeli computer networks, whose operators in turn have hacked Palestinian computer networks. The extent of support for Palestinians has been singled out as a reason behind Israel's recruitment of an "army of cyber-soldiers" (Farago 2006). In monitoring the Gaza war of 2012, the *Washington Post* weighed in with an answer to its question "who is winning the online war?" It said, "the online masses are clearly on the Palestinian side, overcoming the challenge of an IDF armed with more sophisticated and well-funded, optimized posts and 'fancy' graphics and videos" (Sommer 2012).

Conclusion

Several commentators have pointed out that one of the unintended effects of the First Intifada, if not the entire Palestinian-Israeli conflict, is that it has increased reliance on ICT, particularly the Internet for the purpose of reaching beyond the borders of Palestine to convey the texture of life under occupation and maintain contact with Palestinians worldwide. Thus, in spite of poverty and unemployment, the occupied territories have experienced a general increase in the diffusion of ICT, and with this increase has come the need to acquire skills in ICT use.

Based on the historical data and the focus group interviews summarised above, it appears that as of nearly two decades ago, there was considerable familiarity with the Internet and use of the computer among Palestinians in the occupied territories. At the precollege level, the schools did not seem to play an active role in training students in ICT use. The situation may have changed now. At that time, the skills acquired were more a product of "learning by doing" than the result of systematic hands-on instruction in schools. Contrary to the fear expressed by various observers, the home did not appear to exert a controlling effect on Internet and computer usage. This does not mean that Internet usage was not monitored at home, particularly where young users were concerned. But for the young adults in the studies discussed above, both males and females, supervision by parents or older siblings was not an issue. The main impetus for using the Internet was the desire to establish contact with friends and family members. That Palestinians were living under occupation with restricted freedom of movement made virtual technology indispensable. Most of the participants in the qualitative interviews were white-collar workers and students. Those who were in the labour force relied heavily on computers, and most – but not all – had access to the Internet at work. As is the case elsewhere, workers' Internet use was monitored by employers in both the private and public sectors. The cost of the Internet connection was cited as the greatest deterrence against having Internet access. This explains the popularity of Internet cafés, youth clubs, and community centres. Several respondents mentioned the lack of fair competition in the telecommunications sector and were fairly critical of the Palestinian service provider for its high subscription rates and unavailability of land phone lines in remote and rural areas. To remedy the situation, respondents suggested instituting fixed subscription rates for Internet usage, fashioned after television licence fees. One salient feature of Internet usage in Palestine was the issue of privacy, surveillance, and monitoring by foreign nations, particularly Israel and the United States. This concern was raised in almost every location in which the focus group interviews were held. Finally, all respondents noted that privacy and secure information flow on the Internet were nonexistent. Several of the respondents had experienced hackers and had suffered from viruses in their computers. Although they knew about firewalls and installing special antivirus software, the majority chose to change their passwords regularly in order to avoid identity theft.

Israel's conscious attempts to control the flow of information by denying Palestinians access to high-speed and broadband wireless communication practically amounts to what Helga Tawil-Souri (2012a) calls "digital occupation" of the Palestinian territories.

Note

This chapter draws upon a chapter by the author in Elia Zureik, ed., *Information Society in Palestine: The Human Capital Dimension*, report (Ottawa: International Development Research Centre, 2006). The study discussed here and in that chapter was funded by the International Development Research Centre, Ottawa.

CONCLUSION

In the wake of Israel's savage attack on Gaza in late December 2008, historian Avi Shlaim (2009), a seasoned analyst of the Israeli-Palestinian conflict, concluded:

> This brief review of Israel's record over the past four decades makes it difficult to resist the conclusion that it has become a rogue state with "an utterly unscrupulous set of leaders." A rogue state habitually violates international law, possesses weapons of mass destruction and practices terrorism – the use of violence against civilians for political purposes. Israel fulfils all of these three criteria; the cap fits and it must wear it. Israel's real aim is not peaceful coexistence with its Palestinian neighbours but military domination.

As documented in chapter 5, the extent of destruction and ferocity referred to by Shlaim was surpassed in Israel's attack on Gaza in July 2014. In his survey of the disproportionate extent of the destruction, Rashid Khalidi (2014–15, 5) points out the following details:

> During its latest campaign, stretching over a period of fifty days in July and August of 2014, Israel's air force launched more than six thousand air attacks, and its army and navy fired about fifty thousand artillery and tank shells. Together, they utilized what has been estimated as a total of twenty-one kilotons, or twenty-one thousand tons, of high explosives. The attack from the air involved weapons ranging from drones and American Apache helicopters firing U.S.-made Hellfire missiles to American F-16s carrying two-thousand-pound bombs. According to the commander of the Israeli Air Force, there were several hundred F-16 attacks on targets in Gaza, most of them using these powerful munitions. A two-thousand-pound bomb creates a crater 15 meters wide by 11 meters deep and propels lethal fragments to a

radius of 365 meters. One or two of these monsters can destroy a multistory building, and they were used at the conclusion of the Israeli air campaign toward the end of August to level several of Gaza City's high-rises.

In addition to the aerial bombardment, Israel launched equally vicious sea and land attacks against Gaza, which were described by one retired American lieutenant general as "absolutely disproportionate" (in ibid.). Moreover:

> ... over 16,000 buildings were rendered uninhabitable, including entire neighborhoods ... A total of 277 United Nations and government schools, 17 hospitals and clinics, and all 6 of Gaza's universities were damaged, as were over 40,000 other buildings. Perhaps 450,000 Gazans, over a quarter of the population, were forced to leave their homes, and remain displaced as many of them no longer have homes to go back to. (Ibid., 6)

The military doctrine followed by Israel in Gaza was a replica of the blanket-bombing campaign that Israel carried out in Lebanon in 2006. Both strategies involved collective, disproportionate punishment.

There is no escaping the fact that, since its confrontation with settler Zionism in Palestine more than a century ago and given the growth of the Palestinian population from 300,000 in the late nineteenth century to close to 12 million globally in the early part of the twenty-first century, the Palestinians have been plagued by a plethora of problems that continue to dominate their future and frustrate their national aspirations. This book has framed the problem in terms of biopolitics and demography, on the one hand, and state security and control of territory in the context of Palestine's colonial experience, on the other. I have explored the ideological bases of Zionism's brand of settler colonialism along several fronts. It is clear that any critical assessment of the Zionist venture and its implications for the Palestinians in particular is not in the offing. On the contrary, right-wing Zionism, as shown by the adherents of various political stripes, remains trapped in an ideological straightjacket. The push by Prime Minister Benjamin Netanyahu in 2015 to enshrine Israel's brand of Zionism in the Jewishness of the state and his demand that the rest of world, particularly the Palestinians, accept such branding were tantamount to rejecting the notion of citizenship rights along universal lines and to abandoning any peace prospects.

More than a decade ago, the noted historian Tony Judt (2003) singled out Israel's "anachronistic" position with regard to the Jewishness of the state: "The very idea of a 'Jewish state' – a state in which Jews and the Jewish religion have exclusive privileges from which non-Jewish citizens are forever excluded – is rooted in another time and place. Israel, in short, is an anachronism." Like other critics, Jews and non-Jews, Judt opted for a binational state as a way of resolving the impasse with the Palestinians. Similarly, philosopher Judith Butler (2012, 7), who writes that Arab-Jewish "coexistence projects can only begin by the dismantling of political Zionism," is emphatic in rejecting the two-state solution and the continued dominance of a Jewish state over the Palestinians in favour of a binational state.

State violence

> ... the body is ... directly involved in a political field; power relations have an immediate hold upon it; they invest it, mark it, train it, torture it, force it to carry out tasks, to perform ceremonies, to emit signs. (Foucault 1977, 25)

Throughout this book, I have demonstrated that the brutal conduct of the Israeli regime toward the Palestinians in the occupied territories and in the refugee camps of neighbouring Arab countries gives lie to the claim by Netanyahu and others that the Israeli army is "the most moral army in the world" (Keinon 2014). The Palestinians, who have been at the receiving end of Israel's military actions since 1948, hold a diametrically opposed view (M.A. Khalidi 2009–10), and international public opinion no longer gives Israel's official position an automatic seal of approval. Yet Israel is constantly seeking justifications for its use of military force, and as seen in chapter 4, there is no shortage of home-grown legal experts (Asa Kasher, in A. Harel 2009), apologists (Henkin 2003), and others abroad who are prepared to justify the practices of the Israeli army. During military conflicts, Israel is driven by what Karine Hamilton (2011) calls a "moral economy of violence" that is based on a hierarchy of values regarding human life. Reflecting on Israel's extensive bombing of Beirut during its 1982 invasion of Lebanon, Hamilton notes that advanced technology, the so-called "distance technology," tolerates the killing of civilians, such as in aerial bombings, because it is not face-to-face and is carried out from a remote location. Underlying the practice of such asymmetrical warfare is a racist public discourse in Israel that portrays the Arabs as "'savage,' 'sly,' 'cheat,' 'thief,' 'robber,' 'provocateur,' and 'terrorist'" (ibid., 137). This may explain why the minority of the Jewish Israeli public, at 47 per cent, opposes using torture in interrogating suspects, compared to 58 per cent in the United States, 72 per cent in Britain, 49 per cent in China, and 43 per cent in Russia (Ynet 2006).

This book has highlighted several aspects of the Palestinian experience as a colonised population, both in the occupied Palestinian territories and in Israel proper. In referring to Palestinian citizens in Israel, Adriana Kemp (2004, 74) remarks that the "Palestinians stand at the centre of the state's desire for control, discipline, and regulation of the most minute levels of conduct of those who are members of the society and polity, yet do not belong to them" (see also Lowrance 2005). With words that echo Michel Foucault's notions of "capillary power" and the "microphysics of power," Kemp goes on to identify the essence of the inclusion-exclusion contradiction underlying the logic of governmentality facing the Israeli state. On the one hand, discipline and surveillance are applied systematically and minutely to govern the Palestinian community in Israel, and on the other hand, the state limits the community's participation in the body politic as active citizens entitled to take part in the definition of the public good. In pursuit of this objective, the Israeli state has deployed surveillance assemblages since its inception in 1948. These comprise a collection of hard and soft technologies that involve the reporting of information by collaborators as well as spying on the everyday activities of people, both of which are reminiscent of the East German Stasi, as depicted powerfully in the film *The Lives of Others* (Henckel von Donnersmarck 2006). The award-winning documentary *I Love You All* (2004), co-directed by Eyal Sivan of Israel and Audrey Maurion of France, uses the East German Stasi surveillance system allegorically to highlight the experience of Palestinian citizens in Israel at the hands of the Israeli security services (Elazari 2006). Revelations by Israel's elite military security agents have shown that such surveillance is far from being a work of fiction. As a matter of fact, upon seeing *The Lives of Others*, one such agent had a "transformational moment" that resulted in feelings of regret about spying on Palestinians (Rudoren 2014).

A former soldier of the Israeli Haganah has admitted in a television appearance "the deliberate deception of the Zionist movement" in destroying Arab villages in 1948 (Peace Planet 2014). Although such admissions are significant, if not numerous, they do occur every now and then under the weight of moral pangs. Consider, for example, the latest coverage accorded to S. Yizhar's 1949 novel *Khirbet Khizeh*, named for a fictional village that stands in for all the Palestinian villages that were wantonly destroyed by the nascent Israeli army in 1948, their residents expelled to make room for the Zionist settlers. What is galling to the Western reader, according to a *New York Times* book review by Dexter Filkins (2015), is that Smilansky, the protagonist in the novel, "suggests that the Palestinians leaving on trucks resemble the Jews being deported to the Nazi concentration camps. The victims, that is, are now the oppressors." In Smilansky's words:

> I felt that I was on the verge of slipping. I managed to pull myself together. My guts cried out. Colonizers, they shouted. Lies, my guts shouted. Khirbet Khizeh is not ours. The Spandau gun never gave us any rights. Oh, my guts screamed. What hadn't they told us about refugees. Everything, everything was for the refugees, their welfare, their rescue . . . our refugees, naturally. Those we were driving out – that was a totally different matter. Wait. Two thousand years of exile. The whole story. Jews being killed. Europe. We were the masters now. (In ibid.)

The predicament of Palestine

The issue of Palestinian refugees remains at the heart of the conflict, yet this fact is not acknowledged by Israel and its supporters. To this author, the issue of the Palestinian refugees must be brought to the fore and dealt with justly. If this is not done and Israel continues to define the conflict with the Palestinians as part of a zero-sum game in which resolving the refugee issue on the basis of justice is tantamount to surrendering Israeli sovereignty and the Jewishness of Eretz Yisrael (the Land of Israel), the status quo will prevail, with more violence to come.

In this final segment, I rhetorically pose a question: is there a relationship between prolonging the ongoing ethnic and regional conflicts in the Middle East and the unresolved Palestine question? Rarely is the name of Palestine associated with the ongoing conflicts in Iraq, Syria, and Lebanon, let alone with the anti-American sentiment emanating from the Middle East. When mentioned at all, Palestine is usually relegated to the debate about terrorism as formulated by Israel and its supporters in response to Palestinian violent reactions to the occupation of the West Bank and Gaza. What would the Middle East have looked like in the twentieth and twenty-first centuries if the conflict over Palestine had been resolved? Would the level of Muslim and Arab animosity to the West have reached the level that it has? These issues are hardly addressed either in concrete or reflective modes by policymakers. The so-called "Middle East peace process" continues to lurch from one crisis to the next, so much so that many have resigned themselves to accepting this as the normal state of affairs.

In his testimony to the Peel Commission in 1937, Winston Churchill (in A. Roy 2003, 58; see also *Guardian* 2002) had this to say when asked about the rights of the native Palestinians in the face of Jewish illegal immigration to Palestine at the time:

> I do not agree that the dog in a manger has the final right to the manger, even though he may have lain there for a very long time. I do not admit that right. I do not admit, for instance, that a great wrong has been done to the Red Indians of America, or the black people of Australia. I do not admit that wrong has been done to these people by the fact that a stronger race, a higher grade race, a more worldly-wise race, to put it that way, has come in and taken their place.

Such sentiments are not surprising in the light of what we know about the outlook of colonial rule and the racism associated with it. But the gist of Churchill's words must have been music to the ears of the Zionist leadership at the time. The Zionist stance toward the Palestinians, judging by the events of 1948 and the accompanying mass expulsion of Palestinians, has remained entrenched in a Churchillian worldview that belongs to centuries gone by. But it would have been a surprise to the likes of Churchill and his Zionist sympathisers that more than a century after the Zionist settlers first set foot in Palestine, the Palestinians are still around to narrate their story. To quote the title of an article by Edward Said (1984), they cannot be denied the "permission to narrate" their experience. Moreover, in spite of their brutal pursuit by Israel and other Arab regimes, the Palestinians have developed a repertoire of resistance, both discursive and practical.

The denial of any association between the unresolved Palestine issue and the current turmoil in Islamic lands is not new. Israel has always defined the conflict as an interstate conflict between itself and neighbouring Arab countries. The Palestinian dimension is considered tangential. Indeed, the closer Israel has come to normalising its relationship with other Arab countries such as Egypt and Jordan in a public way, as well as with several other Arab countries in the Gulf and North Africa in a less public way, the urgency to resolve the Palestine issue has receded even further into the background. Yet events on the ground involving Palestinians and Israelis have become more deadly, suggesting a correlation between so called "normal politics" at one level and the escalation of violence at another.

Under the Netanyahu government, Palestine has assumed a more perilous position in so far as it has been identified with the global Islamic fundamentalist camp and thus cast as the eternal enemy of the West. Netanyahu personally does not miss an opportunity to lump the fundamentalists of Iraq, Syria, and Al-Qaeda together with radical Palestinian groups such as Hamas as though they were parts of one monolithic entity. We forget, as Shlaim (2009) correctly points out, that Hamas was supported and encouraged during its inception by Israel, which nourished it as a counterweight to Fatah. The association between Palestine and fundamentalism serves Israel's purpose of driving the death nail into the coffin of the two-state solution. The Palestinians are presented as terrorists bent on denying Israel's right to exist. To a very large extent, Israel has succeeded in conveying such an image, particularly in Western media and the US Congress.

There have been attempts to resolve the conflict over Palestine equitably, but the cost would have been unacceptable for Israel in light of its expansionist policies and uncompromising Zionist, fundamentalist attitudes. Its illegal settlement policies would have been curtailed, an outcome deemed undesirable even though Israel would have benefited if it had adhered to the 1949 armistice lines within the 1967 borders, enjoyed tranquillity, and prospered as an industrial country – but maybe without being able to market itself as a main producer of military hardware at the expense of Palestinian lives. For their part, the Palestinians would have gone ahead with the creation of institutions that they deeply needed. They have not lacked the manpower and experience for such a purpose. And above all, they would have relieved themselves of the Israeli occupation.

The most important outcome of such an imagined development would have been to provide young people in the Middle East with an outlet for their blocked aspirations under the status quo. It is their experience of oppression that accounts for the desperation we see in the Middle East, particularly Palestine. No matter how cleverly the roots of the conflict are masked and redefined, unless the Palestinians are acknowledged and dealt with in a serious manner, the turmoil that we now see in the Middle East will only continue. Based on Netanyahu's admissions at the end of his successful and manipulative campaign for re-election in 2015, in which he cultivated fearmongering by warning Israeli Jews that the Arabs of the state were heading in droves to vote, it is clear that the Israeli government does not subscribe to the two-state solution. The most that the Palestinians will get if they accept Israel's conditions regarding the Jewishness of the state is an emasculated entity that lacks a coherent political configuration based on real sovereignty and independence.

REFERENCES

Abdel-Jawad, S. 1996. "Israel's New Historians." Unpublished manuscript, Bir Zeit University, Ramallah.
——. 2005. *Palestinians and the Historiography of the 1948 War*. Ramallah: Muwatin.
Abdo, N. 1991. "Women of the Intifada: Gender, Class and National Liberation." *Race and Class* 32 (4): 19–34.
Abed, G.T., ed. 1988. *The Palestinian Economy: Studies in Development under Prolonged Occupation*. London and New York: Routledge.
Abourahme, N. 2011. "Spatial Collisions and Discordant Temporalities: Everyday Life between Camp and Checkpoint." *International Journal of Urban and Regional Studies* 35 (2): 453–61.
Abowd, T. 2007. "National Boundaries, Colonized Spaces: The Gendered Politics of Residential Life in Contemporary Jerusalem." *Anthropological Quarterly* 80 (4): 997–1034.
Abu Aker, K., and J. Rudoren. 2013. "An Unlikely Path to Palestinian Fatherhood." *New York Times*, 7 February. http://www.nytimes.com/2013/02/08/world/middleeast/palestinian-doctor-describes-plan-to-smuggle-sperm-from-jails.html?_r=0 (accessed 28 February 2013).
Abu Amr, Z. 1994. *Islamic Fundamentalism in the West Bank and Gaza: Muslim Brotherhood and Islamic Jihad*. Bloomington and Indianapolis: Indiana University Press.
Abu El-Haj, N. 1998. "Translating Truths: Nationalism, the Practice of Archaeology, and the Remaking of Past and Present in Contemporary Jerusalem." *American Ethnologist* 25 (2): 166–88.
——. 2002. *Facts on the Ground: Archaeological Practice and Territorial Self-Fashioning in Israeli Society*. Chicago: University of Chicago Press.
——. 2010. "Racial Palestinianization and the Janus-Faced Nature of the Israeli State." *Patterns of Prejudice* 44 (1): 27–41.
——. 2012. *The Genealogical Science: The Search for Jewish Origins and the Politics of Epistemology*. Chicago: University of Chicago Press.
Abujidi, N. 2011. "Surveillance and Spatial Flows in the Occupied Palestinian Territories." In E. Zureik, D. Lyon, and Y. Abu-Laban, eds., *Surveillance and Control in Israel/Palestine: Population, Territory and Power*, 331–54. London: Routledge.

Abu-Laban, Y., and A. Bakan. 2011. "The 'Israelization' of Social Sorting and the 'Palestinianization' of the Racial Contract: Reframing Israel/Palestine and the War on Terror." In E. Zureik, D. Lyon, and Y. Abu-Laban, eds., *Surveillance and Control in Israel/Palestine: Population, Territory and Power*, 276–94. London: Routledge.

Abu-Lughod, I. 1971. *The Transformation of Palestine: Essays on the Origin and Development of the Arab-Israeli Conflict*. Evanston, IL: Northwestern University Press.

Abu-Lughod, J.L. 1980. "Annex 1: Demographic Characteristics of the Palestinian Population: Relevance for Planning Palestine Open University." In *The Palestine Open University Feasibility Study, Part II*. Paris: UNESCO.

Abu-Lughod, L. 1993. *Writing Women's Worlds: Bedouin Stories*. Berkeley: University of California Press.

Abu-Lughod, L., and A. Sa'di. 2007. "Introduction." In A. Sa'di and L. Abu-Lughod, eds., *Nakba: Palestine, 1948 and the Claims of Memory*, 1–24. New York: Columbia University Press.

Abu-Manneh, B. 2006. "Israel in US Empire." *New Formations* 59: 34–51.

Abunimah, A. 2009. "Why Israel Won't Survive." *Electronic Intifada*, 19 January. http://electronicintifada.net/content/why-israel-wont-survive/7999 (accessed 6 October 2014).

Abu-Nimer, M. 1999. *Dialogue, Conflict Resolution, and Change: Arab-Jewish Encounters in Israel*. Albany: SUNY Press.

Abu-Sitta, S. 1999. *Refugee Right of Return: Sacred, Legal and Possible*. London: Palestine Centre.

——. 2005. *Atlas of Palestine, 1917–1966 [1948]*. London: Palestine Land Society.

Abu-Zahra, N. 2008a. "Identity Cards and Coercion: 'Ending Fear or Striking Fear'?" In R. Pain and S. Smith, eds., *Fear: Critical Geopolitics and Everyday Life*, 175–93. Burlington, VT: Ashgate.

——. 2008b. "IDs and Territory: Population Control for Resource Expropriation." In D. Cowen and E. Gilbert, eds., *War, Citizenship, Territory*, 303–26. London: Routledge.

Abu-Zahra, N., and A. Kay. 2005. "Nationalism for Security? Reexamining Zionism." *Arab World Geographer* 8 (4): 220–47.

——. 2013. *Unfree in Palestine: Registration, Documentation, and Movement Restriction*. London: Pluto.

ACRI (Association of Civil Rights in Israel). 2009. *Situation Report: The State of Human Rights in Israel and the OPT, 2009*. http://www.acri.org.il/pdf/state2009en.pdf (accessed 11 April 2010, no longer available).

——. 2012a. "Invasive Email Searches in Airports Contradict Israeli Law." 6 June. http://www.acri.org.il/en/2012/06/06/email-searches-in-airports (accessed 29 August 2012).

——. 2012b. *Situation Report: The State of Human Rights in Israel and the OPT, 2012*. http://www.acri.org.il/en/wp-content/uploads/2012/12/ACRI-Situation-Report-2012-ENG.pdf (accessed 15 September 2013).

——. 2012c. "Update: Anti-Democratic Legislation Initiatives." 2 August. http://www.acri.org.il/en/2012/08/02/update-anti-democratic-legislation-initiatives (accessed 7 May 2014).

——. 2013. *Situation Report: The State of Human Rights in Israel and the OPT, 2013*. http://www.acri.org.il/en/2013/12/10/situation-report-2013 (accessed 7 May 2014).

Adalah. 2012. *New Discriminatory Laws and Bills in Israel*. Updated October. Haifa: Adalah.

——. 2013. *Index of Currently Pending Discriminatory Bills in the 19th Israeli Knesset*. Updated June. Haifa: Adalah.

Agamben, G. 1995. "We Refugees." Trans. Michael Rocke. *Symposium* 49 (2): 114–19. http://www.egs.edu/faculty/agamben/agamben-we-refugees.html (accessed 12 December 2013).

———. 1998. *Homo Sacer: Sovereign Power and Bare Life*. Stanford, CA: Stanford University Press.
———. 2000. *Means without Ends: Notes on Politics*. Minneapolis: University of Minnesota Press.
———. 2002. "Security and Terror." Trans. C. Emcke. *Theory and Event* 5 (4): 1–2.
———. 2005. *State of Exception*. Chicago and London: University of Chicago Press.
Ahren, R. 2009. "South Africa: Israel Actions in East Jerusalem Akin to Apartheid." *Haaretz.com*, 26 November. http://www.haaretz.com/hasen/spages/1130768.html (accessed 3 December 2009).
Ajana, B. 2005. "Surveillance and Biopolitics." *Electronic Journal of Sociology*. http://www.sociology.org/content/2005/tier1/ajana_biopolitics.pdf (accessed 10 August 2009).
Ajluni, S. 2003. "The Palestinian Economy and the Second Intifada." *Journal of Palestine Studies* 32 (3): 64–75.
Akram, S. 2002. "Palestinian Refugees and Their Legal Status: Rights, Politics, and Implications for a Just Solution." *Journal of Palestine Studies* 31 (3): 36–51.
Akram, S., and T. Rempel. 2004. "Temporary Protection as an Instrument for Implementing the Right of Return for Palestinian Refugees." *Boston University International Law Journal* 22 (1): 1–162.
Alatout, S. 1999. "Imagining Hydrological Boundaries, Constructing the Nation-State: A 'Fluid' History of Israel, 1936–1948." PhD diss., Cornell University.
———. 2014. "From River to Border: The Jordan between Empire and Nation-State." In Daniel Kleinman and Kelly Moore, eds., *Routledge Handbook of Science, Technology, and Society*, 307–31. New York: Routledge.
Al-Awda. N.d. http://www.al-awda.org (accessed 11 April 2015).
Al-Haj, M. 1995. *Education, Empowerment and Control: The Case of the Arabs in Israel*. Albany: SUNY Press.
———. 2003. "Higher Education among the Arabs in Israel." *Higher Education Policy* 16 (3): 351–68.
Al-Haq. N.d. http://www.alhaq.org (accessed 11 April 2015).
Al-Haroub, K. 2001. "Palestinian and Israeli New Historians." *Majallat al-Dirasat al-Filastiniyah* 48: 48–62 [Arabic].
Aljazeera. 2013. "Palestinian Inmates 'Sneak Sperm out of Jail.'" 7 February. http://www.aljazeera.com/news/middleeast/2013/02/2013275618777526.html (accessed 27 August 2014).
Alon, G. 2003. "Number of Returning Israelis Continues to Drop." *Haaretz.com*, 19 December. http://www.haaretz.com/news/number-of-returning-israelis-continues-to-drop-1.106142 (accessed 3 August 2014).
———. 2004. "270,000 Israelis Left Country over 10-Year Period." *Haaretz.com*, 22 January. http://www.haaretz.com/print-edition/news/270-000-israelis-left-country-over-10-year-period-1.111323 (accessed 3 August 2014).
Alon, G., and A. Benn. 2003. "Netanyahu: Israel's Arabs Are the Real Demographic Threat." *Haaretz.com*, 18 December. http://www.haaretz.com/print-edition/news/netanyahu-israel-s-arabs-are-the-real-demographic-threat-1.109045 (accessed 3 August 2014).
Amit, E. 2006. "Report: 350,000 Israelis Live in NY." *ynetnews.com*, 2 December. http://www.ynetnews.com/articles/0,7340,L-3214723,00.html (accessed 28 July 2014).
Amnesty International. 2001. *Annual Report, January–December 2000*. London: Amnesty International.
———. 2009. *Israel/Gaza: Operation 'Cast Lead': 22 Days of Death and Destruction*. London: Amnesty International.
———. 2014. "Gaza: Stop the Arms, Stop the Killing." 29 July. http://www.alternativenews.org/archive/index.php/politics/activism/8350-act-gaza-stop-the-arms-stop-the-killing (accessed 16 August 2014).

Anderson, Ben. 2011. "Population and Affective Perception: Biopolitics and Anticipatory Action in US Counterinsurgency Doctrine." *Antipode* 43 (2): 205–36.

Anderson, Benedict. 1994a. "Exodus." *Critical Inquiry* 20 (2): 315–27.

———. 1994b. *Imagined Communities: Reflections on the Origins and Spread of Nationalism.* London and New York: Verso.

Anderson, J. 2000. "Producers and Middle East Internet Technology: Getting Beyond 'Impacts.'" *Middle East Journal* 54 (3): 419–31.

Aner, N. 1994. *Will They Be Refugees Forever? Description of Conditions and Suggestions for a Solution.* Jerusalem: Israel Information Office [Hebrew].

Anthias, F. 1998 "Evaluating 'Diaspora': Beyond Ethnicity?" *Sociology* 32 (3): 557–80.

Aouragh, M. 2011a. "Everyday Resistance on the Internet: The Palestinian Context." *Journal of Arab and Muslim Media Research* 1 (2): 1–20.

———. 2011b. *Palestine Online: Transnationalism, the Internet and the Construction of Identity.* London: I.B. Tauris.

Appadurai, A. 1993. "Number in the Colonial Imagination." In C. Breckenridge and P. van der Veer, eds., *Orientalism and the Postcolonial Predicament: Perspectives on South Asia*, 314–40. Philadelphia: University of Pennsylvania Press.

———. 1996. *Modernity at Large: Cultural Dimensions of Globalization.* Minneapolis: University of Minnesota Press.

Arad, R. 2012. "When Inspectors Become Detectives: Hunting Palestinians on the Beaches of Tel Aviv." *Haaretz.com*, 5 August. http://www.haaretz.com/news/features/when-inspectors-become-detectives-hunting-palestinians-on-the-beaches-of-tel-aviv-1.456145 (accessed 5 August 2012).

Arad, U. 2004. "Demography and Demagoguery." *Haaretz.com*, 6 August. http://www.haaretz.com/print-edition/opinion/demography-and-demagoguery-1.130730 (accessed 3 August 2014).

Araj, B., and R. Brym. 2011. "Intifada." In G. Martin, ed., *Sage Encyclopedia of Terrorism*, 2nd ed., 293–94. Thousand Oaks CA: Sage.

Arendt, H. 1943. "We Refugees." Reprinted in M. Robinson, ed., *Altogether Elsewhere: Writers in Exile*, 111–19. Boston and London: Faber and Faber, 1994.

———. 1978. *The Jew as Pariah: Jewish Identity and Politics in the Modern Age.* New York: Grove.

———. 2006. *Eichman in Jerusalem: A Report on the Banality of Evil.* London: Penguin Classics.

———. 2007. *The Promise of Politics.* New York: Schocken.

Ariel, A. 2013. "Revealed from Archive: Israel's Secret Plan to Resettle Arab Refugees." *Haaretz.com*, 19 December. http://www.haaretz.com/weekend/magazine/.premium-1.564422 (accessed 21 December 2013).

ARIJ (Applied Research Institute of Jerusalem). 2009. *A Geopolitical Atlas of the Occupied Palestinian Territory.* http://www.arij.org/index.php/publications/books-atlases/79-2009/243-a-geopolitical-atlas-of-the-occupied-palestinian-territory (accessed 23 July 2012).

Arnaiz-Villena, A., N. Elaiwa, C. Silvera, A. Rostom, J. Moscoso, E. Gomez-Casado, L. Allende, P. Varela, and J. Martinez-Laso. 2001. "The Origin of Palestinians and Their Genetic Relatedness with Other Mediterranean Populations." *Human Immunology* 62 (9): 889–900.

Asad, T., ed. 1973. *Anthropology and the Colonial Encounter.* London: Ithaca.

———. 1994. "Ethnographic Representation, Statistics and Modern Power." *Social Research* 61 (1): 55–88.

Asad, T., and R. Owen, eds. 1983. *Sociology of "Developing Societies": The Middle East.* New York: Monthly Review.

Ashforth, A. 1990. "Reckoning Schemes of Legitimation: On Commissions of Inquiry as Power/Knowledge Forms." *Journal of Historical Sociology* 30 (1): 1–22.

Ashcroft, B., G. Griffiths, and H. Tiffin. 1998. *Post-Colonial Studies: The Key Concepts*. London and New York: Routledge.

Avineri, S., ed. 1968. *Karl Marx on Colonialism and Modernization*. New York: Doubleday.

——. 1972. "Modernization and Arab Society: Some Reflections." In I. Howe and C. Gershman, eds., *Israel, the Arabs and the Middle East*, 300–11. New York: Doubleday.

——. 1981. *The Making of Modern Zionism: The Intellectual Origins of the Jewish State*. New York: Basic Books.

——. 2002. "Zionism According to Theodore Herzl." *Haaretz.com*, 20 December. http://www.haaretz.com/culture/books/zionism-according-to-theodor-herzl-1.24821 (accessed 30 April 2010).

——. 2007. "Post-Zionism Does Not Exist." *Haaretz.com*, 6 June. http://www.haaretz.com/print-edition/opinion/post-zionism-doesn-t-exist-1.224973 (accessed 24 July 2010).

——. 2009. "Herzl's Vision of Racism." *Haaretz.com*, 9 February. http://www.haaretz.com/print-edition/opinion/herzl-s-vision-of-racism-1.269714 (accessed 29 August 2009).

——. 2010a. "Avineri on Herzl." *Haaretz.com*, 17 June. http://jafi.org/JewishAgency/English/About/Updates/Personal%20Stories/Archive/2010/jun17.htm (accessed 21 May 2014).

——. 2010b. "Israel is the Opposite of Fascist." *Haaretz.com*, 15 November. http://www.haaretz.com/print-edition/opinion/israel-is-the-opposite-of-fascist-1.324727 (accessed 15 November 2010).

Avruch, K. 1998. *Culture and Conflict Resolution*. Washington, DC: United States Institute of Peace.

Avruch, K., and P. Black. 1987. "A Generic Theory of Conflict Resolution: A Critique." *Negotiation Journal* 3 (1): 87–96.

Azoulay, A., and A. Ophir. 2004. "On the Verge of Catastrophe." Paper presented at the conference "The Politics of Humanitarianism in the Occupied Territories," Van Leer Institute, Jerusalem, 20–21 April.

Azoulay, Y. 2007. "Civilians from Military Firms to Learn to Fly Drones." *Haaretz.com*, 26 December. http://www.haaretz.com/print-edition/news/civilians-from-military-firms-to-learn-to-fly-drones-1.235965 (accessed 24 April 2012).

Baboun, J. 2013. "The Digital Ecology and the Palestinian-Israeli Conflict." *Technologist Magazine*, 13 May. http://jennybaboun.wordpress.com/2013/05/13/the-digital-ecology-and-the-palestinian-israeli-conflict (accessed 20 December 2014).

BADIL Resource Center for Palestinian Residency and Refugee Rights. N.d. http://www.badil.org (accessed 11 April 2015).

——. 2009. *Survey of Palestinian Refugees and Internally Displaced Persons, 2008–2009*. Bethlehem: BADIL.

Baev, P. and J.P. Burgess,. 2002. "Editor's Comments." *Security Dialogue* 32 (2): 123–26.

Bakan, A., and Y. Abu-Laban. 2010. "Israel/Palestine, South Africa and the 'One-State Solution': The Case for an Apartheid Analysis." *Politikon* 37 (2–3): 331–51.

Baker, A. 1992. "Gender, Urban-Rural-Camp, and Regional Differences among Self-Esteem Scores of Palestinian Children." *Journal of Psychology* 126 (2): 207–9.

Bales, R. 1955. *Small Groups: Studies in Social Interaction*. New York: Alfred A. Knopf.

Balibar, E. 1991. "Is There A 'Neo-Racism'?" In E. Balibar and I. Wallerstein, eds., *Race, Nation, Class: Ambiguous Identities*, 17–28. London: Verso.

Balzacq, T. 2005. "The Three Faces of Securitisation: Political Agency, Audience, and Context." *European Journal of International Relations* 11 (2): 171–201.

Barakat, H., and P. Dodd. 1968. *River without Bridges: A Study of the Exodus of the 1967 Palestinian Arab Refugees*. Beirut: Institute for Palestine Studies.
Bar'el, Z. 2014. "The Racism Playoffs." *Haaretz.com*, 28 May. http://www.haaretz.com/opinion/.premium-1.595632 (accessed 28 May 2014).
Bar-Gal, Y. 1994. "The Image of the 'Palestinian' in Geography Textbooks in Israel." *Journal of Geography* 93 (5): 224–32.
——. 2003. "The Blue Box and JNF Propaganda Maps." *Israel Studies* 8 (1): 1–19.
Bar-Tal, D., and Y. Teichman. 2005. *Stereotypes and Prejudice in Conflict: Representation of Arabs in Israeli Jewish Society*. Cambridge: Cambridge University Press.
Batniji, R. 2012. "Searching for Dignity." *Lancet* 380 (9840): 466–67. http://dx.doi.org/10.1016/S0140-6736(12)61280-X (accessed 9 February 2015).
Baudrillard, J. 1994. *Simulacra and Simulation*. Ann Arbor: University of Michigan Press.
Bauman, Z. 1989. *Modernity and the Holocaust*. Ithaca, NY: Cornell University Press.
Bayly, C.A. 1996. *Empire and Information: Intelligence Gathering and Social Communication in India, 1780–1870*. Cambridge: Cambridge University Press.
BBC News. 2004. "Former Israeli Army Chief Drowns." 23 November. http://news.bbc.co.uk/2/hi/middle_east/4034765.stm (accessed 6 October 2014).
——. 2005. "Intifada Toll, 2000-2005." 8 February. http://news.bbc.co.uk/2/hi/middle_east/3694350.stm (accessed 23 September 2014).
——. 2014. "Gaza Crisis: Toll of Operations in Gaza." 1 September. http://www.bbc.com/news/world-middle-east-28439404 (accessed 23 September 2014).
Beck, U. 2000. *The Brave New World of Work*. Cambridge: Cambridge University Press.
Be'er, Y., and S. Abdel-Jawad. 1994. *Collaborators in the Occupied Territories: Human Rights Abuses and Violations*. Jerusalem: B'Tselem.
Beinin, J. 2014. "Racism Is the Foundation of Israel's Operation Protective Edge." *Stanford University Press Blog*, 30 July. http://stanfordpress.typepad.com/blog/2014/07/racism-is-the-foundation-of-israels-operation-protective-edge.html (accessed 23 September 2014).
Beit-Hallahmi, B. 1992. *Original Sins: Reflections on the History of Zionism and Israel*. London and Concord, MA: Pluto.
Ben-Gurion, D. 1917. "On Clarifying the Origin of the Fallahim [sic]." Reprinted in *We and Our Neighbours*. Tel Aviv: Davar, 1931 [Hebrew].
Benjamin, W. 1999. *Illuminations*. London: Pimlico.
Benn, A. 2010. "Sharon's Real Legacy – Keeping the Arabs Out of Sight." *Haaretz.com*, 13 January. http://www.haaretz.com/print-edition/opinion/sharon-s-real-legacy-keeping-the-arabs-out-of-sight-1.261361 (accessed 18 January 2010).
Bennett, C., and D. Lyon, eds. 2008. *Playing the Identity Card*. London and New York: Routledge.
Ben-Porath, Y., and E. Marx. 1971. *Some Sociological and Economic Aspects of Refugee Camps on the West Bank*. Santa Monica, CA: Rand Corporation.
Ben-Porath, Y., E. Marx, and S. Shamir. 1974. *A Refugee Camp on a Mountain Ridge*. Tel Aviv: Shiloah Institute, Tel Aviv University [Hebrew].
Ben-Rafael, E. 2004. "Where Stands Israel?" *Ethnic and Racial Studies* 27 (2): 310–16.
Benvenisti, M. 1982. "Letter to Professor Avineri." *Haaretz*, 22 July.
——. 2002. "The Creators of Fictitious Identities." *Haaretz.com*, 29 August. http://www.haaretz.com/print-edition/opinion/the-creators-of-fictitious-identities-1.35646 (accessed 21 December 2013).
Ben-Ze'ev, E. 2000. "Narratives of Exile: Palestinian Refugee Reflections on Three Villages: Tirat Haifa, 'Ein Hawd and Ijzim." PhD diss., University of Oxford.
——. 2009. "Constructing Palestine's Landscape: British Mandate Cartography, 1920–1948." Unpublished paper.

———. 2011. *Remembering Palestine in 1948: Beyond National Narratives*. Cambridge: Cambridge University Press.

Benziman, U. 2003. "Nationalist Tendencies Running Rampant." *Haaretz.com*, 3 August. http://www.haaretz.com/print-edition/opinion/nationalist-tendencies-running-rampant-1.96031 (accessed 21 December 2013).

Benziman, U., and A. Mansour. 1992. *Subtenants: The Arabs of Israel, Their Status and the Policies Toward Them*. Jerusalem: Keter [Hebrew].

Berda, Y. 2012a. *The Bureaucracy of the Occupation in the West Bank: The Permit Regime, 2000–2006*. Jerusalem: Van Leer Institute and Hakibutz Hameuhad Publishing [Hebrew].

———. 2012b. "Categorizing Populations – Forms, Spaces, and Emergencies: The Mundane Administrative Legacies of Colonial Rule in India, Israel and Cyprus." Unpublished manuscript.

———. 2013. "Managing Dangerous Populations: Colonial Legacies of Security and Surveillance." *Sociological Forum* 28 (3): 627–30.

Berkowitz, P. 2004. "Breeding Insecurity: Israel Begins to Confront Its Demographic Problem." *Weekly Standard*, 5 June. https://www.weeklystandard.com/Content/Protected/Articles/000/000/004/185jview.asp (accessed 21 December 2013).

Bernstein, D.S. 1998. "Strategies of Equalization, a Neglected Aspect of the Split Labor Market Theory: Jews and Arabs in the Split Labor Market of Mandatory Palestine." *Ethnic and Racial Studies* 21 (3): 449–75.

Bhabha, H. 1994. *The Location of Culture*. New York: Routledge.

Bhungalia, L. 2012. "Im/Mobilities in a 'Hostile Territory': Managing the Red Line." *Geopolitics* 17 (2): 256–75.

Bill, J.A., and C. Leiden. 1976. *The Middle East: Politics and Power*. Boston: Allyn and Bacon.

Bishara, A. 2004. "A Short History of Apartheid." *Al-Ahram Weekly*, 8–14 January. http://weekly.ahram.org.eg/2004/672/op10.htm (accessed 2 October 2014).

———. 2011. *On a Jewish and Democratic State*. Doha, Qatar: Arab Center for Research and Policy Studies.

Bisharat, G. 1989. *Palestinian Lawyers and Israeli Rule: Law and Disorder in the West Bank*. Austin: University of Texas Press.

———. 1994. "Land, Law and Legitimacy in Israel and the Occupied Territories." *American University Law Review* 43 (2): 467–561.

———. 2005. "Facts, Rights, and Remedies: Implementing International Law in the Israel/Palestine Conflict." *Hastings International and Comparative Law Review* 28 (3): 319–31.

Bisharat, G., T. Crawley, S. Elturk, C. James, R. Mishaan, A. Radhakrishnan, and A. Sanders. 2009. "Israel's Invasion of Gaza in International Law." *Denver Journal of International Law and Policy* 38 (1): 41–114.

Black, E. 2001. *IBM and the Holocaust: The Strategic Alliance between Nazi Germany and America's Most Powerful Corporation*. Westport, CT: Dialog.

Blatman, D. 2011. "Heading toward an Israeli Apartheid State." *Haaretz.com*, 4 April. http://www.haaretz.com/print-edition/opinion/heading-toward-an-israeli-apartheid-state-1.353942 (accessed 5 April 2011).

Blau, U. 2012. "The Settler behind Shadowy Purchases of Palestinian Land in the West Bank." *Haaretz.com*, 8 June. http://www.haaretz.com/weekend/magazine/the-settler-behind-shadowy-purchases-of-palestinian-land-in-the-west-bank.premium-1.435253 (accessed 8 June 2012).

Blau, U., and Y. Feldman. 2009. "Gaza Bonanza." *Haaretz.com*, 11 June. http://www.haaretz.com/gaza-bonanza-1.277760 (accessed 4 January 2014).

Bletcher, R. 2005. "Citizens without Sovereignty: Transfer and Ethnic Cleansing in Israel." *Comparative Studies in Society and History* 47 (4): 725–55.

Bloom, E. 2007a. "The 'Administrative Knight' – Arthur Ruppin and the Rise of Zionist Statistics." *Tel Aviv University Year Book for German History* 35: 183–203.
———. 2007b. "What 'The Father' Had in Mind? Arthur Ruppin (1876–1943), Cultural Identity, Weltanschauung and Action." *Journal for History of European Ideas* 33 (3): 330–49.
———. 2011. *Arthur Ruppin and the Production of Pre-Israeli Culture.* Leiden and Boston: Brill.
Blumer, H. 1986. *Symbolic Interactionism: Perspective and Method.* Berkeley: University of California Press.
Bocco, R., M. Brunner, and J. Rabah. 2001a. *The Role of International and Local Aid during the Second Intifada, Report I.* Geneva: Graduate Institute of Development Studies, University of Geneva.
———. 2001b. *The Role of International and Local Aid during the Second Intifada, Report II.* Geneva: Graduate Institute of Development Studies, University of Geneva.
Bocco, R., I. Daneels, M. Brunner, and J. Rabah. 2002. *An Overview of Palestinian Public Assessment of Its Needs and Conditions Following the Recent Israeli Military Operations in the West Bank.* March-April. Geneva: University of Geneva, Graduate Institute of Development Studies, Report IV.
Bocco, R., M. Brunner, I. Daneels, and J. Rabah. 2001. *Palestinian Public Perceptions of Their Living Conditions, Report III.* Geneva: Graduate Institute of Development Studies, University of Geneva.
Bourdieu, P. 1977. *Outline of a Theory of Practice.* Cambridge, and New York: Cambridge University Press.
Bowman, G. 2003. "Israel's Wall and the Logic of Encystation: Sovereignty Exception or Wild Sovereignty?" *European Journal of Anthropology* 50: 127–37.
———. 2011. "A Place for Palestinians in the Altneuland: Herzl, Anti-Semitism, and the Jewish State." In E. Zureik, D. Lyon, and Y. Abu-Laban, eds., *Surveillance and Control in Israel/Palestine: Population, Territory and Power,* 65–79. London: Routledge.
Brand, L.A. 1988. *Palestinians in the Arab World: Institution Building and the Search for a State.* New York: Columbia University Press.
Braverman, I. 2011. "Civilized Borders: A Study of Israel's New Crossing Borders." *Antipode* 43 (2): 264–95.
Bronner, E. 2008. "Mahmoud Darwish, Leading Palestinian Poet, Is Dead." *New York Times,* 10 August. http://www.nytimes.com/2008/08/11/world/middleeast/11darwish.html?_r=0 (accessed 11 August 2008).
———. 2011. "Israel Leader Outlines Point before US Trip." *New York Times,* 16 May. http://www.nytimes.com/2011/05/17/world/middleeast/17mideast.html?ref=global-home (accessed 17 May 2011).
Brot, T. 2011. "German Passport Popular in Israel." *ynetnews.com,* 31 May. http://www.ynetnews.com/articles/0,7340,L-4076384,00.html (accessed 28 July 2014).
Brown, A. 2004. "Movement Restrictions in the West Bank." *Social and Legal Studies* 13 (4): 501–21.
Brown, W. 2010. *Walled States, Waning Sovereignty.* New York: Zone.
Bryant, C. 2013. "What's the Frequency? For Palestinians Not 3G." *Christian Science Monitor,* 25 July. http://www.csmonitor.com/World/Middle-East/2013/0725/What-s-the-frequency-For-Palestinians-not-3G (accessed 23 December 2014).
Brym, R., and B. Araj. 2006. "Suicide Bombing as Strategy and Interaction: The Case of the Second Intifada." *Social Forces* 84 (4): 1969–86.
———. 2008. "Palestinian Suicide Bombing Revisited: A Critique of the Outbidding Thesis." *Political Science Quarterly* 123 (3): 485–500.
Brynen, R. 2000. *A Very Political Economy: Peacebuilding and Foreign Aid in the West Bank and Gaza.* Washington, DC: United States Institute for Peace.

Brynen, R., and R. El-Rifai, eds. 2007. *Palestinian Refugees: Challenges of Repatriation and Development*. London: I.B. Tauris.

———, eds. 2012. *Compensating Palestinian Refugees: Legal Economic and Political Perspectives*. London: Pluto.

B'Tselem. 1995. *Neither Law nor Justice: Extrajudicial Punishment, Abduction, Unlawful Arrest and Torture of Palestinian Residents of the West Bank by the Palestinian Preventive Service*. Jerusalem: B'Tselem.

———. 1998. *Routine Torture: Interrogation Methods of the General Security Service*. Jerusalem: B'Tselem.

———. 2002. *Operation Defensive Shield: Soldiers' Testimonies, Palestinian Testimonies*. September. http://www.btselem.org/publications?date_filter%5Bvalue%5D%5Byear%5D=2002&tid=All (accessed 19 May 2015).

———. 2011. "Operation Cast Lead, 27 Dec. '08 to 18 Jan. '09." 1 January. http://www.btselem.org/gaza_strip/castlead_operation (accessed 17 September 2014).

———. 2013a. "B'Tselem's Findings: Harm to Civilians Significantly Higher in Second Half of Operation Pillar of Defense." 8 May. http://www.btselem.org/press_releases/20130509_pillar_of_defense_report (accessed 22 September 2014).

———. 2013b. "Checkpoints, Physical Obstructions, and Forbidden Roads." 16 January. http://www.btselem.org/freedom_of_movement/checkpoints_and_forbidden_roads (accessed 22 September 2014).

———. 2014a. "Not Holding out Hope That Investigations into Gaza Hostilities Will Lead to Results Other Than Whitewash." 10 September. http://www.btselem.org/press_releases/20140910_response_to_investigations_launched_by_idf (accessed 25 September 2014).

———. 2014b. "Statistics: Fatalities after Operation Cast Lead." http://www.btselem.org/statistics/fatalities/after-cast-lead/by-date-of-event (accessed 22 September 2014).

Burton, J., and D. Sandole. 1986. "Generic Theory: The Basis of Conflict Resolution." *Negotiation Journal* 2 (4): 333–44.

Butenschon, N.A., M. Hassassian, and U. Davis. 1997. *Citizenship and the State: A Comparative Study of Citizenship Legislation in Israel, Jordan, Palestine, Syria and Lebanon*. Syracuse, NY: Syracuse University Press.

Butler, J. 2007. "I Merely Belong to Them." *London Review of Books* 29 (9): 26–28.

———. 2012. *Parting Ways: Jewishness and the Critique of Zionism*. New York: Columbia University Press.

Buzan, B., and O. Waever. 2003. *Regions and Powers: The Structure of International Security*. Cambridge: Cambridge University Press.

Callon, M. 1995. "Four Models for the Dynamics of Science." In S. Jasanoff, G.E. Markle, J.C. Petersen, and T. Pinch, eds., *Handbook of Science and Technology Studies*, 29–63. Thousand Oaks, CA: Sage.

Caplan, J., and J. Torpey. 2001. *Documenting Individual Identity: The Development of State Practices in the Modern World*. Princeton, NJ: Princeton University Press.

Carmi, S., and H. Rosenfeld. 1974. "The Origins of the Process of Proletarianization and Urbanization of Arab Peasants in Palestine." *Annals of the New York Academy of Sciences* 220: 470–85.

Cervenak, C.M. 1984. "Promoting Inequality: Gender-Based Discrimination in UNRWA's Approach to Palestine Refugee Status." *Human Rights Quarterly* 16 (2): 300–74.

Chomsky, N. 1983. *The Fateful Triangle: The United States, Israel and the Palestinians*. Boston: South End.

Chowers, E. 2012. *The Political Philosophy of Zionism: Trading Jewish Words for a Hebraic Land*. Cambridge: Cambridge University Press.

Cisneros, O. 2001. "The Trouble with Wiring Palestine." *Wired News*, 12 January. http://electronicintifada.net/content/trouble-wiring-palestine/4567 (accessed 5 January 2015).

Clough, P., and C. Willse. 2010. "Gendered Security/National Security, Political Branding and Population Racism." *Social Text* 28 (4): 45–63.

Cohen, H. 2000. *The Present Absentees: The Palestinian Refugees in the State of Israel since 1948*. Jerusalem: Center for Research on the Arabs in Israel [Hebrew].

———. 2004. "The Archive Law, the GSS Law, and Public Discourse in Israel." *Adalah's Review* 4: 45–56.

———. 2006. *Good Arabs: The Israeli Security Agencies and Israeli Arabs, 1948–1967*. Trans. H. Watzman. Berkeley: University of California Press.

———. 2008. *Army of Shadows: Palestinian Collaborators with Zionism, 1917–1948*. Berkeley: University of California Press.

———. 2011. "The Matrix of Surveillance in Times of National Conflict: The Israeli-Palestinian Case." In E. Zureik, D. Lyon, and Y. Abu-Laban, eds., *Surveillance and Control in Israel/Palestine: Population, Territory and Power*, 99–112. London: Routledge.

Cohen, S. 1989. *Crime, Justice and Social Control in the Israeli Arab Population*. Tel Aviv: International Center for Peace in the Middle East.

———. 1991. "Talking about Torture in Israel." *Tikkun* 6 (6): 23–30, 89–90.

———. 1993. "Human Rights and Crimes of the State: The Culture of Denial." *Australian and New Zealand Journal of Criminology* 26 (2): 97–115.

Cohn, B. 1987. "The Census, Social Structure and Objectification in South Asia." Reprinted in *An Anthropologist among the Historians and other Essays*, 224–54. Delhi and Oxford: Oxford University Press, 1996.

———. 1996. *Colonialism and Its Forms of Knowledge: The British in India*. Princeton, NJ: Princeton University Press.

Cole, S. 2002. *Suspect Identities: A History of Fingerprinting and Criminal Identification*. Cambridge, MA: Harvard University Press.

Collings, D. 1988. "Conflict and Identity: Palestinianism and the Politics of Identity." MA thesis, Carleton University.

Collins, J. 2004. "Israel's War on the Milieu." *Electronic Intifada*, 20 December. http://electronicintifada.net/content/israels-war-milieu/5379 (accessed 18 May 2015).

Cook, J. 2006. "The Sinister Meaning of Olmert's Hitkansut." *Counterpunch*, 21 April. http://www.counterpunch.org/2006/04/21/deporting-hamas-members-of-parliament (accessed 31 March 2010).

———. 2013. "'The Lab': Israel Tests Weapons, Tactics on Captive Palestinian Population." *Washington Report on Middle East Affairs*, September, 16–17.

Council on Foreign Relations. 1999. *Strengthening Palestinian Public Institutions*. New York: Council on Foreign Relations.

Courbage, Y. 1999. "Reshuffling the Demographic Cards in Israel/Palestine." *Journal of Palestine Studies* 27 (4): 21–39.

———. 2012. "Demographic Trends and Challenges in Case of Statehood in Palestine, 2012-2016." Birzeit University Working Papers 2012/2013.

Crampton, J. 2001. "Maps as Social Constructions: Power, Communication and Visualization." *Progress in Human Geography* 25 (2): 235–52.

Crampton, J., and S. Elden, eds. 2007. *Space, Knowledge and Power: Foucault and Geography*. Aldershot, UK, and Burlington, VT: Ashgate.

Cronin, A. 1993. "Citizens-in-Waiting in Gaza and the West Bank: The Palestinians, Who Are They?" *New York Times*, 12 September, E3.

Curtis, B. 2002. "Foucault on Governmentality and Population: The Impossible Discovery." *Canadian Journal of Sociology* 27 (4): 505–33.

Dahan, M. 2012. "The Gaza Strip as Panopticon and Panspectron: The Disciplining and Punishing of a Society." In *Proceedings of the Cultural Attitudes towards Technology and Communications Conference*, 25–37. Australia: Murdoch University.

Dalal, M. 2003. *October 2000: Law and Politics before the Or Commission of Inquiry.* Haifa: Adalah.
Darwish, M. 1964. "Identity Card." http://electronicintifada.net/content/remembering-mahmoud-darwish/7663 (accessed 28 March 2015).
Davies, B., and R. Harre. 1990. "Positioning: The Discursive Production of Selves." *Journal of the Theory of Social Behaviour* 20 (1): 43–63.
Davis, M. 2001. "The Flames of New York." *New Left Review* 12: 34–50.
Davis, R. 2007. "Mapping the Past, Recreating the Homeland: Memories of Village Places in pre-1949 Palestine." In A. Sa'di and L. Abu-lughod, eds., *Nakba: Palestine, 1948 and the Claims of Memory*, 53–76. New York: Columbia University Press.
Davis, U. 2003. *Apartheid Israel: Possibilities for the Struggle Within.* London: Zed.
Davis, U., A. Mack, and N. Yuval-Davis, eds. 1975. *Israel and the Palestinians.* London: Ithaca.
Davison, J. 2013. "3G Void Limits West Bank Smartphone Revolution." *Phys.org*, 24 July. http://phys.org/news/2013-07-3g-void-limits-west-bank.html (accessed 6 August 2014).
Defense for Children International Palestine. 2015. *Operation Protective Edge: A War Waged on Gaza's Children.* http://issuu.com/dcips/docs/ope.awarwagedonchildren.160415/17?e=0 (accessed 6 May 2015).
Deleuze, G., and F. Guattari. 2009. *Anti-Oedipus: Capitalism and Schizophrenia.* London: Penguin Classics.
Deleuze, G., and E. Sanbar. 1998. "The Indians of Palestine." *Discourses* 20 (3): 25–29.
DellaPergola, S. 2001. "Demography in Israel/Palestine: Trends, Prospects, Policy Implications." Paper presented at the Twenty-Fourth General Population Conference of the International Union for the Scientific Investigation of Population Problems, Salvador de Bahia, Brazil, August.
Demos, T.J. 2006. "Life Full of Holes." *Grey Room* 24: 72–88.
DiMaggio, P., and E. Hargittai. 2001. "From the 'Digital Divide' to 'Digital Inequality': Studying the Internet Use as Penetration Increases." Working paper, Center for Arts and Cultural Policy Studies, Princeton University, New Jersey.
Dirks, N. 1992. *Colonialism and Culture.* Ann Arbor: University of Michigan Press.
Diwan, I., and R. Shaban, eds. 1999. *Development under Adversity: The Palestinian Economy in Transition.* Washington, DC: World Bank and Palestine Economic Policy Research Institute.
Doumani, B.B. 1994. "The Political Economy of Population Count in Ottoman Palestine, circa 1850." *International Journal of Middle East Studies* 26 (1): 1–17.
Dror, Y., and S. Gershon. 2012. *Israelis in the Digital Age – 2012.* Rishon Lezion, Israel: College of Management Academic Studies (COMAS).
Duffield, M. 2007. *Development, Security and Unending War: Governing the World of Peoples.* Cambridge, UK: Polity.
Dugard, J. 2003. *Report of the Special Rapporteur of the United Nations Commission on the Situation of Human Rights in the Palestinian Territories Occupied by Israel since 1967, Submitted in Accordance with Commission Resolution 1993/2 A.* United Nations Commission on Human Rights, 60th session, Item 8 of the provisional agenda, 8 September.
Dupont, D., and F. Pearce. 2001. "Foucault Contra Foucault: Rereading the 'Governmentality' Papers." *Theoretical Criminology* 5 (2): 123–58.
Economist. 2008. "The Wandering Palestinian." 8 May. http://www.economist.com/node/11332217 (accessed 21 May 2015).
Edelman, O. 2013. "Shin Bet Can Continue to Access Tourists' Email upon Arrival at Ben-Gurion." *Haaretz.com*, 25 April. http://www.haaretz.com/news/diplomacy-defense/shin-bet-can-continue-to-access-tourists-emails-upon-arrival-at-ben-gurion-ag-says.premium-1.517415 (accessed 31 May 2014).
Edelman, O., and R. Arad. 2012. "Report: Police Intelligence Told to Target Israeli Arabs Joining Social Protests." *Haaretz.com*, 30 June. http://www.haaretz.com/news/national/

report-police-intelligence-told-to-target-israeli-arabs-joining-social-protests-1.444790 (accessed 30 June 2012).

Edkins, J. 2008. "Biopolitics, Communication and Global Governance." *Review of International Studies* 34 (S1): 211–32.

Efrat, M. 1976. *The Palestinian Refugees: An Economic and Social Study, 1949–1974*. Tel Aviv: Horowitz Institute, Tel Aviv University [Hebrew].

Ehrlich, A. 1987. "Israel: Conflict, War and Social Change." In C. Creighton and M. Shaw, eds., *The Sociology of War and Peace*, 121–42. London: Macmillan.

Eisenstadt, S. 1967. *Israeli Society*. Reprint, London: Weidenfeld and Nicolson, 1969.

El-Abed, O. 2009. *Unprotected: Palestinians in Egypt since 1948*. Washington, DC: Institute for Palestine Studies.

Elazari, J. 2006. "Filmmaker: Israel Regime Is Like East German Stasi." *ynetnews.com*, 11 June. http://www.ynetnews.com/articles/0,7340,L-3261565,00.html (accessed 31 March 2015).

Eldar, A. 2010. "Don't Confuse Us with Facts." *Haaretz.com*, 20 May. http://www.haaretz.com/weekend/week-s-end/don-t-confuse-us-with-facts-1.291302 (accessed 30 May 2010).

———. 2011. "Netanyahu's Ongoing Acquisition of Lands by Force." *Haaretz.com*, 1 November. http://www.haaretz.com/printedition/features/netanyahu-s-ongoing-acquisition-of-lands-by-force-1.393069 (accessed 11 November 2011).

———. 2012a. "The Government Admits: There Is No Longer a Jewish Majority between the Jordan River and the Sea." *Haaretz.com*, 16 October. http://www.haaretz.com.il/news/politics/1.1843217 (accessed 4 January 2014) [Hebrew].

———. 2012b. "Israel Admits It Revoked Residency Rights of a Quarter Million Palestinians." *Haaretz.com*, 12 June. http://www.haaretz.com/news/diplomacy-defense/israel-admits-it-revoked-residency-rights-of-a-quarter-million-palestinians-1.435778 (accessed 12 June 2012).

El-Haddad, L. 2003. "Intifada Spurs Palestinian Internet Boom." *Al-Jazeera.net*, 11 December. http://electronicintifada.net/content/intifada-spurs-palestine-internet-boom/9428 (accessed 6 January 2015).

Elhaik, E. 2012. "The Missing Link of Jewish European Ancestry: Contrasting the Rhineland and the Khazarian Hypotheses." *Genome Biology and Evolution* 5 (1): 61–74.

Elkins, C., and S. Pedersen. 2005. "Introduction: Settler Colonialism: A Concept and Its Uses." In C. Elkins and S. Petersen, eds., *Settler Colonialism in the Twentieth Century: Projects, Practices, Legacies*, 1–20. London and New York: Routledge.

Elstein, N. 2011. "Israel: Partial Democracy." *Haaretz.com*, 26 December. http://www.haaretz.com/print-edition/opinion/partial-democracy-1.403608 (accessed 23 July 2013).

Endresen, L., and E. Zureik. 1995. *Bibliography of Research on Palestinian Refugees Published in English, French, Hebrew and Arabic since the Madrid Conference in 1991*. Oslo: Fafo.

Ericson, R., and K. Haggerty. 1997. *Policing the Risk Society*. Toronto: University of Toronto Press.

Esmeir, S. 2004. "Introduction: In the Name of Security." *Adalah's Review* 4: 2–10.

Ettinger, Y. 2004a. "Extremism Isn't Growing but Fear Is." *Haaretz.com*, 25 June. http://www.haaretz.com/print-edition/business/extremism-isn-t-growing-but-fear-is-1.123450 (accessed 4 January 2014).

———. 2004b. "There Is No Hurry to Grant Citizenship to Arabs Married to Israelis." *Haaretz.com*, 25 August. http://www.haaretz.com/print-edition/features/there-s-no-hurry-to-grant-citizenship-to-arabs-married-to-israelis-1.132638 (accessed 4 January 2014).

Evans, B. 2010. "Foucault's Legacy: Security, War and Violence in the 21st Century." *Security Dialogue* 41 (4): 413–33.

Eyal, G. 2006. *The Disenchantment of the Orient: Expertise in Arab Affairs and the Israeli State*. Stanford, CA: Stanford University Press.

Fafo. N.d. http://www.fafo.no (accessed 11 April 2015).

———. 2011. *Palestinian Opinions about Public Services: Synthesis of Results of Fafo's Opinion Polls in the West Bank and the Gaza Strip, 2005–2011*. http://www.fafo.no/media/com_netsukii/10129.pdf (accessed 26 April 2015).

Fahmy, K. 2010. "Birth of the 'Secular' Individual: Medical and Legal Methods of Identification in 19th Century Egypt." Paper presented at the workshop "Comparative History of Civil Registration: History and Policy," St. John's College, Cambridge University, Cambridge, England, 7–10 September.

Faist, T. 1998. "Transnational Social Spaces out of International Migration: Evolution, Significance and Future Prospects." *European Journal of Sociology* 39 (2): 213–47.

Falah, G. 1996. "Living Together Apart: Residential Segregation in Mixed Arab-Jewish Cities in Israel." *Urban Studies* 33 (6): 823–57.

———. 2007. "The Politics of Doing Geography: 23 Days in the Hell of Israeli Detention." *Environment and Planning D: Society and Space* 25 (4): 587–93.

Falk, Raphael. 1998. "Response to Pfaff." *New York Review of Books*, 15 January. http://www.nybooks.com/articles/archives/1997/oct/23/eugenics-anyone (accessed 26 July 2014).

———. 2006. *Zionism and the Biology of the Jews*. Tel Aviv: Resling [Hebrew].

Falk, Richard. 2010. *Report of the Special Rapporteur on the Situation of Human Rights in the Palestinian Territories Occupied since 1967*. Report to the United Nations General Assembly, 30 August. New York: United Nations.

Fandy, M. 2000. "Information Technology, Trust and Social Change in the Arab World." *Middle East Journal* 54 (3): 378–94.

Fanon, F. 1967. *The Wretched of the Earth*. Harmondsworth, UK: Penguin.

Farago, Y. 2006. "Israel Backed by Army of Cyber-Soldiers." *Times* (London), 28 July. http://www.thetimes.co.uk/tto/news/world/middleeast/article2605536.ece (accessed 1 February 2007).

Farah, R. 1998. "Palestinian Identity, Refugees and UNRWA: Changing Political Context and Issues." Paper presented at the Annual Conference of the Middle East Studies Association of North America, Chicago, December.

———. 2009. "UNRWA: Through the Eyes of Its Refugee Employees in Jordan." *Refugee Survey Quarterly* 28 (2–3): 389–411.

Fargues, P. 2000. "Protracted National Conflict and Fertility Change among Palestinians and Israelis." *Population and Development Studies* 26 (3): 441–82.

Farsakh, L. 2005a. "Independence, Cantons or Bantustans: Whither the Palestinian State?" *Middle East Journal* 59 (2): 230–45.

———. 2005b. *Palestinian Labour Migration to Israel: Labour, Land, and Occupation*. London: Routledge.

———. 2008. "The Political Economy of Israeli Occupation: What Is Colonial about It?" *Electronic Journal of Middle Eastern Studies* 8: 41–58.

Farsoun, S., and C. Zacharia. 1997. *Palestine and the Palestinians: A Social and Political History*. Boulder, CO: Westview.

Fay, B. 1996. *Contemporary Philosophy of Social Science: A Multicultural Approach*. Oxford and Malden, MA: Blackwell.

Federman, J. 2003. "Cyber Escape: Palestinians Turn to Internet to Cope with Israeli Restrictions." *Associated Press*, 17 November. http://usatoday30.usatoday.com/tech/news/2003-11-18-palestine-online_x.htm (accessed 5 January 2015).

Feldman, I. 2006. "Home as a Refrain: Remembering and Living Displacement in Gaza." *History and Memory* 18 (2): 10–47.

———. 2007. "Difficult Distinction: Refugee Law, Humanitarian Practice, and Political Identification in Gaza." *Cultural Anthropology* 22 (1): 129–69.

———. 2008. "Refusing Invisibility: Documentation and Memoralization in Palestinian Refugee Claims." *Journal of Refugee Studies* 21 (4): 498–516.

———. 2012a. "The Challenge of Categories: UNRWA and the Definition of a 'Palestinian Refugee.'" *Journal of Refugee Studies* 25 (3): 387–406.

———. 2012b. "The Humanitarian Condition: Palestinian Refugees and the Politics of Living." *Humanity: An International Journal of Human Rights, Humanitarianism, and Development* 3 (2) 155–72.

Feldman, Y. 2007. "Dr. Naveh, or, How I Learned to Stop Worrying and Walk through Walls." *Haaretz.com*, 25 October. http://www.haaretz.com/weekend/magazine/dr-naveh-or-how-i-learned-to-stop-worrying-and-walk-through-walls-1.231912 (accessed 22 October 2011).

———. 2009. "Eugenics in Israel: Did Jews Try to Improve the Human Race Too?" *Haaretz.com*, 14 May. http://www.haaretz.com/eugenics-in-israel-did-jews-try-to-improve-the-human-race-too-1.276038 (accessed 4 January 2014).

———. 2013. *The Lab*. Documentary. Produced by Yoav Roeh and Aurit Zamir.

Ferlander, S., and D. Timms. 2001. "Local Nets and Social Capital." *Telematics and Informatics* 18 (1): 51–65.

Fieldhouse, D.K. 1981. *Colonialism, 1870–1945: An Introduction*. New York: St. Martin's.

———. 2006. *Western Imperialism in the Middle East: 1914–1958*. Oxford: Oxford University Press.

Fields, G. 2010. "Landscaping Resistance: Reflections on Enclosure in a Historical Mirror." *International Journal of Middle East Studies* 42 (1): 63–83.

Filkins, D. 2015. "'Khirbet Khizeh,' by S. Yizhar." Book review. *New York Times*, 20 February. http://www.nytimes.com/2015/02/22/books/review/khirbet-khizeh-by-s-yizhar.html?ref=topics&_r=0 (accessed on 31 March 2015).

Finkelstein, N. 2001. *The Holocaust Industry: Reflections on the Exploitation of Jewish Suffering*. London and New York: Verso.

Fischbach, M. 2011. "British and Zionist Data Gathering on Palestinian Arab Landownership and Population during the Mandate." In E. Zureik, D. Lyon, and Y. Abu-Laban, eds., *Surveillance and Control in Israel/Palestine: Population, Territory and Power*, 297–312. London: Routledge.

Fisher, S., D. Rodrick, and E. Tuma. 1994. *The Economics of Middle East Peace: Views from the Region*. Cambridge, MA: MIT Press.

Fisk, R. 2005. *The Great War for Civilisation: The Conquest of the Middle East*. London: Fourth Estate.

Flapan, S. 1979. *Zionism and the Palestinians*. London: Croom Helm.

Forced Migration and Refugee Unit, Bir Zeit University. N.d. http://home.birzeit.edu/ialiis/fmru (accessed 11 April 2015).

Forman, G., and A. Kedar. 2003. "Colonialism, Colonization, and Land Law in Mandate Palestine: The Zor al-Zarqa and Barrat Qisarya Land Disputes in Historical Perspective." *Theoretical Perspectives in Law* 4 (2): 491–540.

Forsyth, D. 1983. "The Palestine Question: Dealing with a Long-Term Refugee Situation." *Annals of the American Academy of Political and Social Science* 467: 89–101.

Foucault, M. 1977. *Discipline and Punish: The Birth of the Prison*. Reprint, New York: Random House, 1995.

———. 1978. *The History of Sexuality*. Vol. 1, *An Introduction*. Trans. R. Hurley. New York: Vintage.

———. 1982. "The Subject and Power." In H.L. Dreyfus and P. Rabinow, eds., *Michel Foucault: Beyond Structuralism and Hermeneutics*, 208–26. Brighton, UK: Harvester.

———. 1985. *The History of Sexuality*. Vol. 2, *The Use of Pleasure*. Trans. R. Hurley. New York: Pantheon.

———. 1988. "The Political Technology of Individuals." In L.H. Martin, H. Gutman, and P.H. Hutton, eds., *Technologies of the Self: A Seminar with Michel Foucault*, 145–62. Amherst: University of Massachusetts Press.
———. 2003. *"Society Must be Defended": Lectures at the College de France, 1975–1976*. New York: Picador.
———. 2007. *Security, Territory, Population: Lectures at the College de France, 1977–1978*. Ed. M. Senellart, trans. G. Burchell. Basingstoke and New York: Palgrave.
Fraser, N. 2013. *Fortunes of Feminism: From State-Managed Capitalism to Neoliberal Crisis*. London: New Left Books.
Freedman, S. 2008. "Culture of Fear." *Guardian*, 22 June. http://www.guardian.co.uk/commentisfree/2008/jun/22/israelandthepalestinians.fear (accessed 19 August 2009).
Freire, P. 1994. *Pedagogy of the Oppressed*. New York: Continuum.
Frister, R. 2011. "Polish-Jewish Sociologist Compares West Bank Separation Fence to Warsaw Ghetto Walls." *Haaretz.com*, 1 September. http://www.haaretz.com/print-edition/news/polish-jewish-sociologist-compares-west-bank-separation-fence-to-warsaw-ghetto-walls-1.381828 (accessed 1 September 2011).
Fulghum, D., and R. Wall. 2002. "UAVs Spotted as Defense Priority." *Aviation Week*, 11 February, 26.
Furani, K., and D. Rabinowitz. 2011. "The Ethnographic Arriving of Palestine." *Annual Review of Anthropology* 40: 475–91.
Galili, L. 2002. "A Jewish Demographic State." *Haaretz.com*, 27 June. http://www.haaretz.com/print-edition/features/a-jewish-demographic-state-1.41134 (accessed August 31 2014).
Gans, C. 2008. *A Just Zionism: On the Morality of the Jewish State*. Oxford: Oxford University Press.
Gavison, R. 2011a. "Israel as a Jewish and Democratic State." Lecture presented at the University of California, Los Angeles, 11 February. http://www.gavison.com/a2624-israel-as-a-jewish-and-democratic-state (accessed 23 July 2013).
———. 2011b. "Partition – for Zionism's Sake." *Haaretz.com*, 10 June. http://www.haaretz.com/print-edition/opinion/partition-for-zionism-s-sake-1.366891 (accessed 11 June 2011).
Gazit, S. 1994. "The Palestinian Refugee Question." Trans. Mira Sucharov. Final Status Issues Study No. 2, Jaffee Centre for Strategic Studies, Tel Aviv University.
Genel, K. 2006. "The Question of Biopower: Foucault and Agamben." *Rethinking Marxism* 18 (1): 43–62.
Gerber, H. 2003. "Zionism, Orientalism, and the Palestinians." *Journal of Palestine Studies* 33 (1): 23–41.
Ghanem, A. 1998. "State and Minority in Israel: The Case of Ethnic State and the Predicament of Its Minority." *Ethnic and Racial Studies* 21 (3): 428–47.
———. 2001. *Palestinian-Arab Minority in Israel, 1948–2000*. Albany: SUNY Press.
———. 2013. *Ethnic Politics in Israel: The Margins and the Ashkenazi Centre*. London and New York: Routledge.
Ghanim, H. 2006. "The Role and Position of Palestinian Intellectuals in Israel." PhD diss., Hebrew University [Hebrew].
———. 2008. "Thanatopolitics: The Case of the Colonial Occupation of Palestine." In R. Lentin, ed., *Thinking Palestine*, 65–81. London and New York: Zed.
Ghanim, H., and M. Shalhat, eds. 2011. *The Meaning of a Jewish State*. Ramallah: Madar.
Giacaman, R. 1988. *Life and Health in Three Palestinian Villages*. London: Ithaca.
Giacaman, R., Y. Rabaia, and V. Nguyen-Gillham. 2010. "Domestic and Political Violence: The Palestinian Predicament." *Lancet* 375 (9711): 259–60.
Giacaman, R., N. Abu-Rmeileh, A. Husseini, H. Saab, and W. Boyce. 2007. "Humiliation: The Invisible Trauma of War for Palestinian Youth." *Public Health* 121 (8): 563–71.

Giacaman, R., Y. Rabaia, V. Nguyen-Gillham, R. Batnijc, L. Punamäki, and D. Summerfield. 2011. "Mental Health, Social Distress and Political Oppression: The Case of the Occupied Palestinian Territory." *Global Public Health* 6 (5): 547–59.

Giddens, A. 1981. *A Contemporary Critique of Historical Materialism*. Berkeley: University of California Press.

———. 1984. *The Constitution of Society: Outline of the Theory of Structuration*. Berkeley: University of California Press.

———. 1987. *The Nation-State and Violence*. Berkeley: University of California Press.

———. 1991. *Modernity and Self-Identity: Self and Society in the Late Modern Age*. Cambridge: Polity.

———. 1995. *Affluence, Poverty and the Idea of a Post-Scarcity Society*. Geneva: United Nations Institute for Social Development.

Gilbert, S. 2013. "Access Denied: Phone Politics in Palestine." *Aljazeera.com*, 22 September. http://www.aljazeera.com/indepth/features/2013/09/20139171334748594.html (accessed 18 October 2014).

Gisha – Legal Center for Freedom of Movement. 2012. *Reader: "Food Consumption in the Gaza Strip – Red Lines."* October. http://gisha.org/publication/1667 (accessed 29 March 2015).

Gladstone, R. 2014. "Gaza Cost by Far Exceeds Estimate, Official Says." *New York Times*, 20 August. http://www.nytimes.com/2014/08/21/world/middleeast/gaza-cost-far-exceeds-estimate-official-says.html?hp&action=click&pgtype=Homepage&module=first-column-region&region=top-news&WT.nav=top-news (accessed 21 August 2014).

Glaser, D. 2010. "Zionism and Apartheid: A Moral Comparison." *Ethnic and Racial Studies* 26 (3): 403–21.

Goffman, E. 1959. *The Presentation of Self in Everyday Life*. New York: Doubleday.

Golan, A. 2001. "European Imperialism and the Development of Modern Palestine: Was Zionism a Form of Colonialism?" *Space and Polity* 5 (2): 127–43.

———. 2010. "More Than a Few Fringe Extremists Threaten Israeli Democracy." *Haaretz.com*, 17 November. http://www.haaretz.com/print-edition/opinion/more-than-a-few-fringe-extremists-threaten-israeli-democracy-1.325114 (accessed 7 May 2015).

Goldberg, D.T. 2008. "Racial Palestinianization." In R. Lentin, ed., *Thinking Palestine*, 25-45. London and New York: Zed.

———. 2009. *The Threat of Race: Reflections on Racial Neoliberalism*. Malden, MA: Blackwell.

Goodman, A. 2014. "Noam Chomsky: Sabra and Shatila Massacre that Forced Sharon's Ouster Recalls Worst of Jewish Pogroms." *Democracy Now!* 13 January. http://www.democracynow.org/2014/1/13/noam_chomsky_sabra_shatila_massacre_that (accessed 11 September 2014).

Goonewardena, K., and S. Kipfer. 2006. "Postcolonial Urbicide: New Imperialism, Global Cities and the Damned of the Earth." *New Formations* 59: 23–33.

Gordon, C. 1991. "Governmental Rationality: An Introduction." In G. Burchell, C. Gordon, and P. Miller, eds., *The Foucault Effect: Studies in Governmentality, with Two Lectures and an Interview with Michel Foucault*, 1–52. Chicago: University of Chicago Press.

Gordon, N. 2002. "Zionism, Translation and the Politics of Erasure." *Political Studies* 50 (4): 811–28.

———. 2004. "Rationalizing Extra-Judicial Executions: The Israeli Press and the Legitimisation of Abuse." *International Journal of Human Rights* 8 (3): 305–24.

———. 2008. *Israel's Occupation*. Berkeley: University of California Press.

———. 2009. "Avigdor Lieberman, Israel's Shame." *Guardian*, 25 March. http://www.theguardian.com/commentisfree/2009/mar/25/avigdor-lieberman-binyamin-netanyahu-israel (accessed 19 May 2015).

———. 2010. "Democracy and Colonialism." *Theory and Event* 13 (2). http://papers.ssrn.com/sol3/papers.cfm?abstract_id=1862012 (accessed 23 July 2013).

Gorenberg, G. 2006. *The Accidental Empire: Israel and the Birth of the Settlements, 1967–1977.* New York: Holt.

Graham, S. 2003. "Lessons in Urbicide." *New Left Review* 19: 63–78.

———. 2010. *Cities under Siege.* London and New York: Verso.

———. 2011. "Laboratories of War: Surveillance and US-Israeli Collaboration in War and Security." In E. Zureik, D. Lyon, and Y. Abu-Laban, eds., *Surveillance and Control in Israel/Palestine: Population, Territory and Power,* 133–52. London: Routledge.

———. 2012. "Foucault's Boomerang: The New Military Urbanism." *Development Dialogue* 58: 37–48.

Gramsci, A. 1991. *Prison Notebooks.* Ed. and intro. J.A. Buttigieg, trans. J.A. Buttigieg and A. Callari. New York: Columbia University Press.

Greenberg, J. 2012. "Double Take: Airport Security Designed to Delay." *Haaretz.com,* 6 July. http://www.haaretz.com/news/features/2.458/double-take-airport-security-designed-to-delay-1.449230 (accessed 29 March 2015).

Gregory, D. 2004. "Palestine and the War on Terror." *Comparative Studies of South Asia, Africa, and the Middle East* 24 (1): 185–98.

———. 2007. *The Colonial Present.* Oxford: Blackwell.

Guardian. 2002. "The Churchill You Didn't Know." 8 November. http://www.theguardian.com/theguardian/2002/nov/28/features11.g21 (accessed 8 May 2015).

———. 2009. "UK Has Led Efforts for Gaza Ceasefire." Letter to the editor. 10 January. http://www.theguardian.com/world/2009/jan/10/letters-gaza-uk (accessed 26 March 2015).

Guego, A. 2006. "'Quiet Transfer' in East Jerusalem Nears Completion." *Forced Migration Review* 26: 26–28.

Guha, S. 2003. "The Politics of Identity and Enumeration in India, c. 1600–1990." *Comparative Studies in Society and History* 45 (1): 148–67.

Gunning, J. 2008. *Hamas in Politics: Democracy, Religion, Violence.* New York: Columbia University Press.

Haaretz. 2008. "Something Bad Is Happening to Us." Editorial. 25 February. http://www.haaretz.com/print-edition/opinion/something-bad-is-happening-to-us-1.240080 (accessed 25 September 2013).

Habibi, E. 1974. *The Secret Life of Saeed: The Ill-Fated Pessoptimist.* Reprint, Haifa: Arabesque, 2006 [Arabic].

Hacking, I. 1999. "Making Up People." In M. Biagoli, ed., *The Science Studies Reader,* 226–30. New York and London: Routledge.

———. 2002. "Inaugural Lecture: Chair of Philosophy and History of Scientific Concepts at the Collège de France, 16 January 2001." *Economy and Society* 31 (1): 1–14.

HaCohen, R., and B. Kimmerling. 2005. "Theodor Herzl: 'My Words Were Taken out of Their Context' (A Footnote in the Zionist Historiography)." Copy in the possession of E. Zureik [Hebrew].

Hadawi, S. 1963. *Palestine: Loss of a Heritage.* San Antonio: Naylor.

———. 1967. *Bitter Harvest: Palestine, 1914–1967.* New York: New World Press.

Hadawi, S., and A. Kubursi. 1988. *Palestinian Rights and Losses in 1948.* London: Saqi.

Hager, N. 2010. "Israel's Omniscient Ears." *Le Monde Diplomatique,* September. http://mondediplo.com/2010/09/04israelbase (accessed 6 November 2012).

Haggerty, K., and R. Ericson. 2000. "The Surveillant Assemblage." *British Journal of Sociology* 51 (4): 605–22.

———, eds. 2006. *The New Politics of Surveillance and Visibility.* Toronto: University of Toronto Press.

Haj, S. 1992. "Palestinian Women and Patriarchal Relations." *Signs* 17 (4): 761–78.

Hajjar, L. 1997. "Cause Lawyering in Transnational Perspective: National Conflict and Human Rights in Israel/Palestine." *Law and Society Review* 31 (3): 473–504.

Haj-Yahia, M.M. 2000. "Implications of Wife Abuse and Battering for Self-Esteem, Depression, and Anxiety as Revealed by the Second Palestinian National Survey on Violence against Women." *Journal of Family Issues* 21 (4): 435–63.

———. 2001. "The Incidence of Witnessing Interparental Violence and Some of Its Psychological Consequences among Arab Adolescents." *Child Abuse and Neglect* 25 (7): 885–907.

———. 2011. "Contextualizing Interventions with Battered Women in Collectivist Societies: Issues and Controversies." *Aggression and Violent Behavior* 16 (4): 331–39.

Haj-Yahia, M.M., B. Leshem, and N.B. Guterman. 2011. "Exposure to Community Violence among Arab Youth in Israel: Rates and Characteristics." *Journal of Community Psychology* 39 (2): 136–51.

Halabi, U. 2011. "Legal Analysis and Critique of Some Surveillance Methods Used by Israel." In E. Zureik, D. Lyon, and Y. Abu-Laban, eds., *Surveillance and Control in Israel/Palestine: Population, Territory and Power*, 199–218. London: Routledge.

Halevi, J. 2010. "The Palestinian Refugees on the Day after 'Independence.'" Jerusalem Centre for Public Affairs, 1 December. http://jcpa.org/article/the-palestinian-refugees-on-the-day-after-"independence" (accessed 18 October 2014).

Hall, A. 2005. *The American Empire and the Fourth World*. Montreal and Kingston: McGill-Queen's University Press.

Hall, S., and P. Du Gay, eds. 1996. *Questions of Cultural Identity*. London: Sage.

Hamilton, K. 2011. "The Moral Economy of Violence: Israel's First Lebanon War, 1982." *Critical Studies on Terrorism* 4 (2): 127–43.

Hammack, P., A. Pilecki, N. Caspi, and A. Staruss. 2011. "Prevalence and Correlates of Delegitimization among Jewish Israeli Adolescents." *Peace and Conflict* 17 (2): 151–78.

Hammami, R. 1995. "NGOs: The Professionalisation of Politics." *Race and Class* 37 (2): 51–65.

Hammami, R., and S. Tamari. 1997. "Populist Paradigms: Palestinian Sociology." *Contemporary Sociology* 26 (3): 275–79.

Hamoked: Centre for the Defence of the Individual [Israel]. 2013. *The Permit Regime: The Human Rights Violations in West Bank Areas Known as the "Seam Zone"*. Jerusalem: Hamoked.

Hanafi, S. 2008. "Virtual and Real Returns." *Cairo Papers in Social Science* 29 (1): 131–56.

———. 2010. "Governing the Palestinian Refugee Camps in Lebanon and Syria: The Case of Nahr el-Bared and Yarmouk Camps." In A. Knudsen and S. Hanafi, eds., *Identity, Space and Place in the Levant*, 29–49. London: Routledge.

Hanafi, S., and T. Long. 2010. "Governance, Govermentalities, and the State of Exception in the Palestinian Refugee Camps of Lebanon." *Journal of Refugee Studies* 23 (2): 134–59.

Hanafi, S., J. Cha'aban, and K. Seyfert. 2012. "Social Exclusion of Palestinian Refugees in Lebanon: Reflections on the Mechanisms that Cement Their Persistent Poverty." *Refugee Survey Quarterly* 31 (1): 34–53.

Handel, A. 2009. "Where, Where to, and When in the Occupied Territories: An Introduction to Geography of Disaster." In A. Ophir, M. Givoni, and S. Hanafi, eds., *The Power of Inclusive Exclusion: Anatomy of Israeli Rule in the Occupied Palestinian Territories*, 179–222. New York: Zone.

Hanieh, A. 2002. "Class, Economy and the Second Intifada." *Monthly Review* 54 (5). http://monthlyreview.org/2002/10/01/class-economy-and-the-second-intifada (accessed 18 October 2014).

Hannah, M. 2000. *Governmentality and the Mastery of Territory in Nineteenth-Century America*. Cambridge: Cambridge University Press.

———. 2011. "Biopower, Life and Left Politics." *Antipode* 43 (4): 1034–55.

Harding, S. 2004. *The Feminist Standpoint Theory Reader: Intellectual and Political Controversies*. New York: Routledge.

Harel, A. 2009. "The Philosopher Who Gave the IDF Moral Justification in Gaza." *Haaretz.com*, 6 February. http://www.haaretz.com/print-edition/news/the-philosopher-who-gave-the-idf-moral-justification-in-gaza-1.269527 (accessed 9 February 2009).

Harel, I. 2003. "Being Driven Out by Demography." *Haaretz.com*, 11 December. http://www.haaretz.com/print-edition/opinion/being-driven-out-by-demography-1.108415 (accessed 4 January 2014).

Harker, C. 2009. "Student Im/mobility in Birzeit, Palestine." *Mobilities* 4 (1): 11–35.

———. 2011. "Geopolitics and Family in Palestine." *Geoforum* 42 (3): 306–15.

Harley, J. 1988. "Maps, Knowledge, and Power." In D. Cosgrove and S. Daniels, eds., *The Iconography of Landscape: Essays on the Symbolic Representation, Design, and Use of Past Environments*, 277–312. New York and Melbourne: Cambridge University Press.

Harlow, B. 1996. *After Lives: Legacies of Revolutionary Writing*. London and New York: Verso.

Hartman, B. 2014. "71st Israeli Fatality of Gaza War: Man Succumbs to Wounds from Rocket Attack." *Jerusalem Post*, 29 August. http://www.jpost.com/Arab-Israeli-Conflict/71st-victim-of-Operation-Protective-Edge-succumbs-to-wounds-from-rocket-attack-sustained-last-week-372744 (accessed 6 October 2014).

Harub, K. 2000. *Hamas: Political Thought and Practice*. Washington, DC: Institute for Palestine Studies.

Harvey, D. 2003. *The New Imperialism*. Oxford: Oxford University Press.

———. 2005. *A Brief History of Neoliberalism*. London: Oxford University Press.

Hashweh, M. 1996. "Palestinian Science Teachers' Epistemological Beliefs: A Preliminary Survey." *Research in Science Education* 26 (1): 89–102.

Hass, A. 1999a. "PA Attempting to Curtail 'Political Activities' of Human Rights Groups." *Haaretz*, 13 June.

———. 1999b. "Targeting Voices of Conscience." *Haaretz*, 16 June.

———. 2006. "In the Name of Security, but Not for Its Sake." *Haaretz.com*, 20 September. http://www.haaretz.com/print-edition/opinion/in-the-name-of-security-but-not-for-its-sake-1.197668 (accessed 17 November 2010).

———. 2007. "Israel Refuses to Allocate Cellular Frequencies to Palestinians." *Haaretz.com*, 28 May. http://www.haaretz.com/print-edition/business/israel-refuses-to-allocate-cellular-frequencies-to-palestinians-1.221559 (accessed 21 December 2014).

———. 2009. "Gaza Strike Is Not against Hamas, It's against All Palestinians." *Haaretz.com*, 29 December. http://www.haaretz.com/print-edition/news/gaza-strike-is-not-against-hamas-it-s-against-all-palestinians-1.260406 (accessed 4 May 2010).

———. 2010a. "Israel's Qassam Strikes on Gaza." *Haaretz.com*, 29 December. http://www.haaretz.com/print-edition/opinion/israel-s-qassam-strikes-on-gaza-1.333950 (accessed 29 December 2010).

———. 2010b. "Israel Releases Papers Detailing Formula of Gaza Blockade." *Haaretz.com*, 26 October. http://www.haaretz.com/print-edition/news/israel-releases-papers-detailing-formula-of-gaza-blockade-1.321154 (accessed 26 October 2010).

———. 2011. "When Israel's Protective Net of Tyranny Tears." *Haaretz.com*, 2 February. http://www.haaretz.com/print-edition/opinion/when-israel-s-protective-net-of-tyranny-tears-1.340720 (accessed 9 January 2012).

———. 2012a. "Defying the Occupation with a Camcorder." *Haaretz.com*, 23 July. http://www.haaretz.com/news/features/defying-the-occupation-with-a-camcorder-1.452880 (accessed 23 July 2012).

———. 2012b. "Israel Airport Security Demands Access to Tourists' Private Email Accounts." *Haaretz.com*, 5 June. http://www.haaretz.com/news/diplomacy-defense/israel-airport-security-demands-access-to-tourists-private-email-accounts.premium-1.434509 (accessed 29 August 2013).

———. 2012c. "2,279 Calories per Person: How Israel Made Sure Gaza Didn't Starve." *Haaretz.com*, 17 October. http://www.haaretz.com/news/diplomacy-defense/2-279-calories-per-person-how-israel-made-sure-gaza-didn-t-starve.premium-1.470419 (accessed 17 October 2012).

———. 2013. "The Israeli-Palestinian Balance of Brutality." *Haaretz.com*, 26 May. http://www.haaretz.com/news/features/the-israeli-palestinian-balance-of-brutality.premium-1.526092 (accessed 6 September 2014).

Hasso, F.S. 1998. "The 'Women's Front': Nationalism, Feminism and Modernity in Palestine." *Gender and Society* 12 (4): 441-65.

Hasson, N. 2009. "Israel Stripped Thousands of Jerusalemite Arabs of Residency in 2008." *Haaretz.com*, 2 December. http://www.haaretz.com/print-edition/news/israel-stripped-thousands-of-jerusalem-arabs-of-residency-in-2008-1.3006 (accessed 3 December 2009).

———. 2012. "The Palestinian Taxi Driver Crucial to Jewish Settlement in East Jerusalem." *Haaretz.com*, 11 May. http://www.haaretz.com/news/diplomacy-defense/the-palestinian-taxi-driver-who-s-crucial-to-jewish-settlement-in-east-jerusalem-1.429579 (accessed 11 May 2012).

———. 2013. "How Many Palestinians Actually Live in the West Bank." *Haaretz.com*, 13 June. http://www.haaretz.com/news/diplomacy-defense/.premium-1.532703 (accessed 26 July 2013).

Hazkani, S. 2013. "Catastrophic Thinking: Did Ben-Gurion Try to Rewrite History?" *Haartetz.com*, 16 May. http://www.haaretz.com/weekend/magazine/catastrophic-thinking-did-ben-gurion-try-to-rewrite-history.premium-1.524308 (accessed 25 September 2013).

Hechter, M. 1975. *Internal Colonialism: The Celtic Fringe in British National Development, 1536–1966*. London: Routledge and Kegan Paul.

Hejoj, I. 2007. "A Profile of Poverty for Palestinian Refugees in Jordan: The Case of Zarqa and Sukhneh Camps." *Journal of Refugee Studies* 20 (1): 120–45.

Henckel von Donnersmarck, F., dir. 2006. *The Lives of Others*. Film. Wiedemann and Berg [German].

Henkin, Y. 2003. "Urban Warfare and the Lessons of Jenin: How Israel's Record in Preventing Civilian Casualties Stacks up against Operations in Grozny, Kosovo, and Mogadishu." *Azure* 15. http://azure.org.il/include/print.php?id=240 (accessed 8 August 2014).

Herman, E.S., and N. Chomsky. 1988. *Manufacturing Consent: The Political Economy of the Mass Media*. New York: Pantheon.

Hersh, S. 2004a. "The Gray Zone: How a Secret Pentagon Program Came to Abu Ghraib." *New Yorker.com*, 24 May. http://www.newyorker.com/magazine/2004/05/24/the-gray-zone (accessed 19 September 2014).

Herzl, T. 1896. *The Jewish State*. Reprint, Northvale, NJ: Jason Aronson, 1997.

Higgs, E. 2001. "The Rise of the Information State: The Development of Central State Surveillance of the Citizen in England, 1500–2000." *Journal of Historical Sociology* 14 (2): 175–97.

Hilal, J. 1974. *The West Bank: Social and Economic Structure, 1948–1974*. Beirut: Palestine Liberation Organization Research Center.

Hill, C., K. Loch, D. Straub, and K. El-Sheshai. 1998. "A Qualitative Assessment of Arab Culture and Information Technology Transfer." *Journal of Global Information Management* 6 (3): 29–38.

Hirsch, D. 2009. "Zionist Eugenics, Mixed Marriage, and the Creation of the 'New Jewish Type.'" *Journal of the Royal Anthropological Institute* 15 (3): 592–609.

Hockstader, L. 2001. "Reports of Torture by Israelis Emerge: Rights Groups Document Frequent Police Abuses against Palestinians." *Washington Post*, 18 August, A01.

Holsti, O. 1969. *Content Analysis for the Social Sciences and Humanities*. Reading, MA: Addison-Wesley.

Home, R. 2003. "An 'Irreversible Conquest'? Colonial and Postcolonial Land Law in Israel/Palestine." *Social and Legal Studies* 12 (3): 291–310.

Horvath, R. 1972. "A Definition of Colonialism." *Current Anthropology* 13 (1): 45–57.

Hughes, S. 2012. "Operation Pillar of Defense: The First Social Media War." *BBC News*, 16 November. http://www.bbc.co.uk/blogs/blogcollegeofjournalism/posts/Operation-Pillar-of-Defense-the-first-social-media-war (accessed 22 September).

Human Rights Watch. 2001. "Second Class: Discrimination against Palestinian Arab Children in Israel's Schools." 30 September. http://www.hrw.org/reports/2001/09/30/second-class (accessed 29 March 2015).

——. 2010. *World Report 2010*. New York: Human Rights Watch.

——. 2012. "'Forget about Him. He's Not Here': Israel's Control of Palestinian Residency in the West Bank and Gaza." 5 February. http://www.hrw.org/reports/2012/02/05/forget-about-him-he-s-not-here (accessed 29 March 2015).

Human Sciences Research Council of South Africa. 2009. *Occupation, Colonialism, Apartheid? A Re-assessment of Israel's Practices in the Occupied Palestinian Territories under International Law*. May. electronicintifada.net/files/090608-hsrc.pdf (accessed 3 April 2015).

ICBS (Israel Central Bureau of Statistics). N.d. http://www.cbs.gov.il (accessed 11 April 2015).

——. 2002. *Statistical Abstract of Israel No. 53*.

——. 2003. "On the Threshold of 2004 – 6,750 Residents in the State of Israel." Press release, 31 December.

——. 2009. *The Arab Population in Israel 2008*.

——. 2010. *Demographic Characteristic, Population by Population Group, Religion, Sex, and Age*.

——. 2012. *Statistical Abstract of Israel No. 63*.

IDI (Israel Democracy Institute). N.d. http://www.idi.org.il (accessed 11 April 2015).

——. 2014. "August 2014 Peace Index." 19 August. http://en.idi.org.il/about-idi/news-and-updates/august-2014-peace-index (accessed 23 September 2014).

Ilan, S. 2005. "Demographically Correct." *Haaretz.com*, 7 June. http://www.haaretz.com/print-edition/features/demographically-correct-1.160632 (accessed 7 June 2005).

——. 2007. "Knesset Okays Establishment of 'Big Brother' Database for Police." *Haaretz.com*, 18 December. http://www.haaretz.com/hasen/objects/pages/PrintArticleEn.jhtml?itemNo=935812 (accessed 19 July 2010).

——. 2008a. "Police Wiretaps Climb Sharply in Peripheral Areas." *Haaretz.com*, 18 May. http://www.haaretz.com/hasen/objects/pages/PrintArticleEn.jhtml?itemNo=984365 (accessed 19 July 2010)

——. 2008b. "Under 'Big Brother Law,' Telecom Firms Would Tell All to Police." *Haaretz.com*, 14 August. http://www.haaretz.com/print-edition/news/under-big-brother-law-telecom-firms-would-tell-all-to-police-1.251864 (accessed 10 August 2010).

——. 2009. "Plan to Introduce Biometric IDs Stirs Privacy Debate." *Haaretz.com*, 13 March. http://www.haaretz.com/hasen/objects/pages/PrintArticleEn.jhtml?itemNo =1070793 (accessed 19 July 2010).

Illouz, E. 2013. "47 Years as a Slave: A New Perspective on the Occupation." *Haaretz.com*, 7 February. http://www.haaretz.com/news/features/.premium-1.572880# (accessed 24 June 2014).

IMFA (Israel Ministry of Foreign Affairs). 1983. *Report of the Commission of Inquiry into the Events of the Refugee Camps in Beirut – 8 February 1983.* http://www.mfa.gov.il/mfa/foreignpolicy/mfadocuments/yearbook6/pages/104%20report%20of%20the%20commission%20of%20inquiry%20into%20the%20e.aspx (accessed 19 May 2015).

———. 2010. "Foreign Minister Liberman Addresses the General Assembly." 28 September. http://www.mfa.gov.il/MFA/Government/Speeches+by+Israeli+leaders/2010/FM_Liberman_Addresses_UN_General_Assembly_28-Sep-2010.htm (accessed 27 September 2011).

———. 2011. "Remarks by PM Benjamin Netanyahu to the UN General Assembly." 23 September. http://www.mfa.gov.il/MFA/Government/Speeches+by+Israeli+leaders/2011/Remarks_PM_Netanyahu_UN_General+_Assembly_23-Sep-2011.htm (accessed 13 May 2014).

Institute for International Security Studies. 2010. *Strategic Assessment: Report on the Second Intifada.* Tel Aviv: Institute for International Security Studies, Tel Aviv University.

Interdisciplinary Center Herzliya [Israel]. 2001. *The Balance of National Strength and Security: Policy Directions.* Conference proceedings, April.

Internet World Stats. 2013a. "Internet Usage Statistics: World Internet Users and Population Stats." December. Miniwatts Marketing Group, Bogota, Colombia.

———. 2013b. "Middle East Internet Users: Population and Facebook Statistics." December. Miniwatts Marketing Group, Bogota, Colombia.

Introna, D. 1997. "Privacy and the Computer: Why We Need Privacy in the Information Society." *Metaphilosophy* 28 (3): 259–75.

Israel Internet Association. 2011. *Internet Use According to Various Sectors of Society.* http://data.isoc.org.il/data/116 (accessed 13 February 2012) [Hebrew].

Issacharoff, A. 2009. "Would Israel Arrest a Jewish Terrorist with Only Arab Victims?" *Haaretz.com*, 2 December. http://www.haaretz.com/print-edition/news/would-israel-arrest-a-jewish-terrorist-with-only-arab-victims-1.4983 (accessed 13 May 2014).

Jabareen, H. 2011. "Why Palestinians Can't Recognize a 'Jewish State.'" *Haaretz.com*, 2 August. http://www.haaretz.com/print-edition/opinion/why-palestinians-can-t-recognize-a-jewish-state-1.382091 (accessed 23 July 2013).

Jacobsen, E. 2012. "Unique Identification: Inclusion and Surveillance in the Indian Biometric Assemblage." *Security Dialogue* 43 (5): 457–74.

Jamal, A. 2001. "Engendering State Building: The Women's Movement and Gender-Regime in Palestine." *Middle East Journal* 55 (2): 256–76.

———. 2008. "On the Troubles of Racialized Time." In Y. Shenhav and Y. Yonah, eds., *Racism in Israel*, 348–80. Jerusalem: Van Leer Institute and Hakibutz Ha-Meuhad [Hebrew].

———. 2013. "Manufacturing 'Quiet Arabs' in Israel: Ethnicity, Media Frames and Soft Power." *Government and Opposition* 48 (2): 245–64.

Jamal, S., and A. Sandor. 2010. "Temporarily Permanent: Agamben and Palestinian Refugee Camps in Lebanon." Paper presented at the Canadian Political Science Association, Concordia University, Montreal.

Jamoul, L. 2004. "Spaces of Oppression and Resistance in Palestine." *Antipode* 36 (4): 581–95.

Jeffries, D. 2012. "Institutionalizing Statelessness: The Revocation of Residency Rights of Palestinians in East Jerusalem." *International Journal of Refugee Law* 24 (2): 202–30.

Jensen, M. 2009. *The Political Ideology of Hamas: A Grassroots Perspective.* London: I.B. Tauris.

Jiryis, S. 1973. *The Arabs in Israel.* Beirut: Institute for Palestine Studies [Arabic].

———. 1977. *The Arabs in Israel.* New York: Monthly Review.

Johnson, N. 1982. *Islam and the Politics of Meaning in Palestinian Nationalism.* London: Routledge and Kegan Paul.

Judt, T. 2003. "Israel: The Alternative." *New York Review of Books*, 23 October. http://www.nybooks.com/contributors/judt-tony (accessed 24 March, 2012).

Judt, T., and T. Snyder. 2012. *Thinking the Twentieth Century*. London: Heinemann.

Kana'neh, R. 2002. *Birthing the Nation: Strategies of Palestinian Women in Israel*. Berkeley: University of California Press.

Kana'neh, S. 1991. "Patterns of Forced Emigration of the Palestinians in 1948." *Qadaya* 8: 35–55 [Arabic].

Kaplan, M. 1995. "Panopticon in Poona: An Essay on Foucault and Colonialism." *Cultural Anthropology* 10 (1): 85–95.

Karpel, D. 2006. "Culture Club." *Haaretz.com*, 19 October. http://www.haaretz.com/misc/article-print-page/culture-club1.202851?trailingPath=2.169%2C (accessed 4 January 2014).

Karsh, E. 2000. *Fabricating Israeli History: The "New Historians."* London: Frank Cass.

———. 2006. *Islamic Imperialism: A History*. New Haven, CT, and London: Yale University Press.

Kashti, O. 2009. "Israel Pulls Textbook with Chapter on Nakba." *Haaretz.com*, 19 October. http://www.haaretz.com/print-edition/features/israel-pulls-textbook-with-chapter-on-nakba-1.5858 (accessed 19 October 2009).

———. 2010. "Poll: Half of Israel's Highschoolers Oppose Equal Rights for Arabs." *Haaretz.com*, 11 March. http://www.haaretz.com/print-edition/news/poll-half-of-israeli-high-schoolers-oppose-equal-rights-for-arabs-1.264564 (accessed 11 March 2010).

———. 2013a. "Israeli Teachers Who 'Impart Values' Get Bonuses – but What Sectors Benefit Most?" *Haaretz.com*, 16 August. http://www.haaretz.com/news/national/.premium-1.541827 (accessed 16 August 2013).

———. 2013b. "Who's Afraid of the Nakba? New Research Challenges the Way History Is Taught in Israeli High Schools." *Haaretz.com*, 28 April. http://www.haaretz.com/news/features/who-s-afraid-of-the-nakba-new-research-challenges-the-way-history-is-taught-in-israeli-high-schools.premium-1.517884 (accessed 20 November 2013).

Kashua, S. 2009. "How to Be an Arab." *Haaretz.com*, 16 October. http://www.haaretz.com/sayed-kashua-how-to-be-an-arab-1.6045 (accessed 20 November 2013).

Kayyali, A. 1981. *Palestine: A Modern History*. London: Croom Helm.

Keinon, H. 2014. "Netanyahu Departs for US: I Will Tell Truth about the IDF, the Most Moral Army in the World." *Jerusalem Post*, 28 September. http://www.jpost.com/International/Netanyahu-meeting-with-Indian-PM-Modi-signals-increased-Israeli-Indian-cooperation-376464 (accessed 9 January 2015).

Kelly, M. 2004. "Racism, Nationalism, and Biopolitics: Foucault's *Society Must Be Defended*, 2003." *Contretemps* 4: 58–70.

Kelman, H. 1998. "Social-Psychological Contributions to Peacemaking and Peacebuilding in the Middle East." *Applied Psychology: An International Review (Psychologie-Appliquée: Revue-Internationale)* 47 (1): 5–28.

Kemp, A. 2004. "'Dangerous Populations': State, Territoriality and the Constitution of National Minorities." In J. Migdal, ed., *Boundaries and Belonging: States and Societies in the Struggle to Shape Identities and Local Practices*, 73–98. Cambridge: Cambridge University Press.

Kershaw, S. 2008. "Culture of Surveillance May Contribute to Delusional Condition." *International Herald Tribune*, 29 August.

Kershner, I. 2012. "Arab Spring Spurs Palestinian Journalists to Test Free Speech." *New York Times*, 7 May. http://www.nytimes.com/2012/05/07/world/middleeast/arab-spring-stirs-palestinian-journalists-to-test-limits.html (accessed 17 December 2014).

———. 2014. "Spectators to War, West Bank Residents Hail the Hamas Fight against Israel." *New York Times*, 25 July. http://www.nytimes.com/2014/07/25/world/middleeast/in-west-bank-hamas-hailed-for-israel-in-gaza.html?hp&action= click&pgtype=Hom

epage&module=first-column-region&region=top-ews&WT.nav=top-news (accessed 6 October 2014).

Khalidi, M.A. 2001. "Utopian Zionism or Zionist Proselytism? A Reading of Herzl's *Altneuland*." *Journal of Palestine Studies* 30 (4): 55–67.

———. 2009-10. "'The Most Moral Army in the World'?: The New 'Ethical Code' of the Israeli Military and the War on Gaza." *Journal of Palestine Studies* 39 (3): 6–23.

Khalidi, R. 1997. *Palestinian Identity: The Construction of Modern National Consciousness*. New York: Columbia University Press.

———. 2014–15. "The Dahiya Doctrine, Proportionality, and War Crimes." *Journal of Palestine Studies* 44 (1): 5-13. http://www.palestine-studies.org/jps/fulltext/186668 (accessed 31 March 2015).

Khalidi, R., and Samour, S. 2011. "Neoliberalism as Liberation: The Statehood Program and the Remaking of the Palestinian National Movement." *Journal of Palestine Studies* 40 (2): 6–23.

Khalidi, W., ed. 1971. *From Haven to Conquest: Readings in Zionism and the Palestine Problem until 1948*. Beirut and Washington, DC: Institute for Palestine Studies.

———, ed. 1984. *Before Their Diaspora: A Photographic Essay of the Palestinians, 1876–1948*. Beirut and Washington, DC: Institute for Palestine Studies.

———. 1988. "Plan Dalet: Master Plan for the Conquest of Palestine." *Journal of Palestine Studies* 18 (1): 1–20.

———, ed. 1992. *All That Remains: The Palestinian Villages Occupied and Depopulated by Israel in 1948*. Beirut and Washington, DC: Institute for Palestine Studies.

———. 1993. "The Jewish-Ottoman Land Company: Herzl's Blueprint for the Colonization of Palestine." *Journal of Palestine Studies* 22 (2): 30–47.

———. 2009. "The Reconquista of Palestine: From the 1947 United Nations Partition Resolution to the First Zionist Congress of 1897." *Journal of Palestine Studies* 39 (1): 24–42.

———. 2014. "Palestine and Palestine Studies: One Century after World War I and the Balfour Declaration." Lecture presented at the School of Oriental and African Studies (SOAS), University of London, 6 March. http://www.soas.ac.uk/lmei-cps/podcasts-and-papers/file91749.pdf (accessed 7 July 2014).

Khalil, A. 2011. "Socioeconomic Rights of Palestinian Refugees in Arab Countries." *International Journal of Refugee Law* 23 (4): 680–719.

Khalili, L. 2005. "Virtual Nation: Palestinian Cyberculture in Lebanese Camps." In R. Stein and T. Swedenburg, eds., *Palestine, Israel and the Politics of Popular Culture*, 126–49. Durham, NC, and London: Duke University Press.

———. 2010a. "The Location of Palestine in Global Counterinsurgencies." *International Journal of Middle Eastern Studies* 42 (3): 413–33.

———. 2010b. "Palestinians: The Politics of Control, Invisibility, and the Spectacle." In M. Khalidi, ed., *Manifestations of Identity: The Lived Reality of Palestinians in Lebanon*, 125–45. Beirut: Institute for Palestine Studies and the French Institute for the Near East.

———. 2013. *Time in the Shadows: Confinement in Counterinsurgencies*. Stanford, CA: Stanford University Press.

Khamaisi, R. 1999. *The Impact of the Trans Israel Highway on Arab Localities: A Threat or Lever?* Jerusalem: Floersheimer Center for Constitutional Democracy [Hebrew].

———. 2011. "Territorial Dispossession and Population Control of the Palestinians." In E. Zureik, D. Lyon, and Y. Abu-Laban, eds., *Surveillance and Control in Israel/Palestine: Population, Territory and Power*, 335–52. London: Routledge.

Khamis, V. 1993a. "Post-traumatic Stress Disorder among the Injured of the Intifada." *Journal of Traumatic Stress* 6 (4): 555–59.

———. 1993b. "Victims of the Intifada: The Psychosocial Adjustment of the Injured." *Behavioural Medicine* 19 (3): 93–101.

———. 2000. *Political Violence and the Palestinian Family: Implications for Mental Health and Well-Being*. New York, London, and Oxford: Haworth.

———. 2008. "Post-traumatic Stress and Psychiatric Disorders in Palestinian Adolescents Following Intifada-Related Injuries." *Social Science and Medicine* 67 (8): 1199–207.

———. 2012a. "Impact of War, Religiosity, and Ideology on PTSD and Psychiatric Disorders in Adolescents from Gaza Strip and Southern Lebanon." *Social Science and Medicine* 74 (12): 2005–11.

———. 2012b. "Post-traumatic Stress and Worry as Mediators and Moderators between Political Stresses and Behavioural Disorders in Palestinian Children." *International Journal of Psychology* 47 (2): 133–41.

Khawajah, M. 1994. "Resource Mobilization, Hardship, and Popular Collective Action in the West Bank." *Social Forces* 73 (1): 190–220.

Khouri, R. 2009. "Sixty Years of UNRWA: From Service Provision to Refugee Protection." *Refugee Survey Quarterly* 28 (2–3): 438–51.

Khoury, J. 2010. "Supreme Court Doubles Jail Term for Police Officer Convicted of Shooting Israeli Arab." *Haaretz.com*, 21 July. http://www.haaretz.com/news/national/supreme-court-doubles-jail-term-for-police-officer-convicted-of-shooting-israeli-arab-1.303206 (accessed 28 September 2011).

Khoury, J., J. Lis, and L. Kyzer. 2009. "Groups Decry Police Undercover Unit 'Targeting Arabs.'" *Haaretz.com*, 14 October. http://www.haaretz.com/print-edition/news/groups-decry-police-undercover-unit-targeting-arabs-1.6165 (accessed 14 October 2009).

Khoury, J., T. Zarchin, and B. Ravid. 2009. "Revised Bill Would Ban Funding Nakba Events." *Haaretz.com*, 20 July. http://www.haaretz.com/print-edition/news/revised-bill-would-ban-funding-nakba-events-1.280370 (accessed 21 May 2015).

Khoury-Machool, M. 2010. "Cyber Resistance: Palestinian Youth and Emerging Internet Culture." In L. Herrera and A. Bayat, eds., *Being Young and Muslim: New Cultural Politics in the Global South and North*, 113–24. Oxford: Oxford University Press.

Khromchenko, Y. 2005. "Ministry Decides Shin Bet Will No Longer Scrutinize Arab Educators." *Haaretz.com*, 6 January. http://www.haaretz.com/print-edition/news/ministry-decides-shin-bet-will-no-longer-scrutinize-arab-educators-1.146265 (accessed 1 June 2014).

Kilibarda, K. 2005. "Access to and Use of ICT in the Balata Refugee Camp: A Preliminary Study." Unpublished report.

Kimmerling, B. 1980. "The Palestinians from Two Research Angles." *Medina Mimshal ve-Yahasim Bein-Leumiim* [*State, Government, and International Relations*] 16: 74–77 [Hebrew].

———. 2002. "Jurisdiction in an Immigrant-Settler Society: The 'Jewish and Democratic State.'" *Comparative Political Studies* 35 (10): 1119–44.

———. 2003. *Politicide: Ariel Sharon's War against the Palestinians*. London and New York: Verso.

Kimmerling, B., and J. Migdal. 1993. *Palestinians: The Making of a People*. New York and Toronto: Free Press.

Kinsella, K. 1991. *Palestinian Population Projections for 16 Countries of the World, 1990–2010*. Washington, DC: Center for International Research, Bureau of the Census.

Kirsh, N. 2003. "Population Genetics in Israel in the 1950s: The Unconscious Internalization of Ideology." *Isis* 94 (4): 631–55.

Kisch, S. 2013. "Israel Launches Controversial Biometric Database." *Privacy International*, 22 July. https://www.privacyinternational.org/?q=node/435 (accessed 29 March 2015).

Klinger, J. 2011. "Israel Is to Start Collecting Fingerprints from All Citizens." +972 Blog, 4 June. http://972mag.com/israel-to-start-collecting-fingerprints-from-all-citizens (accessed 21 November 2013).

Knesset, Centre for Research and Information. 2010. "Project for the Knesset on Digital Gap."

Knight, J. 2011. "Securing Zion? Policing in British Palestine, 1917–39." European Review of History 18 (4): 523–44.

Korn, A. 2000. "Military Government, Political Control and Crime: The Case of Israeli Arabs." Crime, Law and Social Change 34 (2): 159–82.

Kosminsky, P., dir. 2011. The Promise. Television serial. Channel 4.

Kossaifi, G. 1980. "Demographic Characteristics of the Arab Palestinian People." In K. Nakhleh and E. Zureik, eds., The Sociology of the Palestinians, 13–46. London: Croom Helm.

Kretzmer, D. 1990. The Legal Status of the Arabs in Israel. Boulder, CO: Westview.

Kupfer, J. 1987. "Privacy, Autonomy and the Self-Concept." American Philosophical Quarterly 24 (1): 81–87.

Kupfer, R. 2012. "Controversial Film Series on British-Controlled Palestine Comes to Tel Aviv." Haaretz.com, 12 April. http://www.haaretz.com/news/features/controversial-film-series-on-british-controlled-palestine-comes-to-tel-aviv-1.424502 (accessed 17 April 2012).

Kuttab, D. 2013. "Palestinians Face Cell Phone, Internet Limits." Al-Monitor, 20 January. http://www.al-monitor.com/pulse/tr/originals/2013/01/Internet-palestine-israel-itu.html (accessed 18 December 2014).

Lagouranis, T. 2008. Fear Up Harsh: An Army Interrogator's Dark Journey through Iraq. New York: Penguin.

Landau, D. 2010. "Israel Is Sliding Toward McCarthyism and Racism." Haaretz.com, 29 March. http://www.haaretz.com/news/national/israel-is-sliding-toward-mccarthyism-and-racism-1.266782 (accessed 29 March 2010).

Lapeyre, F., J. Al Husseini, R. Bocco, M. Brunner, and E. Zureik. 2011. "The Living Conditions of the Palestine Refugees Registered with UNRWA in Jordan, Lebanon, the Syrian Arab Republic, the Gaza Strip and the West Bank." Social Science Research Network, 16 May. http://papers.ssrn.com/sol3/papers.cfm?abstract_id=1843276 (accessed 18 October 2014).

Lapidoth, R. 1986. "The Right of Return in International Law, with Special Reference to the Palestinian Refugees." Israel Yearbook of Human Rights 6 (1): 65–70.

Latour, B. 1987. Science in Action: How to Follow Scientists and Engineers through Society. Cambridge, MA: Harvard University Press.

Lavie, S. 1996. "Blowups in the Borderzones: Third World Israeli Authors' Groping for Home." In S. Lavie and T. Swedenberg, eds., Displacement, Diaspora, and Geographies of Identity, 55–96. Durham, NC, and London: Duke University Press.

Lazaroff, T. 2002. "28% of Israelis Not Jewish." Jerusalem Post, 12 June.

Lebovic, N., and A. Pinchuk. 2010. "The State of Israel and the Biometric Database Law: Political Centrism and the Post-Democratic State." Israel Democracy Institute, 20 June. http://www.idi.org.il/sites/english/BreakingTheNews/Pages/IsraelAndTheBiometricDatabase.aspx (accessed 9 February 2012).

Lee, C. 2009. "Suicide Bombings as Acts of Deathly Citizenship? A Critical Double-Layered Inquiry." Critical Studies on Terrorism 2 (2): 147–63.

Lee, V. 2012. "Probing the Bureaucracy of Occupation." Haaretz.com, 26 July. http://www.haaretz.com/culture/books/probing-the-bureaucracy-of-occupation-1.453805 (accessed 1 August 2012).

Legg, S. 2005. "Foucault's Population Geographies: Classifications, Biopolitics and Governmental Spaces." *Population, Space and Place* 11 (3): 137–56.

———. 2007. "Beyond the European Province: Foucault and Postcolonialism." In J. Crampton and S. Elden, eds., *Space, Knowledge and Power: Foucault and Geography*, 265–89. Aldershot, UK, and Burlington, VT: Ashgate.

Leibler, A. 1999. "Statistics as Social Architecture: The Construction of Israel's Central Bureau of Statistics as an Apolitical Institution." MA thesis, Tel Aviv University [Hebrew].

———. 2011. "'You Must Know Your Stock': Census as Surveillance Practice in 1948 and 1967." In E. Zureik, D. Lyon, and Y. Abu-Laban, eds., *Surveillance and Control in Israel/Palestine: Population, Territory and Power*, 239–56. London: Routledge.

Leibler, A., and D. Breslau. 2005. "The Uncounted Citizenship: Citizenship and Exclusion in the Israeli Census of 1948." *Ethnic and Racial Studies* 28 (5): 880–902.

Leibovitz-Dar, S. 2009. "Senior Lecturer: The Arabs – Failure of Humanity." *Maariv*, 21 October. http://www.nrg.co.il/online/1/ART1/956/392.html (accessed 21 October 2009).

Lemkin, R. 1944. *Axis Rule in Occupied Europe: Laws of Occupation – Analysis of Government – Proposals for Redress*. Washington, DC: Carnegie Endowment for International Peace.

Lentin, R. 2006. "Migrant Women's Networking: New Articulations of Transnational Ethnicity." http://www.tcd.ie/immigration/css/downloads/Migrant_Women's_Networking.pdf (accessed 2 May 2015).

———. 2008a. "Racial State, State of Exception." *State of Nature*, Autumn. http://www.stateofnature.org/racialState.html (accessed 24 July 2010).

———, ed. 2008b. *Thinking Palestine*. London and New York: Zed.

Lerner, D. 1958. *The Passing of Traditional Society: Modernizing the Middle East*. New York and London: Free Press and Collier-Macmillan.

Leuenberger, C., and I. Schnell. 2010. "The Politics of Maps: Constructing National Territories in Israel." *Social Studies of Science* 40 (6): 803–42.

Levine, M. 1999. "A Nation from the Sands." *National Identities* 1 (1): 15–38.

———. 2005. *Overthrowing Geography: Jaffa, Tel Aviv, and the Struggle for Palestine, 1880–1948*. Berkeley: University of California Press.

Levinson, C. 2011. "Israel Has 101 Different Types of Permits Governing Palestinian Movement." *Haaretz.com*, 23 December. http://www.haaretz.com/print-edition/news/israel-has-101-different-types-of-permits-governing-palestinian-movement-1.403039 (accessed 23 December 2011).

———. 2012a. "Israel to Begin Recording Settler Land Claims, Deny Palestinians' Right of Appeal." *Haaretz.com*, 3 July. http://www.haaretz.com/news/diplomacy-defense/israel-to-begin-recording-settler-land-claims-deny-palestinians-right-of-appeal-1.448379 (accessed 3 July 2012).

———. 2012b. "Settlers Say They Bought Outpost Land, One Year after Palestinian Owner's Death." *Haaretz.com*, 3 July. http://www.haaretz.com/news/diplomacy-defense/settlers-say-they-bought-outpost-land-one-year-after-palestinian-owner-s-death-1.448533 (accessed 3 July 2012).

———. 2013. "Israeli Court: Real Estate Transaction That Evicted Palestinian Family Was Forged." *Haaretz.com*, 15 July. http://www.haaretz.com/news/national/.premium-1.535756 (accessed 21 May 2014).

———. 2014. "The Forgery at the Heart of West Bank Land Transactions." *Haaretz.com*, 20 May. http://www.haaretz.com/news/national/.premium-1.591815 (accessed 28 May 2014).

Levy, G. 2002. "Wombs in the Service of the State." *Haaretz.com*, 9 September. http://www.haaretz.com/print-edition/opinion/wombs-in-the-service-of-the-state-1.34696 (accessed 25 November 2012).

———. 2006. "As the Hamas Team Laughs." *Haaretz.com*, 19 February. http://www.haaretz.com/print-edition/opinion/as-the-hamas-team-laughs-1.180500 (accessed 2 October 2014).

———. 2008. "Stop Watching, Big Brother." *Haaretz.com*, 7 August. http://www.haaretz.com/hasen/spages/1009392.html (accessed 12 January 2010).

———. 2011. "Shin Bet Heads Spearhead the Occupation." *Haaretz.com*, 31 March. http://www.haaretz.com/print-edition/opinion/shin-bet-chiefs-spearhead-the-occupation-1.353218 (accessed 31 March 2011).

———. 2012. "Peace Returning to Normal: Qassam War Goodbye." *Haaretz.com*, 23 November. http://www.haaretz.co.il/news/education/1.1871759 (accessed 25 November 2012) [Hebrew].

Lis, J. 2011. "Knesset Passes Law to Strip Terrorists of Israeli Citizenship." *Haaretz.com*, 28 March. http://www.haaretz.com/news/israel/knesset-passes-law-to-strip-terrorists-of-israeli-citizenship-1.352412 (accessed 12 May 2015).

———. 2014. "The Knesset Passes Bill Distinguishing between Muslim and Christian Arabs." *Haaretz.com*, 25 February. http://www.haaretz.com/news/national/.premium-1.576247 (accessed 5 March 2015).

Livneh, N. 2001. "Post-Zionism Only Rings Once." *Haaretz.com*, 21 September. http://www.haaretz.com/post-zionism-only-rings-once-1.70170 (accessed 7 August 2013).

Lloyd, D. 2012. "Settler Colonialism and the State of Exception: The Example of Palestine/Israel." *Settler Colonial Studies* 2 (1): 59–80.

Lockman, Z. 1996. *Comrades and Enemies: Arabs and Jewish Workers in Palestine, 1906–1948*. Berkeley: University of California Press.

———. 2012. "Land, Labour and the Logic of Zionism: A Critical Engagement with Gershon Shafir." *Settler Colonial Studies* 2 (1): 9–38.

Loewenstein, J. 2006. "Identity and Movement Control in the OPT." *Forced Migration Review* 26: 24–26.

Loshitzky, Y. 2006. "Pathologising Memory: From the Holocaust to the Intifada." *Third Text* 20 (3–4): 327–35.

Lowrance, S. 2005. "Being Palestinian in Israel: Identity, Protest and Political Exclusion." *Comparative Studies of South Asia, Africa, and the Middle East* 25 (2): 487–99.

Lubin, A. 2008. "'We Are All Israelis': The Politics of Colonial Comparisons." *South Atlantic Quarterly* 107 (4): 671–90.

Lustick, I. 1980. *Arabs in the Jewish State: Israel's Control of a National Minority*. Austin and London: University of Texas Press.

———. 1988. *For the Land and the Lord: Jewish Fundamentalism in Israel*. New York: Council on Foreign Relations.

———. 2008. "Abandoning the Iron Wall: Israel and 'the Middle East Muck.'" *Middle East Policy* 15 (3): 30–56.

———. 2011. "Israel's Migration Balance." *Israel Studies Review* 26 (1): 33–65.

———. 2013. "What Counts Is the Counting: Statistical Manipulation as a Solution to Israel's 'Demographic Problem.'" *Middle East Journal* 67 (2): 185–205.

Lynfield, B. 2013. "Palestinians Suffer in Cell Phone Dark Ages – and Point Finger of Blame at Israel." *Jewish Daily Forward*, 27 July. http://forward.com/articles/181138/palestinians-suffer-in-cell-phone-dark-ages-and/?p=all (accessed 18 October 2014).

Lyon, D. 2007. *Surveillance Studies: An Overview*. Cambridge: Polity.

———. 2008. *Identifying Citizens: ID Cards as Surveillance*. Cambridge: Polity.

———. 2010. "National IDs in a Global World: Surveillance, Security, and Citizenship." *Case Western Reserve Journal of International Law* 42 (3): 607–23.

———. 2011. "Identification, Colonialism, and Control: Surveillant Sorting in Israel/Palestine." In E. Zureik, D. Lyon, and Y. Abu-Laban, eds., *Surveillance and Control in Israel/Palestine: Population, Territory and Power*, 49-64. London: Routledge.

Maagar, M. 2009. "A Survey on Establishing a Biometric Database." October. http://www.maagar-mohot.co.il (accessed September 2012, no longer available) [Hebrew].

Macbride, S., A. Asmal, B. Bercusson, R. Falk, G. Pradelle, and S. Wild. 1983. *Israel in Lebanon: The Report of the International Commission to Enquire into Reported Violations of International Law by Israel during Its Invasion of the Lebanon*. London: Ithaca.

Macdonnell, D. 1986. *Theories of Discourse: An Introduction*. Oxford: Blackwell.

MacKenzie, D. 1981. "Eugenics and the Rise of Mathematical Statistics." In J. Irvine, I. Miles, and J. Evans, eds., *Demystifying Social Statistics*, 39–50. London: Pluto.

Mackey, R. 2011. "Palestinians Record West Bank Protests with Cameras Supplied by Israelis." *New York Times*, 17 June. http://thelede.blogs.nytimes.com/2011/06/17/palestinians-film-west-bank-protests-with-israeli-supplied-cameras/?_r=0 (accessed 18 June).

Macro Center for Political Economics [Israel]. N.d. http://www.macro.org.il/english.html (accessed 11 April 2015).

Mada al-Carmel. 2010a. *Israel and the Palestinian Minority: Political Monitoring Report, September through November 2009*, no. 6. http://mada-research.org/en/files/2013/05/pmr6.pdf (accessed 9 April 2010).

———. 2010b. *Israel and the Palestinian Minority: Political Monitoring Report, February through March 2010*, no. 8. http://www.mada-research.org/UserFiles/file/PMP%20PDF/PMR8-ENG/PMR8-Eng_final.pdf (accessed 23 September 2011).

———. 2011. *Israel and the Palestinian Minority: Political Monitoring Report, January through March 2011*, no. 13. http://mada-research.org/en/files/2013/05/pmr13.pdf (accessed 9 April 2010).

Madar Research and Development. 2012. *Arab ICT Use and Social Networks Adoption Report*. Dubai: United Arab Emirates.

———. 2014. *Arab Knowledge Economy Report*. Dubai: United Arab Emirates.

Maital, S. 2013. "The Debilitating Brain Drain." *Jerusalem Post*, 2 June. http://www.jpost.com/Magazine/Opinion/The-debilitating-brain-drain (accessed 31 August 2014).

Major, A. 1999. "State and Criminal Tribes in Colonial Punjab: Surveillance, Control and Reclamation of the 'Dangerous Classes.'" *Modern Asian Studies* 33 (3): 657–88.

Manekin, M., A. Sharon, Y. Israeli, O. Na'aman, and L. Spectre, eds. 2010. *Occupation of the Territories: Israeli Soldiers' Testimonies, 2000–2010*. Jerusalem: Breaking the Silence [NGO].

Mannheim, K. 1991. *Ideology and Utopia: An Introduction to the Sociology of Knowledge*. Ed. B.S. Turner, trans. L. Wirth and E. Shils. London and New York: Routledge.

Mansell, R., and U. Wehn, eds. 1998. *Knowledge Societies: Information Technology for Sustainable Development*. Oxford: Oxford University Press.

Maoz, E. 2013. "Profiting off the War: A Look into the World of Israeli Arms Dealing." *Haokets*, 27 July. http://eng.haokets.org/2013/07/27/profiting-off-war-a-look-into-the-world-of-israeli-arms-dealing (accessed 1 August 2013).

Marcus, E. 1995. "What Comes (Just) after 'Post'? The Case of Ethnography." In N. Denzin and Y. Lincoln, eds., *Handbook of Qualitative Research*, 563–74. Thousand Oaks, CA: Sage.

Margalit, M. 2006a. *Discrimination in the Heart of the Holy City*. Jerusalem: The International Peace and Cooperation Center. http://www.kibush.co.il/downloads/book-hw.pdf (accessed 4 October 2011).

———. 2006b. "Settlements and Settlers in the Old City." *Challenge Magazine*, January-February.

———. 2010. *Seizing Control of Space in East Jerusalem*. Jerusalem: Sifrai Aliat Cag.

Mar'i, S. 1978. *Arab Education in Israel*. Syracuse, NY: Syracuse University Press.

Martin, B., and E. Richards. 1995. "Scientific Knowledge, Controversy, and Public Decision Making." In S. Jasanoff, G.E. Markle, J.C. Petersen, and T. Pinch, eds., *Handbook of Science and Technology Studies*, 506-26. Thousand Oaks, CA: Sage.

Martin, L., H. Gutman, and H. Hutton, eds. 1988. *Technology of the Self*. Amherst: University of Massachusetts Press.

Marx, E. 1991. "Rehabilitation of the Refugees in the Gaza Strip." *International Problems, Society and State* 5: 64–73 [Hebrew].

———. 1992. "Palestinian Refugee Camps in the West Bank and Gaza." *Middle Eastern Studies* 28 (2): 281–94.

Masalha, N. 1992. *Expulsion of the Palestinians: The Concept of Transfer in Zionist Political Thought*. Washington, DC: Institute for Palestine Studies.

———. 2012. *The Palestine Nakba: Decolonizing History, Narrating the Subaltern, Reclaiming Memory*. London and New York: Zed.

Massad, J. 2001. *Colonial Effects: The Making of National Identity in Jordan*. New York: Columbia University Press.

———. 2006. *Persistence of the Palestinian Question: Essays on Zionism and the Palestinians*. London and New York: Routledge.

———. 2010. "The Language of Zionism." *Al-Ahram Weekly*, 6–12 May. http://weekly.ahram.org.eg/2010/997/re9.htm (accessed 13 May 2014).

Mazawi, A. 1994. "Teachers' Role Patterns and the Mediation of Sociopolitical Change: The Case of Palestinian Arab School Teachers." *British Journal of Sociology of Education* 15 (4): 497–514.

———. 1995. "University Education, Credentialism and Social Stratification among Palestinian Arabs in Israel." *Higher Education* 29 (4): 351–68.

———. 1996. "Patterns of Competition over School-Management Positions and the Mediation of Social Inequalities: A Case Study of High Court of Justice Petitions against the Appointment of Principals in Public Schools in Israel." *Israel Social Science Research* 11 (1): 87–114.

———. 1998. "Contested Regimes, Civic Dissent, and the Political Socialization of Children and Adolescents: The Case of the Palestinian Uprising." In O. Ichilov, ed., *Citizenship and Citizenship Education in a Changing World*, 5–97. London and Portland, OR: Woburn.

Mbembe, A. 2003. "Necropolitics." *Public Culture* 15 (1): 11–40.

McCarthy, J. 1990. *The Population of Palestine: Population History and Statistics of the Late Ottoman Period and the Mandate*. New York: Columbia University Press.

McCoy, A. 2009. *Policing America's Empire: The United States, the Philippines, and the Rise of the Surveillance State*. Madison: University of Wisconsin Press.

McKie, R. 2001. "Journal Axes Gene Research on Jews and Palestinians." *Guardian*, 25 November. http://www.theguardian.com/world/2001/nov/25/medicalscience.genetics (accessed 27 July 2014).

Mekerishvili, G. 2008. "Macro-securitization, Sovereignty and Hegemony." Shvoong, 8 January. http://www.eastchance.com/essay/ess_Macro-securitizationSovereigntyandHegemony.asp (accessed 14 May 2015).

Melman, Y. 2008. "Shin Bet to Palestinians: Collaborate or Go to Jail." *Haaretz.com*, 5 September. http://www.haaretz.com/print-edition/features/shin-bet-to-palestinian-collaborate-or-go-to-jail-1.253204 (accessed 14 April 2014).

———. 2010. "Foreign Report: Israel Has One of the Largest 'Eavesdropping' Intel Bases." *Haaretz.com*, 5 September. http://www.haaretz.com/print-edition/news/foreign-report-israel-has-one-of-world-s-largest-eavesdropping-intel-bases-1.312198 (accessed 5 September 2010).

———. 2011. "When the Shin Bet Doesn't Really Want To." *Haaretz.com*, 10 October. http://www.haaretz.com/print-edition/opinion/when-the-shin-bet-really-doesn-t-want-to-1.389072 (accessed 10 October 2011).

Mendel, Y. 2008. "Diary." *London Review of Books* 30 (5): 30–31. http://www.lrb.co.uk/v30/n05/mend01_.html (accessed 23 July 2013).

Mesch, G., and I. Talmud. 2011. "Ethnic Differences in Internet Access: The Role of Occupation and Exposure." *Information, Communication and Society* 14 (4): 445–71.

Mi'ari, M. 1998. "Self-Identity and Readiness for Interethnic Contact among Young Palestinians in the West Bank." *Canadian Journal of Sociology* 23 (1): 47–70.

Michael, B. 2007. "Stupid Big Brother." *ynetnews.com*, 25 December. http://www.ynetnews.com/articles/0,7340,L-3486363,00.html (accessed 26 October 2013).

Milton-Edwards, B. 1999. *Islamic Politics in Palestine*. London: I.B. Tauris.

Mishal, S., and R. Aharoni. 1994. *Speaking Stones: Communiqués from the Intifada Underground*. Syracuse, NY: Syracuse University Press.

Mishal, S., and A. Sela. 2000. *The Palestinian Hamas: Vision, Violence and Co-existence*. New York: Columbia University Press.

Mitchell, T. 1988. *Colonising Egypt*. Cairo: American University in Cairo Press.

Mitchell, T., and R. Owen. 1990. "Defining the State in the Middle East: A Report on the First of the Three Workshops Organized by the Social Science Research Council's Joint Committee on the Near and Middle East." *Middle East Studies Association Bulletin* 24 (2): 179–83.

Mitchell, T., G. Prakash, and E. Shohat. 2003. "Palestine in a Transnational Context." *Social Text* 21 (2): 1–5.

Monmonier, M. 1991. *How to Lie with Maps*. Chicago: University of Chicago Press.

Montag, W. 2002. "Toward a Conception of Racism without Race: Foucault and Contemporary Biopolitics." *Warwick Journal of Philosophy* 13: 111–26.

Morris, B. 1987. *The Birth of the Palestinian Refugee Problem, 1947–1949*. Cambridge: Cambridge University Press.

———. 2002. "A New Exodus for the Middle East?" *Guardian*, 3 October. http://www.theguardian.com/world/2002/oct/03/israel1 (accessed 27 July 2014).

———. 2004. "Survival of the Fittest (cont.)." *Haaretz.com*, 8 January. http://www.haaretz.com/survival-of-the-fittest-cont-1.61341 (accessed 2 October 2014).

Moses, A.D. 2008. *Empire, Colony, Genocide: Conquest, Occupation, and Subaltern Resistance in World History*. New York and Oxford: Berghahn.

Mossawa – The Advocacy Center for Arab Citizens in Israel. 2014. "Disciplinary Bills and Laws in the Israeli Knesset." *Mossawa Newsletter*, March, 6–7. http://www.mossawacenter.org/en/item.asp?aid=1177 (accessed 11 April 2015).

Mozgovaya, N. 2011. "Gaza, the Most Facebook Friendly Place on Earth." *Haaretz.com*, 5 June. http://www.haaretz.com/blogs/2.241/gaza-the-most-facebook-friendly-place-on-earth-1.365970 (accessed 6 August 2013).

Mualem, M. 2002. "New Unit to Toughen Citizenship Process for Arabs." *Haaretz.com*, 15 June. http://www.haaretz.com/print-edition/news/new-unit-to-toughen-citizenship-process-for-arabs-1.42347 (accessed 27 July 2014).

Mulaj, K. 2007. "Ethnic Cleansing and the Provision of In/Security." *Security Dialogue* 38 (2): 335–56.

Muslih, M. 1993. "Palestinian Civil Society." *Middle East Journal* 47 (2): 258–74.

Naqib, F. 1995. *Prospects for Sustained Development of the Palestinian Economy: Strategies and Policies for Reconstruction and Development*. Geneva: United Nations Conference on Trade and Development.

Nashif, E. 2008. *Palestinian Political Prisoners: Identity and Community*. London: Routledge.

Nassar, J., and R. Heacock, eds. 1990. *Intifada: Palestine at the Crossroads.* New York: Praeger.

Near East Consulting. N.d. http://www.neareastconsulting.com (accessed 11 April 2015).

Neff, D. 2003. "Abba Eban (1915–2000): An Idealist Ignored in His Adopted Israel." *Washington Report*, January–February, 43–44.

Neocleous, M. 2003. "Off the Map: On Violence and Cartography." *European Journal of Social Theory* 6 (4): 409–25.

Nesher, T. 2012. "Why Is the Birth Rate in Israel's Ethiopian Community Declining?" *Haaretz.com*, 9 December. http://www.haaretz.com/news/national/ why-is-the-birth-rate-in-israel-s-ethiopian-community-declining.premium-1.483494 (accessed 22 July 2014).

———. 2013. "Israel Admits Ethiopian Women Were Given Birth Control Shots." *Haaretz.com*, 27 January. http://www.haaretz.com/news/national/israel-admits-ethiopian-women-were-given-birth-control-shots.premium-1.496519 (accessed 27 January 2013).

Neumann, A. 2011. *Testimony of Amnon Neumann.* YouTube, 27 December. https://www.youtube.com/watch?v=KS4OXOom_vk (accessed 27 March 2014).

Neumann, B. 2011. *Land and Desire in Early Zionism.* Trans. Haim Watzman. Waltham, MA: Brandeis University Press.

Nir, O. 2002. "We Can't Just Be Shooed Away." *Haaretz.com*, 24 April. http://www.haaretz.com/print-edition/features/we-can-t-just-be-shooed-away-1.46912 (accessed 22 July 2014).

Novik, A. 2011. "60 Years Later, Spies' Lives Revealed." *ynetnews.com*, 2 February. http://www.ynetnews.com/articles/0,7340,L-4031176,00.html (accessed 28 April 2014).

Nugent, D. 2010. "Knowledge and Empire: The Social Sciences and United States Imperial Expansion." *Identities: Global Studies in Culture and Power* 17 (1): 2–44.

Nusse, A. 1998. *Muslim Palestine: The Ideology of Hamas.* Amsterdam, Netherlands: Harwood.

Ophir, A. 2007. "The Two-State Solution: Providence and Catastrophe." *Theoretical Inquiries in Law* 8 (1): 117–60.

Ophir, A., M. Givoni, and S. Hanafi, eds. 2009. *The Power of Inclusive Exclusion: Anatomy of Israeli Rule in the Occupied Palestinian Territories.* New York: Zone.

Or Commission. 2003. *Report of the State Commission of Inquiry to Investigate the Clashes between the Security Forces and Israeli Citizens in October 2000.* Jerusalem: Government Printing Press.

Orwell, G. 1946. "Politics and the English Language." Reprinted in S. Orwell and I. Angus, eds., *The Collected Essays, Journalism and Letters of George Orwell*, vol. 4, 127–40. New York: Brace Harcourt and World, 1968.

———. 1949. *Nineteen Eighty-Four.* London: Secker and Warburg.

Oveida, Y. 2010. "Israel Rabbi Calls for 'Plague' on Mahmoud Abbas." *BBC News*, 30 August. http://www.bbc.co.uk/news/world-middle-east-11127409 (accessed 27 September 2011).

Pacheco, A. 2001. "Flouting Convention: The Oslo Agreements." In R. Carey, N. Chomsky, G. Svirsky, and A. Weir, eds., *The New Intifada: Resisting Israel's Apartheid*, 181–208. London: Verso.

Palestinian Authority. 1998. *Palestine: The Poverty Report.* Ramallah: Ministry of Planning and International Cooperation, Palestinian Authority.

Palestinian Human Rights Monitor Group. 2002. "No Internet, No Protests: Israeli Forces Use Violence to Suppress Protestors and Contact with Outside World." *oznik.com*, 19 August. http://oznik.com/news/020719.html (accessed 10 October 2014).

Palestinian Refugee Research Net, McGill University. N.d. http://prrn.mcgill.ca/research (accessed 19 May 2015).

Panorama. 2003. *Information Technology in Jenin: A Limited Survey of Attitudes to Information Technology among a Sample of 800 People.* Ramallah: Panorama [Arabic].

Pappé, I. 1988. "Zionism as Colonialism: A Comparative View of Diluted Colonialism in Asia and Africa." *South Atlantic Quarterly* 107 (4): 611–33.
——. 1999. *The Israel/Palestine Question.* London and New York: Routledge.
——. 2001. "The Tantura Case in Israel: The Katz Research and Trial." *Journal of Palestine Studies* 30 (3): 19–39.
——, ed. 2003. *The Israel-Palestine Question.* New York: Routledge.
——. 2005. *The Modern Middle East.* London and New York: Routledge.
——. 2006. *The Ethnic Cleansing of Palestine.* Oxford: Oneworld.
——. 2008. "The *Mukhabarat* State of Israel: A State of Oppression Is Not a State of Exception." In R. Lentin, ed., *Thinking Palestine,* 148–69. London and New York: Zed.
——. 2009. "Israel's Message." *London Review of Books,* 14 January. http://www.lrb.co.uk/2009/01/14/ilan-pappe/israels-message (accessed 7 May 2015).
——. 2011. *The Forgotten Palestinians: A History of the Palestinians in Israel.* New Haven, CT: Yale University Press.
——. 2014. *The Idea of Israel: A History of Power and Knowledge.* London: Verso.
Parenti, M. 2003. *The Soft Cage: Surveillance in America from Slavery to the War on Terror.* New York: Basic Books.
Parsons, N., and M. Salter. 2008. "Israeli Biopolitics: Closure, Territorialisation and Governmentality in the Occupied Palestinian Territories." *Geopolitics* 13 (4): 701–23.
Parsons, T., and E.A. Shils. 1962. *Toward a General Theory of Action: Theoretical Foundations for the Social Sciences.* New York: Harper and Row.
Patai, R. 1973. *The Arab Mind.* New York: Scribner.
Payton, L. 2014. "CSEC Snowden Docs: MPs Grill Defence Minister on Spying Revelation." *CBC News,* 31 January. http://www.cbc.ca/news/politics/csec-snowden-docs-mps-grill-defence-minister-on-spying-revelation-1.2518564 (accessed 31 January 2014).
PCBS (Palestinian Central Bureau of Statistics). N.d. http://www.pcbs.gov.ps (accessed 11 April 2015).
——. 2000. "Results of the Visual Information Means and Computer Survey." http://82.213.38.42/Portals/_pcbs/PressRelease/com_use.aspx (accessed 5 January 2014).
——. 2004. *Press Conference on the Survey Results: Computer, Internet and Mobile Phone Survey.* October. http://www.pcbs.gov.ps/Portals/_pcbs/PressRelease/computer_e.pdf (accessed 12 April 2014).
——. 2006. *Household Survey on Information and Communication Technology: Main Findings.* August. http://www.pcbs.gov.ps/Portals/_pcbs/PressRelease/CommTec06e.pdf (accessed 12 April 2014).
——. 2011a. *Press Release on the Main Findings of Household Survey on ICT.* November. http://www.pcbs.gov.ps/Portals/_pcbs/PressRelease/HouseholdICT2011_E.pdf (accessed 12 April 2014).
——. 2011b. *Palestinians at the End of 2011.* http://www.pcbs.gov.ps/Portals/_pcbs/PressRelease/palestineEnd2011E.pdf (accessed 3 January 2012).
——. 2012. *Palestine Statistical Yearbook 2012.* http://www.pcbs.gov.ps/Downloads/Book1949.pdf (accessed February 8, 2015) [Arabic].
PCPSR (Palestinian Center for Policy and Survey Research). N.d. http://www.pcpsr.org (accessed 5 January 2015).
——. 1999. "Public Opinion Poll 43." 2–4 September. http://www.pcpsr.org/en/node/511 (accessed 11 April 2015).
Peace Planet. 2014. "1948: Israeli Soldier Story; Ethnic Cleansing." YouTube, 14 October. https://www.youtube.com/watch?v=Z8EUj-MX_Iw (accessed 21 May 2015).

Peled, H., and Y. Peled. 2011. "Post-Post-Zionism? Confronting the Death of the Two-State Solution." *New Left Review* 67: 97–118.

Peled, N. 2006. "About Educating towards Racism and the Murder of Children." *Mahsanmilim.com: Reports from the West Bank*. http://www.mahsanmilim.com/NuritPeledElhanan.htm (accessed 16 December 2009) [Hebrew].

———. 2010. "Legitimation of Massacres in Israeli School History Books." *Discourse and Society* 21 (4): 377–404.

Peled, Y. 1992. "Ethnic Democracy and the Legal Construction of Citizenship: Arab Citizens of the Jewish State." *American Political Science Review* 86 (2): 432–43.

———. 2005. "The Or Commission and Palestinian Citizenship in Israel." *Citizenship Studies* 9 (1): 89–105.

———. 2007. "Towards a Post-Citizenship Society? A Report from the Front." *Citizenship Studies* 11 (1): 95–104.

Peled-Elhanan, N. 2012. *Palestine in Israeli School Books: Ideology and Propaganda in Education*. London and New York: I.B. Tauris.

Penslar, D. 2005. "Herzl and the Palestinian Arabs: Myths and Counter-Myths." *Journal of Israeli History* 24 (1): 65–77.

———. 2007. *Israel in History: The Jewish State in Contemporary Perspective*. New York: Routledge.

Peretz, D. 1958. *Israel and the Palestine Arabs*. New York: AMS Press.

———. 1990. *Intifada: The Palestinian Uprising*. Boulder, CO: Westview.

Peteet, J. 1994a. "The Graffiti of the Intifada." *Muslim World* 84 (1–2): 155–67.

———. 1994b. "Male Gender and Rituals of Resistance in the Palestinian Intifada: A Cultural Politics of Violence." *American Ethnologist* 21 (1): 31–49.

———. 1995. "Transforming Trust: Dispossession and Empowerment among Palestinian Refugees." In V.E. Daniel and J. Knudsen, eds., *Mistrusting Refugees*, 168–86. Berkeley: University of California Press.

———. 1997. "Icons and Militants: Mothering in the Danger Zone." *Signs* 23 (1): 103–29.

———. 2005. "Words as Interventions: Naming in the Israel-Palestine Conflict." *Third World Quarterly* 26 (1): 153–72.

———. 2008. "Stealing Time." *Middle East Research Report (MERIP)* 38 (248). http://www.merip.org/mer/mer248/stealing-time (accessed 19 May 2015).

———. 2009. "Beyond Compare." *Middle East Research Report (MERIP)* 9 (253). http://www.merip.org/mer/mer253/beyond-compare (accessed 19 May 2015).

Petersen-Overton, K. 2008. "Counting Heads: Israel's Demographic Imperative." *Interdisciplinary Journal of International Studies* 5 (1): 1–25.

Pfaff, W. 1997. "Eugenics, Anyone?" *New York Review of Books*, 23 October. http://www.nybooks.com/articles/archives/1997/oct/23/eugenics-anyone (accessed 26 July 2014).

———. 1998. "Reply." *New York Review of Books*, 15 January. http://www.nybooks.com/articles/archives/1998/jan/15/eugenics-denied (accessed 26 July 2014).

Pfeffer, A. 2012. "Psychological Warfare on the Digital Battlefield." *Haaretz.com*, 19 November. http://www.haaretz.com/news/features/psychological-warfare-on-the-digital-battlefield.premium-1.478984 (accessed 23 December 2014).

Philologos. 2006. "Hitkansut: On Language." *Jewish Daily Forward*, 31 March. http://www.forward.com/articles/1165 (accessed 22 November 2010).

Pipes, D. 2002. *Militant Islam Reaches America*. New York: W.W. Norton.

Piterberg, G. 2001. "Erasures." *New Left Review* 10: 31–46.

———. 2008. *The Returns of Zionism: Myths, Politics and Scholarship in Israel*. London and New York: Verso.

Plascov, A. 1981. *The Palestinian Refugees in Jordan*. Totowa, NJ: Frank Cass.

Potoc, R.N. 1998. "Borders, Exiles, Minor Literatures: The Case of Palestinian-Israeli Writing." In E. Barkan and M. Shelton, eds., *Borders, Exiles, Diasporas*, 291–310. Stanford, CA: Stanford University Press.

Pratt, M.L. 1991. *Imperial Eyes: Travel Writing and Transculturation*. New York: Routledge.

Privacy International. 2007. "PHR2006 – State of Israel." 18 December. http://www.privacyinternational.org/article.shtml?cmd%5B347%5D=x-347-559526 (accessed 12 August 2009).

Pugliese, J. 2010. *Biometrics: Bodies, Technologies, Biopolitics*. London: Routledge.

Punamaki, R.L., and M. Joustie. 1998. "The Role of Culture, Violence, and Personal Factors Affecting Dream Content." *Journal of Cross-Cultural Psychology* 29 (2): 320–42.

Punamaki, R.L., and T. Puhakka. 1997. "Determinants and Effectiveness of Children's Coping with Political Violence." *International Journal of Behavioural Development* 27 (2): 349–70.

Rabinowitz, D. 1998. *Anthropology and the Palestinians*. Ra'nanah, Israel: Institute for Israeli Arab Studies [Hebrew].

———. 2000. "Recognizing the Original Sin." *Haaretz.com*, 17 October. http://www3.haaretz.co.il/eng/scripts/article.asp?mador=4&datee=10/17/00&id=968 (accessed 7 August 2013).

———. 2001a. "Natives with Jackets and Degrees: Othering, Objectification and the Role of Palestinians in the Co-Existence Field in Israel." *Social Anthropology* 9 (1): 65–80.

———. 2001b. "The Palestinian Citizens of Israel, the Concept of Trapped Minority and the Discourse on Transnationalism in Anthropology." *Ethnic and Racial Studies* 24 (1): 64–85.

Rabinowitz, D., A. Ghanem, and O. Yiftachel, eds. 2000. *After the Rift: New Directions for Government Policy towards the Arabs in Israel*. Report submitted to Prime Minister Ehud Barak, November. Copy in the possession of E. Zureik.

Radley, K.R. 1978. "The Palestinian Refugees: The Right to Return in International Law." *American Journal of International Law* 72 (3): 586–614.

Rajiva, L. 2005. *The Language of Empire: Abu Ghraib and the American Media*. New York: Monthly Review.

Ram, U. 1993. "The Colonization Perspective in Israeli Sociology: Internal and External Comparisons." *Journal of Historical Sociology* 6 (3): 327–50.

———. 1995. *The Changing Agenda of Israeli Sociology: Theory, Ideology and Identity*. Albany: SUNY Press.

Ramadan, A. 2009. "Destroying Nahr el-Bared: Sovereignty and Urbicide in the Space of Exception." *Political Geography* 28 (3): 153–63.

Rashed, H., and D. Short. 2012. "Genocide and Settler Colonialism: Can a Lemkin-Inspired Genocide Perspective Aid Our Understanding of the Palestinian Situation?" *International Journal of Human Rights* 16 (8): 1142–69.

Ratner, D. 2003. "Demographer: Save Negev and Galilee Now." *Haaretz.com*, 26 February. http://www.haaretz.com/print-edition/news/demographer-save-negev-and-galilee-now-1.17863 (accessed 26 July 2014).

Rattner, A., and G. Fishman. 1998. *Justice for All? Jews and Arabs in the Israeli Criminal Justice System*. Westport, CT, and London: Praeger.

Ravid, I. 2001. "The Demographic Environment of Israel." Paper presented at the conference "The Balance of National Strength and Security: Policy Directions," Interdisciplinary Center Herzliya, Israel, April.

Raviv, D., and Y. Melman. 2014. *Spies against Armageddon: Inside Israel's Secret Wars*. Tel Aviv: Levant.

Refugee Studies Centre, University of Oxford. N.d. http://www.rsc.ox.ac.uk/resources/library (accessed 11 April 2015).

Reuters. 2008. "World Health Organization: Israel Turns Away Sick Gazans Who Die in 'Avoidable Tragedies.'" *Haaretz.com*, 1 April. http://www.haaretz.com/news/who-israel-turning-away-sick-gazans-who-die-in-avoidable-tragedies-1.243108 (accessed 14 April 2014).

———. 2014. "Gaza Woman Gives Birth to First Baby Born from Smuggled Sperm." *Haaretz.com*, 10 January. http://www.haaretz.com/news/middle-east/1.567966 (accessed 10 January 2014).

Reuveny, R. 2008a. "Colonialism or Something else? A Reply to Ira Sharkansky's Comment." *Independent Review* 13 (2): 293–97.

———. 2008b. "The Last Colonialist: Israel in the Occupied Territories since 1967." *Independent Review* 12 (3): 325–74.

Richter-Devroe, S. 2010. "Palestinian Women's Everyday Resistance: Between Normality and Normalization." *Journal of International Women's Studies* 12 (2): 32–46.

———. 2012. "Defending Their Land, Protecting Their Men." *International Feminist Journal of Politics* 14 (2): 181–201.

———. 2013. "'Like Something Sacred': Palestinian Refugee Narratives on the Right of Return." *Refugee Survey Quarterly* 32 (2): 92–115.

Robertson, R. 1995. "'Glocalization': Time-Space and Homogeneity-Heterogeneity." In M. Featherstone, S. Lash, and R. Robertson, eds., *Global Modernities*, 25–44. London: Sage.

Robinson, G. 2010. "Al-Aqsa Intifada 10 Years Later." *Foreign Policy*, 18 October. http://mideast.foreignpolicy.com/posts/2010/10/18/the_al_aqsa_intifada_10_years_later (accessed 19 July 2011).

Robinson, S. 2013. *Citizen Strangers: Palestinians and the Birth of Israel's Settler State*. Stanford, CA: Stanford University Press.

Rodinson, M. 1973. *Israel: A Colonial-Settler State?* New York: Pathfinder.

Roffe-Ofir, S. 2010. "Report: Current Knesset Most Racist of all Time." *ynetnews.com*, 21 March. http://www.ynetnews.com/articles/0,7340,L3865696,00.html (accessed 21 March 2010).

Rogan, E.L., and A. Shlaim, eds. 2001. *The War for Palestine: Rewriting the History of 1948*. Cambridge: Cambridge University Press.

Rohozinski, R., and D. Collings. 2008. *Palestinian Information Society: Exploring the Dynamics of Security and Development in the Information Age*. Report. Ottawa: International Development Research Centre.

Ron, J. 1997. "Varying Methods of State Violence." *International Organization* 51 (2): 275–300.

———. 2000. "Savage Restraint: Israel, Palestine and the Dialectics of Legal Repression." *Social Problems* 47 (4): 445–72.

Rose, N., and P. Miller. 1992. "Political Power beyond the State: Problematics of Government." *British Journal of Sociology* 43 (2): 173–295.

Rosenfeld, H. 2002. "The Idea Is to Change the State, Not the 'Conceptual' Terminology." *Ethnic and Racial Studies* 25 (6): 1083–95.

Rosenfeld, M. 2004. *Confronting the Occupation: Work, Education, and Political Activism of Palestinian Families in a Refugee Camp*. Stanford, CA: Stanford University Press.

Rouhana, N. 1997. *Palestinian Citizens in an Ethnic State: Identities in Conflict*. New Haven, CT: Yale University Press.

———. 2006. "Zionism's Encounter with the Palestinians: The Dynamics of Force, Fear, and Extremism." In R. Rotberg, ed., *Israeli and Palestinian Narratives of Conflict: History's Double Helix*, 115–41. Bloomington and Indianapolis: Indiana University Press.

Rouhana, N., and A. Sabbagh-Khoury, eds. 2011. *The Palestinians in Israel: Readings in History, Politics and Society*. Haifa: Mada al-Carmel. http://mada-research.org/en/files/2011/09/ebook-english-book.pdf (accessed 20 July 2013).

Roy, A. 2003. *War Talk*. Cambridge, MA: South End.
Roy, S. 2000. *The Gaza Strip: The Political Economy of De-development*. 2nd ed. Washington, DC: Institute for Palestine Studies.
———. 2007. *Failing Peace: Gaza and the Palestinian-Israeli Conflict*. Ann Arbor, MI, and London: Pluto.
———. 2009. "If Gaza Falls . . . " *London Review of Books* 31 (1): 26.
———. 2011. *Hamas and Civil Society in Gaza: Engaging the Islamist Social Sector*. Princeton, NJ: Princeton University Press.
Rudoren, J. 2012. "'Forgotten Neighborhood' Underscores the Poverty of an Isolated Enclave." *New York Times*, 9 September. http://www.nytimes.com/2012/09/10/world/middleeast/forgotten-neighborhood-underscores-growing-poverty-of-gaza.html?pagewanted=all (accessed 10 August 2014).
———. 2014. "In Torn Gaza, If Roof Stands, It's Now Home." *New York Times*, 17 August. http://www.nytimes.com/2014/08/18/world/middleeast/gaza-strip-war-leaves-another-crisis-for-displaced-gazans.html?hp&action=click&pgtype=Homepage&version=LargeMediaHeadlineSum&module=photo-spot-region&region=photo-spot&WT.nav=photo-spot (accessed 18 August 2014).
Rudoren, J., and F. Akram. 2014. "As Truce Holds, Dazed Gazans Get to Work."*New York Times*, 27 August. http://www.nytimes.com/2014/08/28/world/ middleeast/gaza-strip.html?ref=middleeast (accessed 28 August 2014).
Ruppin, A. 1935. *The Sociology of the Jews*. Vol. 2, *The Jews' Struggle for Their Future*. Berlin: Stiebel [Hebrew].
Ryan, C. 2012. "The Subjectified and Resisting Corporeal Body: A Theoretical Framework for Examining Subjugation and Resistance." *Limerick Papers in Politics and Public Administration* 2: 1–25. www.ul.ie/ppa/content/files/Ryan.pdf (accessed 11 April 2015).
Sa'ar, A., and T. Yahia-Younis. 2008. "Masculinity in Crisis: The Case of Palestinians in Israel." *British Journal of Middle Eastern Studies* 35 (3): 305–23.
Sabbagh, S. 1989. "Palestinian Women Writers and the Intifada." *Social Text* 22: 62–78.
Sabbagh-Khoury, A. 2007. "Palestinian Predicaments: Jewish Immigration and Refugee Repatriation." Unpublished manuscript.
Sabet, A. 1998. "The Peace Process and the Politics of Conflict Resolution." *Journal of Palestine Studies* 27 (4): 5–19.
Sa'di, A. 1995. "Incorporation without Integration: Palestinian Citizens in Israel's Labour Market." *Sociology* 29 (3): 429–51.
———. 1997. "Modernization as an Explanatory Discourse of Zionist-Palestinian Relations." *British Journal of Middle Eastern Studies* 24 (1): 25–48.
———. 2005. "The Politics of Collaboration: Israel's Control of National Minority and Indigenous Resistance." *Holy Land Journal* 4 (10): 7–26.
———. 2010. "The Borders of Colonial Encounter: The Case of Israel's Wall." *Asian Journal of Social Science* 38 (1): 46–59.
———. 2011. "Ominous Designs: Israel's Strategies of Controlling the Palestinians during the First Two Decades." In E. Zureik, D. Lyon, and Y. Abu-Laban, eds., *Surveillance and Control in Israel/Palestine: Population, Territory and Power*, 83–98. London: Routledge.
———. 2013. *Thorough Surveillance: The Genesis of Israeli Policies of Population Management, Surveillance and Political Control towards the Palestinian Minority*. Manchester: Manchester University Press.
Sa'di, A., and L. Abu-Lughod, eds. 2007. *Nakba: Palestine, 1948 and the Claims of Memory*. New York: Columbia University Press.
Said, E. 1978. *Orientalism*. New York: Pantheon.
———. 1979. "Zionism from the Standpoint of Its Victims." *Social Text* 1: 7–58.

———. 1981. *Covering Islam: How the Media and the Experts Determine How We See the Rest of the World*. New York: Pantheon.
———. 1982. "Travelling Theory." *Raritan* 1 (3) 41–67.
———. 1984. "Permission to Narrate." *London Review of Books*, 16 February, 3–16.
———. 1985. *After the Last Sky: Palestinian Lives*. New York: Pantheon.
———. 1993. *Culture and Imperialism*. New York: Alfred A. Knopf.
———. 1996. *Representations of the Intellectual*. New York: Vintage.
———. 1999. "Refusal to Surrender Quietly." *Al-Ahram Weekly*, 5–11 August. http://weekly.ahram.org.eg/1999/441/op2.htm (accessed 27 July 2013).
Salih, R. 2013. "From Bare Lives to Political Agents: Palestinian Refugees as Avant-Garde." *Refugee Survey Quarterly* 32 (2): 66–91.
Sand, S. 2009. *The Invention of the Jewish People*. London and New York: Verso.
Sarid, Y. 2009. "Yossi Sarid: If You (or I) Were Palestinian." *Haaretz.com*, 2 January. http://www.haaretz.com/print-edition/opinion/yossi-sarid-if-you-or-i-were-palestinian-1.267316 (accessed 2 October 2014).
Save the Children and Medical Aid for Palestinians. 2012. *Gaza's Children: Falling Behind – The Effect of the Blockade on Child Health in Gaza*. http://www.savethechildren.org.uk/sites/default/files/docs/Gazas-Children-Falling-Behind.pdf (accessed 5 October 2014).
Saumarez Smith, R. 1996. *Rule by Records: Land Registration and Village Custom in Early British Punjab*. Delhi: Oxford University Press.
Sayigh, R. 1977. "The Palestinian Identity among Camp Residents." *Journal of Palestine Studies* 6 (23): 3–22.
———. 1979. *Palestinians: From Peasants to Revolutionaries*. London: Zed.
Schacter, D. 2002. *The Seven Sins of Memory: How the Mind Forgets and Remembers*, Boston: Houghton Mifflin Harcourt.
Scholch, A. 1985. "The Demographic Development of Palestine, 1850–1882." *International Journal of Middle Eastern Studies* 17 (4): 485–505.
Sciadas, G., ed. 2005. *From the Digital Divide to Digital Opportunities: Measuring Infostates for Development*. Montreal: Orbicom and Claude-Yves Charron. https://www.itu.int/ITU-D/ict/publications/dd/material/index_ict_opp.pdf (accessed 3 April 2015).
Scobbie, I. 2009. "Colonialism under International Law and Economic Aspects of Israeli Colonialism in the OPT." Paper presented at the conference "Occupation, Colonialism, Apartheid? A Re-assessment of Israel's Practices in the OPT under International Law," organized by the NGOs Al-Haq and Adalah, Ramallah, Palestine, 16 August.
Scott, J.C. 1987. *Weapons of the Weak: Everyday Forms of Peasant Resistance*. New Haven, CT: Yale University Press.
———. 1998. *Seeing Like a State: How Certain Schemes to Improve the Human Condition Have Failed*. New Haven, CT: Yale University Press.
Segal, R., and E. Weizman, eds. 2003. *A Civilian Occupation: The Politics of Israeli Architecture*. Tel Aviv and London: Babel and Verso.
Segan, L. 1999. "30% of Israelis Wired." *Haaretz.com*, 29 June. http://www.cji.co.il/cji-n059.txt (accessed 7 August 2013).
Segev, T. 2009. "The Makings of History: Revisiting Arthur Ruppin." *Haaretz.com*, 8 October. http://www.haaretz.com/the-makings-of-history-revisiting-arthur-ruppin-1.6433 (accessed 27 August 2014).
Sela, R. 2011. "It Took a Village." *Haaretz.com*, 20 May. http://www.haaretz.com/weekend/magazine/it-took-a-village-1.363015 (accessed 21 May 2011).
Selby, J. 2005. "Post-Zionist Perspectives on Contemporary Israel." *New Political Economy* 10 (1): 107–20.
Selmeczi, A. 2009. "'We Are Being Left to Burn Because We Do Not Count': Biopolitics, Abandonment and Resistance." *Global Society* 23 (4): 519–38.

Seltzer, W., and M. Anderson. 2001. "The Dark Side of Numbers: The Role of Population Data Systems in Human Rights Abuses." *Social Research* 68 (2): 481–513.

Semyonov, M., and N. Lewin-Epstein. 1994. "Ethnic Labor Markets, Gender, and Socioeconomic Inequality: A Study of Arabs in the Israeli Labor Force." *Sociological Quarterly* 35 (1): 51–68.

Sengoopta, C. 2003. *Imprint of the Raj: How Fingerprinting was Born in Colonial India*. London: Pan.

Sfard, M. 2012. "Occupation Double-Speak: Zionism's Amazing Revival of the Hebrew Language Has Morphed into an Insidious Instrument of Repression." *Haaretz.com*, 12 June. http://www.haaretz.com/opinion/occupation-double-speak.premium-1.435982 (accessed 13 June 2012).

Shachtman, N. 2002. "Israel Blocks Palestinian ISP." *Wired News*, 16 July. http://electronicintifada.net/content/israel-blocks-palestinian-isp/4564 (accessed 11 April 2015).

Shafir, G. 1989. *Land, Labour and the Origins of the Israeli-Palestinian Conflict, 1882–1914*. Cambridge: Cambridge University Press.

——. 1996. "Israeli Society: A Counterview." *Israel Studies* 1 (2): 189–213.

——. 2003. "Zionism and Colonialism: A Comparative Approach." In I. Pappé, ed., *The Israel-Palestine Question*, 81–95. New York: Routledge.

——. 2005. "Settler Citizenship in the Jewish Colonization of Palestine." In C. Elkins and S. Petersen, eds., *Settler Colonialism in the Twentieth Century: Projects, Practices, Legacies*, 41–57. London and New York: Routledge.

Shafir, G., and Y. Peled. 2002. *Being Israeli: The Dynamics of Multiple Citizenship*. Cambridge: Cambridge University Press.

Shahak, I., and N. Mezvinsky. 1999. *Jewish Fundamentalism in Israel*. Ann Arbor, MI, and London: Pluto.

——. 2004. *Jewish Fundamentalism in Israel*. New ed. Ann Arbor, MI, and London: Pluto.

Shai, A. 2006. "The Fate of Abandoned Arab Villages in Israel, 1965–1969." *History and Memory* 18 (2): 86–106.

Shalhoub-Kevorkian, N. 1997a. "Tolerating Battering: Invisible Methods of Social Control." *International Review of Victimology* 5 (1): 1–21.

——. 1997b. "Wife Abuse: A Method of Social Control." *International Social Science Research* 12 (1): 59–72.

——. 2004. "The Hidden Casualties of War: Palestinian Women and the Second Intifada." *Indigenous Peoples' Journal of Law, Culture and Resistance* 1 (1): 67–82.

——. 2006. "Negotiating the Present, Historicizing the Future: Palestinian Children Speak about the Israeli Separation Wall." *American Behavioral Scientist Journal* 49 (8): 1101–34.

——. 2012a. "E-Resistance and Technological In/Security in Everyday Life." *British Journal of Criminology* 52 (1): 55–72.

——. 2012b. "The Grammar of Rights in Colonial Contexts: The Case of Palestinian Women in Israel." *Middle East Law and Governance* 4 (1): 106–51.

Shamir, J., and K. Shikaki. 2010. *Palestinian and Israeli Public Opinion*. Bloomington and Indianapolis: Indiana University Press.

Shamir, R. 2000. *The Colonies of Law: Colonialism, Zionism and Law in Early Mandate Palestine*. Cambridge: Cambridge University Press.

——. 2002. "Nation-Building and Colonialism: The Case of Jewish Lawyers in Palestine." *International Journal of the Legal Profession* 8 (2): 109–30.

Shanzer, J. 2008. *Hamas vs. Fatah: The Struggle for Palestine*. London: Palgrave Macmillan.

Shapira, A. 1995. "Politics and Collective Memory: The Debate over the 'New Historians' in Israel." *History and Memory* 7 (1): 9–40.

Sharansky, I. 2008. "Colonialism or Something Else? A Comment on Rafael Reuveny's Analysis." *Independent Review* 13 (2): 289–92.

Shavit, A. 2004. "Survival of the Fittest? An Interview with Benny Morris." *Haaretz Friday Magazine*, 9 January.

Shavit, Y. 1990. "Segregation, Tracking, and the Educational Attainment of Minorities: Arabs and Oriental Jews in Israel." *American Sociological Review* 55 (1): 115–26.

Shaw, M. 2010. "Palestine in an International Historical Perspective on Genocide." *Holy Land Studies* 9 (1): 1–24.

Shehadeh, R. 1985. *Occupier's Law: Israel and the West Bank*. Washington, DC: Institute for Palestine Studies.

——. 2003. *When the Birds Stopped Singing: Life in Ramallah under Siege*. Hanover, NH: Steerforth.

Sheinin, Y. 2003. *Demography and Economics: New Demographic Trends and Their Economic Consequences*. December. Interdisciplinary Center Herzliya, Israel.

Sheinin, Y., and Y. Shagev. 2003. *The Economic Waste of the Demographic Structure*. Summary of task force prepared for a conference of the Interdisciplinary Centre Herzliya, Israel, December [Hebrew].

Sheizaf, N. 2012. "Occupation Comes Home: What Was a Military Surveillance Vehicle Doing in TLV Last Night?" *+972 Blog*, 1 July. http://972mag.com/occupation-comes-home-what-was-an-idf-surveillance-vehicle-doing-in-tlv-last-night/49842 (accessed 6 November 2012).

Sheleg, Y. 2004. "The Demographics Point to a Bi-national State." *Haaretz.com*, 27 June. http://www.haaretz.com/news/the-demographics-point-to-a-binational-state-1.123562 (accessed 10 January 2014).

Shenhav, Y. 2002. "The Phenomenology of Colonialism and the Politics of 'Difference': European Zionist Emissaries and Arab-Jews in Colonial Abadan." *Social Identities* 8 (4): 1–23.

——. 2012. *Beyond the Two-State Solution*. Cambridge: Polity.

——. 2013. "Beyond 'Instrumental Rationality': Lord Cromer and the Imperial Roots of Eichmann's Bureaucracy." *Journal of Genocide Research* 15 (4): 379–99.

Shenhav, Y., and Y. Berda. 2009. "The Colonial Foundations of the State of Exception: Juxtaposing the Israeli Occupation of the Palestinian Territories with Colonial Bureaucratic History." In A. Ophir, M. Givoni, and S. Hanafi, eds., *The Power of Inclusive Exclusion: Anatomy of Israeli Rule in the Occupied Palestinian Territories*, 337–74. New York: Zone.

Shenhav, Y., and N. Gabay. 2001. "Managing Political Conflicts: The Sociology of State Commissions of Inquiry." *Israel Studies* 6 (1): 126–56.

Shenhav, Y., and Y. Yona. 2008. *Racism in Israel*. Jerusalem and Tel Aviv: Van Leer Institute and Hakibbutz Hameuchad.

Sher, H. 2000. "Cyber War I?" *Jerusalem Report* 11 (15): 34–39.

Sherwell, T. 1996. "Palestinian Costume, the Intifada and the Gendering of Nationalist Discourse." *Journal of Gender Studies* 5 (3): 20–33.

Shlaim, A. 2009. "How Israel Brought Gaza to the Brink of Humanitarian Catastrophe." *Guardian*, 7 January. http://www.theguardian.com/world/2009/jan/07/gaza-israel-palestine (accessed 5 September 2014).

——. 2014. "'Man of Peace'? Ariel Sharon Was the Champion of Violent Solutions." *Guardian*, 13 January. http://www.theguardian.com/commentisfree/2014/jan/13/ariel-sharon-no-man-of-peace-israel (accessed 11 September 2014).

Shragai, N. 2001. "Ze'evi: IDF General, Proponent of 'Transfer.'" *Haaretz.com*, 17 October. http://www.haaretz.com/news/profile-ze-evi-idf-general-proponent-of-transfer-1.72123 (accessed 10 January 2014).

Shulman, D. 2014. "Palestine: The Hatred and the Hope." *New York Review of Books*, 2 August. http://www.nybooks.com/blogs/nyrblog/2014/aug/02/palestine-hatred-and-hope/?insrc=hpss (accessed 3 July 2014).

Schulz, H.L., and J. Hammer. 2003. *The Palestinian Diaspora: Formation of Identities and Politics of Homeland*. London: Routledge.

Silberstein, L. 1999. *The Post-Zionism Debates: Knowledge and Power in Israeli Culture*. London: Routledge.
———. 2002. "Problematizing Power: Israel's Post-Zionist Critics." *Palestine-Israel Journal* 9 (3): 97–107.
Silver, J. 2013. "Five Reasons to Say No to Israel's New Biometric Database." *Haaretz.com*, 10 July. http://www.haaretz.com/opinion/.premium-1.534927 (accessed 8 May 2014).
Sinclair, G., and C. Williams. 2007. "'Home and Away': The Cross-Fertilisation between 'Colonial' and 'British' Policing, 1921–85." *Journal of Imperial and Commonwealth History* 35 (2): 221–338.
Sirhan, B. 1975. "Palestinian Refugee Camp Life in Lebanon." *Journal of Palestine Studies* 4 (2): 91–107.
———. 2005. *Transformations of the Palestinian Family in the Diaspora: A Comparative Sociological Study*. Beirut: Institute for Palestine Studies [Arabic].
Sivan, Emmanuel. 2004. "Stop Giving Unwanted Advice to the World." *Haaretz.com*, 12 August. http://www.haaretz.com/print-edition/opinion/stop-giving-unwanted-advice-to-the-world-1.131310 (accessed 3 July 2014).
Sivan, Eyal. 1990. *Izkor, Slaves of Memory*. Documentary. http://eyalsivan.info/index.php?p=elements1&id=4#&panel1-5 (accessed 12 September 2013).
Sivan, Eyal, and A. Maurion, dirs. 2004. *I Love You All*. Documentary. ARCAPIX and Zero Film [German, French].
Skop, Y. 2013. "Israel Is More Jewish Than Democratic: New Civics Textbook Asserts." *Haaretz.com*, 27 September. http://www.haaretz.com/news/national/.premium-1.549258 (accessed 28 September 2013).
Smith, A. 1995. "Zionism and Diaspora Nationalism." *Israel Affairs* 2 (2): 1–19.
Smith, E. 2006. "Privacy in the USA." Background paper commissioned by the Globalization of Personal Data Project, Queen's University, Kingston, Ontario. http://www.queensu.ca/sociology/Surveillance/?q=node/78 (accessed 10 August 2009).
Smith, K. 2010. *Liberalism, Surveillance and Resistance: Indigenous Communities in Western Canada, 1877–1927*. Edmonton: Athabasca University Press.
Smith, R.J. 2011. "Graduated Incarceration: The Israeli Occupation in Subaltern Geopolitical Perspective." *Geoforum* 42 (3): 316–28.
Smooha, S. 2005. *Index of Arab-Jewish Relations in Israel 2004*. Haifa: University of Haifa.
———. 2009. "The Israeli Palestinian-Arab Vision of Transforming Israel into a Binational Democracy." *Constellations* 16 (3): 509–22.
———. 2010. *Arab-Jewish Relations in Israel: Alienation and Rapprochement*. Washington, DC: United States Institute for Peace.
———. 2012. *Still Playing by the Rules: Index of Arab-Jewish Relations in Israel 2012: Findings and Conclusions*. Haifa and Jerusalem: University of Haifa and Israel Democracy Institute.
Sofer, A. and E. Bystrov. 2013. *Israel: Demography 2013–2034: Challenges and Chances*. Haifa: University of Haifa.
Somfalvi, A. 2008. "Biometric Database to Be Formed in Israel." *ynetnews.com*, 3 August. http://www.ynetnews.com/articles/0,7340,L-3577046,00.html (accessed 8 August 2008).
Sommer, A. 2012. "Laptop Warriors Engage in Israel-Gaza Twitter Battles." *Haaretz.com*, 15 November. http://www.haaretz.com/blogs/routine-emergencies/laptop-warriors-engage-in-israel-gaza-twitter-battles.premium-1.478083 (accessed 16 November 2012).
Sorek, T. 2011. "The Changing Pattern of Disciplining Palestinian National Memory in Israel." In E. Zureik, D. Lyon, and Y. Abu-Laban, eds., *Surveillance and Control in Israel/Palestine: Population, Territory and Power*, 113–30. London: Routledge.
Spurr, D. 1993. *The Rhetoric of Empire: Colonial Discourse in Journalism, Travel Writing and Imperial Administration*. Durham, NC: Duke University Press.

Stangneth, B. 2014. *Eichmann before Jerusalem: The Unexamined Life of a Mass Murderer*. New York: Alfred A. Knopf.
Sternhell, Z. 2008. "Colonial Zionism." *Haaretz.com*, 17 October. http://www.haaretz.com/print-edition/opinion/colonial-zionism-1.255642 (accessed 13 May 2014).
———. 2010. "In Defence of Liberal Zionism." *New Left Review* 62: 99–114.
———. 2014. "Unconditional Palestinian Surrender." *Haaretz.com*, 18 April. http://www.haaretz.com/opinion/.premium-1.586127 (accessed 21 April 2014).
Stevens, A. 2011. "Surveillance Policies, Practices and Technologies in Israel and the Occupied Palestinian Territories: Assessing the Security State." November. www.ssc-queens.org/sites/default/files/2011-11-Stevens-WPIV_0.pdf (accessed 21 May 2015).
Stoler, A.L. 1995. *Race and the Education of Desire: Foucault's History of Sexuality and the Colonial Order of Things*. Durham, NC, and London: Duke University Press.
———. 2010a. "By Colonial Design." Statement issued 10 September. http://pulsemedia.org/2010/09/17/eminent-scholar-ann-stoler-endorses-boycott-of-israel (accessed 23 July 2013).
———. 2010b. *Carnal Knowledge and Imperial Power: Race and the Intimate in Colonial Rule*. Berkeley: University of California Press.
Stoler-Liss, S. 2003. "'Mothers Birth the Nation': The Social Construction of Zionist Motherhood in Wartime in Israeli Parents' Manuals." *Nashim: A Journal of Jewish Women's Studies and Gender Issues* 6: 104–18.
Strawson, J. 2002. "Reflections on Edward Said and the Legal Narratives of Palestine: Israeli Settlements and Palestinian Self-Determination." *Penn State International Law Review* 20 (2): 363–84.
Suleiman, J. 1997. "Palestinians in Lebanon and the Role of Non-governmental Organizations." *Journal of Refugee Studies* 10 (3): 397–410.
———. 2010. "Trapped Refugees: The Case of the Palestinians in Lebanon." In *No Refuge: Palestinians in Lebanon*, 7–18. Oxford: Refugee Studies Centre, University of Oxford.
Sullivan, D.J. 1996. "NGOs in Palestine: Agents of Development and Foundation of Civil Society." *Journal of Palestine Studies* 25 (3): 29–100.
Sultany, N. 2003. *Citizens without Citizenship*. Haifa: Mada al-Carmel.
Swedenburg, T. 1990. "The Palestinian Peasant as a National Signifier." *Anthropological Quarterly* 63 (1): 18–30.
———. 1995. *Memories of Revolt: The 1936–1939 Rebellion and the Palestinian National Past*. Minneapolis and London: University of Minnesota Press.
Takkenberg, L. 1998. *The Status of Palestinian Refugees in International Law*. Oxford and New York: Clarendon.
Tamari, S. 1994. "Problems of Social Science Research in Palestine: An Overview." *Current Sociology* 42 (2): 67–86.
———. 1996. *Palestinian Refugee Negotiations: From Madrid to Oslo II*. Washington, DC: Institute for Palestine Studies.
———. 2009. *Mountain against the Sea: Essays on Palestinian Society and Culture*. Berkeley: University of California Press.
Tamimi, A. 2007. *Hamas: Unwritten Chapters*. London: Hurst.
Tami Steinmetz Center for Peace Research, Tel Aviv University. N.d. http://peace.tau.ac.il (accessed 11 April 2015).
———. 2003. *The Peace Index (December)*. http://www.tau.ac.il/peace (accessed 3 July 2014).
Tawil-Souri, H. 2011. "Orange, Green, and Blue: Colour-Coded Paperwork for Palestinian Population Control." In E. Zureik, D. Lyon, and Y. Abu-Laban, eds., *Surveillance and Control in Israel/Palestine: Population, Territory and Power*, 219–29. London: Routledge.

——. 2012a. "Digital Occupation: The High-Tech Enclosure of Gaza." *Journal of Palestine Studies* 41 (2): 27–43.

——. 2012b. "Mapping Israel/Palestine." *Political Geography* 30 (8): 57–60.

——. 2012c. "Uneven Borders, Coloured (Im)mobilities: ID Cards in Palestine/Israel." *Geopolitics* 17 (1): 153–76.

——. 2013a. "The Hi-Tech Occupation of Palestine." In P. Howard and M. Hussain, eds., *State Power and Information Infrastructure*, 57–68. Surrey, UK: Ashgate.

——. 2013b. "Networking Palestine, Creating and Limiting Media and Technology Flows: Television and Telecommunications since 1993." In P. Bauck and M. Moghayyer, eds., *The Oslo Accords 1993–2013: Twenty Years with What Results?* 217–30. London: AUC Press and I.B. Tauris.

Taylor, A. 2014. "Israel Hopes Phone Calls to Palestinians Will Save Lives: It Ends Up Looking Orwellian." *Washington Post*, 17 July. http://www.washingtonpost.com/blogs/worldviews/wp/2014/07/17/israel-hopes-phone-calls-to-palestinians-will-save-lives-it-ends-up-looking-orwellian (accessed 18 October 2014).

Thomas, M. 2008. *Empires of Intelligence: Security and Colonial Disorder after 1914.* Berkeley: University of California Press.

Thompson, J. 1989. "The Theory of Structuration." In D. Held and J. Thompson, eds., *Social Theory and Modern Societies: Anthony Giddens and His Critics*, 56–76. Cambridge: Cambridge University Press.

Thompson, S. 2002. "Returning the Gaze: Culture and the Politics of Surveillance in Ireland." *International Journal of English Studies* 2 (2): 95–107.

Tibawi, A.L. 1956. *Arab Education in Mandatory Palestine: A Study of Three Decades of British Administration.* London: Luzac.

Tilley, V. 2005. *The One-State Solution: A Breakthrough for Peace in the Israeli-Palestinian Deadlock.* Ann Arbor MI: University of Michigan Press.

——. 2009. "The One-State Solution: The Future of Israel and Palestine." *London Review of Books* 25 (21): 13–16.

Toft, M. 2002. "Differential Demographic Growth in Multinational States: Israel's Two-Front War." *Journal of International Affairs* 56 (1): 71–94.

Tönnies, F. 1963. *Community and Civil Society.* New York: Harper and Row.

Torpey, J. 1998. "Coming and Going: On the State of Monopolization of the Legitimate 'Means of Movement.'" *Sociological Theory* 16 (3): 239–59.

Traubmann, T. 2004. "Don't Have Children If They Won't Be Healthy." *Haaretz.com*, 16 June. http://www.haaretz.com/do-not-have-children-if-they-won-t-be-healthy-1.124913 (accessed 5 June 2011).

Turner, B.S. 1976-77. "Avineri's View of Marx's Theory of Colonialism: Israel." *Science and Society* 40 (4): 385–409.

——. 1984. *Capitalism and Class in the Middle East: Theories of Social Change and Economic Development.* Portsmouth, NH, and London: Heinemann Educational Books and Humanities Press.

United Nations. 2002. "Report of Secretary-General on Recent Events in Jenin, Other Palestinian Cities." Press release, 1 August. http://www.un.org/News/Press/docs/2002/SG2077.doc.htm (accessed 3 September 2014).

——. 2013. *Report of the United Nations High Commissioner for Human Rights on the Implementation of Human Rights Council Resolutions S-9/1 and S-12/1.* 4 July. http://ap.ohchr.org/documents/alldocs.aspx?doc_id=22620 (accessed 3 April 2015).

UNCTAD (United Nations Conference on Trade and Development). 2012. "Conditions Worsening for Palestinian People, UNCTAD Report Warns." 4 September. http://unctad.org/en/pages/newsdetails.aspx?OriginalVersionID=244 (accessed 3 April 2015).

UNESCO (United Nations Educational, Scientific, and Cultural Organization). 1980. *Palestine Open University: Feasibility Study*. Paris: UNESCO.
UNHRC (United Nations Human Rights Council). 2008. *Annual Report*. http://domino.un.org/UNISPAL.NSF/9a798adbf322aff38525617b006d88d7/fd246b9c33 182c72852573ed005001d2!OpenDocument (accessed 1 February 2008, now defunct).
UNRWA (United Nations Relief and Works Agency). N.d. a. http://www.unrwa.org (accessed 11 April 2015).
——. N.d. b. "Syria Crisis." http://www.unrwa.org/syria-crisis (accessed 20 September 2014).
——. N.d. c. "Where We Work." http://www.unrwa.org/where-we-work (accessed 24 September 2014).
——. 2008. *Joint Rapid Food Security Survey in the Occupied Palestinian Territory*. May. http://unispal.un.org/pdfs/RapidAssessmentReport_May08.pdf (accessed 19 May 2015).
UNSCO (United Nations Office of the Special Coordinator for the Middle East Peace Process). N.d. "Special Reports." http://www.unsco.org/sr.asp (accessed 11 April 2015).
——. 2011. *Socio-Economic Report*. April. http://unispal.un.org/UNISPAL.NSF/0/3B2F13 E455C73F00852578B7005D3045 (accessed 27 March 2014).
Urry, J. 2000. *Sociology beyond Societies: Mobilities for the Twenty-First Century*. London and New York: Routledge.
Usher, G. 1999. "Crossing the Borders." *Al-Ahram* [Internet weekly English edition of the Arabic Egyptian daily], 30 September to 6 October. http://weekly.ahram.org.eg/1999/449/re2.htm (accessed 6 January 2015).
Van Oord, L. 2008. "The Making of Primitive Palestine: Intellectual Origins of the Palestine-Israel Conflict." *History and Anthropology* 19 (3): 209–28.
——. 2011 "Face Lifting Palestine: Early Western Accounts of the Palestinian Refugee Problem." History and Anthropology 22 (1): 19–35.
Venn, C. 2009. "Neoliberal Political Economy, Biopolitics and Colonialism: A Transcolonial Genealogy of Inequality." *Theory, Culture and Society* 26 (6): 206–33.
Veracini, L. 2006. *Israel and Settler Society*. Ann Arbor, MI, and London: Pluto.
Vilnai, O. 2014. "Arab Teacher Strip-Searched before Flying with Her Jewish Students." *Haaretz.com*, 26 February. http://www.haaretz.com/news/national/.premium-1.576569 (accessed 2 March 2014).
Waever, O. 1995. "Securitization and Desecuritization." In R. Lipschutz, ed., *On Security*, 46–86. New York: Columbia University Press.
Wagner, M. 2007. "Eliyahu Advocates Carpet Bombing in Gaza." *Jerusalem Post*, 30 May. http://www.jpost.com/Israel/Eliyahu-advocates-carpet-bombing-Gaza (accessed 6 October 2014).
Wahbeh, N. 2003. "Teaching and Learning Science in Palestine: Dealing with the New Palestinian Science Curriculum." *Mediterranean Journal of Educational Studies* 8 (1): 135–59.
Wallach, Y. 2011. "Trapped in Mirror-Images: The Rhetoric of Maps in Israel/Palestine." *Political Geography* 30 (7): 358–69.
Warschauer, M. 2002. "Reconceptualizing the Digital Divide." *First Monday* 7 (7). http://ojphi.org/ojs/index.php/fm/article/view/967/888 (accessed 4 April 2015).
——. 2006. "Assessing the Human and Social Capital Dimensions of ICT in Palestine: A Conceptual and Methodological Framework." In E. Zureik, ed., *Information Society in Palestine: The Human Capital Dimension*. Report. Ottawa: International Development Research Centre.
Waugh, L. 2008. "Diary: Living in Gaza." *London Review of Books* 30 (11): 35. http://www.lrb.co.uk/v30/n11/waug01_.html (accessed 5 June 2008).
Webb, M. 2007. *Illusions of Security: Global Surveillance and Democracy in the Post-9/11 World*. San Francisco: City Lights.

Weiler-Polak, D. 2009. "Civil Rights Report Details Racism in Israel in All Its Many Shades." *Haaretz.com*, 6 December. http://www.haaretz.com/print-edition/news/civil-rights-report-details-racism-in-israel-in-all-its-many-shades-1.2730 (accessed 19 December 2009).

Weizman, E. 2002. "Introduction to the Politics of Verticality." *openDemocracy*, 24 April. https://www.opendemocracy.net/ecology-politicsverticality/article_801.jsp (accessed 12 April 2015).

———. 2005. "Walking through Walls: Soldiers as Architects in the Israeli/Palestinian Conflict." Lecture presented at the symposium "Arxipelago of Exception: Sovereignties of Extraterritoriality," Centre de Cultura Contemporània de Barcelona (CCCB), 10–11 November. http://www.publicspace.org/en/text-library/eng/b018-walking-through-walls-soldiers-as-architects-in-the-israeli-palestinian-conflict (accessed 15 October 2011).

———. 2006. "Lethal Theory." *LOG Magazine* 7: 53–77.

———. 2007. *Hollow Land: Israel's Architecture of Occupation*. London and New York: Verso.

———. 2011. *The Least of all Possible Evils: Humanitarian Violence from Arendt to Gaza*. London and New York: Verso.

Weizman, E., and K. Kastrissianakis. 2007. "Beyond Colonialism: Israeli/Palestinian Space." Interview. *Re-public*, 27 September. http://www.nettime.org/Lists-Archives/nettime-l-0710/msg00001.html (accessed 27 January 2012).

Whitaker, B. 2004. "Assassination Method: Surveillance Drone and a Hellfire Missile." *Guardian*, 23 March. http://www.theguardian.com/world/2004/mar/23/israel6 (accessed 4 April 2015).

———. 2011. "Behavioural Profiling in Israeli Aviation Security as a Tool for Social Control." In E. Zureik, D. Lyon, and Y. Abu-Laban, eds., *Surveillance and Control in Israel/Palestine: Population, Territory and Power*, 371–85. London: Routledge.

Wick, L. 2011. "The Practice of Waiting under Closure in Palestine." *City and Society* 23 (S1): 24–44.

Wilkins, K.G. 2004. "The Civil Intifada: The Process and Politics of the Palestinian Census." *Development and Change* 33 (5): 891–908.

Williams, M. 2003. "Words, Images, Enemies: Securitization and International Politics." *International Studies Quarterly* 47 (4): 511–31.

Williams, R. 1976. *Keywords: A Vocabulary of Culture and Society*. London: Collins.

Willis, P. 2000. *The Ethnographic Imagination*. Cambridge: Polity.

Wilson, S. 2013. "Israel's New Biometric Database Would Be Most Expansive in the Western World." *Jewish Journal*, 26 June. http://www.jewishjournal.com/hella_tel_aviv/item/israels_new_biometric_database_would_be_most_expansive_in_western_world (accessed 22 November 2013).

Winer, S. 2012. "Emigration Hits Lowest Mark in 40 Years." *Times of Israel*, 7 August. http://www.timesofisrael.com/emigration-at-its-lowest-for-forty-years (accessed 31 August 2014).

Wolfe, P. 2006. "Settler Colonialism and the Elimination of the Native." *Journal of Genocide Research* 8 (4): 388–409.

———. 2007. "Palestine, Project Europe and the (Un-)making of the New Jew." In N. Curthoys and D. Ganguly, eds., *Edward Said: The Legacy of a Public Intellectual*, 313–49. Melbourne: University of Melbourne Press.

———. 2008. "Structure and Event: Settler Colonialism, Time and the Question of Genocide." In A.D. Moses, ed. *Empire, Colony, Genocide: Conquest, Occupation, and Subaltern Resistance in World History*, 102–32. New York and Oxford: Berghahn.

———. 2011. "Not Another Racism: Zionism, a Logic of Elimination." Keynote speech at the School of Oriental and African Studies (SOAS) Conference, 5–6 March. https://vimeo.com/23615746 (accessed 4 April 2015).

———. 2012. "Purchase by Other Means: The Palestine Nakba and Zionism's Conquest of Economics." *Settler Colonial Studies* 2 (1): 133–37.

Wolfsfeld, G., E. Avraham, and I. Aburaiya. 2000. "When Prophesy Always Fails: Israeli Press Coverage of the Arab Minority's Land Day Protests." *Political Communication* 17 (2): 115–31.

World Bank. 2013. "GNI Per Capita." http://data.worldbank.org/indicator/NY.GNP.PCAP.CD (accessed 7 July 2014).

World Tribune. 2008. "Israel Activates Unmanned Video-Directed Machine Gun Stations on Gaza Borders." 3 April. http://www.worldtribune.com/worldtribune/WTARC/2008/me_israel0017_04_03.asp (accessed 4 April 2015).

Wrong, D. 1994. *The Problem of Order: What Unites and Divides Societies*. Cambridge, MA, and London: Harvard University Press.

Yacobi, H. 2004a. *Constructing a Sense of Place: Architecture and Zionist Discourse*. Aldershot, UK, and Burlington, VT: Ashgate.

———. 2004b. "In-Between Surveillance and Spatial Protest: The Production of Space of the 'Mixed City' of Lod." *Surveillance and Society* 2 (1): 55–77. http://www.surveillance-and-society.org/articles2(1)/lod.pdf (accessed 4 April 2015).

———. 2008. "Separate and Unequal." *Haaretz.com*, 17 October. http://www.haaretz.com/print-edition/opinion/separate-and-unequal-1.255647 (accessed 8 August 2013).

Yahav, G. 2013. "An Intifada Substitute in the Heart of Tel Aviv." *Haaretz.com*, 1 July. http://www.haaretz.com/culture/arts-leisure/.premium-1.532973 (accessed 12 August 2012).

Yahia-Younis, T. 2010. "Social and Political Viewpoints and Attitudes of Arab-Palestinian Youth in Israel." In R. Hexel and R. Nathanson, eds., *All of the Above: Identity Paradoxes of Young People in Israel*, 245–81. Herzliya: Friedrich-Ebert-Stiftung and the Macro Center for Political Economics. http://www.macro.org.il/lib/4809349.pdf (accessed 4 April 2015).

Yaish, M. 2001. "Class Structure in a Deeply Divided Society: Class and Ethnic Inequality in Israel, 1974–1991." *British Journal of Sociology* 52 (2): 409–39.

Yehoshua, A. 2002. "Eleven Degrees of Separation." *Haaretz.com*, 8 February. http://www.haaretzdaily.com (accessed 4 January 2014).

Yiftachel, O. 1998. "The Internal Frontier: Territorial Control and Ethnic Relations in Israel." In O. Yiftachel and A. Meir, eds., *Ethnic Frontiers and Peripheries: Landscapes of Development and Inequality in Israel*, 40–67. Boulder, CO: Westview.

———. 2000. "'Ethnocracy' and Its Discontents: Minorities, Protests, and the Israeli Polity." *Critical Inquiry* 26 (4): 725–36.

———. 2006. *Ethnocracy: Land and Identity Politics in Israel/Palestine*. Philadelphia: University of Pennsylvania Press.

———. 2008. "Epilogue: Studying Naqab/Negev Bedouins – Toward a Colonial Paradigm?" *HAGAR: Studies in Culture, Polity and Identities* 8 (2): 83–108.

Ynet. 2006. "BBC Poll: World against Torture, Israel in Favour." *ynetnews.com*, 19 October. http://www.ynetnews.com/articles/0,7340,L-3316939,00.html (accessed 14 March 2015).

Yoaz, Y. 2007a. "Court in Session in the Wake of Big Brother." *Haaretz.com*, 6 December. http://www.haaretz.com/print-edition/features/court-in-session-in-the-wake-of-big-brother-1.234686 (accessed 26 November 2013).

———. 2007b. "A Major Invasion of Privacy." *Haaretz.com*, 19 December. http://www.haaretz.com/print-edition/opinion/a-major-invasion-of-privacy-1.235536 (accessed 26 October 2013).

———. 2007c. "Secret Clause Lets Shin Bet Get Data from Cell Phone Firms." *Haaretz.com*, 9 January. http://www.haaretz.com/hasen/spages/906489.html (accessed 12 January 2010).

Young, J. 2012. "Otherwise Occupied: An Analysis of the Causes and Consequences of Zionist Carceral Practice." MA thesis, Massey University, New Zealand.

Young, R.J.C. 1995. "Foucault on Race and Colonialism." *New Formations* 25: 57–65. Pages 1–18 at http://robertjcyoung.com/Foucault.pdf (accessed 6 May 2015).

Youssef, M. 2007. "Peace Material: Giorgio Agamben and the Israeli Palestinian Peace Accords." *New Formations* 62: 106–22.

Zacharia, C. 1996. "Power in Numbers: A Call for a Census of the Palestinian People." *Arab Studies Quarterly* 18 (3): 37–52.

Zahlan, A.B. 1980. *Science and Science Policy in the Arab World*. New York: St. Martin's.

———. 1997. *The Reconstruction of Palestine: Issues, Options, Policies and Strategies*. New York: Kegan Paul.

Zarchin, T. 2009. "Secret Police Unit Monitoring Israeli Citizens." *Haaretz.com*, 13 October. http://www.haaretz.com/print-edition/news/secret (accessed 27 November 2013).

———. 2012. "High Court: Israel's Biometric Database Is 'Extreme and Harmful.'" *Haaretz.com*, 24 June. http://www.haaretz.com/news/national/high-court-israel-s-biometric-database-is-extreme-and-harmful-1.453155 (accessed 22 November 2013).

Zartman, I.W., ed. 1980. *Elites in the Middle East*. New York: Praeger.

Zelikovich, Y. 2010. "Poll: 46% of High-Schoolers Don't Want Equality for Arabs." *ynetnews.com*, 3 November. http://www.ynetnews.com/articles/0,7340,L-3861161,00.html (accessed 3 November 2010).

Zimmerman, B., and R. Seid. 2004. *Arab Population in the West Bank and Gaza: The Million and a Half Person Gap*. Washington, DC: American Enterprise Institute.

Zochrot. N.d. http://www.zochrot.org (accessed 11 April 2015).

Zreik, R. 2011. "Why the Jewish State Now?" *Journal of Palestine Studies* 11 (3): 23–37.

———. 2014. "Israel's Desire for Normalcy Is Trumped by Arrogance." *Haaretz.com*, 14 September. http://www.haaretz.com/opinion/.premium-1.615569 (accessed 18 September 2014).

Zureik, E. 1979. *The Palestinians in Israel: A Study in Internal Colonialism*. London: Routledge and Kegan Paul.

———. 1981. "Theoretical Considerations for a Sociological Study of the Arab State." *Arab Studies Quarterly* 3 (3): 229–57.

———. 1988. "Crime, Justice and Underdevelopment: The Palestinians under Israeli Control." *International Journal of Middle East Studies* 20 (4): 411–42.

———. 1992. *Facts and Figures about the Palestinians (Information Paper No. 1)*. Washington, DC: Centre for Policy Analysis on Palestine.

———. 1993. "Review of the Fafo Report *Palestinian Society in Gaza, West Bank and Arab Jerusalem: A Survey of Living Conditions*." *Journal of Refugee Studies* 6 (4): 418–25.

———. 1996. *Palestinian Refugees and the Peace Process*. Washington, DC: Institute for Palestine Studies.

———. 2000. *Palestinian Refugees: An Annotated Bibliography Based on Arabic, English, French and Hebrew Sources, 1995–1999*. Report. Ottawa: International Development Research Centre.

———. 2001. "Constructing Palestine through Surveillance Practices." *British Journal of Middle Eastern Studies* 28 (2): 205–27.

———. 2003. "Demography and Transfer: Israel's Road to Nowhere." *Third World Quarterly* 24 (4): 619–30.

———, ed. 2006. *Information Society in Palestine: The Human Capital Dimension*. Report. Ottawa: International Development Research Centre.

Zureik, E., J. Graff, and F. Ohan. 1990-91. "Two Years of the Intifada: A Statistical Profile of Palestinian Victims." *Third World Quarterly* 12 (3–4): 97–123.

Zureik, E., and K. Hindle. 2004. "Governance, Security and Technology. The Case of Biometrics." *Studies in Political Economy* 73: 113–37.

Zureik, E., D. Lyon, and Y. Abu-Laban, eds. 2011. *Surveillance and Control in Israel/Palestine: Population, Territory and Power*. London: Routledge.

Zureik, E., and A. Mazawi. 2000. "Narratives of Exile and Descriptions of Place: The Experience of Palestinian Refugees in Israeli and Palestinian Discourse." Unpublished report, Queen's University.

Zureik, E., F. Moughrabi, and V. Sacco. 1993. "Perception of Legal Inequality in Deeply Divided Societies: The Case of Israel." *International Journal of Middle East Studies* 25 (3): 423–42.

Zureik, E., and A. Vitullo. 1992. *Targeting to Kill: Israel's Undercover Units*. Jerusalem and Washington, DC: Palestine Human Rights Center and Center for Policy Analysis on Palestine.

Zvika, D. 1986. *The "Arabists" of the Palmach*. Tel Aviv: Hakibutz Hameuchad [Hebrew].

INDEX

Abdo, Nahla 19
Abourahme, Nasser 23, 128
Abowd, Thomas 90n.3
absenteeism, and land ownership 74–5
Abu El-Haj, Nadia 33, 55–6, 142, 163
Abu Ghraib prison 86–7, 161
Abujidi, Nurhan 115, 126
Abu-Laban, Yasmeen and Bakan, Abigail 95
Abu-Lughod, Ibrahim 27
Abu-Lughod, Janet 22
Abu-Lughod, Lila and Sa'di, Ahmad 111
Abu-Nimer, Mohammed 38
Abu-Sitta, Salman 23
Abu-Zahra, Nadia 19, 127
Abu-Zahra, Nadia and Kay, Adah 127
Acceptance Committee Law 77, 93n.19
Adalah 117, 123, 124
Admissions Committee 93n.20, 123
advocacy research 23
Agamben, George 5, 6, 14, 85, 86, 88, 108, 114, 168–9
agency 31, 32, 40, 42, 48
Al-Am'ari refugee camp 199
Al-Aqsa Intifada *see* Intifada
Al-Aqsa Mosque 171
Alatout, Samer 34, 92n.18
Al-Awda 23
Al-'Azariyya 197–8
Al-Haq 23
alienation, of Arabs 156

All That Remains 15
aloofness 120
Altneuland 61, 65
American National Security Agency 107
Amnesty International 175
Anderson, Benedict 5, 40–1, 97
Anderson, Jon 180
Anthias, Floya 45–6
Anti-Oedipus: Capitalism and Schizophrenia 67
anti-Semitism 114, 141
Aouragh, Miriyam 205
apartheid 50, 57, 70, 77–8, 79
Appadurai, Arjun 42, 43, 100, 137
Arab Association for Human Rights (Mossawa) 123
Arab-Jewish relations 156, 157
Arab Mind, The 94n.21, 161
Arab Revolt 1936–39 63, 99
Arab Spring 21, 181, 206
Arad, Uzi 149
Arafat, Yasser 40, 88
Araj, Bader 82, 172
Arendt, Hannah 14, 54, 120, 165, 168
Ariel, Arik 145, 146
Arnaiz-Villena, Antonio 143
Asad, Talal 100
Ashkenazi Jews 142
assassinations *see also* killings; massacres: by drones 132; extrajudicial *see* killings; by

Israel 116, 117; by Jews on Jews 118; targeted 133n.6, 171, 177; by United States 126
Association of Civil Rights in Israel (ACRI) 115, 123, 129, 154
attitudes, Israeli Jews toward Arabs 155, 159
Avineri, Shlomo 61–2, 79, 91n.10
Avruch, Kevin 37
Avruch, Kevin and Black, Peter 37

BADIL 23
Baev, Pavel and Burgess, J. Peter 84
Balata refugee camp 202–3
Balfour Declaration 9, 34, 59, 63, 65, 92n.18, 144
Balibar, Etienne 4, 54
Balzacq, Thierry 83–4
Barakat, Halim 22
Barak, Ehud 88, 167
bare life: of Palestinians 86, 114; of refugees 14, 46, 88, 168, 169
Baron de Rothschild 59
Batniji, Rajaie 109
Baudrillard, Jean 106
Bauman, Zygmunt xiii, 91n.13, 121
Bayly, C.A. 96
Beck, Ulrich 43
Before Their Diaspora 15
Begin, Menachem 88
Beinin, Joel 176
Beit-Hallahmi, Benjamin 70
Ben-Gurion, David 23, 61, 73, 76, 91n.8, 139, 143, 144–5
Ben-Porath, Yoram 24
Ben-Rafael, Eliezer 90n.1
Benvenisti, Meron 91n.10, 159
Ben-Ze'ev, Efrat 25, 104
Berda, Yael 103, 120, 121
Bethlehem 195–6
Bialik, Chaim 76
Big Brother Law 132
biometrics 110, 128–30, 133n.2
bionationalism 144
biopolitics: biometrics as new 128–30; and colonialism 3–4, 5, 6, 121, 135–6; to eugenics 136–43; population balance as 143–58; and racism 4; and surveillance 101, 134n.11; and violence 138; of the weak 136; and Zionism 89
biopower 4, 169

Birthing the Nation: Strategies of Palestinian Women in Israel 136
Birth of the Palestinian Refugee Problem, 1947–1949, The 24
birth rates 149, 153, 154 *see also* demography
Bishara, Azmi 168
Bitter Harvest: Palestine 22
Blatman, Daniel 77
Blau, Uri and Feldman, Yotam 164
Bloom, Etan 140–1
bombing(s): Gaza 162, 175, 178n.1, 206, 209–10; Lebanon 210, 211; refugee camps 162; suicide 13–14, 82, 167–8, 171–2
boomerang effect: colonialism 170; surveillance 98, 130–2
Bourdieu, Pierre 45
Bowman, Glenn 58, 99
Boycott and Divestment Campaign 2–3
Brand, Laurie 25
Britain 80; colonial tools of 98; counterinsurgency measures 99; and India 96, 97, 98, 100, 101; and Israeli army 104; social engineering 136–7; support for Zionism 59, 63, 91n.9, 104
British Emergency Regulations in Palestine 127
British Mandate 138 *see also* Mandate Palestine
Brit-Shalom 65
Brown, Allison 26, 127
Brown, Wendy 3
Brynen, Rex 26
B'Tselem 127, 171, 172, 174–5, 177, 207
bureaucracy, colonial and surveillance 118–22
Burton, John 36–7
Burton, John and Sandole, Dennis 36
Bush, George W. 126
Butler, Judith 210
Buzan, Barry 83
Bystrov, Evgenia 147

calibrated human suffering 162–7
Callon, Michel 33
Canada, surveillance in 103, 109
capital, inflow into Israel 62
carceral practices, Zionist 99, 163–4 *see also* prisons

caste system 101
casualties, of Israeli operations 170–6
categorisation: of Palestinian population 112; as surveillance 97–103
cause lawyering 39, 47
cell phone services 203–4
censuses: and present absentees 35; purpose of 127, 137; and right of return 101–2; and state legitimacy 30; as surveillance 97, 100, 101–2
checkpoints 97, 111, 115, 116, 119, 126, 127, 128
children: killings of 171, 174, 175, 176; Yemenite 142–3
Chowers, Eyal 65, 66, 68, 76
Churchill, Winston 213
Citizenship and Entry Law 93n.20, 124
Citizenship Law 77, 93n.19–20, 123
citizenship loyalty bill 153–4
citizenship rights 90n.2, 101, 210
Civilian Occupation: The Politics of Israeli Architecture, A 124
civil rights 78, 123
class formation, Israel's 62
classification: of Jews 141; of populations 98, 100–1
close settlement 74
Clough, Patricia and Willse, Craig 4
co-agency 48
co-existence 38
Cohen, Hillel 25, 81, 118, 119
Cohen, Stanley 32, 39
Cohn, Bernard 97, 101
Cole, Simon 98
collaborators 116, 117, 118, 119, 211
collateral damage 6, 132, 171, 177
Collings, Deirdre 37–8
colonial bureaucracy, and surveillance 118–22
colonial discourse 74
colonialism: as an analytic concept 27–8; and apartheid 50; and biopolitics 3–4, 5, 6, 121, 135–6; boomerang effect 170; and colonisation 50, 51–2; contours of 49–53; and democracy 57–8, 60, 90n.3; dual-colonialism 54; European 3, 62; internal colonialism 52; nature of 3; non-formal 63; and racism 5, 213; settler colonialism *see* settler colonialism; and space 57, 97; and space/territory 57; and surveillance 28, 57, 95, 96–109; and Zionism 49, 53–4, 56, 64, 69–70, 71–3, 81, 89, 92n.17
colonial knowledge 96, 97
colonial law 6, 59–60
colonial occupation, late-modern 125
colonial power 5, 103–6
colonial present 3
colonial regimes, and identification systems 6
colonies of occupation/settlement 50–1
colonisation: and colonialism 50, 51–2; of the mind 111, 126; Zionist 58–9, 90n.1
colonised population, indifference to/ neglect of 56–7
Colonising Egypt 98
Communal Societies Law 93n.20, 123
communication: electronic 42; and electronic networking 21 *see also* networking; global and social reflexivity 42; and globalisation 41; and Internet use 181
Communication Data Law 130
communication technology, and agency 40
communicative action 84
Communist Party 118
communities: in themselves/for themselves 42; transnational 45
computer and Internet usage, Palestinian 41, 207–8
computer networking, and refugee communities 47–8
computer networks: as social capital 40; worldwide 41
computer ownership, Palestine 186, 187
conflict resolution 14, 36–7
constructivist analysis 33–5, 47
control: dialectic of 32; group control model 2; and identity cards 111; of the Internet 21; Israeli over Palestinians 57; of mobility 6, 116; political 112; population 98; of resources 56, 92–3n.18; social 19; and surveillance 21, 28; systems of 11; of time 115
Coordinator of Government Activities in the Territories (COGAT) 162, 164, 165, 166
Copenhagen School 83, 84
counterinsurgency measures, Mandate Palestine 99
countermapping initiatives 104, 105

Courbage, Y. 15
criminalisation: of Palestinians 112; of refugees 127
criminal justice system, Israeli 87
culturalism 44
cultural studies 12
culture: Arab 94n.21; cyberculture 205–6; of denial 39; fascist in Israel 79; of fear 108; and group identity 44; and ICT 181–2; national and conflict resolution 37; stereotypes of Arab 82
cumulative dispossession 121
cyberculture, of refugees 205–6
cyberwar 207

Darwish, Mahmoud 110
Davis, Mike 108
Davis, Rochelle 105
Davis, Uri 70
Dayan, Moshe 146
Defense for Children International Palestine 171
dehumanisation 86–9, 178n.1
delegitimisation 78
Deleuze, Gilles 67–8
Deleuze, Gilles and Guattari, Félix 67
DellaPergola, Sergio 148–9, 158
democracy, and colonialism 57–8, 60, 90n.3
democratisation, and ICT 181
demography: Arab-Jewish population 79, 152, 159–60; birth rates 149, 153, 154; of Israel 147–8; and modernisation 147–52; of Palestinian refugees 22; of Palestinians 9–10, 12–13; and population management 136, 137; and Zionism 144–7
Demos, T.J. 169
denationalisation, of Palestinians 10
desire for land 67–8
deterritorialised people 42–3
detraditionalisation 42
Dhahiyat Al-Bareed 197–8
dialectic of control 32
diaspora 45–6, 47, 53, 181
difference, and group identity/mobilisation 44
digital divide 179, 181, 182–3
digital occupation, of Palestinian territories 208
digital siege, by Israel 206

dignity, violations of 109
disciplining: of memory 111–15; of Palestinian population 28, 113; of populations 30
discourse: colonial 74; elite 30; nationalist 105–6; Orientalist 95, 96; political 80; population 136, 144–7; and power 73–89; scientific 33, 34, 92n.18; securitisation 83
discrimination: against Arab population 148; and identification systems 6; legal 122–4, 130; against Palestinians 78, 79, 81
dispossession: cumulative 121; of indigenous populations 3, 5, 51, 70, 100, 212; of Palestinians 58–9, 64, 71, 73–4, 81, 86, 104
divide and rule 120
Dodd, Peter 22
dominance, surveillance as 109
double hermeneutic 100
drones 6, 132, 134n.11
dual-colonialism 54
Duffield, Mark 57–8

Eban, Abba 55
economic development, Arab/Jewish sectors 63–4
economic studies 15–16
economy, of Gaza 167
education, of Jewish children 106
education studies 18
Efrat, Moshe 24
Egypt, Palestinian refugees in 10, 23
Ehrlich, Avishai 69
Eitan, Raphael 178n.1
El-Abed, Oroub 23
El-Bureig refugee camp 162
Eldar, A. 58, 59, 152
electronic communication 42
electronic networking 21 see also networking
electronic surveillance 131 see also surveillance
elite discourse 30
elite racism 106
elites, and ICT 181
Eliyahu, Mordechai 178n.1
e-mail nationalism 40–1
Emergency Regulations 86

emigration(s): forced 99; Israeli 146, 151–2; Jewish 159
employment, of Arab population 151
empowerment, and technology-people networks 48
Ericson, Richard and Haggerty, Kevin 107
Esmeir, Samera 81
espionage, of Israel 116–18 *see also* surveillance
Ethiopian Jews 142
ethnic cleansing *see also* assassinations; genocide; killings; massacres: of Palestinians 24, 51, 167; and security 84; and village files 104; as Zionist strategy 61, 64, 71, 89, 92n.15
ethnic conflicts 41, 138
ethnic identity 44, 138
ethnicity, and statistics 140
ethnic markers, use of 34
ethnographic research 28–9
ethnographic studies 12, 22
ethno-nationalism 144
ethno-nationalist conflicts 36
eugenics: biopolitics to 136–43; and nationalism 141; and racism 169; and Zionism 138–40, 159
European colonialism 3, 62
European Court of Human Rights 130
evacuees 112
Evans, Brad 3
exception, state of 85–9, 96, 115, 168
exile xii, xvi, 45
exploitation: of indigenous people 52; of resources 56
expulsion, of Palestinians 73, 74, 89, 104, 114, 145
Eyal, Gil 72
Eytan, Rafael 88

facism, in Israel 78–9
Fafo 16, 17, 29
Faist, Thomas 44
Falah, Ghazi 17, 107
Falk, Raphael 142–3
Falk, Richard 50
family violence 19
Fandy, Mamoun 181
Fanon, Frantz 53
fantasy, and imagination 42
Farsakh, Leila 16

fear: culture of 108; globalisation of 108; from the minority 159; of Palestinians 106; and surveillance 107–9
Feldman, Ilana 26, 113
Feldman, Yotam 98, 139, 173
Ferlander, Sara and Timms, Duncan 40
fertility rates, and modernisation 148–9 *see also* birth rates
Fieldhouse, D.K. 50–1, 61, 65
fingerprinting, as surveillance 98, 100
Finkelstein, Norman 114
Fischbach, Michael 102
Fisk, Robert 88
Flapan, Simha 70
Food Consumption in the Gaza Strip – Red Lines 166
Forman, Geremy 59
Forsyth, David 25
Foucault, Michel: and biopolitics 3–4, 5; and colonialism 130; and governmentality 6; and panopticism 97, 164; and the population problem 8n.3; and populations 135; and power 8n.5, 28, 30–1, 32, 98, 211; and racism/colonialism 8n.2, 169–70; state racism 54; and state violence 211; and thanatopolitics 8n.4; theoretical framework of 57
Freedman, Seth 108
Freire, Paolo 183
From Haven to Conquest 15
functionalism 12, 23
fundamentalism 21, 42, 214
Furani, Khaled 24

Galton, Francis 98, 137
Gans, Chaim 64
Gavison, Ruth 49, 60
Gaza: bombings 162, 175, 176, 178n.1, 209–10; economy of 167; Palestinian refugees in 162, 189, 200–1; siege of 163, 164–7; unemployment 166; war 176
Gaza City, computer and Internet usage 193–5
gaze: civic 113; the imperial 95; Israeli 205
Gazit, Shlomo 25
Gemeinschaft 45
gender studies 19
General Security Service 81
generic needs theory 37

Index

genocide, and settler colonialism 52 *see also* assassinations; ethnic cleansing; killings; massacres
geographical studies 17–18
Gerber, Haim 63, 72
Germany, eugenics thinking 138–9
Ghanem, Asad 13, 78
Ghanim, Honaida 27
ghettoisation 120
Giacaman, Rita xvi, 19
Giddens, Anthony 31–2, 41–2, 100
Gilad, Amos 162, 164, 166
Ginsberg, Asher 76
Gisha Legal Center for Freedom of Movement 166
Glaser, Daryl 50, 79
globalisation 3, 41–7, 52, 108, 151
Golan, Arnon 62–3, 79
Goldberg, David 54, 55–6
Gordon, Colin 30
Gordon, Neve 56, 57, 81–2, 87, 90n.3, 92n.15
Gorenberg, Gershom 69
governance: racism and surveillance as tools of 4; of refugee camps 46; and surveillance 4, 5–6, 101, 102
governmentality: and power 6; and subjectification 32, 46; and surveillance 103
Graham, Stephen 125, 126, 173
Gramsci, Antonio x, xi
Gregory, Derek 3
group control model 2
Guha, Sumit 101

Ha'am, Ahad 76
Habibi, Emile 112–13
habitus 45
Hacking, Ian 100–1, 137
Hadawi, Sami 22
hafrada 75–6, 79
Haganah 104, 117, 212
Haggerty, Kevin and Ericson, Richard 5
Hajjar, Lisa 39
Haj-Yahia, Muhammad 19
Halabi, Usama 111, 119, 130
Hamas 20
Hamilton, Karine 26, 211
Hammami, Rema 29
Hamoked 93n.20, 122

Hanafi, Sari 46, 47
Handel, Ariel 56, 57, 105
Hannah, Mathew 5, 103
Harker, C. 20
Harley, John 103
Harvey, D. 121
Hass, Amira 81, 88, 115, 121, 128, 165–6
Hasson, N. 13, 58, 59
hatred, cultivation of 108–9
Hazkani, Shay 73
health system of Israel, and eugenics 139
Hebrew language 76, 77
Heidegger, Martin 115
Hejoj, Ibrahim 23
Herman, Edward and Chomsky, Noam 84
Hersh, Seymour 161
Herzliya centre 145, 149, 150, 153
Herzl, Theodore 53, 60–9, 72, 144, 160n.3
Hill et al. 181
hipardut 75–6
Hirsch, Dafna 141
historical necessity argument 64–5, 69
historical studies 12, 15, 98
history: revisionist/post-Zionist 24; sundered 66
hitkansut 76
Hollow Land: Israel's Architecture of Occupation 124
Holocaust, the 114
Holsti, Ole 80
homeland, in cyberspace 47
Home, Robert 73, 121
homo sacer 14; Palestinian 86, 88, 168
Horvath, Ronald 49–50
human rights *see also* rights: and biometrics 129; and global lobbying 39–40; of Palestinians 93n.20; research 52; and security 82, 83, 84, 89; and state politics 47; violations *see* human rights violations
Human Rights Council 177
human rights violations: Operation Pillar of Defense 175; and permit regime 122; by the PNA 40; and security 81; by the state 39; and use of statistics 101; wide-scale publicity of 207
Human Rights Watch 18, 102
human suffering, calibrated 162–7

ICT index 184
ICT indicators, Palestine 184, 186, 187

identification systems, and colonial regimes 6
"Identity Card" (poem) 110
identity cards 127; and surveillance 98, 99, 109, 110–11
identity(ies): conflicts involving 36; construction of 159; ethnic 44, 138; formation of 37–8; group 44, 137, 138; national and mobility/communication technologies 40; Palestinian 205; production 46; refugees 205
I Love You All (film) 212
imagination: collective 43; and fantasy 42
immigrants, Yemenite 142–3
immigration: Jewish 146, 148; to/from Israel 151–2, 159
immobility 6, 126–8 *see also* mobility
imperialism 50, 51, 53, 62, 63, 95, 133n.1
India, surveillance in 96, 97, 98, 100, 101, 133n.2
indigenous populations: dispossession of 3, 5, 51, 70, 100, 212; exploitation of 52
indoctrination 114
induced transfer 127
infiltrators 112, 118, 127
information: and security 81; and surveillance 96
information and communication technologies (ICT): adoption of 179–80; and culture 181–2; diffusion in Middle East 183–7; infrastructure and Palestine 184; Israel's control of 206–7; use of by Palestinians 207–8
Institute for Palestine Studies 15, 22
Institute of Contemporary Jewry 77, 148
Institute of Policy and Strategy 149
intelligence service, Israeli 118, 119
Interdisciplinary Center Herzliya 145, 149, 150, 153
intermarriages 154
internal colonialism 52
International Humanitarian Law (IHL) 175
international law, Israel's immunity from 65
Internet: diffusion of technology 180–1; and networking 47–8, 183, 190–1, 193, 195–6, 199, 201; Palestinian access to 186, 187; Palestinian use of 41, 206; penetration in Middle East 183; and political mobilisation 21; political use of 199, 204; and resistance 203; studies of 19; and surveillance 208

Internet cafés 191, 192, 194, 195, 198, 200, 201, 202
Intifada: first 13, 207; second 13, 67, 146, 170, 171, 203, 205, 206
Introna, Lucas 107
invisibility: of colonised people 28; of Palestinians 80; of refugees 109
Iraq: Israeli training of Americans 94n.21; Palestinianization of 126; US invasion of 86, 125–6
Islam, aggressive 90n.6
Islam and the Politics of Meaning in Palestinian Nationalism 20
Islamism, as a science of the soul 46
Israel: as a colonial-settler society 56; as a *Mukhabarat* state 5, 85; as a *Reconquista* state 54; as rogue state 209; as Shin Bet state, 85; as a sovereign colonial power 57
Israel and Settler Society 27
Israel and the Palestine Arabs 25
Israel Archaeological Survey Society 91n.8, 104
Israel Beiteinu 124
Israel Central Bureau of Statistics (ICBS) 12, 17, 34, 35, 147, 151, 187
Israel Council for Demography 154
Israel Democracy Institute (IDI) 175
Israel: Demography, 2013–2034: Challenges and Chances 147
Israeli army: and Britain 104; killings by 81–2; torture by 87; violence by 211
Israeli Centre for the Defence of the Individual 122
Israel Internet Association 17
Israeli-Palestinian conflict 209–10
Israeli secret service 32 *see also* Mossad
Israelis, living abroad 146
Israel Land Administration 91n.8, 104
Issacharoff, Avi 87
Izkor, Slaves of Memory (film) 114

Jabotinsky, Vladimir 72
Jamal, Amal 1, 115, 116
Jamoul, L. 111
Jenin, ICT 186–7
Jenin refugee camp 126, 163, 170, 172–4
Jerusalem, residency rights 58
Jewish-Arab relations 156, 157
Jewish homeland 34
Jewish Labour Movement 65

Index

Jewish National Fund 59, 62, 70, 91n.8, 104, 146
Jewish-Ottoman Land Company 62, 65
Jewish state: co-production of the 34; idea of 210
Jews: Ashkenazi/Mizrahi 142; classification of 141; Ethiopian 142; Yemenite 142–3
Jiryis, Sabri 21
Johnson, Nels 20
Jordan, Palestinian refugees in 168
Judt, Tony 58, 210
justice 37, 38, 88

Kadima Party 76
Kafr Kassim 162
Kana'aneh, Rhoda 136
Kaplan, Martha 96–7
Kasher, Asa 177
Kashti, Or 106
Kashua, Sayed 117
Katz, Theodore 25
Kay, Adah 19, 127
Kedar, Alexandre 59
Kelly, M. 21
Kelman, Herbert 36–7
Kemp, Adriana 211
key words 73–4
Khalidi, M.A. 65
Khalidi, Rashid 126, 209
Khalidi, Walid 15, 54, 62
Khalil, Asem 23
Khalili, Laleh 99, 205
Khamaisi, Rassem 17
Khamis, Vivian 19
Khan Yunis refugee camp 200–1
Khirbet Khizeh 212
Khouri, Rami 23
Kilibarda, Kole 202, 203, 204
killings *see also* assassinations; ethnic cleansing; genocide; massacres: of children 171, 174, 175, 176; extrajudicial 82, 116, 117, 133n.6, 163; by Israeli army 81–2; to necropolitics 170–1; suicide bombings 13–14, 82, 167–8, 171–2; targeted 81, 133n.6
Kimmerling, Baruch 71–2
Kirsh, Nurit 139
Klinger, Jonathan 129
Knesset 78–9, 123, 124

Knight, John 63
knowledge: colonial 96, 97; and power 33, 37, 75; production and conflict situations 47; scientific 34
Kochavi, Aviv 173, 174
Korn, Alina 111–12, 119–20
Kosminsky, Peter 100
Kretzmer, David 81
Kubursi, Atef 22
Kufr Al-Labad 196–7
Kupfer, Joseph 107

Lab, The (film) 98
Lacan, Jacques 95
land: acquisitions and surveillance 117, 118; appropriation of Arab 35, 61; confiscations by Israel 74; dispossession of 59; exchange 158; expropriation and the occupation wall 99; Jewish desire for 67–8; land swap 158; land transfers 74; ownership 62, 74–5, 123; and security 81
Landau, David 78
Landau, Moshe 32
Land Day protests 82
Land, Labour and the Origins of the Israeli-Palestinian Conflict 71
language: analysis of 80–1; colonial 75; of dehumanisation 86–9; double-speak 77; Hebrew 76, 77; political 73–80; of security 80–5; as a tool of spiritual revival 76
Lapidoth, Ruth 24
Law of Return 78, 86, 93n.20, 122
law(s): Acceptance Committee Law 77, 93n.19; and Arab citizens 87; Big Brother Law 132; Citizenship and Entry Law 93n.20, 124; Citizenship Law 77, 93n.19–20, 123; colonial 6, 59–60; Communal Societies Law 93n.20, 123; Communication Data Law 130; discriminatory 123–4, 130; International Humanitarian Law (IHL) 175; Israeli 87; Israel's immunity from international law 65; land ownership 123; Law of Return 78, 86, 93n.20, 122; Loyalty Oath Law 93n.20, 124; Nakba Law 77, 93n.19; nation-states power to suspend 169; racist 77, 78–9, 93n.19–20, 153–4
Least of All Possible Evils: Humanitarian Violence from Arendt to Gaza, The 164

Lebanese Christian Phalange 162
Lebanon: bombings 210, 211; Palestinian refugees in 46, 81, 162, 168, 199, 205–6
Lee, Charles 13–14, 26
Legal Centre for Arab Minority Rights in Israel (Adalah) 117, 123, 124
legal discrimination 122–4, 130
legal studies 12
Legg, S. 4, 7, 21
Leibler, Anat 35, 101
Leibler, Anat and Breslau, Daniel 34
Leibowitz, Yeshayahu 85
Lemkin, Raphael 52
Lentin, Ronit 27, 54
lethal theory 173
Levinson, Chaim 119
Levy, Gideon 154
liberal Zionists 50
Lieberman, Avigdor 88, 124, 178n.1
life: under duress 19; management of 4, 5
liminality 20
literacy model 183
Lives of Others, The (film) 212
living conditions, documentation of 16–17
Lockman, Z. 65
Loshitzky, Yosefa 114
Loyalty Oath Law 93n.20, 124
Lubin, Alex 95
Lustick, Ian 1, 2, 21, 151–2
Lyon, David 52

Macdonnell, Diane 32
Macro Center for Political Economics 17
macro-securitisation 83
Mada-al-Carmel 93n.20, 123
Making of Modern Zionism, The 61
Malthus, Thomas 137
management, of life 4, 5
Mandate Palestine 54, 58, 64, 74, 99, 102, 104
Mannheim, Karl x
Mapai 118
Mapam Party 70, 119
maps: and colonial power 103–6; and surveillance 97
Margalit, M. 59
marginalized populations, and the world polity 39
Marx, Emmanuel 24
Marxism 12, 39

Marx, Karl 61
Masalha, Nur 12, 15, 62, 145
massacres *see also* assassinations; ethnic cleansing; killings: of Palestinians 162; of refugees 169
Massad, Joseph 81
mass media, and agency 42
materialist perspective, colonisation of Palestine 71
Maurion, Audrey 212
Mazawi, Andre 18
Mbembe, Achille 5, 125
McCoy, Alfred 97–8, 130
media: Israeli 81–2; mass and agency 42; role of in social movements 20–1
medical sociology 12
Meir, Golda 69, 177
Meir, Joseph 139
memory: disciplining of 111–15; forced 114; and mobilisation 205
Mendel, Yonatan 81
mental health, and nation building 140
mental hygiene 141
Mezvinsky, Norton 21
microphysics of power 30
Middle East, Internet penetration in 183–7
Middle East peace process 213
military, Israeli 81 *see also* Israeli army
military operations, of Israel 170–6
military rule, Israeli 111–12
Mill, John Stuart 58
Milton-Edwards, B. 21
Minerva Humanities Centre 176
Ministry of Defense 166
Ministry of Health 166
Ministry of Immigration and Absorption 146
Ministry of Interior 154
mista'rivm units 117
Mitchell, Timothy 98
Mitchell, Timothy and Owen, Roger 137
Mizrahi Jews 142
mobility *see also* immobility: control of 6, 116; immobility 126–8; virtual 205
modernisation: and demography 147–52; reflexive/simple 42
modernity 41, 43
Monmonier, Mark 103
moral aloofness 120
Morris, Benny 24, 167–8

Moses, Dirk 168
Mossad 149 *see also* Israeli secret service
Mukhabarat state, Israel as a 5, 85
multicultural epistemology xi
multiculturalism 138
Musawa Centre for Arab Rights in Israel 87

Nablus: computer and Internet usage 192–3; history of resistance 203; refugee camp 163, 173
Nakba Bill 93n.20, 123
Nakba (Catastrophe): causes of 24–5; censorship of references to 76, 79; commemoration of 113; denial of 114; and establishment of Israel 10, 11; representation of 75; sharing memories of 205
Nakba Law 77, 93n.19
Nakba: Palestine, 1948, and the Claims of Memory 114
narratives, historical 55
Nashif, Esmail 164
national culture, and conflict resolution 37
national identities, and mobility/communication technologies 40
nationalism: bionationalism/ethno-nationalism 144; diaspora nationalism 53; e-mail nationalism 40–1; and eugenics 141; Jewish 59, 68; long-distance 41; Palestinian 72; race as marker of 142; settler 64
nationalist discourse 105–6
national security, and surveillance/control/violence 6
nation building 34, 92n.18, 140
nation-state racism 4–5 *see also* state racism
nation-states: power to suspend law 169; and the world polity 39
Naveh, Shimon 173, 174
Nazi eugenic doctrines 142
Nazism 169
necropolitics 56, 121, 125, 170–1
necropower 5, 125
negotiations, politics of 38
Neocleous, Mark 103
neocolonialism 52
neoliberalism 56
neoliberal social science 3
neo-racism 4–5
Netanyahu, Benjamin 88, 123, 146, 152–3, 210, 211, 214

networking: electronic 21; and the Internet 47–8, 183, 190–1, 193, 195–6, 199, 205
network society 41–7
networks, transnational and resistance 47
Neumann, Amnon 24–5
Neumann, Boaz 66–7, 68
new technology: electronic networking 21; and surveillance 5
9/11 82, 83, 96, 108, 183
Nineteen Eighty-Four 109
nongovernmental organisations 21, 204

Obama, Barack 82, 109, 132
objectification, of populations 101
occupation wall 99 *see also* separation wall
Olmert, Ehud 76
"On Clarifying the Origin of the Fallahim" 144
Oord, Lodewijk van 24
Operational Theory Research Institute 173
Operation Autumn Clouds 170
Operation Cast Lead 170, 174
Operation Defensive Shield 170, 171–4
Operation Pillar of Defense 170, 174–5
Operation Protective Edge 170, 171, 175–6
Operation Summer Rains 170
Operation Warm Winter 170
oppression, of Palestinians 86
Or Commission 87, 157
order, problem of 35–41
Orientalism 3, 72, 95, 96, 161
Original Sins: Reflections on the History of Zionism and Israel 70
Orwell, George 109
Oslo agreement 12–13, 14, 29, 75, 121, 143
Oslo peace process 16, 22
Oslo refugee talks 146
Other, the 84, 95, 96, 97, 159
Ottoman land code 74, 75
Oveida, Yosef 88

Palestine in Israeli School Books 106
Palestine Liberation Organization (PLO) 13
Palestine: Loss of Heritage 22
Palestine Mandate 74
Palestine, partitioning of 9
Palestinian Authority 13, 40, 143, 165
Palestinian Center for Policy and Survey Research (PCPSR) 17, 184, 186
Palestinian Central Bureau of Statistics (PCBS) 13, 17, 186, 191

Palestinian Diaspora: Formation of Identities and Politics of Homeland, The 26
Palestinian National Authority (PNA) *see* Palestinian Authority
Palestinian Population Projections for 16 Countries of the World, 1990–2010 26
"Palestinian Refugee Camp Life in Lebanon" 22
Palestinian Refugees: An Economic and Social Study, 1949–1974, The 24
Palestinian Refugees in Jordan, The 24
Palestinian Rights and Losses in 1948 22
Palestinian Scientists and Technologists Abroad (PALESTA) 19
Palestinians, demography of 9–10, 12–13
Palestinians: From Peasants to Revolutionaries, The 22
Palestinians in Israel: A Study in Internal Colonialism, The 2, 70
Palestinians in the Arab World: Institution Building and the Search for a State 25
Palestinians: The Making of a People 71
Palmach 117
panopticism 96, 97, 98, 112, 113, 124, 125
Panorama in Ramallah 186
Pappé, Ilan 5, 25, 27, 69–70, 71, 85–6, 114, 178n.1
paranoia, and surveillance 109
Parenti, Christian 109
Patai, Raphael 94n.21, 161
peace process, Middle East 213
Pearson, Karl 137
Peel Commission 213
Peled-Elhanan, Nurit 18, 106
Peled, Nurit 53
Peled, Yoav 53, 90n.2
Penslar, Derek 72, 92n.17
Peretz, Don 25
permit system 122, 127
Peteet, Julie 31, 44, 75, 78, 79, 80, 115
Pfaff, William 142
Pfeffer, Ashnel 206
Philippines, surveillance in 98, 130
Pinson, Halleli 106
Piterberg, Gabriel 64, 65, 73
Plan Dalet 15
Plascov, Avi 24
police: electronic surveillance by 131; violence 157
policy(ies): criticism of Israeli as anti-Semitism 114; national ICT 180; of racism 79; securitisation 84; separation 80, 176; settlement 51; terrorist label justifying 80, 214
policymaking, and survey research 29
political acquiescence, of Palestinian Arab community 1
political control 112
political culture, of fascism 79
political discourse 80
political language 73–80
political mobilisation, and the Internet 21, 199, 204
political other, state terrorization of 84
political rights, erosion of 123
political violence 19
political Zionism 68
politicide, against Palestinians 71
politicization thesis 156–7
politics: biopolitics *see* biopolitics; and literacy 183; necropolitics 56, 121, 125, 170–1; and necropower 5; of negotiations 38; state and human rights 47
population balance, as biopolitics 143–58
population containment 93n.20, 152–4
population control, and censuses 98
population demographics *see* demography
population discourse 136, 144–7
population exchange 158
population homogenisation 84
population management, and demography 136, 137
population of Israel 147–8
population registration 126
population(s): categorisation and enumeration of 96; classification of 98, 100–1; dangerous 5; disciplining of 28, 30, 113; and the state 135
population separation 146–7
population statistics 137
population targeting, reverse targeting 101
population transfer 62, 74
positioning of self x, xi, xiii, xiv
postcolonialism 3, 8n.2, 96–109
postmodern violence 172–4
post-Zionism 70–1, 72
post-Zionist history 24
power: analysis of 30, 32; asymmetrical and Oslo agreement 14; biopower 4, 169; colonial 5, 103–6; and discourse 73–89; and governmentality 6; and knowledge 33, 37, 75; and literacy 183; and maps

103–6; microphysics of 30; necropower 5, 125; and resistance 30–1; of social statistics 100, 101; sovereign 4; state 119; and surveillance 107; of words 75
power relationships, asymmetrical 14, 37, 38, 75, 95, 157–8
practice, and knowledge/power 33
Pratt, Mary Louise 97
prejudice 108–9
present absentees 34, 35, 101, 112
Present Absentees: The Palestinian Refugees in Israel since 1948, The 25
primordial 36, 44, 45, 54, 62, 137
primordialist approaches 38, 103
prisons *see also* carceral practices: Abu Ghraib prison 86–7, 161; Israeli 164; and resistance 136
Privacy International 131, 132
privacy violations 83, 107–8, 130, 132 *see also* surveillance
privatisation, of land ownership 74
Promise, The (TV program) 100
propaganda, Israeli 106
property: appropriation of Arab 35; of refugees 75, 91n.8, 101–2
protofascism 78
psychiatry, and social engineering 139–40
psychological effects, of surveillance 112–13
psychosis, and surveillance 109
public opinion 17, 29, 156, 176, 178n.1, 211
punishments, of Palestinians 163–4

Qibya 162
quantification, as surveillance 97–103
quantitative-qualitative divide, research 28–30
quarantining, of Palestinians 99

Rabinowitz, Danny 23, 38, 72
Rabin, Yitzhak 75
race 55, 141, 142
racial hierarchy 120
racialisation, of the native 95
racialised time 115–16
racialism 3, 54, 120
racial Palestinianization 55
racial profiling 3
racial purity, of Jews 142
racism: and biopolitics 4; and colonialism 5, 213; and colonial states 4; and eugenics 169; Israeli 55, 78–9, 154–5, 159, 176, 178n.1; of Israeli leaders 88; Jewish 78, 87; Jewish elite 106; neo-racism 4–5; policies of 79; state 4–5, 53, 54; as tool of governance 4
racist laws 77, 78–9, 93n.19–20, 153–4
radical movements, rise of 20
Radley, Kurt René 25
Rafah refugee camp 201–2
Ramallah 189–92
Ram, Uri 69, 70
Ravid, Itzhak 149–50
Reconquista state, Israel as a 54
record keeping, as surveillance 100, 102, 119
reflexive modernisation 42
Refugee Camp on a Mountain Ridge, A 24
refugee camps 168–70; Al-Am'ari 199; Balata 202–3; bombings 162; computer and Internet usage 189–91; El-Bureig 162; governance of 46; Israel's incursions into 126; Jenin 126, 163, 170, 172–4; Khan Yunis 200–1; Nablus 163, 173; Rafah 201–2; Sabra and Shatila 162, 169; as spaces of exception 46; state of exception in 168; Yarmouk 169
refugees: bare life of 14, 46, 88, 168, 169; bibliographies 22; camp refugees 189, 190; categorisation of 112; compensation issue 25; computer and Internet usage 41, 199–204; and computer networking 47–8; criminalisation of 127; cyberculture of 205–6; demography of 22; identity of 205; invisibility of 109; Israel's responsibility for 60, 65; losses incurred by 22; loss of dignity 109; massacres of 169; numbers of 9; Palestinian 10, 22; Palestinian in Egypt 10, 23; Palestinian in Gaza 162, 189, 200–1; Palestinian in Jordan 168; Palestinian in Lebanon 46, 81, 162, 168, 199, 205–6; Palestinian in Syria 46, 168, 169; Palestinian in West Bank 168, 189, 199–200, 202–3 *see also* Jenin refugee camp; prevention of the return of 23; property of 75, 91n.8, 101–2; right of return 23, 24, 25, 60, 65, 144, 145, 153; studies of 21–2; surveillance of 169, 205; targeted killings of 81
relativism xi
religion, defining citizenship 159
Report of the Commission of Inquiry into the Events of the Refugee Camps in Beirut – 8 February 1983 178n.3

repression 162–3
reproduction: and eugenics 142; and resistance 136
research: advocacy 23; ethnographic 28–9; human rights 52; on Palestinians 26–7; quantitative-qualitative divide 28–30; securitisation 83–4; on technology adoption 180
reserve system, United States 103
residency rights, Arab Jerusalem 58
resistance: and agency/structure 32; analysis of 30; and censuses 102; and computers/telecommunications 41; countermapping as a tool of 104, 105; and the Internet 203; to Mandate 102; memory as act of 113; of Palestinians 127–8; and power 30–1; and reproductive strategies/prison policies 136; studies of 20; to surveillance 133; tactics of 126; technologized 204–7; and technology-people networks 48; theory of 31; and transnational networks 47
resources, control of 56, 92–3n.18
Reuveny, Rafael 27, 54
reverse targeting, of populations 101
revisionist history 24
Richter-Devroe, Sophie 20, 26
right of return: and censuses 101–2; refugees 23, 24, 25, 60, 65, 144, 145, 153
rights *see also* human rights: citizenship rights 90n.2, 101, 210; civil rights 78, 123; erosion of political 123; of non-Jewish citizens 144
risk, and surveillance 107–8, 109
River without Bridges 22
Robinson, Shira 53
Ron, James 39, 162, 163
Rosenfeld, Maya 25
Rothschild, Baron de 59
Rouhana, Nadim 13, 27
Roy, Sara 16, 17
Ruppin, Arthur 140–3, 159
Ryan, Caitlin 26

Sabbagh-Khoury, Areej 112
Sabet, Amr 38
Sabra and Shatila refugee camps 162, 169
Sa'di, Ahmad 119, 120
Said, Edward 3, 27, 41, 49, 58, 68, 75, 213
Salih, Ruba 14, 23
Salter, Mark 21, 127
Sarid, Yossi 167

Sayigh, Rosemary 22
Schueftan, Dan 88
Schulz, Helena Lindholm 26
science: of calibrated human suffering 162–4; in the service of suffering 164–7; and society 18–19
scientific discourse 33, 34, 92n.18
scientific knowledge 34
Scobbie, Ian 16
Scott, James C. 30, 136
seam zone 122
second modernity 43
securitisation, research 83–4
security: conflicts involving 36; and ethnic cleansing 84; and human rights 82, 83, 84, 89; and information 81; justifying policies 80; language of 80–5; logic of 6, 80–5; and risk 108; and settlement 81; and the state of exception 85–9; and surveillance 108
Security, Territory, Population: Lectures at the College de France, 1977–1978 6
Segev, Tom 142
segmentation, of Palestinian population 112
segregation 125 *see also* apartheid
Sela, Rona 104
Selby, Jan 72
self: positioning of x, xi, xiii, xiv; and society 42
self-determination 38
self-disciplining 113
self-victimisation, of Palestinians 78
separation, of populations 146–7 *see also* apartheid
separation policies 80, 176
separation principle 56
separation wall 77, 80, 116, 122 *see also* occupation wall
settlement(s): building of 77; close settlement 74; Israeli 20, 99, 124–5; policies of Israel 51; and security 81; West Bank 147; and Zionism 58, 80, 89
settler colonialism: consequences of 52; and dispossession of indigenous populations 3, 5, 51, 70, 212; and logic of elimination 5; methods of 99; and territoriality 6, 51; Zionist 59, 63, 64, 70
settler nationalism 64
Sfard, Michael 77
Shabak 118, 119

Index

Shachtman, N. 21, 206
Shafir, Gershon 65, 69, 71
Shafir, Gershon and Peled, Yoav 53, 65
Shahak, Israel 21
Shai, Aron 91n.8, 104
Shalhoub-Kevorkian, Nadera 19, 205
Shamir, Ronen 54
Shamir, Shimon 24
Shaml Center in Ramallah 23
Sharansky, Ira 54, 90n.6
Sharon, Ariel 71, 76, 80, 99, 146, 162, 169, 171
Shas Party 88
Shehadeh, Raja 168
Sheinin, Yacov 149, 150
Shenhav, Yehouda 52, 120, 121
Shikaki, Khalil 17
Shin Bet 81, 115, 117, 119, 133n.8
Shin Bet state, Israel as 85
Shlaim, Avi 209, 214
Shulman, David 154
siege: digital by Israel 206; of Gaza 163, 164–7; strategy of Israel 164–7
Silver, Jonny 130
Sirhan, Basem 22
situationalist approaches 38
Sivan, Emmanuel 149
Sivan, Eyal 114, 212
Smith, Keith 103
Smith, Richard Saumarez 100
Smith, Ron 20, 26, 99
Smooha, Sammy 155, 156–7, 159
Sneh, Efraim 158
social capital: computer networks as 40; and social spaces 45
social class, and ICT access 182
social control, studies of 19
social Darwinism 137, 139, 142, 159
social engineering 136–7, 139–40
social media 21
social movements 20–1
social networking see networking
social reflexivity, and global communication 42
social reproduction 31
social science, neoliberal 3
social sorting, of Palestinians 10–11
social statistics, power of 100, 101
society: and self 42; as a web/network 46
Society Must be Defended 4, 8n.5
sociology, medical 12
Sociology of the Jews 142

Sofer, Arnon 146, 158
Soft Cage: Surveillance in America from Slavery to the War on Terror, The 109
solipsism xi
Some Sociological and Economic Aspects of Refugee Camps on the West Bank 24
Sorek, Tamir 113
South Africa: apartheid 50, 77–8, 79; condemnation of Israel 77–8
sovereignty, right of 4
space: and colonialism 57, 97; transnational sense of 44–5
spaces of exception, refugee camps as 46
Special Night Squads 63
speech act approach 83
spillover effect, surveillance 98
Spurr, David 97
state building, in conflict zones 20
state creation, studies of 20
state of emergency 85, 88
state of exception: and control of time 115; in refugee camps 168; and security 85–9; and surveillance 96
state racialism 54
state racism 4–5, 53, 54
state repression, and suicide bombing 82
state(s): hegemony 30; and ICT 181; intelligence states 5; legitimacy of 30, 39; and the population 135; power of 119; surveillance by 28; surveillance states 5, 97; terrorization of political other 84
state violence 32, 39, 84, 157, 161–2, 177, 211–12
stationary transfer 155, 158
statistics: dark side of 101; and ethnicity 140; power of 100, 101; as surveillance 100
stereotyping: of Arabs/Arab culture 82, 211; of the Other 96
Sternhell, Ze'ev 64
Stevens, Andrew 131
Stoler, Ann 2, 54, 67, 101
Stoler-List, Sachlav 139
"Story of the Fish That Understands All Languages, The" 112–13
strategic resources, water as 34
Strawson, John 3, 59
structuration theory 31
studies: Israeli contributions 23–5; Palestinian/Arab contributions 22–3; Western contributions 25–7

subaltern 14, 43, 80, 95, 99
subjectification 31, 32
suffering, calibrated human 162–7
suicide bombings 13–14, 82, 167–8, 171–2
Sultany, Nimer 155
sundered history 66
surveillance: and biopolitics 101, 134n.11; boomerang effect 98, 130–2; in Canada 103, 109; censuses as 97, 100, 101–2; cloak-and-dagger operations 116–18; and colonial bureaucracy 118–22; and colonialism 28, 57, 95, 96–109; constructivist aspect of 102; and control 21, 28; as dominance 109; electronic surveillance 131; and fear 107–9; fingerprinting as 98, 100; and governance 4, 5–6, 101, 102; and governmentality 103; and identity cards 98, 99, 109, 110–11; and imperialism 95; in India 96, 97, 98, 100, 101, 133n.2; and information 96; and the Internet 183, 208; by Israel 98, 206–7, 211–12; and maps 97; material, corporeal, and discursive forms 5; of Palestinians 5, 10; and paranoia 109; in Philippines 98, 130; postcolonial/colonial 96–109; and power 107; psychological effects of 112–13; and psychosis 109; quantification/categorisation as 97–103; record keeping as 100, 102, 119; of refugees 169, 205; resistance to 133; and risk 107–8, 109; and securitisation 84; and security 6, 108; spatial 124–6; spillover effect 98; spy networks 116–17; and state of exception 96; statistics as 100; technologized 5, 204–7; and trust 107; United States 82, 107
surveillance drones 134n.11
surveillance states 5, 97
surveillant assemblage 5
Swedenburg, Ted 56
Swiss Agency for Development and Cooperation (SDC) 16
Syria, Palestinian refugees in 46, 168, 169

Tamari, Salim 22, 29
Tami Steinmetz Center for Peace Research 17, 156
Tawil-Souri, Helga 26, 111, 208
technology: electronic networking 21; and surveillance 5, 204–7
technology-people networks 48

territoriality, and settler colonialism 6, 51
territory: and colonialism 57; ethno-nationalist conflicts over 36
terrorism: and suicide bombing 167; and surveillance 108; and surveillance of the internet 183
terrorist label, justifying policies 80, 214
thanatopolitics 5, 8n.4
"The Way of Life, the Division of Labour and the Social Roles of Palestinian Refugee Families: The Case of Dheisheh Refugee Camp" 25
Thinking Palestine 27
Thomas, Martin 97, 100
threat, of Arab citizens 156, 160
Tibawi, Abdul 18
Tilley, Virginia 16
time: racialised 115–16; theft of 128
Toft, Monica 138
Tönnies, Ferdinand 45
torture: by Israeli army 87; by the PNA 40; of prisoners 32; public opinion on 211; by United States 86
traditions 42
transfer: land/population 74; of Palestinians 153, 155–6
Transfer of Knowledge Through Expatriate Nationals (TOKTEN) 19
transnationalism 44–5, 47
transnational networks, and resistance 47
transnational social spaces 45
trust, and surveillance 107
Turner, Bryan 62
two-state solution 147, 210, 214

underdevelopment, of Palestinians 150
unemployment, Gaza 166
Unit 101 162
United Kingdom *see* Britain
United Nations Development Programme 19
United Nations Educational, Scientific, and Cultural Organization (UNESCO) 18
United Nations General Assembly, nonmember status for Palestine 20
United Nations Human Rights Council 177
United Nations Relief and Works Agency (UNRWA) 12, 23, 102, 167, 168
United States: assassinations by 126; imperialism of 133n.1; influence of

Israel on 125–6; and Iraq 86, 94n.21, 125–6; and the Philippines 98; reserve system 103; support of Israel 65, 162; surveillance by 82, 107; surveillance in 103, 132; torture by 86
urban-economic development, Arab/Jewish sectors 63–4
urbanisation, Zionist in Palestine 63, 64
urban warfare 125, 126, 173
urbicide 18, 125, 173
Urim military base 131
Urry, John 40

Venn, Couze 170
Veracini, Lorenzo 27
village files 104, 127
villages: computer and Internet usage in 196–8; destruction of 212
Vilnai, Matan 178n.1
violence: and biopolitics 138; family violence 19; of Israel 164; Israel's justification of 177; and national security 6; political 19; postmodern 172–4; as a spectacle 32; state violence 32, 39, 84, 157, 161–2, 177, 211–12; of Zionism 65

Waever, Ole 83
Wallach, Yair 104–5
wall, separation wall 77, 80, 116, 122
war: cyberwar 207; Gaza 176
warfare: asymmetrical 211; economic 167; urban 125, 126, 173; urban guerrilla warfare 173
war on terror 84, 107, 108, 126
Warschauer, Mark 182, 183
water resources 34, 92–3n.18
Waugh, Louisa 163
Weapons of the Weak 136
Weber, Max 39, 120
Weissglass, Dov 163
Weitz, Yosef 145–6
Weizman, Eyal 57, 85, 124, 125, 164, 173–4
Weizmann, Chaim 53, 58
West Bank: Palestinian refugees in 168, 189, 199–200, 202–3; settlements 147
Wick, Livia 26, 128
Wilkins, Kevin 102
Williams, Michael 84

Williams, Raymond 73
Willis, Paul 28, 29
Will They Be Refugees Forever? Description of Conditions and Suggestions for a Solution 24
Wingate, Orde 63
Wolfe, Patrick 1, 5, 6, 27, 50, 51
women: and closures/curfews 128; and ICT 187, 191
World Zionist Organization 94n.20, 140
Wretched of the Earth, The 53

Yacobi, Haim 64, 125
Yahia-Younis, T. 17
Yalon, Moshe 88
Yarmouk refugee camp 169
Yemenite Jews 142–3
Yiftachel, Oren 54
Yizhar, S. 212
Young, Jane 26
Young, Robert 4, 169
Youssef, Maissa 14

Zacharia, Christine 102, 137
Zahlan, Antoine 18–19
Zalashik, Rakefet 139
Ze'evi, Rehavem 88
Zionism: and apartheid 50; and biopolitics/settlements 89; British support for 91n.9, 104; and co-existence field 38; and colonialism 49, 53–4, 56, 64, 69–70, 71–3, 81, 89, 92n.17; and colonisation 58–9, 90n.1; critical perspective 65–6; and diaspora nationalism 53; and ethnic cleansing 61, 64, 71, 89, 92n.15; and eugenics 138–40, 159; ideology 25; and Israeli writers/scholarship 23–4; and Jewishness of the state 210; logic of 58–60; as a national liberation movement 62–3; and Orientalism 72; political 68; and population discourse 144–7; project of 1–2, 59; as a revolutionary movement 61; and scientific knowledge 34; settlement policies 58, 80, 89; as a settler colonial movement 59, 63, 64, 70; violence of 65
Zochrot 24
Zreik, Raef 176